Voices in Flight: RAF Fighter Pilots In WWII

Voices in Flight: RAF Fighter Pilots In WWII

Martin W. Bowman

Pen & Sword
AVIATION

First Published in Great Britain in 2015
and reissued in this format in 2025
by Pen & Sword Aviation
an imprint of
Pen & Sword Books Ltd
Yorkshire – Philadelphia

Copyright © Martin W Bowman, 2015

ISBN 978 1 39907 817 7

Type right of Martin W Bowman to be identified as author of this work
has been asserted by him in accordance with the Copyright,
Designs and Patents Act 1988.

A CIP catalogue record for this book is
available from the British Library.

All rights reserved. No part of this book may be reproduced, transmitted, downloaded, decompiled or reverse engineered in any form or by any means, electronic or mechanical including photocopying, recording or by any information storage and retrieval system, without permission from the Publisher in writing. NO AI TRAINING: Without in any way limiting the Author's and Publisher's exclusive rights under copyright, any use of this publication to "train" generative artificial intelligence (AI) technologies to generate text is expressly prohibited. The Author and Publisher reserve all rights to license uses of this work for generative AI training and development of machine learning language models.

Typeset in 10/12pt Palatino by GMS Enterprises
Printed and bound in England by CPI Group (UK) Ltd, Croydon, CR0 4YY

MIX
Paper | Supporting responsible forestry
FSC www.fsc.org FSC® C013604

The Publisher's authorised representative in the EU for product safety is Authorised Rep Compliance Ltd., Ground Floor, 71 Lower Baggot Street, Dublin D02 P593, Ireland.
www.arccompliance.com

For a complete list of Pen & Sword titles please contact
PEN & SWORD BOOKS LIMITED

47 Church Street, Barnsley, South Yorkshire, S70 2AS, England
E-mail: enquiries@pen-and-sword.co.uk
Website: www.pen-and-sword.co.uk
or
PEN AND SWORD BOOKS
1950 Lawrence Road, Havertown, PA 19083, USA
E-mail: uspen-and-sword@casematepublishers.com
Website: www.penandswordbooks.com

Contents

Acknowledgements

I am thankful to all the contributors for their words and photographs.

Thanks also go to my fellow author, friend and colleague, Graham Simons, for getting the book to press ready standard and for his detailed work on the photographs; to Pen & Sword and in particular, Laura Hirst; and Jon Wilkinson, for his unique jacket design once again.

Chapter 1
Legless Ace

On a raw November day in 1932 a young RAF fighter pilot drove his little red MG sports car along the winding A505 in Cambridgeshire to take up a new posting at Duxford airfield just south of the University City of Cambridge. This RAF fighter station forty miles north of London was home to 19 Squadron flying Bristol Bulldog IIA biplane fighters. At weekends the airfield hosted undergraduate members of the Cambridge University Air Squadron who were learning to fly and to become officers in the RAF. Duxford would normally have been a Mecca too for the 22 year old ex RAF College Cranwell graduate, accomplished pilot and all-round sportsman who had flown Gloster Gamecocks in tied together aerobatics at Hendon air displays. But for Douglas Bader his posting to 19 Squadron was a bitter pill to swallow. Both his legs had been amputated following a horrific crash during low level aerobatics at Reading Aero Club at Woodley airfield on 14 December 1931 when the wingtip of his Bulldog clipped the grass and the aircraft smashed into the ground. Lesser men would have died but expert medical care and his own tremendous fighting spirit and a strong will to live pulled him through. He endured the long ordeal of operations and rehabilitation and when given artificial legs Bader confounded the doctors who said that he would never walk unaided again. He not only proved them wrong, he proved to his RAF superiors that he could still fly aircraft but the service was unable to pass him fit for flying because 'there was nothing in King's Regulations which covered his case'. Instead, he was posted to Duxford and on his arrival the wing commander in charge of the station told him, 'Glad to have you here Bader. You're taking over the Motor Transport Section.

Duxford and the Big Wings 1940-45[1]

The fascination exercised by the sea over sailors is well-known and there is no doubt that the air exercises a similar fascination over many airmen who have fought and trounced the German legions in the skies. Just as the born sailor feels in his element when he is at sea, so must Wing Commander Bader feel in his element in the air, for his eagerness to fly at all times was always impossible to conceal.[2]

Born in London in the neighbourhood of Regent's Park in 1910, Douglas Robert Stewart Bader went to St. Edward's School at Oxford to receive his education. By the time he was eighteen years old he had thoroughly made up his mind that he wanted to be a pilot in the Royal Air Force. Accordingly he went from school at Oxford to the Royal Air Force College at Cranwell as a cadet to receive a thorough grounding in the theory and practice of flight and in 1930 he received with pride his commission as a Pilot Officer in the Royal Air Force.

The very keenness and mastery of the air which he displayed almost led to his undoing. Taking off in a Bristol Bulldog on the morning of 14 December 1931 he flew around and diving low, started to stunt about ten feet from the ground. A slight misjudgement, a touch of the aircraft on the grass and Pilot Officer Bader who had been stunting so joyously a second earlier lay mangled among the wreckage. He was shockingly injured. His right leg was nearly severed above the knee, his left terribly smashed below, with broken ribs and an injured lung to make his recovery seem almost impossible. The extraordinary thing is that he remained conscious all the time. His body was shattered, but his mind remained clear. It was a significant fact which showed the beginning of that strength of mind which was later to become manifest to the world.

Tenderly he was extricated from the wreckage and rushed by ambulance to the Royal Berkshire Hospital at Reading where his clothes were cut from him and he was put upon the operating table and under an anaesthetic without delay. With the right leg practically off, there was nothing to be done except amputate it. Deftly the surgeon tied up the blood vessels and applied the dressings. The left leg was carefully examined, the fractured bones set, in the hope of preserving it.

Somehow his wonderful vitality enabled him to survive the shock, but it became increasingly evident that his left leg could not be saved, so it was amputated a week after the accident. During the following fortnight death hovered very near, his black hair making more pronounced his pallid face which was as white as the pillow. The lamp of life burned very dimly indeed in his body throughout those three weeks.

Then a most pronounced change took place. He started to improve and, once on the way to recovery, made rapid progress. His well-developed, sturdy body gathered strength, the stumps of his legs healed. The day came when a wooden peg was strapped to his leg and he took a pair of crutches and began to get about again. It felt strange to a young man who had been used to playing games, whose whole temperament was keyed up to rapid movement. Without legs, condemned to getting about on crutches - the disability must have been very bitter. Yet, strangely enough, he was not depressed. The kindness all about him in the hospital helped him more than he knew.

Directly after the accident the main concern of the doctors was to save his life. They were compelled to do the best they could with his maimed limbs in order not to add to the shock, which would otherwise have killed him, although it was plain that his limbs would need further attention later on. In three months when he was fit and strong again, he was wheeled once more to the operating theatre where the stumps of his legs were re-amputated for permanent healing. His physical condition at that time was so good that in a fortnight he had his wooden peg on his leg again and was moving about on crutches. He spent two more months in the hospital at Reading, amid the kindness of doctors and nurses that will ever remain in his memory.

It seemed rather ironical that while he was lying in bed without legs his promotion to Flying Officer should have been gazetted, yet so it was. Most men in his position would have been convinced beyond all doubt that his flying career was at an end. Flying Officer Bader was the one young man in the world who was not convinced. On, the contrary there was in his mind the idea that somehow at sometime he would once more climb into the clouds and be as free as the birds on the wing.

Five months after his accident, he went off to Roehampton to be fitted with his two duralumin legs. That was his testing time, when the strength of his mind alone triumphed over the disabilities of his body. He was determined, no matter what happened, that once his legs were fitted he would never make use of a stick to help him to walk. He never did. The first time his legs were fitted, he rose upon them unsteadily and walked a step or two. He strove to walk again, just like a baby, falling down sometimes, but rising with his determination to succeed growing stronger than ever. Occasionally he would take the arm of another patient for support, but always there was the inflexible mind to drive his body to do his bidding. Time and again he tried, learning how to balance his body upon his metal legs.

Only he knows the difficulties he surmounted. Sometimes he was depressed beyond words. No one could help him. He had to fight the fight alone and win the victory in his mind, to abolish all doubts, to feel sure beyond peradventure that he could stand as firmly upon his artificial legs as he once stood upon his own. Orderlies and the boys in the hospital watched him fighting his battle. They lent what aid they could and he was filled with gratitude to them; but they could not know the depths he plumbed, he who had been so active.

It took him three weeks to learn to walk, three of the most depressing weeks of his life. By then he had largely mastered the technique, the art of balancing; all the little movements of walking and sitting and rising from a chair. By then he began to feel that the seemingly insuperable difficulty had been overcome and that the rest would follow... it was just a matter of time and practice.

Following that month in hospital at Roehampton, he was granted two months leave, part of which was spent at his home in Yorkshire. Then he went off to spend some of his holiday with his friend Sir Philip Sassoon.[3] While there he experienced the greatest thrill of his life. An aircraft stood before him - it was an Avro 504K and he climbed in, not with the old agility, perhaps, but with considerably greater ease than most people exercise the first time they clamber into an aircraft. He settled himself into place, had a good look round the cockpit, waggled the stick, fingered the throttle and swung the rudder from side to side with his artificial legs just to get the feel of it.

He was going to fly again. He felt sure he could do it. There was no doubt about it. Perhaps, far, far back in his mind there lurked the merest shadow of uncertainty, so slight as to be almost unnoticed. So he took off, as he had done hundreds of times before to enjoy the ecstasy of flight, landing perfectly to demonstrate to the world that a man, given the will and skill, can fly as well with artificial legs as with his own. He had no trouble at all. That day he proved to himself that the so-called impossible is possible.

In September 1932 he went back to duty at Uxbridge. Later he was posted to the Central Flying School where he was permitted by the medical board to fly in dual controlled aircraft. It soon became obvious that he flew as competently and confidently with his artificial legs as any pilot could fly with his own legs. The accident had not affected his nerve. He could do all the aerobatics with the same joy and abandon as of old. The result was that he flew all the normal service types of aircraft without any difficulty and went off from the Central Flying School with a letter written to the Air Ministry saying he was 100 per cent competent as a pilot.

Fortified by his recent flying experience, with such a letter to back him, he went up for his final medical examination before the Central Medical Board, thinking it would be merely a formality and that he would at once be passed as fit. Physically he was as fit as any man alive. To his consternation the Board refused to pass him. He could hardly believe his ears. 'I'm sorry we cannot pass you fit, because there is nothing in the King's Regulations which covers your case,' said the President.

It was true. There was nothing in the King's Regulations to cover the case of the one man in the world who was genius enough to fly as well with artificial legs as the ordinary pilot flies with his own legs.

The iron will which had sustained the brilliant young pilot through all those dark days and had enabled him to accomplish a miracle broke down before that verdict. He lost his temper. The injustice of deluding him by letting him go back to fly and then rejecting him when he had proved himself fit was too much for him to suffer in silence. His protests, however, made no difference. A few weeks later he received a letter from the Air Ministry asking him to resign on the grounds of ill-health. In the circumstances there was nothing else he could do, so Flying Officer Bader was forced to relinquish the career he loved, the one which he had chosen above all others, the one in which he had sacrificed his limbs and nearly his life and for which he had learned to do what no other man had ever done. It was a black day for him when he dropped his resignation in the post.

So the young pilot gave up his career in the Royal Air Force and in May 1933, joined the staff of the Asiatic Petroleum Company[4] donning a hard hat and the clothes of a city man in place of the air force blue, reaching the office at 9 o'clock in the morning and leaving for home at 5 o'clock. But if his artificial feet were anchored to the earth his heart was still in the sky. Now and again in the course of his duties on the aviation side of the business he flew in a passenger liner to the continent. Then the urge to fly must have welled up in him stronger than ever. At very rare intervals he took up an aircraft for a short time to taste again the joys of flying.

Determined in 1935 to get back to the Royal Air Force, he had an interview with Air Vice-Marshal Sir Frederick Bowhill, who was then Air Member for Personnel and later became the Chief of the Coastal Command. Sir Frederick Bowhill received him most sympathetically, but the earlier ruling seemed to preclude all possibility of the pilot rejoining the Royal Air Force. Bader bowed to the decision, but in his heart he did not accept it. Meanwhile he continued to live the life of a city man and go to his office regularly.

The tense atmosphere of Munich in 1938 drove him once again to try to get back to the Royal Air Force. Air Chief Marshal Sir Charles Portal, who is now Chief of Air Staff, was then Air Member for Personnel and to him Bader wrote a letter asking if he could be taken back on the reserve in order to be in flying practice if war broke out. The reply he received from Sir Charles Portal set his mind at rest. Although it pointed out that the Medical Board would not hear of it, Sir Charles added that he could rest assured that in the event of war they would accept his services. The young city man, who longed to don the Royal Air Force blue again, was content. For a year he continued to go to the office, while the European skies grew darker under the menace of German might. In the six years since he had left the Royal Air Force he had flown for perhaps five hours, no more. But he had no doubt about his ability to fly. At the outbreak of war his application to rejoin the RAF was answered by an appointment to see Air Vice-Marshal Frederick Crosby Halahan CMG of the Royal Air Force Volunteer Reserve Selection Board.[5] Fortunately for Bader and for the country, this officer was his Commanding Officer while he was at Cranwell and was therefore well aware of his outstanding abilities and the miracle he had accomplished in learning to fly with artificial legs. This time the Medical Board was instructed to see if he was organically sound, apart from the loss of his legs and as he was in perfect health he was passed as fit. Off to the Central Flying School he went for a test, which gave him no trouble at all and on 26 November 1939 he took out his uniform and donned it once more as Flying Officer D. R. S. Bader.

Since his resignation from the service six years earlier, aircraft had made big strides; Spitfires and Hurricanes were coming into production, so he went to the Central Flying School for a refresher course on modern aircraft and flew like a bird - his artificial legs caused him no difficulty.

Posted as Flying Officer in February 1940 to 19 Spitfire Squadron, he was promoted to Flight Lieutenant two months later and posted to 222 Squadron with which squadron of Spitfires he fought and patrolled over Dunkirk. During patrols over Dunkirk he proved his ability by shooting down a Messerschmitt 109 and 110; but strangely enough although patrolling with the rest of his flight twice a day looking for the enemy, they did not often make contact, while other squadrons at different times of the day ran into flocks of German aircraft.

From high in the sky he saw Dunkirk ablaze. He stated afterwards that one of the most remarkable things was the sight of a great column of solid black smoke from the oil tanks pushing through a blanket of cloud over which he was flying at 10,000 feet. There was the great white level sea of cloud, with a dense peak of black smoke thrusting through the surface. It was an unusual sight that he will not soon forget. His graphic description of the evacuation from Dunkirk calls up the whole picture in a few words: 'The sea from Dover to Dunkirk was like the Great West Road on a Bank Holiday. It was covered with shipping of all descriptions.'[6]

His dash and leadership over Dunkirk brought him further promotion on 24 June 1940, when Air Chief Marshal Trafford Leigh-Mallory gave Bader command of 242 (Canadian) Squadron languishing at RAF Coltishall having been decimated in the Battle of France. In late September 1939 when Lord Gort's BEF moved across the English Channel to France, four Hurricane squadrons - 1, 73 85 and 87 went with them. By mid November 607 and 615, equipped with Gloster Gladiators were sent to reinforce them. All political attempts to persuade the RAF to send Spitfires to France were resisted but the movement of the Hurricanes and the Gladiators left Dowding with about 35 on paper for the defence of Britain. On 15 May 1940 Winston Churchill promised France's Premier, Paul Reynaud ten fighter squadrons. On 16 May any thoughts of sending fighter squadrons to France was vetoed emphatically by Sir Cyril Newall, Chief of the Air Staff. He told Churchill that he did not think that a few more fighter squadrons would make any difference between victory and defeat in France. By then the ten Hurricane squadrons in France had lost 195 Hurricanes. Some squadrons were down to two and three fighters and another had lost 26 pilots. One of the worst hit was 242 Squadron. Between May and June 1940 the all-Canadian fighter squadron had lost every pilot of Flying Officer rank and middle echelon officers, over enemy territory. Canadian Flying Officer Russ Wiens had noted: 'The war in the air today makes shows like Dawn Patrol look like Sunday School.'[7]

These were the fighters whom he led so brilliantly throughout the Battle of Britain. Their Hurricanes tore through the German masses and wrought terrible havoc. So cleverly were they led, so fiercely did they fight that their losses were trifling compared with the losses they inflicted.

On 11 July Squadron Leader Bader claimed his second victory, a Dornier Do 17Z off Cromer. It was the first of eleven victories Bader scored while leading 242 Squadron before he was promoted to Wing Commander Flying of the Tangmere Wing in March 1941.

The German air offensive began to flare up in earnest on 30th August when the Canadian fighters shot down twelve of the enemy without loss to themselves. Fighter Command lost 39 fighters on 31 August, when the RAF flew 2,020 sorties and the Luftwaffe almost 2,800 sorties against London's sector airfields. These were the worst losses of the Battle so far and they brought the number of RAF pilots killed and wounded that week to 115 with 65 of the fighters downed on the 30th and 31st. By Friday 6 September, a huge German invasion fleet appeared to be ready to sail. British forces were put on 'Alert No. 2' meaning that an attack was probable in the next two days. On Saturday 7 September 984 Hurricane and Spitfire pilots were flying with the squadrons, a deficiency of nearly 22 pilots per squadron and of these 150 were only partly-trained.

Bader's firmly-held belief that more damage could be done by large formations of fighters led directly to the 'Big Wing' argument between his AOC, Trafford Leigh Mallory and the 11 Group Commander, Keith Park. By September 1940 he was frequently leading a mixed Hurricane and Spitfire Wing of five squadrons into action with controversial results. AVM Trafford Leigh-Mallory told Bader that 242 and 310 Squadrons' Hurricanes would use Duxford daily. Together with 19 Squadron operating out of the satellite at nearby Fowlmere, they would form the 'Big Wing'. At first there was no 'trade' for Bader to pursue and he practiced with the 'Duxford Wing' for four days, reducing take-off times to just three minutes, the same as a squadron, climbing 242 on a straight course followed by 310 Czech Squadron and 19 Squadron. Though they were not called into action on 1 September, Fighter Command sent up 147 patrols involving 700 fighters and lost fifteen aircraft from which nine pilots survived. The Luftwaffe lost fourteen aircraft. The Duxford Wing began to operate on the morning of Friday 6 September but no contact was made with the enemy. (Later, the Wing was joined by 302 'City of Poznań' with Hurricane Is and 611 'West Lancashire' AAF, with Spitfires. On paper this was the equivalent of sixty or more fighters). On Monday 9 September they chased the enemy bombers over London and came up with them over the Thames at Hammersmith - I happened to be in a train packed solid with passengers when bombs were dropped and that fight was going on overhead, but people were so interested in the air battle that they completely ignored their own danger - that day the 'Duxford Wing' drove the enemy aircraft towards Enfield around which eleven [of the 28 enemy aircraft officially destroyed this day] all crashed, while only one pilot of 242 Squadron was lost [sic].[8]

On Saturday 14th September the Canadian squadron destroyed twelve. On 15 September claims by the Duxford Wing at the end of the day were 44 enemy aircraft shot down, with eight probables. Overall, Fighter Command claimed to have shot down 185 aircraft, but the true figure was 56 German aircraft shot down for the loss of 26 RAF fighters but thirteen pilots were saved. On the 18th they shot down eleven without any losses to themselves. Altogether, the Duxford Wing claimed thirty destroyed, six probables and two damaged in the air battle. Ten were claimed by 242 Squadron while 19 and 302 Squadrons had claimed seven each and 310, six. Despite the Duxford Wing's claims, only nineteen Luftwaffe aircraft had been shot down during that memorable afternoon with II./KG77 losing nine Ju 88s over the Thames Estuary. Twelve British fighters were lost but only three of the pilots were killed, in the course of 1,165 sorties.

The last 'Big Wing' 'thrash' came on Friday 27 September when the Luftwaffe mounted heavy attacks on London and one on Bristol and made phased attacks on airfields in Nos. 10 and 11 Groups. The Canadians shot down six for a loss of one pilot.[9] Total claims by the 'Duxford Wing' for 27 September were twelve destroyed. This brought Bader's Big Wing claims to 152 aircraft shot down for the loss of thirty pilots. The Luftwaffe lost 55 aircraft including 21 bombers and 19 Bf 109s. The RAF lost 28 fighters. In all, during the Battle of London, Squadron Leader Bader's Canadians destroyed 63 aircraft and lost only three of their own pilots. It was a magnificent record.

While those battles were raging, Squadron Leader Bader himself shot down ten of the enemy aircraft. Two of them were fighters, Messerschmitt 109s[10] but the remainder were all bombers, twin-engined aircraft, Junkers 88, Dornier 17 or Messerschmitt 110. Once he was leading eight pilots of his squadron when they ran into 100 of the enemy at about 15,000 feet. The Hurricanes promptly sailed in to such good effect that the nine fighters between them shot down twelve of the enemy, completely breaking up the formations and sending the survivors fleeing for their lives. From that battle the Canadians emerged unscathed.

Once a friend asked Bader if he was ever bored. 'I'm never bored except by lack of fighting,' he replied. 'The Germans never dodge - they always run away.'

During the mass attacks on London, he saw one German bomber shot down and crash right into the heart of a fiery furnace. There was another day when his eagerness to get at the enemy might easily have ended his life if the little god of chance had not been watching over him.

Notification of an impending attack reached him a little late and he and his squadron were unable to take off in time to reach the required altitude. In his anxiety to come to grips with the enemy he gave his Hurricane full boost and shot ahead so rapidly that he left the rest of his formation, with the exception of one pilot who kept up with him, trailing out behind him. Approaching him over the Thames Estuary were 36 bombers, with attendant Messerschmitt fighters above. Without hesitation he and the pilot who followed him made a beam attack. As he swept past the formation, he turned in behind the bombers. At once the German bombers opened up with all their guns upon the two Hurricanes. In the concentrated gunfire of the 36 bombers their destruction appeared to be certain. The squadron leader said afterwards that he could see the tracers streaming past him like hail. To make his position more deadly some Messerschmitt 109s dived down and started to fire on the Hurricanes from behind, so the two British fighters were fairly caught between two fires. Instantly Squadron Leader Bader did the sensible thing and broke off the attack. In turning away a Messerschmitt 110 came right into his sights and he immediately shot it down. As his companion swerved to avoid colliding with another German bomber he gave it a burst which sent it crashing, so they took their toll in the very act of escaping. When the two Hurricanes landed they were simply riddled with bullet holes - they were in fact unfit to fly, although the two pilots managed to fly them safely home. The other pilot got a bullet right through his reflector sight, yet it did not touch him; Squadron Leader Bader got an explosive bullet in the cockpit which missed him by just two inches. Anyone seeing those two aircraft would have sworn it was impossible for the pilots to escape, yet neither was touched. The little god of chance was certainly looking after them that day. To see the Canadians lounging in their chairs at the dispersal point, with the yellow dope on their Mae Wests almost rubbed away by continual usage and to watch the way they were galvanized into life by the entrance of their squadron leader and his terse: 'Come on!' was to witness a living example of leadership. He was the captain of their team and they would have followed him anywhere, as they did. They flew into the fury of the fight undismayed by any odds. It must have been a sad blow to them and to him when his promotion to the rank of Wing Commander in March 1941 compelled him to relinquish his command and go elsewhere.

As the Battle of Britain entered its final phase it was clear that the Duxford Wing was unlikely to see much further action as speed of reaction was essential when trying to intercept incoming high level fighter sweeps. For another fortnight the Duxford Wing assembled each day at Duxford and patrolled London, usually twice a day, but the Luftwaffe had been reigned in during the daylight hours and victories were few and far between. On 12 October Hitler postponed Operation 'Sea Lion' [the intended invasion of Britain] until the following spring.

Honours and promotion have come to Wing Commander D. R. S. Bader DSO and Bar and DFC and Bar for his fearless leadership and the many victories he has won in the air. But his greatest triumph of all was won when, deprived of his legs, he determined to prove that if the will be strong and the spirit be right, the gravest physical disabilities of man can be overcome.

He has proved it to the world and most relentlessly of all to the fifteen Germans whom he has sent flaming out of the skies down to the earth they have defiled.

Endnotes Chapter 1

1 *Duxford and the Big Wings 1940-45; RAF and USAAF Fighter Pilots At War* by Martin W. Bowman (Pen & Sword 2009). Later Bader brought his wife Thelma down to stay at the 'Red Lion' at Whittlesford just outside Duxford. 'Her landlady was a formidable woman known as 'The Sea Lion' because of a tendency to a straggling black moustache. She dominated everyone and Thelma was getting a little restive until Douglas gave 'The Sea Lion' the benefit of his overwhelming personality, fixing her eyes with his glittering eyes and speaking a few forceful words. 'The Sea Lion' and he became great friends after that and Thelma was happy.' *Reach for the Sky* by Paul Brickhill (Collins 1954).

2 Douglas Robert Stewart Bader was born in St. John's Wood, North London on 21 February 1910, spending the early years of his life in India, before being sent home to school. He gained a prize cadetship to the RAF College at Cranwell in September 1928, and on graduation was posted to 23 Squadron in July 1930, flying Gloster Gamecocks. He played rugby for the RAF, Harlequins, Surrey and Combined Services teams, and cricket for the RAF. In 1931 he represented the squadron in the pairs' aerobatic competition at Hendon, now flying Bristol Bulldog IIAs.

3 Sir Philip Albert Gustave David Sassoon, 3rd Baronet, PC GBE CMG (born 4 December 1888) was a British politician, art collector and social host, entertaining many celebrity guests at his homes, Port Lympne Mansion, Kent and Trent Park, Hertfordshire. Sassoon died on 3 June 1939, aged 50, of complications from influenza.
4 Later renamed Shell. And he got married, to Thelma.
5 AVM Halahan died on 17 October 1965 aged 85. Flight Lieutenant Michael Frederick Crosby Halahan his son was killed while serving on 74 Squadron on 18 March 1941 at age 29.
6 On 1 June he scored the first of his twenty aerial victories when he shot down a Bf 109E over Dunkirk and also was awarded a half share in a He 111 'probable'.
7 *The Few, Summer 1940, the Battle of Britain,* by Philip Kaplan and Richard Collier (Orion 2002). Flying Officer Russell Henry Wiens (22), who was wounded in the Battle of Britain, was killed in an Anson he was flying on 20 May 1941 at No.31 ANS, Port Albert, Canada. The crew was flying a navigation exercise and whilst the aircraft was at 4,000 feet, Wiens tried to fire a Very cartridge but it did not ignite. He withdrew the pistol and examined the cartridge which fell on the floor and ignited. The crew's attempts to extinguish the fire were unsuccessful and four RAAF men abandoned the aircraft safely. Wiens then attempted a forced landing in a small field 5 miles North of Listowel, Ontario but the aircraft crashed and he received fatal injuries.

On 11 July 1940 Squadron Leader Bader claimed his second victory, a Dornier Do 17Z off Cromer. It was the first of 11 victories Bader scored while leading 242 before he was promoted to Wing Commander Flying of the Tangmere Wing in March 1941.
8 The 242 Squadron ORB (Operational Record Book) for 9 September said: Squadron Leader Bader leading wing consisting of 242, 310 and 19 Squadrons patrolling over London encountered large formation of e/a bombers and fighters. 242 Squadron led the attack and shot down ten aircraft. 310 (Czech) Squadron shot down seven and 19 Squadron two. One pilot of 242 killed [Pilot Officer Kirkpatrick MacLure Sclanders a Canadian died when he crash landed his Hurricane I (P3087) near Rye after being attacked in the air]. One pilot [Sergeant Robert Henry Lonsdale, who was shot down by Bf 109s] bailed out and returned to the Squadron the next day unhurt. Congratulations received from Air Officer Command and Chief of the Air Staff.
9 Pilot Officer M. G. Homer in Hurricane P2967 who was shot down and crashed near Sittingbourne in Kent after combat with Bf 109s near Dover.
10 One of the two Bf 109Es Bader claimed on 27 September was credited as a victory; the other was recorded as a probable. On 1 June he was credited with a Bf 109E and a third share in a Heinkel 111 probable. From 11 July to 18 September 1940 Bader's claims totalled ten aircraft destroyed and three Do 17s damaged. His final wartime score reached 20 and 4 shared destroyed, 6 and 1 shared probables, 11 damaged. *Aces High.*

Chapter 2

Heavy Odds

An American-born fighter pilot tells something of his experiences and excitements he's been through while serving in the RAF. He has shot down eight enemy aircraft and badly crippled three or four more and for these feats he was awarded the DFC yesterday. He is a Flight Lieutenant and his squadron has shot down more than fifty enemy planes.

BBC Broadcast, 9 June 1940.

James William Elias Davies was born of Welsh parents in Bernardsville, near Morristown, New Jersey, in 1913. His father ran a big farm there. James went to school first at the Morristown High School and when the family left there for Connecticut, he went to the Gilbert School in Winstead, Connecticut. The Davies' lived for a long time in New Hertford, Connecticut and James had many friends over there. He left the United States when he was about eighteen or nineteen years old. His parents, who had gone out to America two years before he was born, returned to Europe and settled down in Bridgend, South Wales. James went to Cardiff College to study wireless for a while and after doing 'this and that' for a year or two, he took a short service commission in the RAF. That was in 1936. Flying Officer Davies was posted to 79 Squadron immediately he had finished training - in March 1937 - and the fighter pilot liked it more and more each day.

'I got my first German on 21 November 1939' said Davies in a BBC radio broadcast. 'It was the first enemy aircraft to be shot down in the Straits of Dover in this war. I was on patrol between Deal and Calais, leading a section of Hurricanes from my squadron when we spotted, at 12,000 feet, a Dornier 17 'flying pencil'. He was about 2,000 feet below us and as we hadn't seen a German machine up to then, we went down carefully to make sure. We soon recognised him as an enemy and as I turned to attack he tried to attack me. My Hurricane quickly outmanoeuvred him. I got on his tail and gave him three sharp bursts of fire. Another member of the section got in three bursts too, as he dived towards the clouds. The last I saw of him was just above sea level. He had turned on his back and a moment later crashed into the sea. When we got back to the mess we were handed a parcel. It contained a bottle of champagne - with the compliments of the Station Commander. You see it was our first fight - and we'd won. In those days, one German aircraft was something to celebrate.[11]

'On 10 May, when Hitler invaded the Low Countries we went over to France [operating from Vitry for a period and then over Dunkirk, Davies acting as 'A' Flight Commander]. We went up that same afternoon. That time we didn't see anything, but the next day we really started. We carried out three patrols east of Brussels and on the third patrol we saw three Heinkel 111s. We shot down one and badly damaged the other two. The day after that we got two Heinkel 111s, one of which was credited to me.[12] I shot mine down from 12,000 feet.

'All the same, those skirmishes were child's play to what was to come later. On 14 May, after we had escorted a number of Blenheim bombers into enemy territory, we were on our way back when we saw three Dornier 17 'Flying Pencils'. It was a trap, for when we gave chase to the Dorniers, we suddenly found ourselves in the middle of between fifty and sixty Messerschmitt 109s and 110s. I was leading the flight that day and when I realised how hopelessly outnumbered we were, I gave orders to the boys to sort out their own targets and not to keep formation. We broke up and began to set about the Messerschmitts. I got four Me 110[13] and other members of the flight got four more. On the way back to our base, I saw two Heinkel 126s, one of which I shot down and damaged the other with the rest of my ammunition. It was a good day. We routed an overwhelming number of enemy fighters, beat up two of their Army reconnaissance planes and we all got home safely. Our bag on that day was six. There were six of us, so we averaged one each.

'There were several other days when we ran into heavy odds of enemy fighters[14] It is really amazing, looking back, that we should have had the success we had. But it certainly was a success each day. We never ran into the Germans without shooting some down. When we were patrolling Dunkirk, for instance, giving protection day after day to the BEF we always got a few. I remember once [on 7 June, in the Abbeville area], when we found ourselves in the thick of six squadrons of Me 109s and 110s, we saw an unusual type of enemy fighter. They were the new Heinkel 113s. Naturally we couldn't resist the appointment. We got one of each type and three or four of what we call 'probables'. I was attacking a Me 110 when I suddenly realised that there were six Heinkel 113s on my tail. I made a very quick turn to get away from them and then shot down the Heinkel 113 on the extreme left of that particular formation. That was in the afternoon. We had an 'appetiser' before lunch, when we met twenty Heinkel 111 bombers. I got one. He went down in flames.[15] And others of the squadron got their share. 'The smoke from innumerable fires in Dunkirk and other French coast towns was terrific about that time. A fellow pilot described it as being like a gigantic piece of cotton-wool lying right across the seashore, following the coast down the Channel as far as he could see, even from two or three miles up. There were times when we found that same smoke of great assistance in outwitting enemy fighters.

'One of our squadron, for instance, used up all his ammunition in shooting down two Me 110s one day and found himself being chased by two more. Without ammunition he could do nothing, so he dived into the smoke over Dunkirk. He emerged above the smoke a few miles away and there the Messerschmitts were still waiting for him. They simply stuck above the smoke waiting for him to emerge, a victim for their guns. But he outwitted them by diving back into the smoke and was able to slip away home, only to be off again into battle the same evening.

'We were stationed in France for eleven days. I remember that when we went away the roses were in bud; and when we came back they were in full bloom. In between we'd had eleven glorious days of action, but it was very hard work.'

'On 27 June James Davies was returning from escorting a formation of six Blenheims to St Valery in France when the 79 Squadron was 'bounced' by Bf 109s and he failed to return. A second Hurricane pilot bailed out and a third escaped. The award of a DFC was announced on 8 June and the medal was due to be presented to him by the King at Biggin Hill on the day he was lost.

Endnotes Chapter 2

11 Davies was awarded a half-share in the destruction of the Dornier Do 17.

12 His claim for a second Heinkel 111 was unconfirmed.

13 Davies was awarded with just one Bf 110.

14 Davies was awarded a Do 17 on 18 May to take his score to four and one shared destroyed. On 27 May he was awarded a Bf 110 destroyed and a Bf 110 damaged.

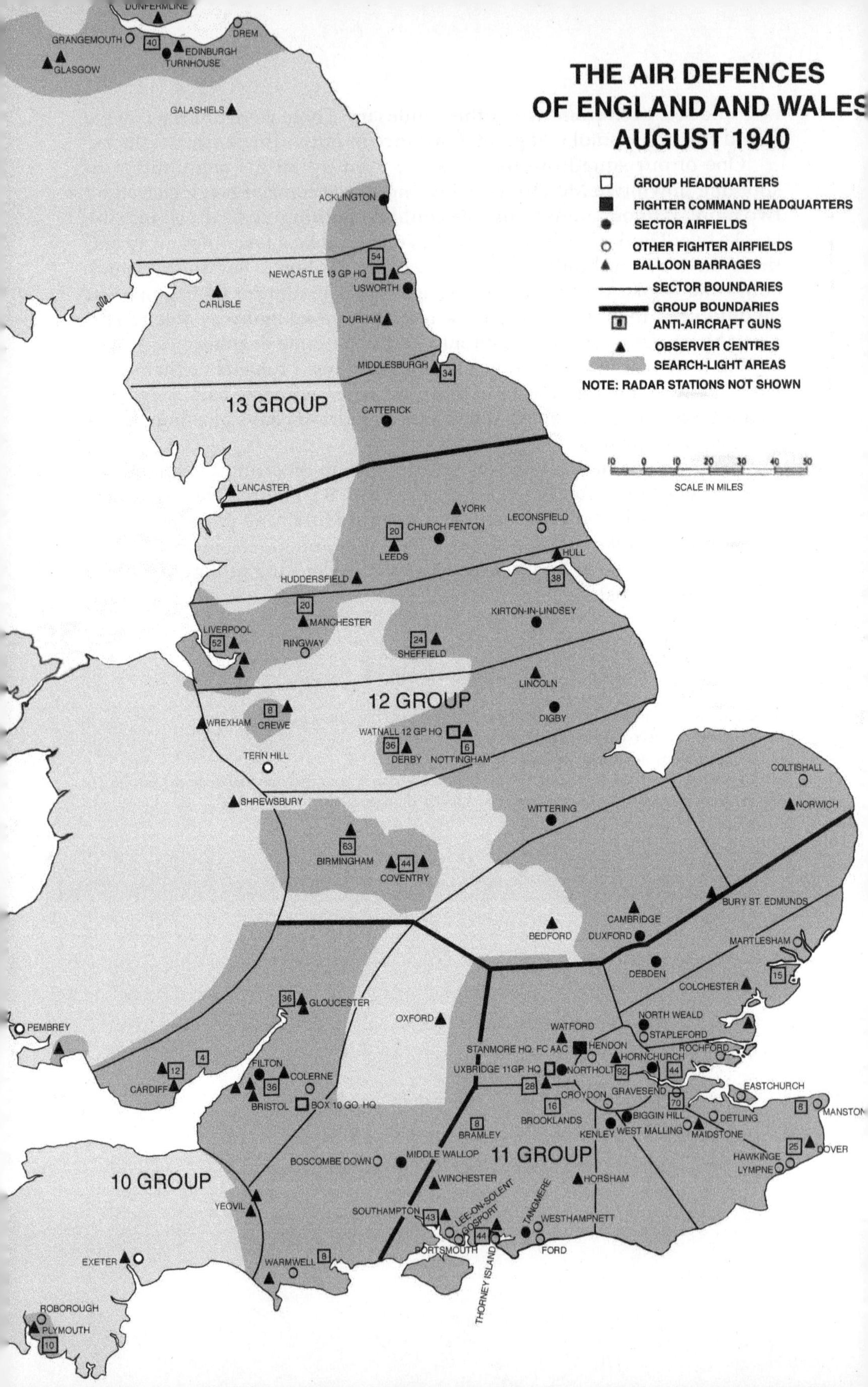
THE AIR DEFENCES OF ENGLAND AND WALES AUGUST 1940
GROUP HEADQUARTERS
FIGHTER COMMAND HEADQUARTERS
SECTOR AIRFIELDS
OTHER FIGHTER AIRFIELDS
BALLOON BARRAGES
SECTOR BOUNDARIES
GROUP BOUNDARIES
ANTI-AIRCRAFT GUNS
OBSERVER CENTRES
SEARCH-LIGHT AREAS
NOTE: RADAR STATIONS NOT SHOWN
10 0 10 20 30 40 50
SCALE IN MILES
13 GROUP
12 GROUP
11 GROUP
10 GROUP
DUNFERMLINE
DREM
GRANGEMOUTH
EDINBURGH
TURNHOUSE
GLASGOW
GALASHIELS
ACKLINGTON
NEWCASTLE 13 GP HQ
USWORTH
CARLISLE
DURHAM
MIDDLESBURGH
CATTERICK
LANCASTER
YORK
CHURCH FENTON
LECONSFIELD
LEEDS
HULL
HUDDERSFIELD
KIRTON-IN-LINDSEY
MANCHESTER
LIVERPOOL
RINGWAY
SHEFFIELD
LINCOLN
DIGBY
WREXHAM
CREWE
WATNALL 12 GP HQ
DERBY
NOTTINGHAM
TERN HILL
SHREWSBURY
COLTISHALL
NORWICH
WITTERING
BIRMINGHAM
COVENTRY
BURY ST. EDMUNDS
CAMBRIDGE
BEDFORD
DUXFORD
MARTLESHAM
DEBDEN
COLCHESTER
GLOUCESTER
OXFORD
PEMBREY
NORTH WEALD
STAPLEFORD
WATFORD
STANMORE HQ. FC AAC
HENDON
ROCHFORD
HORNCHURCH
UXBRIDGE 11GP. HQ
NORTHOLT
CARDIFF
FILTON
COLERNE
BRISTOL
BOX 10 GO. HQ
GRAVESEND
EASTCHURCH
CROYDON
MANSTON
BROOKLANDS
BIGGIN HILL
DETLING
BRAMLEY
KENLEY
WEST MALLING
MAIDSTONE
DOVER
HAWKINGE
LYMPNE
BOSCOMBE DOWN
MIDDLE WALLOP
WINCHESTER
HORSHAM
YEOVIL
SOUTHAMPTON
LEE-ON-SOLENT
GOSPORT
TANGMERE
WESTHAMPNETT
PORTSMOUTH
FORD
THORNEY ISLAND
EXETER
WARMWELL
ROBOROUGH
PLYMOUTH

Chapter 3

Eagle Squadron

'An unidentified Pilot Officer RAF'

This is the story of 'Red' Tobin. Late in 1939 three Americans - Andrew 'Andy' Mamedoff, a 29-year old Jewish-American whose family were White Russian émigrés from Siberia and Eugene Quimby 'Red' Tobin and 26-year old Vernon Charles 'Shorty' Keough crossed into Canada, the three soldiers of fortune, some would have called them mercenaries, intending to head for Europe and fly for the Finns in the Russo-Finnish war. Tobin was a lanky 6 foot redhead from Los Angeles, the son of a real estate broker, who had learned to fly in the late 1930s, paying for his lessons by working as a guide and messenger at the MGM studios in Hollywood. Peter Townsend remembered that 'He was a fine and gentle man who might have stepped straight out of a Western. His language was coloured with phrases like 'Saddle up boy; I'm ridin' that sent his fitter running to start up his Spitfire.' Keough was a 4 feet 10 inch New Yorker from Brooklyn. He had been a professional parachutist and stunt pilot, had made more than 500 jumps and had logged several hundred flying hours, scraping by as a barnstormer. Apparently he was so short because he had two vertebrae removed after a parachute accident. When Finland fell they were told that they would be able to join the Armée de l'Air so they had set sail for St. Nazaire on the French Atlantic coast, arriving in Paris on 4 June. From then on their escapades read like a Hemingway novel.

'I expect it must seem a long hop from guiding visitors round the movie studios in Culver City to fighting in an eight-gun Spitfire over London. But that's just how it happened to me and all within a little more than a year, with some exciting adventures in between. It was only my second air fight when I helped rout Goering's mass attack on September 15th. And I had the good luck to shoot down my first raider.

During the battle, the air over Surrey, Kent and Sussex was full of bombers and fighters. At 20,000 feet I met a formation of Me 110s. I gave one a burst and saw him giving out smoke. But I lost him in the cloud before I could press home my attack. Then below me I saw a big Dornier 215 bomber trying to seek the safety of some clouds. I followed it down and gave it a long squirt. Its left motor stopped and its right aileron came to bits. Smoke was pouring from it as the bomber disappeared in a cloud. I followed. Suddenly the clouds broke and on the ground I saw a number of crashed aircraft. It was an amazing sight. They had all crashed within a radius of about twenty miles from our fighter station. My Dornier was there too. I was quite sure I could see it. A little later I learned that the Intelligence Officer's report on the damage to the crashed Dornier agreed with my own, so I knew I had claimed my first definite German victim.

That was a great day for England. I thought this little island was going to sink under the weight of crashed enemy planes on that day. And was I proud to be in the battle! It was the fulfilment of a year's ambition.

But let me go back and tell you the story of this momentous year.

My home is in Hollywood. It was in the wonderful Californian climate that I was born, educated and learnt to fly. I don't suppose there are more than seven days in a year when you can't take the air in California. I learnt to fly at the Mine Fields, Los Angeles. I was always pretty keen on flying and whenever there were no classes at school I hurried out to the airfield to put in all the time I could learning about aircraft and their vices. My instructors were mostly army people. I went through the various graduations and by July last year I was a fully qualified charter pilot.

For nearly two months last year I flew parties up to the High Sierras in California on hunting and fishing expeditions. It was pretty tricky flying, because you get some fierce down drafts and you can't be too careful.
I had a civilian job of course in the MGM studios at Culver City; I finally acted as guide for visitors to the studios. I used to meet all the film stars and found them nice ordinary folk. But my studio jobs didn't keep me from flying and in the winter of 1939 I took a course in aerodynamics at evening school.

Then a number of us met Colonel Sweeny, whose name you will know from his association with the 'Escadrille Lafayette' in the last war.[16] With him we decided it would be a grand idea to form a flight and go out and fly for Finland. But, I guess, that war was over before we could get going.

In May of this year we decided to form a squadron of all American flyers, another Escadrille Lafayette. The adventure was off. Several of us went by train from Los Angeles, through the States to Canada. Finally we finished up at Halifax, Nova Scotia, where we got split up. I joined a large French motor vessel, which was part of a big convoy sailing for France. My boat could do about sixteen knots but she had to travel at only six. In front of us was a boat with 400 mules on board. The stench from the mules was something awful and so was the weather. We had pursuit planes, bombers and munitions of all sorts on board, cargo worth in all about seven and a half million dollars. We rolled and pitched all the way across the Atlantic and were mighty thankful after seventeen days to tie up at St. Nazaire.

All our plans went haywire at St. Nazaire. I had no passport and had lost my birth certificate. Naturally the French treated me with suspicion.
Incidentally, there's a story about that birth certificate. In all my journeys up and down France, I stuck to an old shirt just in case I wanted a spare one any time. Only last week I took out that shirt and from it dropped my birth certificate.

The next thing was to get to Paris and meet the rest of the boys. I took three and a half days to reach the capital and there I met my friends who had disembarked at Bordeaux. Just outside Paris while in the train I had my first experience of being bombed. The scream of the bombs dropping on the suburban houses from about 20,000 feet was awful.

We made our way to the French Air Ministry, saw high officials there and were given our physical examination. The French didn't hurry and we were in and out of the Ministry for three days. They kept telling us that all would be well and that we would be flying any day soon. Actually we spent a whole month in Paris, doing nothing, for nothing could be done for us.

Then suddenly one day we realised that Paris was going to be evacuated. As the Air Ministry had gone, we made up our minds to get going as well - to Tours. A pall of smoke - which might have been a smokescreen - covered the city and you couldn't see more than a block away. There must have been 10,000 people at one station, all patiently waiting for trains to take them to safety - staunch solemn queues all around the station - men, women and children.

It took us a day and a half to reach Tours and it was an awful journey. Sometimes we had to ride between the cars to get a breath of fresh air. But there was no panic among the refugees, just fear and depression. We didn't lose a bit of luggage on this journey. We spent a week at Tours and were bombed by Heinkels and Dorniers every day. There was a pretty big party of us by now, most of them belonging to the French Air Force. We left Tours by bus for Chinon, about an hour's ride away. We got away just in time, for the Nazis bombed and machined -gunned the main bridge out of Tours just as it was packed with refugees. The bridge was completely destroyed and very many refugees were killed.

Things weren't looking at all good. We were tired and food was getting scarce. We set out for Arcay about four hundred of us of all ranks and from there walked another fifteen miles to Air Vault. Our boots were completely worn out and we had no food and no water. Dog-tired, we lay down in some fields at Air Vault, but not for long. At nearly midnight we were ordered by an elderly French officer to get going once again, this time to Bordeaux. It took us three and a half days in a packed train to reach Bordeaux and when we got there we found that the French Air Ministry could do nothing for us. We Americans were pretty sore by this time and thought that the best thing we could do would be to take some aircraft and fly to England. But that little plan didn't come off and we began our travels again determined to get out of the country.

Our little bunch went by bus to Bayonne. The British consul had left. We had no money and were starving. Eventually we made our way to Ste-Jean-de-Luz and were lucky enough to get the American consul. He was a fine guy and treated us pretty handsomely. But he told us the situation was pretty bad and advised us to quit. There was a crowd pouring into Ste-Jean-de-Luz and the quayside was crowded with refugees. They came any old way they could, in cars, on motorcycles and cycles. The cycles they did not bother to park, but simply threw them in the water.

We boarded a British ship, *Baron-Nairn*, a little old-timer of seven knots. We were a mixed crowd on board. Our number included seven hundred Polish refugees. A tragedy occurred as we were going on board. We had only one suitcase between our little bunch. The handle came off and into the water she went with all our belongings. All the extras I had then were a pair of shorts and a couple of shirts. We sailed across the Bay of Biscay. It was a three-day journey and all we had to eat was a dog biscuit - even the one dog on board wouldn't eat them. The boat had no cargo and rolled pretty badly. But the crew were rather kind and did all they could for us. Eventually we made Plymouth, although I thought at one time we were bound for South Africa judging by the ship's course.

I guess we weren't too popular at Plymouth. We had no papers and we were evacuated straight away to London. We were put in an ice-skating rink and had to stay there for three days. We weren't allowed out at all. We rang up the Air Ministry, who sent round an officer to see us. He was very kind but didn't hold out much hope that the Air Force could use us at the moment. We talked it over between us and made up our minds to return to America. We rang the Embassy who sent round a representative to see us. He got our particulars, checked them over with Washington, fixed us up with passages to America and lent us £15 for food and clothing. It looked as if the adventure was over. Then, I forget how, we met a very fine English lady, who after hearing our story told us she was sure that a friend of hers, a well-known Member of Parliament, could do something for us. We met him next day in the Houses of Parliament and he sent us to the Air Ministry. We were given our physical examination at once. All passed and so we were in the Volunteer Reserve of the Royal Air Force for the duration of the war.

We felt pretty good when we went to the American Embassy. The officials there were mad with us at first for upsetting all the arrangements, but we soon smoothed that out. Things moved rapidly. Three of us, all in RAF uniforms, were sent north to an Officers' Training Unit. I had not flown for two months, but after twenty minutes in an advanced trainer I was put into a Spitfire.[17]

After twenty hours' flying in Spitfires I was attached to a station in the south, just in time for the opening of the big Blitz. But I had several weeks' training before I became operational that is, fit to fight. And I guess my first fight was lucky. I was patrolling high over an English port on the South Coast when I saw some Me 110s. I went into them and hit the first guy with my first burst. He was quickly lost in a cloud. Then another Me 110 shot ahead of me. I gave him a long burst and saw my stuff entering his fuselage. He climbed steeply then and then as steeply dived in a sort of spin. I couldn't turn on oxygen and suddenly had what they call over here a blackout. I went into a sort of dream from which I awakened when I was only 1,000 feet from the ground. I think I heard myself say 'you'd better come to, you're in trouble.' Anyway, I landed safely with two probables in my 'bag'.

And now, we Americans are a separate squadron. We wear RAF uniforms with the American Eagle on the shoulder. It's a grand idea this Eagle squadron of all American flyers[18] We must try and make a name for ourselves, just like the famous 'Escadrille Lafayette'. After all, we're all on the same side and all fighting in the same cause. The fellows in the squadron come from various parts of America - New York, Idaho, Minnesota, Oklahoma, Illinois and California. We're all flyers and very keen. We have got a lot to learn yet, of course and that is why I'm so glad to have been with an English fighter squadron, first. These English pilots certainly know their fighting tactics. My old squadron has brought down at least one hundred German aircraft. The German airmen may be pretty good formation flyers, but the British pilot has got the initiative in battle. He thinks quickly and gets results. He knows how to look after himself.

And are we lucky with our fighter planes? I guess the Spitfire is the finest fighter aircraft in the world. It's rugged and has no vices. I'd certainly rather fight with than against one.

We like England and its people who are cheerful and very easy to get on with. I miss the Californian weather, of course and if I could only have the English people and the Californian weather combined, everything would be grand. Everyone in the Royal Air Force is most kind to us all. They somehow seem to understand us and go out of their way to be helpful.

It's grand to say hello to everyone on behalf of the Eagle squadron. You can be sure we will do our very best, because we're in this business to try and do a little job of work for England.'

On 4 July 1941 'Andy' Mamedoff and 'Red' Tobin marked another death in the Eagle family when on that Independence Day afternoon they and the pilots of 71 Squadron bade their farewells to Billy Fiske, the first of the Eagles [sic] to fall, at a Memorial Service at St. Paul's cathedral in London.[19] Mamedoff became the first of the Eagles to take a war bride when he married Penny Craven, one of the most eligible young women in England, the daughter in the wealthy Craven cigarette family. Vic Bono, his best man, persuaded several members of the squadron to fly two 'honour guards' of the cannon armed Hurricanes after the church ceremony at Epping! The new bridegroom was posted to Coltishall on 1 August 1941 to be a flight commander in 133. A month later, on 7 September 'Red' Tobin went missing on 71 Squadron's first fighter sweep over France when six pilots of JG26 including Oberstleutnant Adolf Galland over claimed the three Eagle Squadron's Spitfires that were shot down. It is possible that the gangly 24-year old tangled with 22-year old Joachim Müncheberg commanding 7th Staffel, JG26 who downed the Spitfire northwest of Montreuil for his 53rd Abschuss (victory). Gone too were Hillard Fenlaw, like Mamedoff, recently married and Pilot Officer Bill Nichols, who shot up and forced to crash-land was soon captured. Tobin's sister Helen was visiting relatives in Denver when she received word that Gene was reported missing in action. His girlfriend in Los Angeles, 24-year old Anne Haring, a tall Irish beauty, contacted the International Red Cross as soon as she learned that he was missing. It was not until late October that she finally received confirmation that Tobin was dead. Mamedoff was now the only surviving member of the three brave, brash musketeers who had set out full of spirit and adventure to fight in Europe.

Early in October 1941 133 Squadron fled the Eagle's nest at Duxford and moved to Fowlmere. The Eagles' winter sojourn was short because on the

8th the fifteen Hurricanes piloted by American nationals left for Eglington, eight miles from Londonderry in Northern Ireland where they were to take further instruction amid rain, more rain and mud. At Fowlmere Mamedoff took off first and led them to Sealand to refuel. In less than hour they touched down at the transit station but overhead, storm clouds began rolling in from the Irish Sea. Only six of the Hurricane pilots that took off again reached RAF Andreas on the Isle of Man, a tiny pinprick in the Irish Sea, having missed several hilltops by only a few feet. Three landed at an intermediate airfield. Two more turned back for Sealand. The other four Eagles never arrived. One of them was Mamedoff. Local farmers found the 28-year old's broken body and blazing Hurricane in a field near the village of Maughold, southeast of Ramsey. On 14 October a telegram arrived at Lev and Natasha Mamedoff's Russian Bear restaurant in Connecticut telling them of their only son's death and that he was to be buried in Brookwood Military Cemetery in Woking.[20]

After the attack on Pearl Harbor on 7 December 1941 most of the Eagle Squadron pilots wanted to immediately join the fight against Japan. Representatives from 71 and 121 Squadrons went to the American Embassy in London and offered their services to the United States. The pilots from 71 Squadron decided they wanted to go to Singapore to fight the Japanese and a proposal was put to RAF Fighter Command, but it was turned down. The Dieppe Raid on 19 August 1942 was the only occasion that all three Eagle Squadrons saw action operating together. 71 Squadron moved from Debden to Gravesend in mid-August in anticipation of the Dieppe action, while 121 operated from Southend. 133 Squadron moved with 401 Squadron RCAF from RAF Biggin Hill to Lympne on the south coast. 71 Squadron claimed a Ju 88 shot down, 121 a FW 190, while 133 claimed four FW 190s, a Ju 88 and a Dornier Do 217. Six 'Eagle' Spitfires were lost, with one pilot taken prisoner and one killed.

By the end of September 1942 the three Eagle squadrons had claimed 73½ German aircraft destroyed while 77 American and five British members were killed. 71 Squadron claimed 41 victories, 121 Squadron, eighteen and 133 Squadron, 14½. On 29 September the three Eagle squadrons were officially turned over by the RAF to the fledgling Eighth Air Force and became the 4th Fighter Group, with the American pilots becoming officers in the USAAF. The Eagle pilots had earned twelve Distinguished Flying Crosses and one Distinguished Service Order. Of the thousands that volunteered, only 244 Americans served with the three Eagle Squadrons; sixteen Britons also served as squadron and flight commanders. About 100 Eagle pilots had been killed, were missing, or were prisoners and only four of the 34 original Eagle pilots were still present when the squadrons joined the USAAF. They retained their Spitfires until P-47 Thunderbolts became available in January 1943, conversion being completed in April 1943.

Endnotes Chapter 3

16 Charles M. Sweeny - soldier of fortune who fought in seven wars under five different flags - was born in Spokane, Washington on 26 January 1882. He enlisted as a Private in the Spanish American War fought in the Philippines and received an appointment to the USMA class of 1905 but dropped out around 1903. He then went to South America and participated in several revolutions there. In 1908 he joined the French Foreign Legion and was the first American ever to serve as a commissioned officer. He had a hand in organizing the 'Lafayette Escadrille' and may have flown with them. When America entered WWI he received a direct appointment to Major in the US Army and commanded an Infantry Battalion in the AEF. After WWI he served as a Brigadier in the Polish Army fighting the Bolsheviks. Later he served as a Brigadier with the White Russians fighting the Reds in the Russian Civil War. In 1920 he fought as a General with Gamal Atta Turk and helped organize and run the Turkish Revolution. Around 1925 he was back in the French Foreign Legion as a Colonel and fought Abdel Krim in North Africa. When WWII began he helped organize the Eagle Squadrons and served as a Group Captain in the RAF. When America entered WWII he moved to Switzerland to help Allen Dulles run agents in and out of the occupied countries. After WWII he was back in the French Foreign Legion fighting the Viet Minh in Indochina. He reportedly died of cancer, a wealthy man, in Las Vegas on 27 February 1963 and his tombstone supposedly reads 'Charles Michael Sweeny: Fought in every war worthy of the name War since 1898.'

17 On 26 September 1940 the three inseparable American soldiers of fortune were posted to Drem in Scotland where they became the proud founder members of 71 'Eagle' Squadron. The three Americans were posted to 609 Squadron at Warmwell in Dorset where they took part in the fighting. Tobin shared in the destruction of a Do 17 on 8 August and Keough shared in the destruction of a Do 17 on 18 September. 'Shorty's lack of height had never proved to be an impediment. 'Barring circus freaks', Keough was the smallest man some men had ever seen, had to be given a leg up into his Spitfire and he almost failed his medical board because of his lack of height. They thought that he would never ever reach the rudder bar in a Spit but Keough produced two seat cushions that he had brought with him all the way from the States via France especially for the purpose. One went under his parachute and raised him up, the other he wedged in the small of his back. Now he was able to see out of the cockpit and reach the bar! During a protection convoy just off the east coast on 15 February 1941 Keough failed to pull out of dive and his Hurricane smashed into the sea at over 500 mph. Vertigo was suspected but he had simply forgotten to turn on his oxygen and had blacked out for lack of air. The 29-year old died instantly he hit the water.

18 A total of three Eagle Squadrons were formed between September 1940 and July 1941. The first (71 Squadron) was formed in September 1940 and became operational on 5 February 1941 at Church Fenton, before a move to Kirton-in-Lindsey. In April, the squadron transferred to RAF Martlesham Heath in Suffolk for operations over Europe. During May they suffered their first loss when Mike Kolendorski was killed during a fighter sweep over the Netherlands. Intensity of operations stepped up with a move into 11 Group at North Weald by June 1941. On 2 July, William J. Hall became the first Eagle Squadron pilot to become a PoW when he was shot down during an escort operation. The squadron's first confirmed victory came on 21 July 1941 when Pilot Officer William R. Dunn destroyed a Bf 109F over Lille. In August, the Spitfire Mk II replaced 71 Squadron's Hurricanes, before quickly re-equipping with the latest Spitfire V. Numerous air kill claims were made on fighter sweeps over the continent during the summer and autumn of 1941. In December the Squadron was rested at Martlesham Heath, before a move to Debden in May 1942.

The second Eagle Squadron, 121 Squadron, was formed at RAF Kirton-in-Lindsey in May 1941, flying Hurricanes on coastal convoy escort duties. On 15 September 1941 it destroyed its first German aircraft. The Hurricanes were replaced with Spitfires and the Spitfire Mk V arrived in November 1941. The following month the Squadron moved to RAF North Weald, replacing 71 Squadron. In 1942 its offensive activities over the English Channel included bomber escorts and fighter sweeps.

The third and final Eagle Squadron - 133 - was formed at RAF Coltishall in July 1941, flying the Hurricane Mk IIb. A move to RAF Duxford followed in August and re-equipment with the Spitfire Mk V occurred early in 1942. In May the Squadron became part of the Biggin Hill Wing. On 31 July 1942 during a bomber escort to Abbeville, 52-victory 'Experte' Oberleutnant Rudolf Pflanz of 11./JG 2 engaged in combat with 133's Spitfires and after shooting down one was then shot down and killed in his Bf 109G-1 over Berck-sur-Mer. 133 Squadron claimed 3 destroyed and one probable while losing three aircraft. Pilot Officer 'Jessie' Taylor claimed a Bf 109F and a FW 190 and Pilot Officer W. Baker was credited with a FW 190 destroyed. On 26 September eleven of the unit's twelve new Spitfire Mk IXs were lost over Morlaix, when escorting 8th Air Force B-17 Flying Fortresses in heavy cloud cover. Strong winds blew the unit further south than realised and short of fuel, the Squadron let down directly over Brest. Six of the squadron were shot down and taken prisoner, four were killed; one bailed and evaded capture, while one crash landed in England. (Flight Lieutenant Gordon Brettell; one of the British pilots taken prisoner, was to be shot as one of the escapees in The Great Escape from Stalag Luft III in 1944).

19 Billy Fiske died of his wounds in hospital 48 hours after being shot down on 16 August 1940. He was never an 'Eagle' Squadron pilot but flew only with the RAF, on 601 Squadron.

20 *The Few; The American 'Knights of the Air' who risked everything to fight in the Battle of Britain,* by Alex Kershaw (Da Capo Press 2006).

Chapter 4

First Of Our First

Captain John R. 'Tex' McCrary[21]

I was so very anxious to fly. When the RAF airman told me it would be 7/6d a day (seven shillings and sixpence, or about 37 pence) I told him I couldn't afford it. You see, I thought I had to pay them. I had always heard that to be a member of British Armed Forces you had to have a bit of money.
'The airman laughed at me and said: 'No, we pay you 7/6d a day.'
I said: 'You loveable fool. You could've had me for nothing. I really thought they were crazy to pay me to fly.

James E. 'Goody' Goodson wanted to see the world in the summer of 1939, so he boarded a ship and made his way across the Atlantic to Europe by working as a pantry boy. A few months after Goodson arrived, Joseph P. Kennedy Sr., the US ambassador to England, urged all American expatriates to return home because of the looming threat of war. Goodson booked passage on the Athenia, one of the last ships to leave England before Europe convulsed into world war. On 3 September the liner was torpedoed and shelled by a German U-boat off the Scottish coast. Goodson was on the Athenia's deck when the torpedo struck and he assisted with rescue efforts as the ship listed and its lights went dark. More than 100 of the roughly 1,300 passengers and crew members perished before rescue boats arrived. Goodson and other survivors were taken to port in Galway, Ireland where children from the ship wept for their missing parents and many adults were inconsolable. One woman said she saw two children fall from a lifeboat as it was lowered into the chilly water. They were never seen again. The sinking of the Athenia helped turn world opinion against Germany. For Goodson, it was the moment when he decided to do his 'bit to stamp out Nazism.' He joined the RCAF in 1940 and in England was posted to 133 Eagle Squadron RAF before transferring to the 4th Fighter Group on 25 September 1942. Lieutenant Colonel James 'Goody' Goodson destroyed 14 enemy aircraft before being shot down by flak on 20 June 1944. He was taken prisoner. an unabashed Anglophile he once said: *During the war the music hall joke was that 'Yanks' were 'Overpaid, Oversexed and Over here.' I'm still here and I'm overpaid ... Two out of three ain't bad'* Goody Goodson died on 1 May 2014. He was 93 years old.

'You've heard of the Eagles, the American kids who formed three squadrons in the RAF and then transferred back to the Eighth US Air Force. They flew Spitfires in the RAF and kept them for a while when they shifted from blue to khaki. They loved those Spits, as one of them put it, 'with the kind of love that makes babies.' It's possible to feel that way about a Spitfire.

Those were the kids who were given the big-bellied Thunderbolts to take into battle. There was damn near mutiny. Orders had to be issued instructing the Eagle pilots to keep their opinions about the plane to themselves. 'Don't talk to newspapermen!' It was like that for almost a month. And perhaps the most violent critic was a kid named Avey Clark - nephew of Tommy Hitchcock[22] He used cuss words that seamen reserve for U-boats, to describe the Thunderbolt. That was in the beginning.

Then one evening, I ran into Avey. He was with a girl, at a London night club, obviously celebrating something, with a big, almost drunken grin on his face, but he wasn't drinking. I sat down beside him. What goes, Avey? The story tumbled out:

'It happened today - first crack at the Jerries - short, but we found out - hell, I could out-dive him and turn inside him. Couldn't climb with him, but it's okay because I can do all I need to do. Did I get one? Those fifties just ate him up. I saw it in the film.'And that's what happened to all the Eagles. You know how it is: a man will be faithful to a plane, until he finds another that can kill for him and then his love learns another song.

Now the Eagles have still another plane - you know the one, even better than the Thunderbolt. It had to pass the Eagles' test, too. There is no better test than 'Do the Eagles like it?'

A lot of people have tried to tell the story of the Eagles since Quentin Reynolds first struck gold with them. Their story can never be 'told out,' because it's still going on. Let's bring it up to date:

I crossed the Eagles' trail first in 1940 when Bob Scheftel got me to write some stuff in the Mirror about his good friends, the Sweeny's and about an idea of theirs. The idea was the Eagles. Next time I got tangled up with their story was in January 1941. I went up beyond the Eastern Hump of England to the Eagles' nest. They weren't on combat yet; almost, but not quite. Bill Taylor was their acting CO then; their actual CO was Walter Churchill, an Englishman.[23] I spent that first night in his rooms. I prowled around and looked at the things I could see without breaking locks, to find out what I could about this Englishman who was worshipped so by these typical American boys.

I talked too many of the Eagles, sopped up their stories and then began to ask the question to which I have not yet found a universal answer:

'Why did you go to war before your country did?'

There were perhaps four times as many answers as there were Eagles. I like this one best: it is the story of Don Willis, from Fort Leavenworth, Kansas, now a Captain in the Eighth Air Force, married to an English girl.

One evening, out in Chicago, he heard a guy playing a violin in a night club and the music the guy made with his fiddle was beautiful. Don talked and drank with this man late into the evening and early into the morning. The man came from Finland and Finland was at war with Russia then. Don decided he wasn't drunk - that any country that could produce men who could make music like his new friend, such a country must be a helluva fine country. So he went to Finland and joined her air force and fought wing to wing with the Finns. Just like that. It wasn't idealism. He'll call you an idiot or a liar if you say it was. It was just that 'this guy with the fiddle made such goddamn beautiful music and he was a Finn.'

He fought with the Finns until Germany muscled in on the war with Russia. Then Don decided that something was wrong, so he joined the Norwegian Air Force. He doesn't know why he did, but he did. Norway fell and he came to England and joined the RAF. And then, along with all the others, he swapped the blue for the khaki of the Eighth.

I went up to the ceremony at their station, when RAF Air Marshal Leigh Mallory of Fighter Command gave each of the transfers a special silver emblem to be worn on the right - it meant they had fought with the RAF before America got into the ring. Run through the list of the names of the boys who got those medallions that day - you'll see how the story of 'the first of our first' was rooted in every corner of America.

Now these boys were not all in the Eagles, nor were they all the boys who did make up the Eagles. They were just the ones who had been in the RAF and were now in the Eighth Air Force Group that did hold most of the Eagle transfers.

The present commanding officer of that Group is perhaps the most famous of the Eagles - Lieutenant Colonel Chesley G. Peterson, 23 years old, from an alfalfa farm in Utah.[24]

Quent Reynolds made some of the Eagles who died more famous than Pete - boys like Anderson and Fenlaw and Flynn and Kolendorski and Mays and McGerty and Olson and 'Red' Tobin. They had more of what you call 'color' than Pete.

Don't know when Pete started being serious; must have been early. He's a student of air combat, just as some people are students of history and mathematics and physics and chemistry and astronomy. Pete is a student of killing at 400 mph. More than a student, he's a Ph.D. But he still studies.

Pete saw his first Jerry killed at his first training field after he came to England. Squadron Leader and later Group Captain Walter Churchill was the 'professor'. The Americans had just arrived at the field. It was near Liverpool. A Heinkel roared over and dropped its bombs one day. Churchill went up and knocked it down, almost on the field.

'That's a damn fine way to teach,' says Pete. He's done a lot of the same kind of teaching. But first, he learned a lot from others. For instance, from Churchill, he learned many of the things a leader must know: Study tactics. Never stop studying, because they always change. You hear a lot about the Germans making frontal attacks on our Flying Fortresses today, but that is not new with the Germans. Churchill knocked down the first bomber with a frontal attack, a Jerry, in 1940. It is important for a leader to do first what he recommends that others do.'[25]

'I suppose the first time this stringy blond boy ever studied flying was about fifteen years ago, when a barnstorming outfit with a ramshackle plane tried to rent his father's alfalfa field - for selling short hops to the local yokels in Utah at $2.50 a ride. Young Peters prodded his Pop into this barter: 'You fellers can use my alfalfa field for your flying machine, but you are gonna have to pay me rent the way I say. You're gonna have to take this boy of mine for a ride until he says we been paid off.'

That was the first of many hours in the air for Pete. You probably know the middle part of his story: two years in Brigham Young University, quit to go into the Air Forces, lied about his age by two years and was nailed for it. To spare him more serious charges, a kind officer bounced him out with this verdict - 'lack of inherent flying ability.' Twice he tried to get around our neutrality laws to join the Canadians; and then, the way a busted jockey would drift to a job on a stud farm, Pete took a job in the Douglas plants out in California.

And finally - because his story had to end this way - along with a bunch of other American boys who could get into the air no other way, he sailed for England on 13 August 1940. Their passage was paid by a man named Colonel Charles Sweeny. These were the first of the Eagles.

Actually, they weren't the first Americans in the RAF. There is a plaque in St. Paul's Cathedral in London and a small headstone beside an English fighter field, that commemorate the very first of our first to die in the RAF.

He was Billy Fiske. But Fiske was not like these Eagles - though he came from Chicago, he had spent much of his time in Europe; he married a famous English beauty, the former Countess of Warwick; and most of his best friends were English boys already in the famous 601 Squadron of the RAF.

These Eagles were far more American than Fiske. They were Main Street. Take a boy like 'Gus' Daymond - he was a make-up man in Hollywood; he made the first kill for the Eagles, when he was only nineteen. Before he finished, he destroyed eight.[26] Pete's score was six.[27]

Pete and Gus were two of the Eagles' seven COs; they were the last two before all the Eagles put on the khaki of the Eighth, on 29 September 1942.

There were three Eagle Squadrons; and before they transferred, in eighteen months of combat they destroyed 73 ½ Jerries - the half they shared with the RAF. Of that 73½, the original Squadron killed 45 Huns. Of the boys in that Squadron, eight were killed in action and 17 on active service, three are missing and six are Prisoners of War.

As I told you, Pete is the CO now. He had been CO before, but in the Dieppe show, while they were still flying in the RAF, Pete got the first of his two dunkings in the Channel. He was shot down on 19 August. It wasn't bad. Pete had time to take off his new boots and reluctantly throw them away and he tossed away a pistol he always carried, but not before he emptied it on the way down' in the general direction of the Jerries. He was quickly picked up by a launch of the Air-Sea Rescue.

I'm convinced that Destiny puts the finger on some boys and marks them for survival - Pete is one of them. He was drying in the wind on the deck of that launch, sitting and talking to a Canadian who had been fished out just before him, when a Focke Wulf came dusting over the waves and sprayed the deck of the launch with cannon shells. The Canadian was killed instantly. Pete was not touched.

Once more Pete was shot down, in one of the first brushes between the Thunderbolts and the Jerries. This time, he came out with two black eyes - slapping his face against the water in the fall did it. After that, he was grounded.

Pete is married. To a Hedy Lamarr type of girl with a wonderful sense of humor - Audrey Boyes she was, from South Africa. A movie star over here.[28] After he was grounded he was sent to US Fighter Command and given a staff job that permitted him to commute to work from a London flat. But you know enough about guys who fly to know that you could never keep Pete out of a plane.

Last time I saw him he was coming through town, on the way to make a speech to some British factory workers who were making the 'drop-tanks' that give our Thunderbolts the extra range. It was to be one of those pep talks the British use to boost production. Pete dreaded it. As he got into the elevator, I kidded him about the brief case he carried. 'That's really the mark of a settled old man, Pete - you'll wind up a brief case brigadier if you aren't careful.' Pete just laughed and patted the worn brief case.

'You know, I've carried that ever since I came to England. Makes me look older, but I've never carried anything in it except a toothbrush. That's all that's in it now.'

I suppose Pete knows the British and gets along with them better than any other American I know. They like him and respect him. I've tried to get out of Pete an answer to my question 'Why did you come to war - before our country did?' No luck. Nor is he sure why he fought for' the British instead of for the Chinese, for instance and Pete is generally pretty sure of why he does whatever he does.[29]

The Eagles can't tell you why they came ahead of the rest of US; but none of them have ever been guilty of the crime that some of us committed when we came to England and our manner shouted: 'Okay, Britain, relax - we'll win the war for you.'

Endnotes Chapter 4

21 Captain John R. 'Tex' McCrary was a war reporter (as well as a Photographic Officer) for 8th Air Force Public Relations. He had once worked on the *New York Mirror,* which always specialized in 'Rape, riot and ruin'. Born John Reagan McCrary in 1910 in Calvert, Texas, the son of a cotton farmer hurt by the Depression later attended Phillips Exeter Academy and Yale where he was a member of Skull and Bones. He started in journalism as a copy boy at the New York *World-Telegram*. He left to join the *Daily Mirror,* later becoming its chief editorial writer. After divorcing his first wife in 1939, McCrary began writing the column '*Only Human*' and in 1941 met Jinx Falkenburg. When he interviewed her; she was starring in Broadway tuner *Hold Onto Your Hats* with Al Jolson. In 1945 he was one of the first Americans to visit Hiroshima after the atomic bomb was dropped. He advised journalists not to write about what they had seen because he did not think Americans could stand to know 'what we've done here.' After John Hersey published his account in the *New Yorker*, McCrary said, 'I covered it up and John Hersey uncovered it. That's the difference between a PR man and a reporter.' After the war McCrary edited the American *Mercury* magazine. He soon renewed his friendship with Jinx Falkenburg, who had become a star under contract at MGM and was one of the nation's highest-paid models. They were married in June 1945. Although they were separated years later, they never divorced. McCrary and his wife had two radio talk shows, *Hi Jinx* and *Meet Tex and Jinx* and a TV show, sometimes broadcasting from Gotham's Waldorf-Astoria Hotel where they could nab celebs, as they stopped to pick up their room keys. McCrary died aged 92 in New York.

22 James Averill 'Jim' Clark Jr, born on 7 September 1920 in New York City. Clark received his wings from the RAF on 20 November 1941. He joined 71 'Eagle' Squadron on 9 June 1942, which became the 334th Fighter Squadron on 15 September 1942. He was Squadron Operations Officer from 22 May 1943 and Squadron CO from 26 October 1943 to 15 March 1944. He married Lady Bridget Elliot on 19 April 1944. By war's end he had scored 10½ kills. He died on 11 January 1990.

23 Walter Myers Churchill born in Amsterdam in 1907. His father was William Algernon Churchill (1865-1947), a British Consul who served in Mozambique, Amsterdam, Pará in Brazil, Stockholm,

Milan, and Algiers. His father was also an art connoisseur, and author of what is still the standard reference work on early European paper and papermaking *Watermarks in Paper*. His mother was Violet Churchill (née Myers). Walter was educated at Sedbergh School and Cambridge University where he read Engineering after which he started an aviation precision engineering company Churchill Components (Coventry) Ltd in 1937. The company worked for Sir Frank Whittle, the jet-engine pioneer and it machined compressor blades for the gas-turbine engines in the early 1940s. Churchill was commissioned as a pilot officer in the Auxiliary Air Force on 11 January 1932 and appointed to 605 (County of Warwick) Squadron. He was promoted to flight lieutenant in June 1937 and transferred from the AAF to the Auxiliary Air Force Reserve of Officers in January 1939. He was recalled to 605 Squadron and full-time service in August 1939. Churchill later served on 3 Squadron and 71 (Eagle) Squadron and took part in the Battle of Britain as a squadron leader. He was subsequently promoted to wing commander, then group captain. Churchill was credited with seven victories and was awarded a DSO and a DFC. He also evaluated various makes of fighter aircraft for the RAF, and played a key role in getting Spitfire aircraft to the defence of Malta. In August 1942 he was stationed in Malta as group captain. On 27 August Churchill was KIA while leading a raid in a Spitfire on Biscari airfield near Gela in southern Sicily. He was 35 years old. Churchill was the elder brother of Peter Churchill and Oliver Churchill, both of whom were Special Operations Executive officers during the Second World War. His company continued under the management of his wife, Joyce, and subsequently by his second son, James. The company is now known as J.J. Churchill Ltd.

24 Peterson was born on 10 August 1920 at Salmon, Idaho, but moved to Utah in his childhood. He joined the Utah National Guard in 1937. In 1939, he joined the Army Air Corps and was selected for air cadet training, but was dismissed before graduation from flight school. He moved to Los Angeles after being dropped from flight school and was working at Douglas Aircraft when he became interested in flying for the RAF, who were at that time recruiting Americans to fight the Germans. Peterson arrived in England in late 1940 and was assigned to 71 Squadron, one of the three Eagle squadrons made of volunteer American pilots. The Americans would fly Hurricanes and Spitfires against the Luftwaffe. In time, he was promoted to flight lieutenant and given command of 71 Squadron. Flight Lieutenant Peterson completed 42 sorties while flying with the RAF. When he was given command of 71 Squadron he was only 21 years old and the youngest squadron commander in the RAF.

25 Churchill suffered a severe case of sinus trouble which caused his removal on 23 January 1941 and he was promoted Wing Commander and put in charge of RAF Valley, Anglesey, He was fit for flying again the following year and he went out to Malta aboard *HMS Furious* as part of the 'Pedestal' convoy, flying off to the island on 11 August 1942. Now a Group Captain, he took command of Takali airfield, where he planned early offensive action over Sicily. On 27 August he led a major sweep over Axis airfields on that island by the full wing of Spitfires, but as he approached Biscari, his Spitfire received a direct hit from flak and blew up, crashing in flames.

26 Gregory Augustus 'Gus' Daymond was born on 14 November 1920 at Great Falls, Montana. He joined the RAF and earned his wings on 15 October 1940. He was posted to 71 (Eagle) Squadron and scored 7 destroyed and 1 damaged flying Hurricane IIs and Spitfire Vbs in 1941 and 1942. He was awarded a DFC and bar. When the Eagle Squadrons transferred to the USAAF he was CO of 334th Fighter Squadron from 29 September 1942 to 3 March 1943 when he returned to the US. He retired from the Army Reserves on 3 August 1945 with the rank of Major. He died in 1966. *Stars & Bars.*

27 These were scored while flying a Hurricane IIb and Spitfire Vbs on 71 Squadron. His total wartime score was seven victories, four probables and seven damaged. These included a FW 190 on 15 April 1943 while flying P-47 Thunderbolts and a FW 190 probable and FW 190 damaged on 14 May 1943). *Stars & Bars.*

28 Audrey Boyes was born in 1914. She was an actress, known for Banana Ridge (1942). She died on 1 June 2007.

29 Chesley Peterson died on 28 January1990 (aged 69) at Riverside, California.

Chapter 5

Adventure's Best Ending

Captain John R. 'Tex' McCrary

William Meade Lindley Fiske III was born in New York in June, 1911, the son of a successful international banker. His family was wealthy, and Fiske attended private schools, and then Trinity College Cambridge. While in England he developed a love for the country and the people. Fiske showed an early interest in sports and speed and he also took part in numerous driving rallies and competitions, including the Le Mans 24 Hour Race when aged just 19. After leaving Cambridge Fiske took up a post with the international bankers Dillon, Reed, & Co., working mainly in Europe. This gave him the chance to indulge and develop his sporting interests, and his growing love of the British. He became a member of the exclusive White's Club in London, where he met and socialised with many members of 601 Squadron, Auxiliary Air Force (AAF). In 1938 he met Rose Bingham, the former Countess of Warwick, whom he later married. Encouraged by his new friends in the AAF, he also learned to fly.

He was one of those who fought in the 'thin blue line' of the RAF to beat back the Luftwaffe in the Battle of Britain. He was an American. The first American to join the RAF. The first American to die in the RAF [but only if one discounts James William Elias Davies who was born in the USA but of British parents and was killed on 27 June 1939]. Very few, too few Americans know his name. On the Roll of Honor in Westminster Abbey that lists 375 airmen who died in the Battle of Britain, you will find it. That Roll is symbolic of that Battle. The first name is an English one - Pilot Officer Hugh Charles Adams. Born, raised, shot down and buried in an English village.[30] The last name on the list is a Polish one - Pilot Officer Aleksy Zukowski, from Vilna, Poland. Zukowski was a giant of a man. Oddly enough, he was raised in Japan and became a skiing champion out there. But when the Huns slashed into Poland, Zukowski was in the air against them. When the Huns slashed into France, Zukowski was in the air against them again. And when they tried to smash into Britain, Zukowski died to stop them.[31]

This first American's name is on still another scroll in England, in St. Paul's Cathedral. Below the tablet that bears his name is a glass case with his RAF wings in it. Some friend had saved them from his tunic and sent them along to the Dean of St. Paul's. The inscription on the tablet reads like this:

PILOT OFFICER WILLIAM MEADE LINDSEY FISKE, RAF;
AN AMERICAN CITIZEN WHO DIED THAT ENGLAND MIGHT LIVE.

His name lives in one other place in England; in a rambling little house that rises off an alleyway between the two places Americans know best in London, Grosvenor and Berkeley Squares. It was a famous house in the last war. The fabulous Canadian, Mike Edgar, lived there.

Rose Fiske lives there now - Mrs. William Fiske. American officers know 125B Mount Street well, on Thanksgiving and Christmas and New Year's Day and in the late afternoon when work is done. And 'Fisky' watches and approves, from a picture frame. Americans who never knew Fisky get a warm picture of him from Rose. Amazing girl, tall, lean, erect, dark, tremendous strength in her face, determination in her walk. She was certainly beautiful at twenty. At thirty, distinguished. Her dark hair is streaked with grey. She likes to talk about Fisky.

'We lived in a house by the field. He came home to lunch one day, furious with me. It seems that he had been up at dawn that morning got on the tail of a Heinkel out over the Channel and herded it right across our house so I could watch him shoot it down. He was in a rage because I wouldn't get out of bed to look. He couldn't understand why I couldn't tell his Hurricane from all the others, just by the sound of it.'

I suppose a first essential of understanding the story of Fisky's brief three weeks of ops with the RAF is to know his story from the beginning. He was born in Chicago, but he was raised all over Europe. His father was the European representative of a great investment banking firm, Dillon-Read, Wall Street. As a boy he had brief schooling at a private ranch school in California. Then to England.

At fifteen, he spent a year on a sheep ranch in the Argentine. At seventeen he went to Cambridge. Spent his vacations in Switzerland, became a great skier, racing driver, set records on the bobsled and Cresta runs.[32]

Out of Cambridge, he went twice around the world, once with the elder Douglas Fairbanks. And then he took a fat inheritance to Hollywood, collected a cast and a crew, sailed for Tahiti and settled down to make a picture about the islands. His stars spent more time in splints than on sets, more time putting liniment on sore muscles than Max Factor makeup on wrinkles and double chins. Fisky had invented a game of riding bamboo rafts through rapids on a river. The movie was a flop.

And so he went to Paris and worked in a bank for almost a year. A bank was a cage. He went back to Hollywood, formed a small company, made shorts and Westerns, good ones, profitable. That was typical of Fisky. First thing wildly, then well.

Then he went back to banking in London. That was 1937. The year he married Rose, once Countess of Warwick, but never really happy until she was Mrs. Fiske.[33] And all his friends were young Englishmen. They were all wealthy - call them playboys. Perhaps they were. But not the nightclub brand. They drove fast cars, skied, flew fast planes, lived as dangerously as their money could permit.

Most of Billy Fiske's best friends belonged to an RAF Volunteer Reserve Squadron - 601, the City of London Squadron. Whitney Straight[34] and Billy Clyde[35] and Roger Bushell[36] and Willie Rhodes-Moorhouse[37] and

Beaverbrook's tough son, little Max Aitken. Fisky flew, too - had about 90 hours to his credit. But he wasn't in 601. He was American, remember. But as the meaning of Munich grew clearer, he told these friends of his: 'If war comes, count me in.'

In August, 1939 Fisky was living and working in New York. Hated it.

Billy Clyde was working in America, too. Clyde got a cable from London, calling him into active service with 601. Fisky phoned a friend in London. 'Is this it? Yes. I'll be there.'

Rose booked passage on every boat that sailed during the following week as Fisky scrambled to settle his affairs. War seemed imminent - he didn't want to get caught in America by the Neutrality Act. On September 3, when England went into the war, Fisky was on the *Aquitania*, one day at sea.

Rose followed as soon as she could. They took a house close to the station where he got his secondary training. And on bad-weather days, the house was full of eighteen-year-old kids from Australia and Canada and South Africa.

'They were such babies. They all looked up to Fisky, told him all their troubles, everything from their debts to their blind dates. You must understand that everybody loved Fisky. I mean that literally. I never really understood it until he died. And then the cables and letters came from all around the world, from all kinds of people. They all loved Fisky.'

Fisky was posted to 601 when he finished his training. That was in July, just about three weeks before he was shot down.

'The day Fisky got his first Hun, he was so happy. Never before had he been half so happy as when he was in 601. He never could have been again.'

They fought all day, went up again and again, the pilots of the Spits and hump-backed Hurricanes, as our own boys fought in the Pacific in the beginning.

'There were such wonderful guys in 601. They wore red linings in their tunics and mink linings in their overcoats. They were arrogant and they looked terrific and probably the other Squadrons hated their guts. But by God they did fight. Look at the records. None better. And they always did everything without any apparent effort. They had always been like that at everything, all their lives.'

She told me a lot of all this about Fisky one night after we went to a play called *Flare Path* together. There was a scene where three RAF wives, living in an inn on the edge of a bomber field, looked out and saw a Wellington crash and burn.[38]

'Fisky was killed in August.[39] I had gone up to London that morning. His field was in the south of England. I phoned him about lunch time - we weren't supposed to call the field, but you know how it was.

'I called him again right after lunch. I couldn't get any information except that I could hear over the phone that the field was being bombed. I called back again in fifteen minutes. They told me that Fisky was being taken to a hospital. I drove down as fast as I could and all the time I told myself that this was so lucky because surely he had done no more than perhaps to break an arm or a leg and that would keep him out of the war for a while and maybe he would get through the whole war all right. Over and over, I said that - '

At about that time; Fisky was lying in an ambulance, quizzing the doctor that rode with him: 'Listen, I'm not going to die, am I? Tell me.'

Not frightened, just worried. Maybe he knew. They took him to a new hospital. A military hospital, built for such things. By the time Rose got there, Fisky had been to the operating room. They had covered his legs and arms and most of his face and head with black goo. He was burnt to cinders.

'He was conscious for a little while. He didn't die until next morning. And when he was delirious, all he would talk about was his plane. He wanted me to go and see if it was all right. They told me afterwards that he could never have walked again if he had lived and he would have hated that.'

He landed his plane. Didn't crash. It was blazing. His willpower or maybe it was instinct, made him get out. He walked a few steps and then he fell.

Fisky was buried in a country churchyard near a corner of the field from which he flew.[40] When Spitfires take off now to give air cover for our invading troops, they fly across Fisky's grave...'

Endnotes Chapter 5

30 Sergeant pilot Hugh Charles Adams on 501 Squadron died on 6 September 1940 while flying Hurricane (V6612) at 9am over Ashford Kent. The aircraft crashed at Eltham. He is buried in the north-west part of Tandridge churchyard. Son of John Coker Adams, and Grace Adams of Chaddleworth, Berkshire. He was 22.

31 Pilot Officer Aleksy Zukowski was killed on Friday 18 October 1940. He was one of four Hurricane pilots on 302 (Poznan) Squadron who ran out of fuel, crashed and were killed returning to Duxford in adverse weather. Zukowski became lost and ran out of fuel and his Hurricane (V6571) crashed at Bluebell Hill near Horsley, Surrey.

32 At the 1928 Winter Olympics in St. Moritz, Switzerland, as driver of the first five-man US Bobsled team to win the Olympics, Fiske, aged just 16 years became the youngest gold medalist in any winter sport. Fiske competed again at the 1932 Winter Olympics at Lake Placid, New York where he carried the United States' flag at the opening ceremony. Now a four-man team event, Fiske and his three team-mates again took gold. Fiske declined to lead the bobsled team in the 1936 Winter Olympics in Garmisch-Partenkirchen in Germany, probably because he disagreed with the politics in Germany at the time. Fiske was also a Cresta Champion and was well known for jumps from the Badrutt's Palace Hotel's bar chandelier in St. Moritz.

33 Rose Bingham was born on 14 March 1913. She was the daughter of Lieutenant David Cecil Bingham and Lady Rosabelle Millicent St. Clair-Erskine. She married Charles Guy Fulke Greville, 7th Earl of Warwick, son of Leopold Guy Francis Maynard Greville, 6th Earl of Warwick and Elfrida Marjorie Eden on 11 July 1933. They divorced in 1938. She married, secondly, William M. L. Fiske III, son of William M. L. Fiske II on 8 September 1938. She married, thirdly, on 17 March 1945 Lt Colonel Sir John Charles Arthur Digby Lawson, 3rd Baronet. They divorced in 1950. She married, fourthly, Theodore Sheldon Bassett in 1951 and they too divorced. As a result of her marriage, Rose Bingham was styled as Countess of Warwick on 11 July 1933. She died on 29 December 1972 at age 59.

34 Born in New York, the son of Major Willard Dickerman Straight and heiress Dorothy Payne Whitney, he was almost six years old when his father died in France of influenza during the great epidemic while serving with the US Army during WWI. Following his mother's remarriage to British agronomist Leonard K. Elmhirst in 1925, the family moved to Dartington Hall England where he attended the progressive school founded by his parents. His education was completed at Trinity College, Cambridge. On 17 July 1935 he married Lady Daphne Margarita Finch-Hatton, daughter of the 14th Earl of Winchilsea and they had two daughters. While still an undergraduate at Cambridge,

he became a well known Grand Prix motor racing driver and competed at events in Britain and Europe. He competed in more Grands Prix than any American until after WWII. Flying was also a passion and while 16 years old (still too young for a pilot's licence) he had already accumulated over 60 hours solo flight. In his early 20s, as head of the Straight Corporation Limited, he operated airfields throughout Britain and ran flying clubs. In 1936 he helped develop the Miles Whitney Straight aircraft. He became a naturalised British citizen that year. On 18 October 1938 the Straight Corporation purchased control of Norman Edgar (Western Airways) Ltd and renamed it Western Airways Ltd. His commercial airline business in the later 1930s was reputed to be carrying more passengers than Imperial Airways. Whitney Straight was sent to Norway in April 1940 to find frozen lakes suitable for use as airfields. Lake Lesjaskog was utilised by 263 Squadron during the Norwegian Campaign as a result. Straight was seriously wounded during a German bombing raid in Norway. After convalescing he next served on 601 Squadron. From September 1940-April 1941 he was credited with two aircraft destroyed. He then became CO of 242 Squadron, taking his total to 3 and 1 shared and 2 probables by late July 1941. Early in 1941 he was awarded a MC for his work in Norway. He was shot down by flak over France on 31 July and made his way through the French Underground to unoccupied Vichy France where he was captured and put in a PoW camp. He escaped on 22 June 1942 and with the aid of the French Resistance reached Gibraltar. In September 1942, now as an Air Commodore he was sent to HQ 216 Group in the Middle East as AOC. In June 1945 he returned to England, becoming AOC 46 Group. In late 1945 he became chairman of the Royal Aero Club in 1946 was appointed deputy chairman of British European Airways Corporation. In July 1947 he became managing director and CEO of BOAC. In 1949 was appointed deputy Chairman of the board and also joined the board of Rolls-Royce. When the Soviet Union was given 40 Rolls-Royce jet engines by Clement Attlee's Labour government and the Russians copied the technology to produce their own version jet engine to power their MiG fighters he sued the Soviet government for copyright infringement. The figure claimed was £200 million which he never received. Straight died in Fulham in 1979 aged 66.

35 William Pancoast 'Billy' Clyde joined the Auxiliary Air Force in 1935 and also skied for Britain at this time. In February 1938 he went into the RAFVR and left Britain to settle in Mexico. With the outbreak of war he returned to England in September 1939, joined 601 Squadron and saw action over Dunkirk and the Battle of Britain. His score during this time was 9 and 1 shared destroyed, 2 probables, 1 and 1 shared damaged. Group Captain Clyde DFC left the RAF in 1945 and returned to Mexico.

36 Roger Joyce Bushell was born in Springs, Transvaal, South Africa on 30 August 1910 to English parents Benjamin Daniel and Dorothy Wingate Bushell. His father, a mining engineer, had emigrated to the country from Britain and he used his wealth to ensure that Roger received a first class education. He was first schooled in Johannesburg. Then, aged 14 went to Wellington College in Berkshire, England. In 1929, Bushell then went to Pembroke College, Cambridge to study law. Keen on pursuing non-academic interests from an early age, he excelled in athletics and skied for Cambridge in races between 1930 and 1932 - captaining the team in 1931. One of Bushell's passions and talents was skiing: in the early 1930s he was declared the fastest Briton in the male downhill category. He even had a black run named after him in St. Moritz, Switzerland, in recognition of the fact that he had set the fastest time for the run. He also won the slalom event of the annual Oxford-Cambridge ski race in 1931. At an event in Canada, Bushell had an accident in which one of his skis narrowly missed his left eye, leaving him with a gash in the corner of it. Although he recovered from this accident, he still had a dark drooping in his left eye as a result of scarring from his stitches. Bushell became fluent in French and German, with a good accent, which became extremely useful during his time as a prisoner of war. Despite his sporting prospects, one of Bushell's primary wishes was to fly and in 1932 he joined 601 Squadron Auxiliary Air Force, often referred to as 'The Millionaires' Mob' because of the number of wealthy young men who paid their way solely to learn how to fly during training days at weekends.

37 William Henry 'Willie' Rhodes-Moorhouse was born on 4 March 1914 at a house in Brompton Square, Kensington in London. When he was less than a year old, his father, William Barnard Rhodes-Moorhouse, who was the first airman to be awarded the Victoria Cross, was wounded in action and died of his injuries. The Rhodes-Moorhouse family enjoyed considerable wealth and circulated in the top echelons of upper-class society of the time. William was educated at Eton College, where he was able to obtain his pilots licence aged 17. In October 1933, William inherited his father's estate of over £250,000 (a huge sum for the time). After travelling extensively, on 15 September 1936 at Marylebone Rhodes-Moorhouse married Amalia Demetriadi, who had been approached to be screen-tested for the role of Scarlett O'Hara in the film *Gone with the Wind*. She declined. A keen sportsman, Rhodes-

Moorhouse was selected for the British Winter Olympics team for the 1936 Winter Olympics, but an accident on the ski jump prevented him from competing. Flight Lieutenant 'Willie' Rhodes-Moorhouse DFC was killed in action aged 26 over Tunbridge Wells in his Hurricane at 0930 on 6 September 1940. His score stood at 7 and 4 shared destroyed, 4 probables.

38 *Flare Path* is a play by Terence Rattigan, written in 1941 and first staged in 1942. Set in a hotel near an RAF Bomber Command airfield, the story involves a love triangle between a pilot, his actress wife and a famous film star. The play is based in part on Rattigan's own wartime experiences. In writing the play, Terence Rattigan drew on his experiences as a tail gunner in RAF Coastal Command. He was suffering from writer's block, but on a mission to West Africa in 1941 he started writing Flare Path. He managed to save the incomplete manuscript when his plane was damaged in combat and the crew ordered to jettison excess weight. Flare Path was initially rejected twice because it was thought that the public would not want to see a play about the war. It was accepted by producer Binkie Beaumont of H.M. Tennent, Ltd. The play opened at the Apollo Theatre in London on 13 August 1942. The role of Teddy Graham was played by Jack Watling and his wife Patricia was played by Phyllis Calvert. The director was Anthony Asquith, who later directed the film adaptation *The Way to the Stars*.

39 On 16 August 1940 601 Squadron were scrambled to intercept a squadron of German dive-bombers. Fiske was flying a Hawker Hurricane (P3358) The Squadron destroyed eight Junkers Ju 87 Stukas, but after just 15 minutes of flying time, a German gunner put a bullet through Fiske's fuel tank. With his aircraft badly damaged and his hands and ankles burnt, instead of bailing out, Fiske nursed his Hurricane home, gliding over a hedgerow to the airfield. Although he landed his aircraft safely back at Tangmere, Fiske had to be extracted from the aircraft by ambulance attendants. Shortly after, his fuel tank exploded. Fiske was taken to the Royal West Sussex Hospital in Chichester for treatment, but he died 48 hours later from surgical shock. Fiske was 29 years old.

40 Billy Fiske's funeral was conducted with full military honours and took place at Boxgrove Priory on 20 August 1940 near RAF Tangmere. Six members of Tangmere's ground staff carried Fiske to his final resting place. As his coffin, covered in the Union Jack and the Stars and Stripes, was borne on a bier to Boxgrove Priory Church, members of the Central Band of the RAF played funeral marches.

Chapter 6

Their Finest Hour

'Even though large tracts of Europe and many old and famous States have fallen or may fall into the grip of the Gestapo and all the odious apparatus of Nazi rule, we shall not flag or fail. We shall go on to the end, we shall fight in France, we shall fight on the seas and oceans, we shall fight with growing confidence and growing strength in the air, we shall defend our island, whatever the cost may be, we shall fight on the beaches, we shall fight on the landing grounds, we shall fight in the fields and in the streets, we shall fight in the hills; we shall never surrender...

Winston Churchill, a speech to the House of Commons, 4 June 1940.

'The English have lost the war, but they haven't yet noticed it; one must give them time, but they will soon come around to accepting it.

Adolph Hitler, 17 June 1940, on the fall of France.

Air Marshal Sir Hugh Caswall Tremenheere Dowding had, on 14 July 1936, become the first Air Officer Commander in Chief of Fighter Command. Early in 1939, faced with taking early retirement, he wrote to the Air Ministry and said: 'I can say without fear of contradiction that since I have held my present post I have dealt with and am in the process of dealing with a number of vital matters which generations of Air Staff have neglected for the last fifteen years: putting the Observer Corps on a war footing, manning of Operations Rooms, identification of friendly aircraft, unserviceability of aerodromes and adequate Air Raid Warning System. This work had to be carried out against the inertia of the Air Staff, a statement which I can abundantly prove if necessary... In spite of my intense interest in the Fighter problems of the immediate future ... there is little in my past or present treatment at the hands of the Air Ministry to encourage me to undertake a further period of service.' Dowding's retirement was deferred, but only until the end of March 1940.

While radar was fundamental, a great deal more was involved in the air defence system. Between the radar 'plots' of approaching hostile aircraft and the fighters which climbed to intercept them and the guns, searchlights, balloons and air-raid sirens (all of which had their vital functions) there existed a highly intricate system of communications manned by hundreds of men and women. Once the raiders crossed the coast tracking them was the responsibility of the Observer Corps, which was made up of 32 centres whose 30,000 volunteers manned over 1,000 posts around the clock monitoring the height, speed and strength of the enemy formations overhead. The Observer Corps plotted the 'hostiles' by sight or sound, depending on the visibility and passed their plots by landline to their own Group HQ, which relayed them to the Fighter Command Filter room for onward transmission throughout the system. The filter room concept was developed by Squadron Leader Hart at Bawdsey where the first one was built but parts were later removed and taken to Bentley Priory in October 1938. The first filter training school opened in March 1940 at Bawdsey.

'It is midnight at one of the posts of the Observer Corps near a small country town somewhere in England. I am one of the crew on duty. My mate has just said it isn't a bad night but he wishes it were a bit warmer. And so do I for I call it decidedly chilly, even for an English midsummer. It's dark, too, for the waning moon has not yet risen and the stars don't seem to have much brightness about them. We came on duty at ten o'clock, just as it was getting dark and since then we've been watching the skies and listening, as we have watched and listened since the war began. But the night is quiet. The wind has blown away the rain-clouds which threatened a wet night and has now died down. My mate and I discuss the prospects of a raid. He thinks it most likely that Jerry will come over a bit later on - when the moon rises.

Suddenly our telephone bell rings. A message from headquarters: 'Keep a sharp lookout - we're expecting a spot of trouble.' My mate and I stand-to with increased vigilance. But all is quiet. A little breeze brings the scent of new-mown hay across the meadows. The river murmurs as it wanders below us on its way to the sea. All is as it has been for centuries-the war is a thousand miles away.

'The bell rings again. This time the voice at the other end is a little more explicit. Jerry, the gentleman who drops the bombs, is definitely about. Certain figures and directions are given and on the map we are able to trace his course from the spot where he last disclosed his unwelcome presence. The telephone is very busy now and we hear our neighbouring posts take up the tale as they pick up the sound of the raider and pass him on to the next post and the next. Still we can hear no sound of him - he is too far away yet. Suddenly the air-raid sirens - a melancholy sound at the best of times but in the dead of night a most depressing performance. And when they have died away we are able to listen again. Our nearest neighbour now has the raider within his hearing and, on the telephone, we hear him reporting the track of the plane across the sky. Will he come towards us? we wonder. At last we hear him, but he is still a long way off and our neighbour hasn't finished with him yet. Faintly and intermittently at first, then louder we hear him and finally our neighbour passes him on to us. And now we start to track him; we hear him quite plainly now. There's no gunfire yet, but we can picture the anti-aircraft gunners behind their guns waiting for the moment when he comes within the probing beams of those searchlights. On and on comes the raider-a lone machine, we decide. Suddenly there's a flash and a report and a light in the sky. He's dropped a bomb - and another - and another.

'My mate and I are very busy now. It is vitally important that every movement of the raider should be followed and reported and we watch and listen for every change in his height or direction. Ah, he's turning now, coming straight towards us - his engine becomes suddenly louder. On he comes, louder again now, turning again till he strikes his course for home. Fainter and fainter grows his engine and at last we pass him back to our neighbour, a little regretfully. We had hopes he would have shown himself for just one moment - just long enough, as my mate puts it, for the boys to crack off at him. But he is a long way from home yet and he has many perils of British fighters and anti-aircraft guns to face before he can say he is safe. On the telephone we hear him being passed on from one post to the next.

'Before long the sirens sound again - this time the long sustained note of the 'all clear'. Gradually the sound of activity in the little town beneath us dies away. The worthy country folk return to their beds and my mate and I settle down once again to our routine job of watching and listening.'

***The Observer Corps Waits for the Enemy*, by a member of the Observer Corps, BBC radio broadcast, July 1940.**

'I was visiting a big aircraft factory the other day and I was talking to a crowd of workers. I was not quite sure how they were reacting to my remarks, so I turned to a little old man who looked particularly 'surly' and said to him, 'How long do you think you can stick this war?' Without hesitation the chap said, 'One week longer than the bloody Germans'.

***Father of the RAF*, Lord Trenchard.**

'I suppose many people who watched the air battle from the shore on 10 July 1940 saw a lot more than I did, although I was in it. As you can imagine, you don't see anything but your own particular part of the show when you are actually fighting. Treble One Squadron was ordered to fly to the spot where ships were being attacked. In a few minutes we had reached the scene. We were at 8,000 feet, the clouds were about 2,000 to 3,000 feet above us and below we saw very clearly a line of ships and a formation of bombers about to attack.

'The bombers were between 100 to 200 feet below us. There were twenty-four Dorniers altogether and they apparently intended to attack in three ways. The first bunch of bombers had already dropped their bombs when we got there and the second formation was about to go in. The third wave never delivered an attack at all. It was a thrilling sight I must confess, as I looked down on the tiny ships below and saw two long lines of broken water where the first lot of bombs had fallen. There were two distinct lines of disturbed water near the ships and just ahead were fountains of water leaping skywards from bombs newly dropped. In a second or two the sea down below spouted up to the height of about 50 feet or more in two lines alongside the convoy.

'Our squadron leader gave the order to attack. Down we went. He led one flight against a formation of bombers and I led my flight over the starboard side. It was a simultaneous attack. We went screaming down and pumped lead into our targets. We shook them up quite a bit. Then I broke away and looked round for a prospective victim and saw, some distance away, a Dornier lagging behind the first formation. I flew after it, accompanied by two other members of my flight and the enemy went into a gentle dive turning towards the French coast. He was doing a steady 300 mph in that gentle dive, but we overtook him and started firing at him. He was in obvious distress. When fifteen miles out from the English coast we turned back to rejoin the main battle.

'I was just turning round when I saw a Me 109 come hurtling at me. He came from above and in front of me, so I made a quick turn and dived after him. I was then at about 5,000 feet and when I began to chase him down to the sea he was a good 800 yards in front. He was going very fast and I had to do 400 mph to catch him up, or rather to get him nicely within range. Then, before I could fire, he flattened out no more than 50 feet above the sea level and went streaking for home. I followed him and we still were doing a good 400 mph when I pressed the gun button. First one short burst of less than one second's duration, then another and then another and finally a fifth short burst, all aimed very deliberately. Suddenly the Messerschmitt's port wing dropped down. The starboard wing went up and then in a flash his nose went down and he was gone. He simply vanished into the sea.

'I hadn't time to look round for him because almost at the precise moment he disappeared from my gun sights I felt a sting in my leg. It was a sting from a splinter of my aircraft, which had been hit by enemy bullets. There were some Messerschmitt 109s right on my tail. Just as I had been firing at the enemy fighter which had now gone, three of his mates had been firing at me. I did a quick turn and made for home, but it wasn't quite so easy as all that. My attacker had put my port aileron out of action, so that I could hardly turn on the left side. The control column went rough on that side too and then I realised that my engine was beginning to run not quite so smoothly.

'There were no clouds to hide in except those up at 10,000 feet and they seemed miles away. Practically all my ammunition had gone, so it would have been suicide for me to try and make a fight of it. All I could hope for was to get back home. I watched my pursuers carefully. When they got near me I made a quick turn to the right and saw their tracer bullets go past my tail. I gained a bit on them and then they overtook me again and once more I turned when I thought they had me within range. I did that at least twelve times. All the time I was climbing slightly and when I reached the coast I was at 2,000 feet. My course had been rather like a staircase. They had not hit my aircraft after that first surprise attack and finally, on the coast, they turned back.

'I went on and landed at Croydon, my home aerodrome, got a fresh Hurricane and rejoined my squadron before going on another patrol.'

Flying Officer Henry Michael Ferriss was awarded a 1/8 share in the destruction of a Do 17 of I/KG2 and a Bf 109E of 2/JG 3 confirmed destroyed. Born on 1 August 1917 in Lea, London, he was educated at St Joseph's, Blackheath and Stoneyhurst College. He began flying with the University Air Squadron while he was at London University in 1935. Subsequently he became a medical student at St Thomas' Hospital. In July 1937 he joined the RAF on a short service commission and after completing training, was posted to 111 Squadron at Northolt on 7 May 1938. After the Dunkirk evacuation, he was awarded a DFC. On 16 August 1940, over Marden, Flight Lieutenant Ferriss crashed head-on into a Do 17 of 7./KG2 which he was attacking. He crashed on Sheephurst Farm. The Dornier crashed at Moatlands, Benchley, Paddock Wood. All were killed. His score stood at 9 and 2 shared destroyed, 1 shared u/c destroyed, 1 probable, 2 damaged and 1 He 59 floatplane destroyed on the water. Ferriss is buried in St Mary's churchyard, Chislehurst, Kent.

'Yes, it really was a good day for the squadron. We caught about twenty-five Junkers 87 dive bombers attacking ships off Orford Ness [sic]. We shot down fifteen of them into the sea, probably destroyed seven others and damaged one more. So that out of the twenty-five dive-bombers making the attack, only two escaped us without bullet-holes in them.

'We all seemed to have a hunch that there were going to be fireworks that afternoon and decided to stay in the crew-room instead of going across to the mess for tea. We were quite right; for at about ten minutes past four, we had orders to take off and patrol over one of our convoys. We were all in the air within three or four minutes. We had been patrolling the convoy for about ten minutes, when looking towards the south I suddenly saw the bursting of anti-aircraft shells about twelve miles away, some distance from the coast. I called up the other boys on the radio telephone and off we went towards the bursting shells. We were a few miles away when I saw the first of the enemy bombers diving down on some objective we could not see. The weather was not very good; there was a sea fog reaching up to 2,000 feet but at 10,000 feet where we were the sun was shining brightly. So I led the squadron round to get the advantage of the sun and down we went on to the enemy. We found that three or four of them at a time were dive-bombing ships from 7,000 feet; they were taking it in turn to go down vertically, one behind the other. I told the squadron to attack from somewhere below 2,000 feet and to choose their targets. Down we went, taking the enemy completely by surprise as we did their escort of Messerschmitt fighters.

'We dived down and got within range of our targets below a thousand feet and then we gave them 'the works'. We attacked them in pairs, one of us giving the enemy a good burst and the other doing what he could to finish him off. And this is what happened to me: first of all I went after one Junkers - a sergeant-pilot followed when I broke away and did him a lot more damage. The bomber went waffling out to sea, looking very sorry for himself. Bits had been shot off him, so we claimed him for a probable as he didn't look as though he would get very far. Then looking round again I saw another bomber at only a few hundred feet above the sea. So I got right behind him and opened fire and kept on firing all the time I was overtaking him. I could see my bullets hitting him and his rear-gunner stopped firing almost immediately. Then I got really close to him and shot him up again. Suddenly the Junkers blew up in the air. I think I must have hit a bomb, for there was a yellow flash and a cloud of black smoke. The explosion gave me a bump for as I broke away, blinded by the smoke, my Hurricane shuddered and dropped quite a distance. I couldn't see what happened to the bomber after that, but some of the boys said afterwards that it fell in little pieces over quite a big area of the sea. It was an extraordinary show - one moment the bomber was there, the next there was a big cloud of black smoke in its place. After that I circled round for a few minutes searching for something else to take on and soon found another bomber which I attacked with the last of my ammunition. When I had used it all up and had broken away, another of my Hurricanes took over and attacked him. He was so badly damaged that he became one more of our probables.

'While this had been going on, the rest of my squadron had been doing grand work and that day was definitely the best day for the squadron that I can remember. It was such a quick job and took only five minutes' fighting to clear the air of Germans. I mentioned just now that we took off at ten minutes past four and at a quarter to five we had landed on our aerodrome again.'

'*A Hurricane Squadron Attacks Twenty-Five Junkers 87s* by 'a Flight Lieutenant', which was broadcast on the BBC Home Service in November 1940. It describes the events of 8 August 1940 when 22 Stukas were claimed by 143, 145, 609 and 43 Squadrons. The 'flight lieutenant' was most likely one of the Hurricane pilots on 145 Squadron at Westhampnett whose claims later totalled ten of the dive bombers, including three damaged. Flight Lieutenant Adrian Hope Boyd claimed five (two Bf 109Es and 2 Bf 110s and a Ju 87) and one Stuka damaged during three sorties. Flight Lieutenant Roy Gilbert Dutton claimed 3 Stukas and a Bf 109E damaged. 143 Squadron claimed nine Stukas, including two damaged. The convoy codenamed 'Peewit' by the RAF consisting of twenty mostly coal-bearing merchant ships with nine naval escort vessels which had sailed in the previous evening's tide from the Medway and attempted to pass through the Dover Straits under cover of darkness was decimated. Only four ships sailed into Swanage virtually unscathed. Most of 145's victories were in fact off the Isle of Wight. On 18 August the Stukas were decimated again, losing sixteen shot down by 43, 602 and 152 Squadrons. Two more Ju 87s crash-landed at their bases in France and another four of the dive-bombers were damaged.

'We waited for the bombers at around 3,000 metres [10,000 feet] and then accompanied them in the direction of England. My Staffel was positioned to the left rear of the bombers. Oberleutnant Henrici, my Rottenführer, flew at the rear of our Staffel and we were thus at the cad of the entire formation. As we crossed the English coast, Henrici and I saw about four or five Hurricanes approaching us. We left the formation and attacked the British aircraft. During the battle, I found myself behind a Hurricane and opened fire. At that same moment, I was hit in the back, at the level of my shoulder harness. I must have lost consciousness immediately. When I came to, my hands were covered in oil and I thought only of bailing out. I found the emergency release for the canopy, unfastened my parachute harness from the seat and shot from the aircraft. Shortly thereafter, I again passed out. I don't know for how long; I came to my senses only long enough to pull the parachute handle. I can recall nothing of striking the ground, being discovered, or being transported to the hospital. I next regained consciousness in a hospital near Dover, following an operation....'

Feldwebel Gerhard Kemen, JG 26, shot down on 14 August 1940 by Pilot Officer Rupert Frederick Smythe on 32 Squadron at Hawkinge, whose Hurricane was immediately shot down by a Messerschmitt. Smythe force-landed at Hawkinge without injury but his Hurricane was scrapped. Kemen was transported to a Canadian PoW camp in 1941, was repatriated with several other wounded pilots in 1943 and returned to active duty in time for the final battles for the Reich - this time on a ground staff. Smythe, from Killiney, County Dublin, had joined the RAF on a short-service commission

in October 1937, being posted to 29 Squadron on completion of training in October 1938. In September 1939 he was posted to 504 Squadron, moving, in May 1940 to 32 Squadron. He was shot down and wounded by Bf 109s over South London on 24 August, crashing at Lyminge. He was taken to Royal Masonic Hospital, Hammersmith. Awarded a DFC, he did not return to operations. He left the service in 1946 as a Flight Lieutenant.

'It was very hectic at Hawkinge. When the Hurricanes or Spitfires came in, we automatically guided them in with our hands, into the right positions on dispersal. The next thing we were all over them, getting them refuelled, rearmed; ready again for take-off. It was quite fast working to get them off. I think the recognised fastest time was seven minutes to get six aircraft refuelled and rearmed, from the time of touch-down to take-off. It wasn't always for the same pilot - in fact it was different squadrons coming in all the time. Hawkinge really was an advance fighter base. The planes came to us during the daytime and we operated them right through the day, then they went back to their bases at Kenley, Northolt, Biggin Hill, Gravesend, West Malling - and if they went up on a scramble, they would probably be up for a half hour or three-quarters of an hour, then come back in to us for refuelling and rearming. We'd probably work the same squadron, perhaps, until about 2 or 3 o'clock in the afternoon. They would probably go back to base and another squadron would come in. There would be Hurricanes and Spitfires and also we had 141 Squadron, which was a Defiant squadron operating from Hawkinge, but I'm afraid they lost nearly all their aircraft.

When the aircraft came in, the first thing we did was check their petrol, oil and oxygen bottles. Naturally the armourers checked the guns and the wireless people checked the radios. They all did their very quick check, and then we had to get them off again. We got the starter trolleys in position to get them away again. At that time there would be about forty of the trades on a dispersal. You had all the ancillary staff, the petrol bowser drivers and so on.

It certainly happened that we got machine-gunned and bombed with them on the 'drome. If they were coming in, the pilots would scramble straight away and try to get them off the ground. Most of the time we had already got them refuelled and they were waiting to go. It was just a matter of starting them up. It was not like today, when you have a push-button starter - you had the trolley jack, which had to be operated by the fitters and riggers.

There were quite a few crash landings - it was a grass strip - and when they took off, they didn't take off singly, there were six of them at a time, right across the field. The squadrons were not only fighting the aircraft, they were protecting the airfields as well. Personally, I didn't like bombing, but I hated machine-gunning across the 'drome more than anything. If the squadrons had scrambled and we came under fire, the station used to put a call out, 'Station under attack,' and they'd try to get something back round us. Sometimes the first thing we knew was the bombs landing or the machine guns going - they used to come in so quick you didn't even get a warning. But, naturally, if they knew, they would get the sirens going. They bombed the strip quite a few times, and they smashed the hangars and a lot of the buildings.

One day there three, Messerschmitts came round. They were very low and I think some of the guns had to pack up firing because they were so low that they were firing across one another. I think all three would have landed if there had not been so much fire directed at them, however, one of them landed -and he had no hope of getting up again. The plane was intact, and they captured him. Whether he came in because he thought he'd been damaged, I don't know - but the overall impression you got was that all three would have landed. Maybe it was to get out of the war, or perhaps they had lost their direction and thought that it was the occupied coast - I don't know. The pilot can't have been anymore than 18 or 19 years of age. He handed over his revolver, got his little box out of the cockpit and they waltzed him off to the guard-room.'

Wilf Dykes, a flight rigger at Hawkinge, a forward airfield just outside Folkestone.

'Treble One Squadron had a very enjoyable time on 13 August before breakfast. We had a lovely party somewhere off the Isle of Sheppey in the Thames estuary. It was a beautiful morning and twelve of us were flying very high over Beachy Head. We were told to patrol below clouds over Dover and then we had orders to intercept enemy aircraft between us and the North Foreland. So we went down to about 3,000 feet just below clouds. We turned north and came over the Thames estuary. It was very misty so we went up again above the clouds to about 6,000 feet. The sun was coming up from the east and so were the enemy. We saw two formations of bombers - two lots of twelve aircraft, one behind the other, with about two miles between them. They were 1,500 feet lower than we were, so we had an immediate advantage. Our squadron leader gave his orders quickly and clearly over the radio telephone. He would lead his flight of six Hurricanes round the back of the first formation and the other flight of six, which included me, was to deliver a head-on attack.

'As soon as the leader of my flight went down towards the first formation, the enemy darted down for the clouds. The squadron was in four sections of three each in line astern. The CO [Squadron Leader J. M. Thompson] led the first two sections and I was leading the last section of three. It is one of the duties of the last section to give warning of approach of enemy fighters.

'Anyway, when the Dorniers went into cloud, I led my section down after them and when we emerged at the bottom of the clouds I found we were ahead of them. So I swung completely round and led a head-on attack on the second formation of Dorniers which had now appeared. I'm sure they got an awful shock. They didn't expect an attack from the front like that. You could see that they didn't like it.

'My section came up from below and slightly to one side of the bombers and we blazed away for all we were worth. It was impossible to miss them. We simply sprayed them with bullets and then we broke away to the left. One of them was badly hit and he broke away. I pounced on him right away, fired from dead astern and after another pilot had fired at him I believe he went down to crash into the sea.

'In a battle you don't often have time to see what happens to every enemy aircraft you shoot at. But you usually have a chance to look round and see what is happening near you. I looked around after my head-on attack and saw a grand sight. My flight-leader was leading his section up at the bombers head-on. I could see their machine-gun bullets spurting from their wings and I could see the Germans losing their formation under this terrific fire.

'After that we began to look for odd enemy bombers which were now wheeling about in the sky and trying to form up together. I went up above the clouds again with another pilot and we saw three Dorniers, looking very sorry for themselves, heading for home. We took one each and the one I fired at shed a lot of pieces from his wings and fuselage. I saw the other pilot - Sergeant John Craig - later when he landed. I asked him how he got on and he said: 'Fine! I got him nicely. First the rear gunner bailed out and then I saw the Jerry plane go into the sea.'

'We had quite a good breakfast that morning, for including what we got the squadron's bag contained four certainties and a number of others probably destroyed or damaged.

'I think my best day was one over Dunkirk [on 31 May] during the evacuation of the BEF. Our squadron was patrolling Dunkirk at more than 10,000 feet I doubt if our troops could see us at that height - when we saw a formation of about twenty Heinkel 111s. High above them were a lot of Messerschmitts 109 acting as a fighter escort. We were told to attack the fighters, but before we could reach them they sheered off and left the bombers to us. We went down on them like a shot.

'I got two of the easiest enemies of my life that afternoon. I dived on one Heinkel and gave him an incredibly short burst of fire. My thumb was still on the gun button when both his engines immediately caught fire. He put his nose down and to my surprise, I must confess, he went straight down into the sea with a tremendous splash. He just went straight in from 10,000 feet.

'I climbed up a bit and looked round. Then I saw another Heinkel going east, having attacked shipping in Dunkirk harbour. I started chasing him, climbing after him all the time. When I got fairly near I just crept up to him - we were doing just over 200 mph - that is what I call 'creeping' in a Hurricane. Anyway, I crept after him for a few minutes and I'm sure he didn't see me until I opened fire from close in. I just let him have it - a long burst of five seconds. The rear gunner opened fire at me almost at the same moment that I started firing. He was silenced immediately, yet he managed to put half a dozen bullets into my aircraft. The Heinkel began to emit black smoke and dived vertically towards the sea. I watched him crash.

'There was another day in France when we ran into ten Messerschmitts and only one of them got away. That was a good scrap. If I remember rightly, it was our first morning in France, too.

'One afternoon, in France, when on patrol, we saw anti-aircraft shells bursting high above us. I spotted a German aircraft and reported it to the leader of the squadron. He as good as said, 'Well, go and get it then, if you can see it'. I went up to 15,000 feet and found it was a Dornier 17. I attacked from behind and below and in a few moments the machine caught fire and a second or two later, began a dive which ended on the ground. Then I rejoined the rest of the squadron to continue the patrol. I was just lucky to be the one who happened to see the enemy.

'I have about 850 flying hours altogether on my log book, half of them on Hurricanes. I have been with the squadron longer than any other pilot. A few have joined since the war, but most of the pilots came in two or three years ago. There isn't one of them who hasn't got a Hun. It's a grand squadron to be in, I can assure you.'

22-year old Sergeant William Lawrence Dymond on 111 Squadron talking about his two victories on Tuesday 13th August 1940. He had been in action at least thirty times. Born in Twickenham, Middlesex, Bill Dymond was a pre-war NCO pilot, who joined the RAF in September 1935 and he was posted to 111 Squadron in August 1936. He was awarded a DFM, gazetted on 6 September, for eight destroyed and three probables. On 2 September 1940 he was shot down in his Hurricane over the Thames Estuary and was killed. He would have been 23 in November. His total score was 10 and 1 shared destroyed, 1 probable and 6 damaged. Sergeant John Teasdale Craig was born in Newcastle-upon-Tyne, but lived in Witton-le-Wear, Isle of Man before joining the RAF. He saw considerable action on 111 Squadron over Dunkirk in May and June 1940 and during the first part of the Battle of Britain. He was credited with a Do 17 over Herne Bay on 13th August. On 31 August he was shot down over Felixstowe by Bf 110s and bailed out injured. He was awarded a DFM on 6 September 1940. He was killed on 2 June 1941, aged 27, in a mid-air collision in his Hurricane whilst instructing at 56 OTU. His score stood at 5 destroyed, 4 probables and 8 damaged.

August 16th was a glorious day. The sun was shining from a cloudless sky and there was hardly a breath of wind anywhere. 249 Squadron was going towards Southampton on patrol at 15,000 feet when I saw three Junkers 88 bombers about four miles away flying across our bows. I reported this to our squadron leader and he replied: 'Go after them with your section.' So I led my section of aircraft round towards the bombers. We chased hard after them, but when we were about a mile behind we saw the 88s fly straight into a squadron of Spitfires. I used to fly a Spitfire myself and I guessed it was curtains for the three Junkers. I was right and they were all shot down in quick time, with no pickings for us. I must confess I was very disappointed, for I had never fired at a Hun in my life and was longing to have a crack at them.

'So we swung round again and started to climb up to 18,000 feet over Southampton, to rejoin our squadron. I was still a long way from the squadron when suddenly, very close in rapid succession, I heard four big bangs. They were the loudest noises I had ever heard and they had been made by four cannon shells from a Messerschmitt 110 hitting my machine. The first shell tore through the hood over my cockpit and sent splinters into my left eye. One splinter, I discovered later, nearly severed my eyelid. 1 couldn't see through that eye for blood. The second cannon shell struck my spare petrol tank and set it on fire. The third shell crashed into the cockpit and tore off my right trouser leg. The fourth shell struck the back of my left shoe. It shattered the heel of the shoe and made quite a mess of my left foot.

But I didn't know anything about that, either, until later. Anyway, the effect of these four shells was to make me dive away to the right to avoid further shells. Then I started cursing myself for my carelessness. What a fool I had been, I thought, what a fool!

'I was just thinking of jumping out when suddenly a Messerschmitt 110 whizzed under me and got right in my gun-sights. Fortunately, no damage had been done to my windscreens or sights and when I was chasing the Junkers, I had switched everything on. So everything was set for a fight. I pressed the gun button, for the Messerschmitt was in nice range; I plugged him first time and I could see my tracer bullets entering the German machine. He was going like mad, twisting and turning as he tried to get away from my fire. So I pushed the throttle wide open. Both of us must have been doing about 400 mph as we went down together in a dive. First he turned left, then right, then left and right again. He did three turns to the right and finally a fourth turn to the left. I remember shouting out loud at him when I first saw him: 'I'll teach you some manners, you Hun,' and I shouted other things as well. I knew I was getting him nearly all the time I was firing.

'By this time it was pretty hot inside my machine from the burst petrol tank. I couldn't see much flame, but I reckon it was there all right. I remember looking once at my left hand which was keeping the throttle open. It seemed to be in the fire itself and I could see the skin peeling off it. Yet I had little pain. Unconsciously too, I had drawn my feet up under my parachute on the seat, to escape the heat, I suppose.

'Well, I gave the Hun all I had and the last I saw of him was when he was going down, with his right wing lower than the left wing. I gave him a parting burst and as he had disappeared, started thinking about saving myself. I decided it was about time I left the aircraft and bailed out, so I immediately jumped up from my seat. But first of all I hit my head against the framework of the hood, which was all that was left. I cursed myself for a fool, pulled the hood back (wasn't I relieved when it slid back beautifully) and jumped up again. Once again I bounced back into my seat, for I had forgotten to undo the straps holding me in. One of them snapped and so I only had one to undo. Then I left the machine.

'I suppose I was about 12 to 15,000 feet when I bailed out. Immediately I started somersaulting downwards and after a few turns like that I found myself diving head first for the ground. After a second or two of this, I decided to pull the rip-cord. The result was that I immediately straightened up and began to float down. Then an aircraft - a Messerschmitt, I think - came tearing past me. I decided to pretend I was dead and hung limply by the parachute straps. The Messerschmitt came back once and I kept my eyes closed, but I didn't get the bullets I was half expecting. I don't know if he fired at me; the main thing is that I wasn't hit.

'While I was coming down like that I had a look at myself. I could see the bones of my left hand showing through the knuckles. Then for the first time I discovered I'd been wounded in the foot. Blood was oozing out of the lace-holes of my left boot. My right hand was pretty badly burned, too. So I hung down a bit longer and then decided to try my limbs, just to see if they would work - thank goodness they did. I still had my oxygen mask over my face, but my hands were in too bad a state to take it off. I tried to, but I couldn't manage it. I found, too, that I had lost one trouser-leg and the other was badly torn and my tunic was just like a lot of torn rags, so I wasn't looking very smart. Then, after a bit more of this dangling down business, I began to ache all over and my hands and legs began to hurt a lot.

'When I got lower, I saw I was in danger of coming down in the sea. I knew I didn't stand an earthly if I did, because I wouldn't have been able to swim a stroke with my hands like that. So I wriggled about a bit and managed to float inland. Then I saw a high tension cable below me and thought it would finish me if I hit that. So I wriggled a bit more and aimed at a nice open field.

'When I was about 100 feet from the ground I saw a cyclist and heard him ring his bell. I was surprised to hear the bicycle-bell and realised that I had been coming down in absolute silence. I bellowed at the cyclist, but I don't suppose he heard me. Finally, I touched down in the field and fell over. Fortunately it was a still day. My parachute just floated down and stayed down without dragging me along, as they sometimes do.

'I had a piece of good news almost immediately. One of the people who came along and who had watched the combat, said they had seen the Messerschmitt 110 dive straight into the sea, so it hadn't been such a bad day after all.

Flight Lieutenant James Nicolson, a Hurricane pilot on 249 Squadron at Boscombe Down. He was awarded the first and only VC awarded to Fighter Command and later in the war was also decorated with the DFC. In the Far East on 2 May 1945 Wing Commander Nicolson flew on a Liberator on 355 Squadron attacking Japanese gun positions in Burma. The aircraft took off from Salbani, Bengal at 0051 hours and at 0330 hours it radioed its position as approximately 130 miles south-east of Calcutta. It was assumed from this message that the Liberator was returning to base and that it would arrive there at about 0630 hours. When it became overdue an ASR search was instituted and, at 1505 hours, twelve hours after the message, two members of the Liberator's crew were found clinging to the wreckage of the aircraft. The body of another crew member was later recovered from the sea but no trace of Wing Commander Nicolson or the remaining occupants was ever found. From a statement made by one of the survivors it is known that one of the Liberator's engines caught fire and the order was given to jettison the bomb load. This was carried out and the aircraft turned about and headed for base. Height could not be maintained, however and the captain warned the crew that a forced landing would have to be made on the sea. Neither of the survivors could remember anything after that until they found themselves floating in the water.

'At 1300 we took off from Caffiers. Our mission was to escort a bomber formation in an attack on Kenley, an airfield near London. Flying at about 6,000 meters [19,500 feet] altitude, we reached the target without being attacked and were only then engaged by British fighters, which were primarily interested in the bombers and Bf 110s. I was still right beside the bombers when a Spitfire immediately beneath me attacked a circling Bf 110 from behind. It was simple for me to get behind the attacker by a short manoeuvre. We then had a Bf 110, a Spitfire and a Bf 109 (myself), flying in a row. While the rear gunner fired at the Spitfire and the Spitfire in turn attempted to silence the rear gunner, I found it easy to put a long burst into the Spitfire and which immediately smoked and broke away in a split-S. I had approached very near the 110, whose gunner was firing continuously and turned away to keep from ramming it. At this moment I felt a blow beside my left foot in the cockpit and my engine quickly came to a stop. Good Lord! The Bf 110 gunner, seeing me, had taken me to be another enemy and had hit my aircraft.

'Streaming a white cloud of fuel, I feathered my prop and glided unmolested in the direction of the French coast, hoping that I might reach the water of the Channel and eventually be fished out by a German rescue aircraft. The sun shone brightly; the seconds seemed like hours. Around me, the bitter combats continued to rage. Damaged German bombers, British and German fighters fell away, smoking, burning, or breaking up. Parachutes opened or failed to open - it was a gruesome but also an exciting spectacle. I had never before been able to observe such an air battle. My glide took me ever nearer the ground; I would never be able to reach the water of the Channel. I glanced at my watch; it was about 1400. I was aware that this was the end of my fighting career and tears streamed down my face. I finally crashed my loyal Bf 109 (into many pieces) near Rye, south of Folkestone and woke up later in the hospital, suffering from back and head injuries.

'About a week later, I was taken by subway to the interrogation camp in London. The caption to a photograph an English photojournalist took of me and my guards stated that I had quite a sense of humour for a German. I had cheerfully told the ticket taker that I did not need a ticket, as I had a season pass – a season that stretched into six years of imprisonment as a guest of the British King.'

Oberleutnant Jupp Buerschgens a ten-victory Experte of 7th Staffel, JG26, shot down flying a Geschwader escort to the London area in the Battle of Britain, 1 September 1940.

'Red 1 (Squadron Leader D.R. S. Bader) on sighting e/a opened full throttle and boost and climbed and turned left to cut off the enemy and arrived with Red 2 (Sub/Lieutenant Richard John 'Dickie' Cork) only, on the beam slightly in front. Squadron Leader Bader gave a very short beam burst at about 100 yards at e/a, which were then flying section of 3 line astern in a large rectangle. Then accompanied by Red 2 gave short bursts at the middle of e/a of back section. The e/a started smoking preparatory catching fire. Squadron Leader Bader did not notice result, which was later confirmed by Pilot Officer Turner as diving down in flames from the back of the bomber formation. At the time of Squadron Leader Bader's attack on the Me 110 a yellow-nosed Me 109 was noticed reflected in his mirror and he turned to avoid the e/a. Big bang was heard by him in the cockpit of his Hurricane. An explosive bullet came through the right-hand side of fuselage touching map case knocking the corner off the undercarriage selector quadrant and finished up against the petrol priming pump. Squadron Leader Bader executed a steep diving turn and found a lone

Me 110 below him, which he attacked from straight astern and above him and saw e/a go into a steepish straight dive finishing up in flames in a field just north of railway line turning approximately East. (West of Wickford due North of Thameshaven).

'Red 2 sighted e/a to East and above. He climbed to meet e/a and carried out a beam attack of the leading section of bombers, firing at a Do 215 on the tail end of the formation. Port engine burst into flames after two short bursts and crashed vertically. Red 2 was then attacked by e/a from rear and hit a starboard mainplane. He broke away downwards and backwards nearly colliding head on with an Me 110. Red 2 gave short burst before pulling away and saw front cabin of 110 break up and machine go into vertical dive. Two of the crew bailed out. Whilst Red 2 was following e/a down, e/a was stalling and diving. An Me 109 attacked Red 2 from the rear, one shot from the e/a going through the side of Red 2's hood, hitting bottom of reflector sight and bullet proof windscreen. Red 2 received a number of glass splinters in his eyes so broke away downwards with half roll and lost sight of e/a.'

242 Squadron Combat report 7 September 1940. The Bf 110 destroyed by Squadron Leader Douglas Bader and Sub/Lieutenant Cork, crashed at Downham Hall, near Wickford. Leutnant Hans Dietrich Abert and Unteroffizier Hans Scharf were killed. Early in 1941 Bader began leading squadrons of Hurricane IIs on offensive sweeps over France from North Weald. In March 1941 he was appointed Wing Commander Flying at Tangmere flying Spitfires on offensive sweeps over the continent. He had been awarded a DFC in January 1941 for ten victories and a bar to his DSO followed in July for 15 and a bar to his DFC came in September, for four more. On 9 August Bader was shot down over France on a fighter sweep and he spent the rest of the war in German prison camps until finally being released from Colditz Castle in April 1945. His final score stood at 20 and 4 shared destroyed, 6 and 1 shared probables, 11 damaged. He led the 1945 Battle of Britain flypast over London and then took command of the North Weald Sector. He left the RAF in 1946. He was knighted in 1976. Douglas Bader died on 5 September 1982.

In October 1940 'Dickie' Cork was awarded a DFC, which at the insistence of the Admiralty was exchanged for a Distinguished Service Cross. When he returned to the FAA, Cork served with 880 Naval Air Squadron in the Arctic, Mediterranean and Indian Ocean. It was during Operation 'Pedestal' in 1942 that he became the only Royal Navy pilot to shoot down five aircraft in one day and was the leading naval ace flying the Hawker Hurricane. He was given command of the 15th Naval Fighter Wing aboard HMS *Victorious* but was killed in a flying accident on 14 April 1944 (aged 27) in a F4U Corsair over China Bay, Ceylon. His final score was nine destroyed, two shared, one probable, four damaged and seven destroyed on the ground.

'In the halcyon, carefree days of 1938 when I landed my flight of six Hurricanes in v-formation on the grass at Biggin Hill, my bull terrier 'Merlin' - what else could I call him for he was a wizard; - would rush out, identify my aircraft and run alongside as I taxied in. How did he know? Had my engine a different sound? He never divulged his secret and in wartime always picked out my Spitfire from others.

'Flying Hurricanes until early 1941 and Spitfires until the end of the war inevitably I am asked the perennial question, 'Which was the better fighter?' Each had its advantages and disadvantages. The Hurricane with its hump back was the bruiser, tough and rugged, a better gun platform with its curved nose enabling deflection shots without losing sight of the target. The Spitfire was the slim dainty lady with the better overall performance and a name to provoke and excite attention. You paid your money and made your choice.

'Having a little success in a battle over Dover one day, I hastened to Hawkinge to refuel and rearm; with the airman refuelling whilst standing on the wing beside me I watched the battle overhead. He shouted suddenly, 'Look, we've got one! as a Me 109 burst into flames. Then we saw a parachute blossom and the airman turned to me with a look of disgust and said, 'The jammy bastard.'

Pete Brothers, who Laddie Lucas once described as: 'one of those distinctive Fighter Command characters, full of bonhomie, humour and decorations, who made light of the serious things, no matter what his innermost thoughts might be saying. And in his war there was plenty to be serious about. Having entered the Service in the mid-1930s, he was necessarily in at the start, yet he was still in operational play near the end ... The Battle of Britain, the offensive years over occupied Europe and then D-Day and all that went with it, it was an inevitable progression which took him to several squadron and wing commands - and to a healthy bag of enemy aircraft destroyed to show for it. There was little rest. At one point along the way, he formed - and led into battle - 457, the second Australian fighter squadron to serve in the UK. Pete Brothers was exactly the sort of Pom whom those discerning Cobbers would follow.

'In the summer of 1940 there is no question that Germany intended to invade this country and that air supremacy was needed to make this feasible. But by no means the whole of the summer of 1940 qualifies, to the historians, as constituting the Battle of Britain. Some knowledgeable authorities, presumably in the Air Ministry, decided that the Battle of Britain should be spanned by the period 12 July to 31 October. This was indeed the critical period but it was not the only period when there was intense fighting.

'Your average man or woman knows that a few dashing young British officers flying Spitfires defeated the enemy and prevented the invasion. Thereafter they were known as 'The Few', but this alone was a misnomer because it assumes that only the few who flew in fact contributed to victory whereas what ensured it was the performance, not just of the RAF aircrew, but of the population of the whole country.

'Until the mid 1930s, Guernica and other places like it surrendered when they were heavily bombed. The British did not - they were the first population to stand up to heavy bombing although, to do them justice, it must be acknowledged that the Germans later sustained even heavier bombing without surrendering. Clearly everybody in this country contributed to victory in the Battle of Britain, from the RAF ground crew to the anti-aircraft gunners, the transport workers, the miners and, in particular, the Merchant Navy crews. All played a critical part - it was by no means a victory for the few. Indeed, it was the many who won by their outstanding and unexpected performance under fire. Nor, indeed, were 'The Few' all that few. Nearly 2,000 aircrew (and let us not forget the gunners in the Defiants and the observers in the Blenheims) officially qualified for the Battle of Britain clasp. Nor were they all 'dashing'. The more dash the less likelihood of survival. It was the prudent pilot who knew when to save his skin and when the odds were not just heavy but ridiculous and he lived to fly another day. Nor were all the pilots 'young'. Men like Broadhurst, Beamish[41] and Bader were all well into their 30s when the Battle was fought and many of our gallant Polish allies were past 40 - although they never admitted it. Mention of the Poles reminds us how many nationalities other than the British fought in the Battle. There were, of course, the outstanding pilots from the Commonwealth, men like Alan Deere and 'Sailor' Malan, but there were also others who by no stretch of the imagination could be called British. Everyone seems to know about the Poles and Czechs who contributed large contingents; but many are surprised to hear that the French made a contribution, as did many other countries - even Israel.

'Nor were the Germans faced only by commissioned officers. Non-commissioned officers such as 'Ginger' Lacey, George Unwin[42] and 'Sticks' Gregory[43] were NCOs and before the war the NCO fighter pilot formed the hard professional backbone of the majority of RAF fighter squadrons. Later, these NCOs were joined by the newest of the new but in early 1940 the proven and expert NCO pilot contributed enormously, not only to the numbers but also to the efficiency of such squadrons. Finally, 'Spitfires'? The statistics show that there were twice as many Hurricanes fighting in the Battle as Spitfires and they shot down twice as many aircraft. But the Spitfire has somehow appealed to the public imagination as the Hurricane has not and even now, in talking of 1940, we talk about 'Spitfire Summer'. Even the Germans contributed to this phenomenon. For some reason, they seemed to resent being shot down by a Hurricane. It was somehow infra-dig and they always heatedly denied it when all the evidence showed that it was a Hurricane that had been their undoing. So much of the history that we learn about the Battle of Britain is inaccurate. Was the Battle worth fighting at all? The best evidence that we have on this came from Field Marshal von Rundstedt. After the end of the war he was interrogated and one of the most important questions asked of him was when he felt that the tide was beginning to turn and when the uninterrupted catalogue of German victories became more and more doubtful. Was it Stalingrad or Leningrad or even El Alamein? 'Oh no' replied the Field Marshal, 'it was the Battle of Britain'. This answer certainly surprised his interrogators and they questioned him further. 'Well you see', he said, 'that was the first time I realised that we were not invincible'. So it was worthwhile having the Battle, whatever the cause and it was as critical as is portrayed. The one thing that should never be forgotten about the Battle is that we won it.'

Sir Christopher Foxley-Norris, who served operationally throughout

World War II, starting on Lysanders during the withdrawal from France in 1940, through Hurricanes in Scotland during the Battle of Britain and finishing on Beaufighters and Mosquitoes in the Eastern Mediterranean and the Baltic. He rose to the rank of Air Chief Marshal and became Commander-in-Chief RAF Germany/Commander 2nd Allied Tactical Air Force.

'Even the Germans got to respect the Spitfire. I remember Peter Townsend went to see one of the German pilots which he had shot down, close to the base. The German pilot said to him, 'I'm very glad to meet the Spitfire pilot who shot me down.'

'And Peter said, 'No, no - I was flying a Hurricane. I'm a Hurricane pilot.'

'The German kept arguing with him and Peter kept saying, 'No - you were shot down by a Hurricane.'

'The German pilot said, 'Would you do me a favour? If you ever talk to any other Luftwaffe pilots, please tell them I was shot down by a Spitfire?'

Sergeant James A. Goodson 43 Squadron.

'Saturday was certainly a grand day. It started as most days for fighter pilots start - with the dawn. We were up at a quarter past four. I felt in my bones that it was going to be a good day. We were in the air just after five o'clock. Shortly before half-past eight we were in the air again looking for enemy raiders approaching the South Coast from France. We saw three or four waves of Junkers 88s, protected by a bunch of Me 109s above them. We were flying at 15,000 feet, between the bombers and the fighters. The fighters did not have much chance to interfere with us before we attacked the bombers. I attacked one of the waves of bombers from behind and above. I selected the end bomber of the formation which numbered between fifteen and eighteen. I gave this Junkers a burst of fire lasting only two seconds, but it was enough. It broke away from the formation, dived down and I saw it crash into the sea.

'I then throttled back so that I would not overtake the whole formation. I was getting quite a lot of crossfire from the other bombers as it was, though none of it hit me. If I had broken away after shooting down the first bomber, I should have exposed myself to the full force of the enemy formation's crossfire, so I throttled back and stayed behind them. I didn't have time to select another bomber target, for almost immediately an Me 109 came diving after me. As I had throttled back he overshot me. He simply came along and presented me with a beautiful target. He pulled up about 150 yards in front of me, so I pressed the gun button for two seconds. He immediately began to smoke and dived away. I followed him this time and saw him go straight into the sea. When the sky was clear of German planes, we went home for breakfast. We had a nice 'bag' in that combat before the other Germans escaped.

'As a matter of fact, I didn't get any breakfast at all. I only had time for a hot drink before we were ordered to stand by again and by half-past eleven that morning we were patrolling the Southeast Coast. We were attacked by half a dozen Me 109s and of course we broke up to deal with them individually. I had a dogfight with one, both of us trying to get into position to deliver an attack, but I outmanoeuvred him. I got on his tail and he made off for the French coast as hard as he could go. The fight started at 10,000 feet and we raced across the Channel like mad. As were going like that, I saw one of our fellows shoot down another Me 109, so I said to myself: 'I must keep the squadron's average up and get this one.' I didn't fire at him until we were actually over the French coast. Then I let him have it - three nice bursts of fire lasting three seconds each, which, as you may imagine, is an awfully long time! I started that final burst at 8,000 feet and then he began to go down and I followed until I saw him crash into a field in France. Then I went back home without seeing any enemy at all. I carefully examined my Spitfire when I landed, certain that I must have been hit somewhere. But, no, not a mark. It was very satisfactory.

'Our third show began just before four o'clock in the afternoon. We were flying towards the Thames estuary at 5,000 feet, when we saw antiaircraft shells bursting in the sky to the northeast. We changed course and began to climb for the place where we thought we should meet the enemy. We did. They were flying at 12,000 feet - twenty Ju 88s in tight formation accompanied by about twenty Me 109s, above them. They were flying towards the London area and we could see the balloons shining in the sun. When we spotted the fighters we pulled up towards them. I got under one Me 109 and gave him two bursts. Smoke started to pour out of him and he went down out of control. Suddenly, tracer bullets started whizzing past my machine. I turned sharply and saw an Me 109 attacking one of our pilots. I turned on the attacker and gave him a quick burst. Immediately he began to slow down and the aircraft began to smoke. I pressed the gun button a second time and he caught fire. I fired a third time and the whole machine became enveloped in flames and pieces began to fly off. Finally, as it went down, more pieces came off, all burning. As it tumbled down towards the Thames estuary it was really a bunch of blazing fragments instead of a whole aircraft. It was an amazing sight. That was my fifth for the day and the squadron's ninety-ninth! The squadron brought the score over the century the next day, as a matter of fact. The squadron has damaged a lot more, of course.

'There is a lot of luck about air fighting - by which I mean it's a matter of luck whether you get into a good scrap or not. I was right through the Dunkirk show and didn't get a thing. But recently I seem to have been lucky. These fights are over so quickly that unless you are there right at the beginning, you are liable not to see anything at all. None of the fights on Saturday lasted more than five minutes each.'

Sergeant (later squadron leader) Ronald 'Ronnie' Fairfax Hamlyn on 610 Squadron, who on 24 August claimed five victories in a day, an achievement which he described in a BBC radio broadcast when he was portrayed as 'an unidentified sergeant pilot of a fighter Command Spitfire squadron who shot down five enemy aircraft in three air battles on one day in August 1940'. He followed this on 26 August with a Bf 109E and a Bf 109E probable. Born in Harrogate, North Yorkshire on 26 February 1914, Ronnie Hamlyn joined the RAF by direct entry in 1936 and was serving as a Sergeant with 72 Squadron when war broke out. He was posted to 610 Squadron early in June

1940 and was with this unit throughout the Battle of Britain. His score was 10 and 1 shared destroyed, 1 probable, 1 damaged. On 29 August he was awarded a DFM, the citation recording eight successes. He was commissioned on 7 February 1941. On 13 June he went to 242 Squadron to fly Hurricanes, mainly on anti-shipping duties. Promoted to command a flight late in July, he remained with the unit until 15 October, when he was taken off operations. He remained in the RAF until October 1957.

'On 31 August the squadron was scrambled from Fowlmere - a satellite of Duxford - at about 7.30 am. There were only nine aircraft serviceable and we climbed to the east to about 25,000 feet in sections of three in loose line astern. Flight Lieutenant Clouston led the squadron.[44] I led the second section and Flight Lieutenant Brinsden the third.[45] About ten miles east of Duxford, I sighted a large formation - fifteen Do 215s escorted by a reported sixty fighters. Clouston 'instructed Brinsden to climb and engage the fighters while we attacked the bombers head-on. My foot was shot off when closing, causing no pain but just a dull thud and I saw my bare foot on the floor of the cockpit, almost severed. The aircraft controls were damaged and the aircraft went out of control, bunting into a steep dive.

'On bailing out, my parachute got caught and I was forced back along the fuselage, my gloves being blown off. I tried to do a delayed drop from about 20,000 feet because I was losing blood very quickly, but was unable to stand the pain of the foot twisting in the slip-stream, so I pulled the ripcord and put on a tourniquet using my helmet wireless lead.

'I drifted across Duxford airfield at about 10,000 feet towards Royston and I saw the squadron land. Eventually the wind changed and I sailed back across Duxford and came down in a field near the roundabout at Whittlesford on the Royston/Newmarket Road, where I was met by a youth of fifteen with a pitchfork, who thought I was a German. When my language convinced him that I wasn't, he went off at high speed to find a doctor.[46] Fortunately the first car he met contained a doctor and in about half an hour I was picked up by an RAF ambulance from Addenbrooke's, suffering no great pain.

'My aircraft crashed just beyond my home village of Little Shelford and my wife was told about it by the milkman. Fortunately the service doctor called in and told her I was all right and she arrived at the hospital before I recovered from the anaesthetic after the amputation.[47]

'The bombers' objective was presumably Duxford airfield, but on being attacked they jettisoned their bombs which fell in fields south of the high ground to the east of Duxford and then turned off to the south. Three of them were claimed as shot down and I learned from Flight Lieutenant Clouston that our lack of success was due to the fact that the cannons with which we had just been equipped had some teething troubles and very few rounds fired due to stoppages. In my own case, the guns went 'boom boom' and stopped.'

Flying Officer James Baird Coward on 19 Squadron was leading 'Green Section' in 'B' Flight. He was born in Teddington, Middlesex on 18 May 1915 and educated at Sutton High School. He joined the RAF on a short service commission in October 1936. After completing elementary, intermediate and

advanced flying training from February to September 1937, he was posted to 19 Squadron at Duxford. On 6 November 1939 Coward was appointed 'A' Flight Commander in 266 Squadron, then forming at Sutton Bridge. *Men of the Battle of Britain.* On 29 December 1939 he had married Cynthia Bayon, who lived at her parent's huge house at King's Farm at Little Shelford, four miles from RAF Duxford. After a spell in hospital to have his tonsils removed, her husband had rejoined 19 Squadron, then at Fowlmere. Over Dunkirk on 2 June 1940 he had claimed a Bf 109 probably destroyed. After Dunkirk seven or eight exhausted soldiers were billeted at King's farm for a spell. Cynthia's sister, who had married Bill, also a RAF pilot and their brother Michael H. A. T. Bayon, who wanted to be a fighter pilot, all lived at the house, which soon became known as 'RAF King's Farm'. Every morning after breakfast Cynthia would give her husband a farewell kiss, saying, 'See you later'. After flying for hours a day James and Bill would arrive for the three course evening meal served on a white damask table cloth with its huge silver soup tureen and Mike Bayon well remembers both of them falling asleep on the dinner table between courses. James Coward was eventually taken by ambulance to Addenbrooke's Hospital in Cambridge where his leg was later amputated below the knee. Three weeks later he was discharged from Ely RAF Hospital just in time for the birth of his first child, a daughter, Janice. After receiving an artificial limb and fit again, James Coward was posted to Mr Churchill's personal staff, in charge of roof spotting at Chequers and Chartwell. In early January 1942 he went on a three month's refresher course at Hullavington, after which he was posted to 52 OTU Aston Down to command a squadron. In October 1942 Coward went as CFI to 55 OTU where, incidentally, he taught the young man who had found him. On 21 November 1943 he took command of I ADU at Croydon. Coward was sent on a course at RAF Staff College on 17 June 1944, following which he was posted to the Air Ministry, in charge of Fighter Operational Training. After the war he held a series of staff appointments and commands and was awarded the AFC in 1954. He retired from the RAF on 8 September 1969, as an Air Commodore.[48] Air Commodore James Baird Coward AFC died on 25 July 2012.

'At lunchtime on Sunday 15th September, my squadron was somewhere south of the Thames estuary behind several other squadrons of Hurricanes and Spitfires. The German bombers were three or four miles away when we first spotted them. We were at 17,000 feet and they were at about 19,000 feet. Their fighter escort was scattered around. The bombers were coming in towards London from the south-east and at first we could not tell how many there were. We opened our throttles and started to climb up towards them, aiming for a point well ahead, where we expected to contact them at their own height.

'As we converged on them I saw there were about twenty of them and it looked as though it were going to be a nice party, for the other squadrons of Hurricanes and Spitfires also turned to join in. By the time we reached a position near the bombers we were over London - central London I should say.

We had gained a little height on them, too, so when I gave the order to attack we were able to dive on them from their right.

'Each of us selected his own target. Our first attack broke them up pretty nicely. The Dornier I attacked with a burst lasting several seconds began to turn to the left away from his friends. I gave him five seconds and he went away with white smoke streaming behind him.

'As I broke away and started to make a steep climbing turn I looked over the side. I recognised the river immediately below me through a hole in the clouds. I saw the bends in the river and the bridges and idly wondered where I was. I didn't recognise it immediately and then I saw Kennington Oval. I saw the covered stands round the Oval and I thought to myself: 'That is where they play cricket.' It's queer how, in the middle of a battle, one can see something on the ground and think of something entirely different from the immediate job in hand. I remember I had a flashing thought - a sort of mental picture - of a big man with a beard, but at that moment I did not think of the name of W. G. Grace. It was just a swift, passing thought as I climbed back to the fight.

'I found myself very soon below another Dornier which had white smoke coming from it. It was being attacked by two Hurricanes and a Spitfire and it was still travelling north and turning slightly to the right. As I could not see anything else to attack at that moment, I went to join in. I climbed up above him and did a diving attack on him.

Coming in to attack I noticed what appeared to be a red light shining in the rear gunner's cockpit, but when I got closer I realised I was looking right through the gunner's cockpit into the pilot and observer's cockpit beyond. The red light was fire.

'I gave it a quick burst and as I passed him on the right I looked in through the big glass nose of the Dornier. It was like a furnace inside. He began to go down and we watched. In a few seconds the tail came off and the bomber did a forward somersault and then went into a spin. After he had done two turns in his spin his wings broke off outboard of the engines, so that all that was left as the blazing aircraft fell was half a fuselage and the wing roots with the engines on the end of them. This dived straight down, just past the edge of a cloud and then the cloud got in the way and I could see no more of him.

'The battle was over by then. I couldn't see anything else to shoot at, so I flew home. Our squadron's score was five certainties - including one by a sergeant pilot, who landed by parachute in a Chelsea garden.

'An hour later we were in the air again, meeting more bombers and fighters coming in. We got three more - our squadron, I mean. I started to chase one Dornier which was flying through the tops of the clouds. Did you ever see that film *Hell's Angels*? You remember how the Zeppelin came so slowly out of the cloud. Well, this Dornier reminded me of that.

'I attacked him four times altogether. When he first appeared through the cloud - you know how clouds go up and down like foam on water - I fired at him from the left, swung over to the right, turned in towards another hollow in the cloud, where I expected him to reappear and fired at him again. After my fourth attack he dived down headlong into a clump of trees in front of a house and I saw one or two cars parked in the gravel drive in front. I wondered whether there was anyone in the doorway watching the bomber crash.

'Then I climbed up again to look for some more trouble and found it in the shape of a Heinkel 111 which was being attacked by three Hurricanes and a couple of Spitfires. I had a few cracks at the thing before it made a perfect landing on an RAF aerodrome. The Heinkel's undercarriage collapsed and the pilot pulled up, after skidding fifty yards in a cloud of dust. I saw a tall man get out of the right-hand side of the aircraft and when I turned back he was helping a small man across the aerodrome towards a hangar.'

Squadron Leader John Sample DFC on 504 Squadron, was born in 1913. Before the war Sample, of Morpeth had been an estate agent in Northumberland. It was Sergeant Raymond Towers Holmes who bailed out and landed in a Chelsea garden, in Hugh Street; his Hurricane crashing and burning out outside Fountain Court, Buckingham Palace. 'Ray' Holmes was feted by the press as a war hero who saved Buckingham Palace from being severely damaged by German bombing. Born in Liverpool on 20 August 1914, Holmes worked initially as a journalist before joining the RAFVR in 1937. In June 1940 he joined 504 Squadron. On 15 September Holmes spotted a damaged Dornier Do 17 of KG76 apparently making a bombing attempt on central London. Avoiding the bomber's return fire, Holmes made a head-on attack on the Dornier, however upon firing discovered his machine guns failed. Holmes decided to ram the bomber hoping his plane could withstand the impact and cut through it. He cut the tail off the bomber with his wing, causing the bomber to crash near Victoria tube station. When recovered, Holmes joined 81 Squadron and was sent to the Northern Front near Murmansk in Russia to help train the Soviet air force in flying the Hurricane. Here he claimed a further kill; a Bf 109F. He was commissioned as a Pilot Officer on 10 June 1941, promoted to Flying Officer on 10 June 1942 and Flight Lieutenant on 10 June 1943. Returning from Russia, Holmes served as an instructor with 2 FIS, Montrose from 1942 until 1944. He then flew PR Spitfires on 541 Squadron from February 1945. After the war he was a King's Messenger, personally delivering mail to Winston Churchill, and later a journalist. 65 years later, the wreckage of Holmes' Hurricane was discovered and successfully excavated from the streets of London. Ray Holmes died on 27 June 2005; aged 90.

In March 1941 Sample was posted to 10 Group HQ as a controller. In September 1941 he was given the job of forming 137 Squadron on Whirlwinds at Charmy Down. On 24 October 137 Squadron flew its first operation, a 'Mandolin'. The target, several trains carrying fuel containers in railway sidings at Landernau, near Brest were not found, but Squadron Leader Sample attacked several wagons and Flying Officer Clark destroyed a locomotive. On 28 October Sample and Sergeant M. J. Peskett took off from base at 1745 for a formation practice south of Bath, with practice attacks to be carried out by Sergeant J. F. Luing who took off ten minutes later. All three aircraft carried out turns at about 1,000 feet for some minutes and Luing broke away on Sample's orders to carry out the first attack. On approaching for the second attack, Luing saw Sample's aircraft going down out of control, with part of the tailplane coming off. The machine was in a

spin and when close to the ground, Luing observed Sample leave his machine and his parachute open, but his canopy did not open and Sample landed on the roof of some farm buildings at Manor Farm near Englishcombe. The aircraft landed on the same buildings and burst into flames. Sample was killed. Peskett reported that his aircraft was 'bumped' but remained under control and he returned immediately to base and landed. His aircraft was found to be damaged but repairable on the unit. He did not see anything of the Sample's crash. Later examination of Peskett's aircraft suggested that the starboard propeller had hit the tail of Sample's aircraft. Both sets of undercarriage doors and the central bulge of the Fowler flap also showed signs of contact.

'In July 1940 the Battle of Britain began. As Hitler stepped up his campaign to annihilate the RAF Fighter Command as a necessary prelude to his planned invasion of Britain, we witnessed more and more aerial activity. Within viewing distance of the action in the skies over Biggin Hill we watched encounters between German and British planes. We followed many a dogfight between Messerschmitts and Spitfires, sometimes directly overhead, cheering whenever an enemy plane was chased off or shot down. Dad was stationed at Kenley airfield, not too far away. He worked as an aircraft mechanic. During the Battle of Britain the ground crews were frantically busy, refuelling and repairing planes between sorties. As the conflict intensified, ground crews and pilots alike were perpetually exhausted. When a Spitfire came to a stop one day at the airfield, no one climbed out. 'Something's wrong!' shouted Dad to the other ground staff. They ran over and Dad climbed up onto the wing. The pilot was fast asleep. Sometimes the pilots were so worn out; they fell asleep as they ate.

'...As the battle in the skies escalated we learned to identify the different aircraft. 'See the glazed nose of the Heinkel, there? That's one of theirs.' We became adept at recognizing the different planes before we saw their identification marks. The Spitfires were our favourites; they moved with such speed and panache. We watched in awe one day in August when nine Dornier 17s swept in to bomb the airfield at Biggin Hill. They were intercepted by two Hurricane squadrons and a great fight ensued. Two of the Dorniers were downed and the rest were driven off. Throughout that month the Luftwaffe launched a thousand planes a day across the channel. On August 15, they mounted their maximum effort with eighteen hundred sorties. The skies seemed always to be filled with planes and the noise was tremendous. It was a different world from the peaceful skies of Sussex we had known.

'In September Clare and I started back to school at Hawes Down junior. If the air raid siren sounded while school was in session, we picked up our books and marched down the steps into the underground shelter to continue our work. The light was dim and when winter came it was bitterly cold with water running down the bare brick walls. A dank smell permeated everything. Air raids were frequent. One day we went to the shelter three times...If there was an air raid at night and the all clear sounded before midnight then school was open as usual next day. If the raid occurred after midnight, school was closed.

Mother always sent us to school. Several times Clare and I walked the mile to school, only to find it closed. Once the school was closed for two days because of an unexploded bomb in The Mead, a nearby street. It was all very stressful and confusing. As the assaults on London escalated, we ceased going to school very much at all.

'On September 7 hundreds of bombers targeted the London docks, setting them ablaze, lighting the way for more destruction throughout the night. We lay listening to wave after wave of bombers passing overhead. The racket of the anti-aircraft barrage was tremendous, but we found it comforting. The noise gave us the impression that something, at least, was being done to deter the bombers. Because of the din we couldn't hear the noise of the bombs whistling down, but neither could we sleep. The morning after a raid, Clare and I would rush outside to pick up pieces of shrapnel. We vied with each other to see who had the more interesting shapes.

'West Wickham didn't escape damage. A bomb fell in the High Street, completely demolishing one shop and damaging several others. Houses on residential streets were bombed. There was great excitement when a Messerschmitt was shot down and the pilot captured. On the afternoon of September 15, when every plane that the RAF could muster was flown to fight off the Luftwaffe attacks on London, the Battle of Britain was on its way to being won. Two days later, Hitler postponed the invasion of Britain. It never did take place...'

Annette June Coppard, East London schoolgirl.

Peter Wood was living in Tulse Hill in south London and working in the City for a shipping company. On 7 September he was playing football near Crystal Palace when he heard some unseasonal thunder. He looked up to see the sky full of German bombers - but the game went on.

'Literally dozens of Germans, accompanied by smaller aircraft which I took to be fighters, were going over at about 500 feet. There didn't seem to be any gunfire from our defending forces at all. Fortunately for us, they overflew us, because they were obviously heading for the docks, for what was, as we know now, the first bombing of the docklands at that time. We shrugged our shoulders and carried on to finish our game of football. After that the bombing of London increased in volume and the routine was to sleep in a reinforced cellar where my wife's family lived in Tulse Hill and when the all-clear went in the morning, you just got up, washed and dressed and went to work.

'After just over a month of this, I remember the all-clear going, and it was still dark. We came up out of the cellar and went out into the street and I literally walked up a hill. A 500lb bomb had peeled the road up about 50 yards from the house where I lived. This was, I suppose, the nearest thing to bombing that we got - except that about a month later I was walking my wife to her place of work, and we saw a hole in the gutter. We both peered down it, wondering what it was and then when we came back in the evening, that road was all blown up. It was an unexploded bomb, which had gone off during the day, and a bus had actually gone into the hole - that was how big the crater was.

'Like all of us still living and working in London, we were members of the ARP and did our stint of fire-watching and generally helping the fire brigade and police as best we could. When we were in the shelters we played pontoon or poker most of the night and drank tea or cocoa. We didn't sleep very much because the anti-aircraft guns were going constantly. We could feel the shocks in the ground from the bombs hitting the area. The extraordinary thing was, when the 500-pounder came so close to us, we didn't actually feel much from it. We must have been so close to the epicentre of the explosion that we didn't actually feel it. That was why it was a shock when I came upstairs [in the morning] and went into the street.

'Working in the City, sometimes you had a normal run through on the bus or tram - we had trams in those days - sometimes you would be diverted and you wouldn't get to the office for four or five hours. Or even, on some days, the damage was so bad that you just gave up and went back home because you couldn't get to the office.

'Our area was not as badly affected at this time as later on, in '44 when the V1 and V2 attacks were going on. That was much more devastating than even the [Blitz] bombing although that was very bad. The incendiary bombs were serious because they would start the fires going, then they would drop high explosives into the fires to stop you from putting the fires out.

'Life went on as normally as possible. People got to the stage where as soon as they had had tea or supper, they would take their bedding and go to the Anderson shelter - it became a way of life. The extraordinary thing was that people were not badly demoralised - the more they suffered, the more determined they seemed to be that they would beat this thing.'

'The first air-raid warning was the worst. Before this war began the experts were predicting that when the Nazis made mass air attacks on London the casualties would be from 30,000 to 35,000 a day. We believed them. So, when the Banshees began their howling on that sunny Sunday morning of September 1939, my knees shook. So did a lot of other people's.

'A year ago the bombing raid had been a vague terror. Now it had been experienced and measured and, as H. G. Wells wrote: 'Our remarkable people seem to enjoy being at last, all of them, under fire. They feel that they are doing their bit and no longer being 'protected' by the men in uniform.'

'Even more, since Wells wrote that, we have seen letters from soldiers in camps in the West Country and Scotland, actually pleading to be allowed to come back to London. They did not want to feel safe, they insisted, when they knew their wives and children were in danger.

'But since Wells wrote that, on September 15th, 1940, there has been a change in the temper of London's people. It does not mean any diminution of courage. On the contrary, from what Tom and I saw and heard in the various shelters, down Thames River and among the debris of bombings, we believe that the courage with which the Londoner carries on - carries on, mind you - is much more to be admired than the original instinctive gutfulness with which nearly everybody in this amazing city reacted to the first downpour of disaster.

'I have never known the river in such a lovely mood. The Thames, these days, seems ready, even anxious, to take on anybody. You see this in the dramatic way so many of the wheel-houses of passing ships have been turned into armoured pill-boxes. Grey, armoured plating, with narrow apertures to enable the helmsman to look out. All the river ambulances and many of the tugs are transformed like this. Fire-tugs have Lewis guns sticking upwards from their sterns. Ocean liners have three-inch and high-angle guns tilted skywards from steel round-houses on their poops.

'*The Spero*, with a bad list to port, comes limping up-river from Newcastle with a cargo of coal; she has a gun which her crew are just covering up. A sailor on the bridge of the Cedric, from Hull, amuses himself practice-aiming a machine-gun as she waits to go out on the turn of the tide. A tramp comes up-river with her bridge sand-bagged. The Lodestone, rusty with salt rime, is berthed by two puffing tugs - also gunned. A big black ship, with a Dutch name, lies close to a brick wharf with half a dozen cranes bending and dipping for her cargo; part of her dun superstructure has been carried away - 'It was a time-bomb,' said the barge-tender. 'Took seven tugs to bring her in; but they're making repairs on her now as she unloads.' Here and there a small boat is anchored off the wharves, bearing a green flag with the white letters WRECK.

'It's over a barge, or something, sunk,' says the tram conductor – 'to mark an obstruction, you see.'

'And the parent ship of these' WRECK' small craft has the remains of a Spitfire or a Hurricane (which it has apparently fished out of the river) dangling from her forward boom. A nasty sight.

'Hope he bailed out!' says the barge-tender.

'See that, mate? ...well, a bomb blew two of them up on the top of that warehouse over there.' And, encouraged by my open mouth, he sang out to a man standing on the pier to which we were tying up: 'Hi, mate, how'd you find last night?'

'Oh, we all just die here!' rang out the cheery reply. 'Cannons to the right of us, cannons to the left - Gor blimey!'

'That's the way it is,' said a local man, as I waited beside him in a bus queue; 'some of the women this morning looked a bit knocked about - sort of white - but they've got a reason for it. You see, we're on the main route to London from Dover and the coast. If our Spitfires get them coming, then they drop their bombs here. If they get chased out of London, then they drop 'em on the way back. People around here's got a right to look flustered. First drink I ever had in me life was in the pub that used to stand there. Got it... three weeks ago.'

'The smoke from the dying dock-fires made a false sunset. The silver balloons became pink and a glowing ball hung at an angle of thirty degrees at 4.30 pm. The white turrets on the towers of Tower Bridge were ghost-like in the haze. St. Paul's dome rose undaunted above the murk. It was high tide now, with the red tramcars running along almost level with us on the Embankment. The yards of Captain Scott's *Discovery* rose over the plane trees along the drive.

'It had been a fine day - for September.'

***Bomber's Moon* (1941) by James Negley Farson.**

'At approximately 1440 hours AA fire was sighted to the south and at the same time a formation of about thirty Do 215s was seen. I climbed up astern of the enemy aircraft to engage the fighter escort, which could be seen above the bombers at about 30,000'. Three Me 109s dived on our formation and I turned to starboard. A loose dogfight ensued with more Me 109s coming down. I could not get near to any enemy aircraft so I climbed up and engaged a formation of Me 110s without result. I then sighted ten Me 109s just above me and attacked one of them. I got on his tail and fired several bursts of about two seconds. The enemy aircraft was taking violent evasive action and made for cloud level. I managed to get in another burst of about five seconds before it flicked over inverted and entered cloud in a shallow dive, apparently out of control. I then flew south and attacked two further formations of about 30 Do 215s from astern and head on. The enemy aircraft did not appear to like the head on attack as they jumped about a bit as I passed through. I observed no result from these attacks. Fire from the rear of the enemy aircraft was opened at 1,000 yards. Me 110s opened fire at similar range but appeared to have no idea of deflection shooting.'

Squadron Leader Brian J. 'Sandy' Lane DFC, CO, 19 Squadron Spitfires, Duxford, 15 September 1940. Flight Sergeant George 'Grumpy' Unwin, Lane's Red 3; reported sighting 'thousands of 109s'. At close range 'Grumpy' fired a 3-second burst at a 109 which half-rolled and dived steeply into the clouds. Although the Spitfire pilot pursued his prey, he lost the 109 at 6,000 feet when his windscreen froze up. Climbing back up to 25,000', a Rotte of 109s (the basic fighting unit, consisting of a leader and a wingman) appeared above him, flying south. Unwin gave chase and caught both over Lydd. The first consequently burst into flames and went down vertically and the second crashed into the sea. It is likely that these two 109s were from I/JG77: Oberleutnant Kunze, of the Geschwaderstabschwarm, was killed when his aircraft crashed at Lympne, as was Unteroffizier Meixner who crashed into the sea off Dungeness. This brought Unwin's total of 109s destroyed this day to three.

Brian John Edward 'Sandy' Lane was born on 18 June 1917 in Harrogate, North Yorkshire, joining the RAF on a short service commission in 1936 when he lost his job as a supervisor in an electric bulb factory. On completion of training he was posted to 66 Squadron in January 1937 but in June moved to 213 Squadron. Shortly after the outbreak of war he was posted to 19 Squadron as a flight commander, becoming temporary commanding officer when the existing CO was killed over Dunkirk on 25 May 1940. His actions over Dunkirk brought the award of a DFC at the end of July and on 5 September he became commanding officer formally when the next CO was lost. He left the unit early in June 1941 on posting to the Staff of HQ, 12 Group, when he wrote a classic book *Spitfire* under the pseudonym B. J. Ellan (John Murray, 1942). In November 1941 he was posted to the Middle East, serving at Air HQ, Western Desert and then with HQ, Middle East, from February 1942. In June he returned to the UK and took command of fir OTU until early December 1942, when he was given command of 167 Squadron. Four days after his arrival he led three other

Spitfires off on a 'Rhubarb' operation over the Dutch coast. FW 190s were engaged and he disappeared, being reported missing; he had been shot down west of Schouwen Island by Oberleutnant Walter Leonhardt of 6/JG1.

'The gratitude of every home in our island, in our Empire and indeed throughout the world, except in the abodes of the guilty, goes out to the British airmen, who, undaunted by odds, unweary in their constant challenge and mortal danger, are turning the tide of the world war by their prowess and their devotion. Never in the field of human conflict was so much owed by so many to so few.'

Winston Churchill, 20 August 1940.

'I am very proud of having fought in the Battle of Britain. It is thought of as being a considerable achievement. You shouldn't say it but I thoroughly enjoyed it. I think that most of the other chaps enjoyed it. After all, a lot of us were Volunteer Reserve. We joined to fly and here we were flying one of the best aircraft as many times a day, more or less as you could wish for. It was good fun.

'Air to air combat was a complete shambles. Suddenly you would get a 'scramble' and we would be off. Sometimes you would find the enemy; other times it was a wasted trip. It was really a bit chaotic. There were times we know when Hurricanes and Spitfires shot down Hurricanes and Spitfires; it was almost inevitable.'

Sergeant (later Wing Commander) Paul Caswell Powe Farnes, 501 Squadron Hurricane pilot, 7 and two shared victories. On 30 September Farnes met Oberleutnant Friedrich Oeser the pilot of a Ju 88A-1 of 2/KG77 who crashed at Gatwick moments after he shot him down. Unteroffizier Klasing the gunner was killed. 'I don't suppose many people had the luxury of landing to meet the pilot' recalls Farnes. 'Whether we like it or not and the Navy do not, but if you talk sensibly about it people accept it as an iconic occurrence.

Paul Farnes was born in Boscombe, Hampshire on 16 July 1918. He joined the RAFVR in April 1938 and was called up in July 1939, being posted to 501 Squadron on 14 September 1939 from the 11 Group Fighter Pool at St. Athan. He then accompanied the squadron to France in May 1940, seeing action here and then in the Battle of Britain. He was awarded a DFM in October and was commissioned the following month. Farnes total score was 8 victories (7 and 2 shared destroyed, 2 'probables' and 11 damaged).

Pilot Officer (later Squadron Leader) Basil Gerald 'Stapme' Stapleton was born in Durban, South Africa on 12 May 1920 and his nickname came from a phrase used in his favourite cartoon 'Just Jake'. He travelled to England to take up a short service commission in the RAF in January 1939, being posted to 603 Squadron in Scotland in October of that year. He was to see action with this unit first off the coast of Scotland and then over southeast England during summer and autumn 1940. On 3 July he and two other members of 'Green' Section shared in the destruction of a Ju 88A-2 of 8/KG 30 Adler-Geschwader over the sea near Montrose. On 20 July Stapleton, his closest friend, Flying Officer Robin Waterston and Flight Lieutenant J. L. G. 'Laurie' Cunningham shared in the destruction of a Dornier Do 17P reconnaissance aircraft of 1 Staffel, AufklärungsGrüppe / 120 off Peterhead. Leutnant Heuer and two of his crew were reported missing. 603 Squadron's Spitfire Is arrived at Hornchurch from Scotland on 27 August and they were in the action the very next day, losing three pilots killed. Pilot Officer Donald K. MacDonald and Laurie Cunningham died when they were bounced by 109s whilst still trying to gain a height advantage. MacDonald was on his first patrol and had just fifteen hours on Spitfires while Laurie Cunningham was experienced with over 160 hours. On their last patrol of the day the squadron was bounced again and Pilot Officer Noel J. V. 'Broody' Benson, who had over 160 hours on type, was shot down after being bounced unseen. In an attempt to avoid this happening again, the CO, Squadron Leader 'Uncle' George Lovell Denholm, climbed the squadron on a reciprocal heading to that given by the controllers after take-off. Only when he believed that they had gained sufficient altitude did they turn towards the enemy.

On 29 August Stapleton was credited with two Bf 109E 'probables' at Deal and Manston and two days later he was awarded a third Bf 109E 'probable' north of Southend. On 31 August the death in combat of Robin Waterston, who was described as the Squadron's 'brightest character' was a great blow. While 603 were airborne RAF Hornchurch was attacked by fighter-bombers and three Staffeln of Ju 88s and Bf 110s, which dropped about thirty bombs on the station and at Biggin Hill. Four ground crew at Hornchurch were killed and two Spitfires were destroyed. Stapleton says. 'With no time to grieve we just got on with our job. We had to - we were fighting for our lives, our freedom and our country. Despite the casualties, I recall that we also had great fun. It was an exciting time and we lived life to the full. Each day was treated as if it were our last.'

On 3 September 'Stapme' Stapleton was credited with his first outright victory when he shot down a Dornier Do 17 15 miles southwest of Harwich. Stapleton's second victory followed on 5 September when the Squadron lost 'a good friend and an excellent Flight Commander'. Flight Lieutenant Fred 'Rusty' Rushmer had refused 'Uncle' George Denholm's orders to rest and exhaustion was probably a contributing factor when he was shot down and killed in combat with 109s. Stapleton recalls.

'We had taken off from our forward base at Rochford when, at about 29,000 feet, we spotted a number of Dorniers below us escorted by 109s. I dived to attack the bombers but was engaged by a pair of Messerschmitts. I certainly hit one as I saw glycol streaming from the radiator but in my attempt to finish him off I was fired on by another German so I broke off my attack and continued my dive. In the heat of the battle I didn't see anything of Rusty but Bill 'Tannoy' Read later said he saw Rusty's Spitfire dive straight down vertically from altitude, through the bomber formation. He had obviously been hit. Rusty's grave in the churchyard at All Saints, Staplehurst, Kent was only officially confirmed as being his in 1998 (marked 'Unknown' until then). That day I was reunited with a number of my former ground crew at the rededication ceremony. Rusty made the national news 58 years after his death.

'A short while later I managed to shoot down a Messerschmitt 109 which, unlike my first attack, was possible to confirm. During my dive from altitude I spotted a Spitfire at about 6,000 feet diving vertically towards the ground, its tail shot away. I then spotted a lone 109 in the same airspace as a RAF pilot descending by parachute. I latched onto the German and pursued him at low-level over the Kent countryside. As I fired short bursts he attempted to shake me off but I could see my tracer striking his aircraft and I closed in. I remember at one stage being concerned that there was a village in my line of fire. He had nowhere to go but down and eventually force-landed in a field. I flew low over the site. The German was soon apprehended, initially by the unarmed cook from the local searchlight battery! A short time after the war I learned that the pilot was Oberleutnant Franz von Werra, his exploits made famous in the book and film The One That Got Away, as the only German pilot to escape captivity (from Canada) during WWII and return to Germany. By all accounts he was an arrogant little man who was willing to lie to enhance his reputation. Well, he didn't get away from me!' Stapleton was also awarded a Bf 109E 'probable' in addition to the confirmed Bf 109 victory.

On 7 September Stapleton's Spitfire was hit in combat with 109s as he recalls. 'Having escaped the mêlée I managed to nurse my damaged aircraft back over the Channel, applying throttle intermittently so as not to overheat the engine, gradually losing height in the process. I eventually managed to force-land in a ploughed field adjacent to a hop garden. On climbing out of my aircraft I slid the canopy shut and turned to look for the nearest road. I spotted a couple having a picnic in the gateway to the field, their Austin Ruby saloon parked close-by. As I approached a sergeant-pilot who had landed by parachute joined me in a nearby orchard. The couple offered us a cup of tea and then a lift, not back to my aerodrome but to the nearest pub. What a contrast to fighting for our lives just a short time before!'

On 11 September Stapleton was credited with a Bf 110 'probable' and a Bf 109E 'damaged'. Four days later he scored his third victory when he destroyed a Do 17 and he was also awarded a Bf 109E 'damaged'. A Bf 109E 'probable' followed on 17 September and on the 30th; he scored his fourth victory when he destroyed a Bf 109E. During October he again claimed a Bf 109E and he was credited with two Bf 109E 'probables'. The South African's sixth and final victory came on 11 November when he shot down a Bf 109E 20 miles northeast of Ramsgate. The award of a DFC was announced on 15 November.

'Stapme' Stapleton left 603 Squadron in April 1941 and served in various units, including flying 'Hurricats' with the MSFU, as a Flight Commander with 257 Squadron in February 1942 and as an instructor at Central Gunnery School. In August 1944 he took command of 247 (China-British) Squadron, flying Hawker Typhoons, receiving the Dutch Flying Cross for his part in the Arnhem operations. On 23 December 1944 as a part of a force of sixteen Typhoons on 247 and 137 Squadrons at Eindhoven, he attacked a train, using rockets. One of his projectiles must have entered the firebox, as there was a terrific explosion and his radiator was punctured as he flew through the debris. Stapleton tried to nurse his Typhoon back at low level but he ran out

of height and he force-landed two miles inside German lines near Mönchengladbach. He spent the rest of the war in Stalag Luft I at Barth on the Baltic coast. Leaving the RAF in 1946, he flew for BOAC until late 1948, when he returned to South Africa. In 1994 he returned to the UK with his wife, Audrey to live at Ketton. He died on 13 April 2010.

'After coming down from Cambridge, I decided to join the RAF. I took a Short Service Commission in 1932. Eventually I did my flying training at No.3 FTS. The course was normally one year. At the end of that time I was lucky enough to be presented with a Challenge Cup for being judged likely to be the best fighter pilot of the course. After passing out from Grantham I was sent to the Operational Training Unit at Digby where we did formation flying and, generally speaking, more advanced flying training. My first operational Unit was 25 Fighter Squadron which was based at Hawkinge in Kent. Having learnt that the Squadron had been given the task of taking part in the 1934 Hendon Air Display, there was competition among pilots to be chosen for the Squadron Tied-Together Aerobatics with nine aircraft. I was lucky enough to be selected as one of them. The Hawker Fury was, at that time, the first-line fighter of the day with a top speed of about 150 mph. We did our display fairly well I think by looping the loop in formation and rolling the aircraft. Each aircraft was tied with the one next to it by a thin elastic cord with bunting on it so that it could be seen from the ground. If one aircraft went too far from the next the elastic broke fairly easily.

'It was just after the New Year that I was posted to act as Personal Assistant, or more normally called ADC, to Sir Arthur Longmore, the Chief of Coastal Command and after one year went back as a Flight Commander at 25 Squadron. Promotion was fairly fast in those days as it was the time when expansion of the RAF began in earnest. My wife agreed to marry me, much to my joy and the marriage took place at Watford, which was her home, on 22 February 1936. I had been posted to 600 Auxiliary Squadron at Hendon as Assistant Adjutant. The pilots were all civilians and flew at weekends. 600 Squadron was named the City of London Squadron and most of the pilots had jobs in Lloyds Insurance. My wife and I had a flat near Hendon and after about a year I went to a Flying Training School at Netheravon on Salisbury Plain as an instructor, where I remained to the end of my Short Service Commission on 25 April 1938 and was then placed on the Reserve. These were six very enjoyable years which I look back on as being the best of the RAF.

'I cannot admit that I enjoyed, at this time, my first experiences in a civilian life, being fairly sure that in the end there was bound to be a war. Sure enough it began in September 1939 and I was recalled to the RAF towards the end of August of that year. I was sent first of all to the Flying Training School in Cheshire as an instructor and then went on to the Headquarters of the Group at a place called South Cerney. It did not take me long to put in an application to be posted to a Fighter Unit, where I felt I had good experience. First of all I was told in a reply that I was too old as at that time the senior RAF Officers, such as Lord Dowding who was in charge of the whole of Fighter Command, had stated that Squadron Leaders should not be more than 26. However, minds were changed and I was posted to do a refresher course on Hurricanes and Spitfires in May 1940. After the course I was posted, first of all, to 213 Squadron and informed that I would be taking over a Squadron shortly. By this time expansion of the RAF was going ahead, not only with aircraft but also with personnel. 213 Squadron was stationed at the civilian airfield at Exeter, which was no more than a grass field and had no accommodation. The Squadron Commander, Hector McGregor, with whom we became very friendly, rose to a high rank later on in the war and was knighted.[49]

'I was posted to form and command the first Czech Fighter Squadron in June 1940 at Duxford. Dunkirk was over and so was the French fighting spirit. A number of Czech pilots had reached France to help the French Air Force and after considerable problems on their part, had flown French fighters well although most had been sent elsewhere and some had found themselves in the French Foreign Legion.

'When France gave in, most Czechs who wanted to continue the fight against the aggressor did all they could to come to this Country as the only free country, so Czech pilots came too. 310 Czech Squadron was formed at the end of June 1940 and one of the immediate problems for aircrew was RAF uniforms and getting kitted up with parachutes etc. Most of the officers were still wearing Czech or French uniforms and it was all a bit chaotic for a while. Another problem at the time was the lack of a common language, although we were able to converse, to a certain extent, in a rather muddled French, which most of them spoke pretty well. The morale of the Czech Pilots was excellent but it was not easy to make them understand that things had to be done in a British way and not necessarily in their way. We had, beside myself, two experienced British Flight Commanders and one Junior Pilot, who was a qualified flying instructor, to help the Czechs to learn about flying the Hurricane aircraft. Unfortunately he was killed in September, as was one of the British Flight Commanders although not with us.

'We classified ourselves operational on about 20 August and intercepted our first enemy aircraft on 26 of that month over Essex. This was a Squadron of Dorniers who had been bombing a nearby airfield escorted by Messerschmitt 110s. We attacked the Dorniers and destroyed, I think, three of them with a loss of three of ours but our pilots escaped by parachute, including myself having been set on fire with an incendiary bullet in the main petrol tank from a tail gunner in one of the Dorniers which I was attacking. One problem was a severe shortage of VHF radios. I had one but the other pilots had older sets and therefore they could not hear what I or the Ground Controller said.

'We carried on rising in experience for the rest of August and into September. I remember one occasion in particular when leading some aircraft in the early morning just after a heavy night raid. Most of the centre of London was covered in smoke from fires from the oil tanks in the Thames Estuary but I could see quite clearly [from 25,000 feet over North Weald] St. Paul's Cathedral. Close to it I was able to distinguish the remains of my father's office in Paternoster Road and hoped that he was able to salvage some of his things.

'Later we began operating as a Wing of aircraft, i.e. three Hurricane Squadrons and a Spitfire Squadron above us. This Wing, called the Bader

Wing, was led by the bravest man I am ever likely to know. I knew him well and we used to play squash together in the evenings at Duxford. On one occasion he announced while playing a ball, 'Sorry Douglas, I must stop as I have broken my leg.' He went off to his room and got another and we then went on playing. He had a remarkable spirit in whatever he was doing, whether fighting the enemy or playing games. It rightly won him many decorations. Unfortunately, he was shot down over France in 1942 leading a Wing of Spitfires 'looking for trouble', as he would express himself. He always said that if he was shot down, he would never be able to make use of his parachute because he would not be able to get his tin legs out of the cockpit. He left one leg behind but managed to escape and was naturally taken prisoner and very carefully guarded by the Germans. He was eventually sent to Colditz. He came back to this country in 1945 and led the formation of aircraft saluting the King and the Nation in the victory parade.

'Raids went on with more and more aircraft in the formations. I remember very well the continuing good weather that summer and feeling the longing for the weather to change to the more normal cloud and rain. It would have given us all a bit of a rest from the continuous 'Standing By' from dawn until dusk. It was a long day most of it sitting in ones aircraft or close to a telephone waiting for a call to take off. It seems silly now but it was very exhausting flying most of the time with oxygen on, high up and searching the skies for the possibility of being pounced upon by an enemy aircraft.

'The pilots stationed in the south at airfields like Biggin Hill and Tangmere were even more relieved than we were when, early in September, the Germans changed their tactics by more or less giving up the daylight raids on Fighter Stations and Radar Installations etc. and decided to attack London and other big cities, mostly by night. It was a memorable sight to see these huge raids flying over London. Bader used to lead us in to break up these formations and then we used to pick our own aircraft and do our best to destroy them. We fired at many but it was never as easy as it might sound to be sure of hitting them unless they should be seen to burst into flames or otherwise go out of control. I remember seeing one Me 110 going away with smoke pouring out of one of its engines but try as I did, I could not catch it up to get close enough to see it going down but lost it going across the Channel to France. The 110 was a good deal faster than the 109 and the Hurricane.

'To revert to October, there was still a great shortage of pilots and they had to be borrowed from other Commands such as The Fleet Air Arm, who supplied quite a few who came to Duxford, although we had enough Czechs to manage necessary replacements.

'In various books a lot has been written about the gallantry of those pilots who were expert at shooting down aircraft but to the more ordinary person, such as myself, we were relieved when the attack changed to night instead of day, although very sorry for the inhabitants of the big cities.

'So far as 310 Squadron were concerned, the highlight of October was when the President of Czechoslovakia in exile came to visit the Squadron. President Benes awarded some of us, including myself, with the Czech War Cross, which is the equivalent of the DFC. It called for a celebration party that evening.

'After saying goodbye to my Squadron at the beginning of January 1941 I was posted to Group Headquarters for six months and after that was sent to 84 Group in Northern Ireland where we were housed in Stormont Castle in the most king-like offices. It was early in 1941 that America came into the war and I was given the job of liaising with a Senior American Officer who commanded American pilots who were to take over Spitfires for the joint invasion of North Africa. As a Group they were a grand lot of chaps, but they had not flown monoplanes to say nothing of any aircraft equivalent to a Spitfire. Their CO, Colonel Bill Allison, was excellent and asked me to go to London with him to show him the way. We flew over in a couple of Spits and he was very impressed by his first visit to our capital city. On return he was absolutely furious to find a number of his aircraft scattered round the airfield in various damaged conditions. After calling all the pilots to a meeting, he proceeded to tell them exactly what he thought of them and threatened to send home the next pilot to do any damage. The talk did the trick and although the Group had terrible causalities when they got to North Africa, the Invasion was successful.

'So far as I was concerned I went back to Stormont Castle for my duties there until I was posted to command a small airfield called Culmhead in the Exeter Sector. My wife and daughter lived in a small cottage in Blagdon where our son Michael was born.[50] It was at Culmhead that 134 Wing was formed for the eventual invasion of Normandy. There were by then three Czech Fighter Squadrons and we went into the Tangmere Sector in a grassy area called Appledram where at the time no wives or non-service people were allowed. The Squadrons went on flying over to France to escort bombers and do the occasional beating up of German or French transport. I flew over to France once or twice myself and once the Invasion had taken place, it was very interesting to see the actual bombing that was taking place over areas that one used to know in peacetime.

'My part in the war ended rather abruptly by the decision to abandon 134 Wing because it was felt that there were not enough Czech replacements available to replace casualties and so ended my long association with the Czechs. I was presented in London by Jan Masarik, who was at that time Foreign Secretary of the Czech Nation in exile, with the Czech Order of Merit First Class. He thanked me personally for what I had done for his country and I was eventually presented with the Award of King George of Podebrad, which is a high award in the present Czech Republic, signed by the President J. Havil.'

George Douglas Morant Blackwood, born 11 October 1909 a great-great-grandson of William Blackwood who founded William Blackwood & Sons the publishers and Blackwood's Magazine. He was educated at St Cyprian's School, Eastbourne and Eton. On completing his education, he had little choice but to follow his father into the family firm. He held a short service commission in the RAF from 1932 to 1938 and had it not been for the outbreak of war, he would have returned to Edinburgh to work for his father and uncle. On 18 July 1940 Squadron Leader Blackwood arrived from 213 Squadron to take command of the three dozen Czech pilots on 310 Squadron

at Duxford. On Monday 26 August he shot down Do 17Z-2 north-east of Chelmsford. Leutnant Krieger and three of his crew were killed. Blackwood was shot down by a Bf 110 at 1530 and bailed out near Maldon unhurt. On 9 September he shot down Bf 110C 2137 2N+FM of III/ZG 76 near Croydon at 1740 hours. Unteroffizier Bierling and Unteroffizier Weiher were killed. Blackwood left the RAF in 1945 and found the publishing business to be in a shocking state.[51] George Douglas Morant Blackwood died on 2 March 1997.

A neglected area of the Battle of Britain is the courage and heroism shown on the ground by RAF and WAAF[52] personnel and also the casualties suffered during attacks. Squadron Leader Tony Pickering, a Hurricane pilot in the Battle said that his major memory of 1940 was of the young WAAFs who endured the bombing of the aerodromes such as Biggin Hill and Kenley and carried on at their posts with great bravery.'

'I don't suppose airwomen on stations feel any different during raids from what ordinary people do in towns when they are bombed' recalled Corporal J. D. M. Pearson in a BBC broadcast. 'If you've got a job of work to do you get on with it. Otherwise most people go to the shelters, except of course, those who are on station defence duty.

'You'll want to know which of the Women's Auxiliary Air Force are on duty during a raid. Well, the switchboard operators for one; they are usually airwomen. Then there are first-aid workers, sick quarter attendants, anti-gas squads and of course the plotters in the operations room.

'Plotters particularly have proved that those members of the RAF were justified who said that women could be trusted to carry out operational work in air raids. They have shown they have plenty of nerve. So too, have the telephone operators. These WAAF who got the Military Medal this week were all telephone operators and it was a good thing they kept their heads and stuck to their job, because the station defence really depends a great deal on them. As for the plotters, I know of one who had half a table where she was working bombed away, but she went on with her job. Two others had a shed blown down over them, but when they were dug out they were still sticking to what they had been doing before the bomb fell.

'And it isn't only on the station that airwomen show how cool they can be in an emergency. One WAAF was coming back from leave by train when an incendiary bomb fell in the carriage. Her cap was burnt, all but the badge. She herself was almost unhurt and only suffered slightly from shock. She was off work for one day, but was quite recovered by evening and came on duty again ready for the next raid that night.

'There seems to have been something about that train. When it stopped during the raid, another WAAF ran out into the fields. A bomb came very close so she threw herself on her face and felt that she had landed on something hard. When she had got to her feet she picked up the object and asked an airwoman who was with her if she had dropped it. They looked more closely at it and found it was an unexploded bomb. The little crowd who had gathered round scattered in no time, while the WAAF very calmly replaced the bomb on the ground and walked away.

'We rather like to feel, you know, that members of the Women's Auxiliary Air Force keep their heads in a crisis. We are proud to feel that we have been trusted to work in the front line helping the RAF.'

***WAAF In Air Raids* by Flight Officer Daphne Pearson quoted in *Winged Words*. In May 1940 Corporal Pearson at the Coastal Command station at Detling, Kent, dragged the badly injured pilot of a crashed Anson clear of the burning wreckage and shielded him as bombs exploded. She was awarded the EGM, later converted to the George Cross.**

During the Battle of Britain, Military Medals were awarded to six WAAFs. During the big attack on Biggin Hill on 18 August Sergeant Elizabeth Mortimer, a telephone operator who was also in charge of the despatch of ammunition to the gun positions, remained at her very dangerous post throughout the raid, then, as soon as the bombs stopped falling - and long before the 'all clear' - began planting red flags round the craters in which there were unexploded bombs. That same day at Poling, Sussex CH station, diminutive Corporal Avis Hearn ignored the order to take cover as a large Luftwaffe formation approached Poling because she 'had a lot of plots to send and I loved my country.' Avis, who was only 4 feet 10½ inches tall, was soon promoted to Flight Sergeant and sent to a top training establishment. Her mother had once chided 'you'll never amount to anything'. Her standard reply given to puzzled soldiers who approached was always: 'Yes that is the ribbon of the MM and yes, apparently women can win it.'

On 1 September, two telephone operators at Biggin Hill, Sergeant Helen Turner and Corporal Elspeth Henderson, continued to maintain communications even after the operations block in which they were working received a direct hit. Such calm behaviour, to which the superb example of the WAAF officer in charge - Assistant Section Officer Felicity Hanbury - greatly contributed, was an inspiration not only to airwomen on other stations but also to their male comrades. Felicity was awarded a military OBE.

The two other MM awards were made to Sergeant Jean Youle who was on duty in a Station telephone exchange when the Station was attacked and bombed by five enemy aircraft and Corporal Josephine 'Josie' Robins who was in a dug-out which received a direct hit during an intense enemy bombing raid. Josie recalled in a radio programme for the BBC.

'I really do not know why I have been given the Military Medal, as I only did what everyone else would have done. The actual raid was a lightning one; we saw the German planes coming and at first thought they were our own as they were so very low, then we made for the nearest shelter as the bombs rained down on us. Two of us were literally blown into the dug-out by the blast of a bomb which burst just behind us and the next nearly blew us out again as it was a direct hit on the shelter, killing four men and injuring others. We helped some out of the dug-out which was full of awful dust and fumes from the explosion and got a stretcher for a seriously injured man ... The morning after the raid we turned into carpenter and demolition squads, as each section had to make the building habitable. The roof of ours was decidedly impaired so we climbed up to investigate and were forced into a perilous slide to the ground every time the siren sounded or there were signs of air activity overhead.'

In January 1941 Squadron Leader Alexander Vallance Riddell 'Sandy' Johnstone DFC Commanding 602 (City of Glasgow) Squadron wrote the following account of his time on the Auxiliary Squadron:

'After four months' fighting in the South of England 602 has just come out of the front line, as it were, to an aerodrome in a quieter part of the country up north. And it is good to be able to relax a bit. We have had our casualties in those four months; six pilots in the squadron were lost. But not one was actually killed in the air by the enemy. During this time scarcely a day passed without a combat. On many days we were sent up half a dozen times to fight battles, often against large formations of the enemy. In the circumstances we consider our losses were astonishingly light. On the other hand our 'bag' of enemy aircraft was eighty-nine destroyed and confirmed; many probables and damaged. So the Germans paid a stiff price for our losses and each new successful engagement gave us fresh heart for more.

'I joined the City of Glasgow Squadron in 1936, shortly after leaving school and began my flying career with them. The squadron had already been in existence for nine years and for four years after my entry continued to engage in bomber training. Then, to the delight of every member, we became single-seater fighters. At once we got down to some really serious training. We had our civil occupations to attend to, but every week-end and several evenings a week we put in learning all we could about fighter tactics. It was just as well we did, for six months after this development the war broke out. Within six weeks of hostilities, the squadron was engaged in the first Fighter Command action of the war - the raid on the Firth of Forth on 16 October 1939. In that action the squadron helped to shoot down the first enemy aircraft to be lost in the war over British soil. I had nothing to do with it personally. In fact, I distinguished myself by being about the only person in the squadron who did not fire his guns at something Teutonic that day. Truth is, I never saw any German aircraft in the air while I was up. My record up till early this summer consisted of having seen two German aircraft in the air when I was on the ground and two on the ground when I was in the air. But not one sausage did I see in the air while I was flying.

'One night in June however, when I was on patrol, a Heinkel came my way - caught in the beams of several searchlights. This turned out to be my first victim. When the target aircraft is brightly illuminated, as this one was, it becomes fairly easy to shoot it down, as you have the advantage of seeing without being seen. The one difficulty I did find was to be able to gauge the height of the target, since there is no background to it. It looks like something sitting stationary in mid-air, when, in fact, it is travelling at 200 mph or thereabouts.

'After my debut, as one might call this combat, the squadron had several encounters with reconnaissance aircraft, mostly in ones and twos, over the North Sea. But it was not until my squadron moved south [to Tangmere's satellite airfield at Westhampnett], sometime after I had been given command of it, that we encountered the real 'Blitz'. On one particular patrol [18th August] we were told to intercept a raid of about one hundred enemy aircraft which were coming in from the south. We were informed that their height was about 8,000 to 10,000 feet and that just about that height there was a heavy layer of cloud. Consequently we split into two flights. One flight, which I was leading, went above the clouds. The other remained below to make sure we did not miss the raid by being on the wrong side of the cloud layer.

'As you can well understand it is not possible for a pilot when flying an aircraft to hear any outside noises and one has to rely entirely on seeing one's quarry. As it happened, on this occasion, we did hear something of our prey. The enemy were using a wireless frequency which must have been very nearly the same as our own, for presently we began to hear them chattering away to each other like a lot of monkeys in a box. Up to this time we had seen nothing of our quarry and as we approached them the chatter grew louder and louder. Then, suddenly, we spotted them. They were straggled out in large 'vics' of about eighteen aircraft in each, just above the clouds. As we were only six in number, against their one hundred or so, we saw them a long time before they saw us - which, of course, gave us a big initial advantage. We were able to climb above them and get out in front of their leading formation. As we approached nearer, the Huns suddenly spotted us and, above all their chatter, a somewhat agonized voice came through as clear as daylight - *Achtung! Achtung! Schpeetfiren!* At that, an amazing transformation took place - and the straggling formation closed up into a formidable mass, the Me 110s wheeling out from the front to form a protective circle round the bombers.

'Thanks to the advantage we had in position, three of us were able to dive head-on into the leading formation, whilst the other three stayed behind to play with the fighters. The leading formation of bombers broke up after our attack and in ones and twos they sought refuge either in or below the clouds. Those who were stupid enough to go below the layer of cloud were pounced on by our other flight which was still waiting for them. Theirs was a sort of vulture's job and like vultures they did it. And then we all returned safely.

'Which reminds me. A very great friend of mine, who was one of the best fighter pilots in the country - but who unhappily was killed in action recently - once said to me: 'Napoleon used to say 'Don't give me clever men - give me lucky ones'.' Well, there seems to be a good sprinkling of lucky ones in the RAF. Touch wood, I've been pretty lucky myself. I've forgotten how many combats I've fought. But, with a score of eight, confirmed, as a result of my fighting, I've never once been hit. Nor has my aircraft. Even more remarkable, another member of my squadron, with a score of twelve enemy aircraft to his credit, all confirmed, has never once been hit either. There was a dent on his tailplane one day, but it appears that the mark was caused by a stone.

'The best 'bag' the squadron had in one single action was on a day in August [the 25th], when we were detailed to intercept a raid coming in over Dorset. Once again we had the advantage of height and this time of the sun also and arranged to knock down twelve of the enemy with a loss to ourselves of only two aircraft - the pilots of both of them safe. The enemy were very strong in numbers, but they split up and fled back to France. One of the two pilots of my squadron who bailed out landed in a farmyard where he was promptly cornered by a lot of irate farmers armed with pitchforks. That reception, the pilot said, was much more frightening than the bailing out.[53] Actually, on that day, so many people were floating down by parachute at the same time - mostly Germans I'm glad to say - that it must have looked rather like an invasion army being landed.

'While on the subject of coming down by parachute a rather amusing incident occurred on another occasion. A very fat man bailed out of a Dornier which the squadron had intercepted at about 25,000 feet. Needless to say everyone thought it was our old friend Goering doing another of his celebrated reconnaissance trips over this country! We circled around him while he was coming down - and it was ludicrous to see this enormously fat man dangling at the end of his parachute harness with his two podgy arms stretched above his head. His landing was even more ludicrous. He touched down on the roof of an outhouse in a garden in Kent, went crashing through the roof and remained there with only his head sticking through. The last we saw of him was his parachute - descending slowly on top of him, obscuring the whole picture.

'Finally, I would like to take this opportunity of saving a word about the ground crews. It is usually the pilots who get the praise and the thanks. But the job we do is little in comparison with the excellent and unremitting work done by the fellows who keep us in the air. They work for us day and night and I never hear a grumble from any of them. They are just grand and if any of them are listening in just now I would like to say, speaking, I am sure, for all pilots; 'We take off our hats to them.'[54]

Endnotes Chapter 6

41 Francis Victor Beamish was born in Dunmanway, County Cork, on 27 September 1903, but lived at Coleraine in Ulster before joining the RAF. He attended the College at Cranwell, receiving his commission in 1925 and being posted to India where he served on 31 Squadron at Anbala and then 60 Squadron at Kohat. He returned to the UK late in 1926, attending an instructor's course at CFS, Wittering and then going to 5 FTS as an instructor. In 1927 he joined the staff at Cranwell until 1929, when he went to Canada on an exchange with the RCAF. He first flew fighters with 25 Squadron as a flight commander from 1931, whilst the next year he was Personal Assistant to the AOC in C of ADGB. When a severe case of tuberculosis struck him he was forced to retire from the service in October 1933. After making a recovery he became a civilian instructor at 2 FTS. In 1936 he returned to Northern Ireland where he became the civilian adjutant at RAF Aldergrove. In January 1937 his health had improved and he was reinstated in the RAF as a Flight Lieutenant. At the end of the year he was given command of 64 Squadron, being awarded an AFC. After attending a Staff College course, he took command of 504 Squadron in September 1939. He was sent on a mission to Canada in mid January 1940 and then on 7 June became an airfield commander at North Weald on his return, a post he held throughout the Battle of Britain, flying with the squadrons at the airfield on every opportunity. On 7 November he collided with a 249 Squadron Hurricane flown by Flying Officer Tom Neil, the propeller of his aircraft cutting off the tail. Neil was able to bail out to safety. Beamish was awarded a DSO on 23 July 1940 and a DFC on 8 November. In March 1941 he was posted to HQ 11 Group, but returned to North Weald later in the year, being awarded a Bar to his DSO in September and being promoted Group Captain. On 12 February 1942 on a morning sortie with his Wing Commander Flying, Finlay Boyd, he made the first sighting of the German capital ships, Scharnhorst and Gneisenau, heading through the English Channel at the start of the famous 'Channel Dash'. On 28 March 1942 he was again leading the Wing over France when his Spitfire was seen to be hit and damaged by a Bf 109. It disappeared into cloud near Calais and he was not seen again. His total score was 10 destroyed, 11 and 1 shared probables, 5 damaged. *Aces High*.

42 George Cecil 'Grumpy' Unwin was born on 18 January 1913 in Bolton-on-Dearne, Yorkshire. He joined the RAF in 1929, becoming an apprentice clerk in Records. Promoted LAC in April 1931, he served as a clerk in HQ, Fighting Area at Uxbridge until November 1935 when he was selected for pilot training. He joined 19 Squadron as a sergeant pilot in 1936 and became one of the first pilots in the RAF to fly Spitfires. On 3 March 1939 he deliberately crashed one of these following an engine failure to avoid hitting some children playing in a field in which he was attempting to force-land. On 25 May 1940 the unit moved to Hornchurch for operations over Dunkirk. Now an experienced Flight Sergeant, he was left out of the first sortie next day, due to shortage of aircraft. It was his anger at this that gained him his nickname, which remained with him thereafter. He was in action next day however and when the unit withdrew had claimed five, two of them unconfirmed. During the summer and autumn battles he was to claim a further ten and two shared, receiving a DFM on 1 October and a Bar to this on 6 December having just been promoted Warrant Officer. He was commissioned in July 1941and he joined 613 Squadron in April 1944. His total score stood at 13 and 2 shared destroyed, 2 unconfirmed destroyed, 2 probables and 1 damaged. *Aces High*.

43 So called because he was a once a drummer in Debroy Somers' band. (Somers was born in 1890 in Dublin as William Debroy Somers. He died in 1952 aged 62). Gregory was Air Interception (AI) radar operator to night fighter ace Wing Commander Bob Braham. Gregory's superb radar skills helped Braham to destroy 29 German aircraft. Wing Commander William James 'Sticks' Gregory AFC DSO DFC DFM* died aged 87 on 9 October 2001.

44 Wilfred Greville 'Wilf' Clouston, a New Zealander who joined 19 Squadron in June 1937, who on 24 June had been awarded a DFC. The 24-year old New Zealander and former clerk from Auckland had joined the Squadron in June 1937. In constant action over Dunkirk in May and June, he had destroyed two Stukas, a couple of Bf 109s and a Dornier Do 17 as well as being awarded half shares in three other victories. Clouston died on 24 May 1980 following a fall.

45 Flying Officer Francis Noel Brinsden. a 21-year old New Zealander from Auckland. Brinsden was posted to 54 OTU Charter Hall in February 1943 for a night-fighting-conversion-course and then joined 25 Squadron flying Mosquito 'Intruder' fighter-bombers at Church Fenton. On a sortie

to Westerland on 17 August 1943 on the night of the Peenemünde raid he bombed Sylt airfield and successfully attacked the hangars at rooftop height. He was then picked up and blinded by searchlights. With vision almost lost he headed out to sea but struck the surface of the water and broke both airscrews. Brinsden ditched the aircraft and he and his navigator Flying Officer P. G. Fane-Sewell, got into their dinghy and attempted to sail out of the bay under an offshore breeze. Dawn brought a wind change and at mid-day on the 18th they were blown ashore into the arms of German troops who had been watching them for six hours. Eventually Brinsden found himself in Stalag Luft III.

46 A young lad of sixteen came dashing up with a pitchfork, obviously thinking that he was a German. He was told to 'piss off' and 'fetch a doctor!' In due course a medical officer from the local AA unit who was en route to Duxford for breakfast, turned up but he was unable to administer any morphine because the orderly corporal had gone on leave and taken the key to the poisons' cupboard with him.

47 His Spitfire crashed in flames near Little Shelford where his wife Cynthia, now seven months' pregnant, was bathing her sister's baby at King's Farm. Mike Bayon, who was in a field feeding chickens, vividly recalls the events of that clear, dewy Saturday morning. 'The German planes came winging over in tight formation, pretty high. Three Spitfires beamed into attack. I could hear the gunfire and see the absurdly pretty cotton wool bursts of the cannon shells. One of the Spitfires was hit. I was not to know that it was James. He was pressing home an attack on a Dornier when a Messerschmitt from behind completely removed his foot with a cannon shell. Glycol from burst hydraulics was burning his face and hands and soon he realized that the plane was out of control. He bailed out and with every heartbeat he could see a gush of blood from his severed foot and at that height and in that cold thin air, the blood spread out almost pink in curious spirals, rather like a long sinuous chiffon scarf. He decided not to pull the ripcord yet or he would have bled to death before he could land.' Mike Bayon wanted to be a fighter pilot but he eventually became a Mosquito navigator in 8 Group and flew Mosquito raids before the war in Europe ended. He was awarded the DFC.

48 *Men of the Battle of Britain* by Kenneth G. Wynn. (CCB Associates 1999).

49 A New Zealander, Hector Douglas McGregor was born in Wairoa on 15 February 1910. He joined the RAF in 1928 and was awarded a Permanent Commission in 1932. On completing his training in April 1929, he served for two years with 111 Squadron and then with 401 Fleet Fighter Flight on HMS *Courageous*. After attending an engineering course, he went to the School of Naval Co-operation at Lee-on-Solent in 1933, and then to the Engineer Section at HQ, Coastal Command. After a spell at Air Ministry, 1936-38, he went out to Egypt where he became commander of 33 Squadron, operating against dissidents in Palestine during early 1939, for which he was awarded a DSO. Returning to the UK early in 1940, he took command of 213 Squadron, but was shot down over Dunkirk on 31 May, bailing out to be picked up by a destroyer. During the Battle of Britain he claimed six victories. Sir Hector McGregor retired from the RAF in September 1964 and died in England on 11 April 1973. *Aces High* by Christopher Shores and Clive Williams (Grub Street, London 1994).

50 He had married Phyllis Caulcutt, an equestrian rider and an expert exponent of dressage in 1936 and they had a son and daughter. On his death his son Michael, a former naval pilot, succeeded him in the business but by then the firm had amalgamated to concentrate on printing.

51 The Blitz had destroyed millions of books as well as Blackwood's base in London and heralded a decline in the firm's fortunes. Before the war William Blackwood & Sons had been one of Britain's leading literary publishers, but in the post-war world its name and literary reputation counted for little. Blackwood was managing director of the firm and editor of Blackwoods Magazine 1948-1976. Blackwoods had to deal with an increasing number of mass-production rivals and with a decline in interest in monthly literary magazines. By the 1970s Blackwoods and its magazine appeared out-of-date and failed to attract a younger generation of writers and readers. It was an achievement that the magazine survived until 1980. Blackwood retired from the editorship in 1976, being the last member of his family to edit the magazine which bore his name. He remained chairman of the publishing house until 1983.

52 The Women's Auxiliary Air Force was established in June 1939 with the aim of freeing men for operational roles. Its members became known as 'WAAFs'. Previously the Women's Royal Air Force had existed briefly at the end of the First World War. This name was used again from 1949,

when the WAAF was re-formed and it continued until the women's service became fully integrated into the RAF.

53 The two pilots who bailed out were Flying Officer William Hugh Coverley who was shot down by Bf 109s near Dorchester and Sergeant Mervyn. Herbert Sprague who was shot down south of Dorchester. Both pilots were unhurt. Coverley was KIA on 7 October 1940. Sprague was KIA on 11 September 1940.

54 'Sandy' Johnstone was born in Glasgow on 2 June 1916. He had joined 602 in late 1934 and became its CO on 12 July 1940. He was awarded the DFC on 1 October 1940. His score stood at 7 and 2 shared destroyed, 1 probable, 6 and 1 shared destroyed. He left 602 in mid-April 1941 and became Controller at Turnhouse. Air Chief Marshal Johnstone CB retired from the RAF on 1 December 1968.

Chapter 7

Biggin Hill 1940

A. J. C. Pelham-Groom

'Angels One Five' refers to RAF radio procedure words indicating the altitude of a radar contact is 15,000 feet. The film of the same name is a 1952 British film based on the book What Are Your Angels Now? by actor and writer Pelham Groom (who was also technical advisor to the film under his full title of Wing Commander Arthur John Pelham Groom; born on 27 January 1906 in Hackney, London. The plot centres on a young fighter pilot immediately before and during the Battle of Britain. Some scenes in the film were shot at RAF Uxbridge, home to a wartime operations room. The film begins with a replacement, Pilot Officer T. B. 'Septic' Baird (John Gregson), landing his Hawker Hurricane at 'Pimpernel' Squadron's airfield. Just as he touches down however, a straggler from an earlier mission taxis across his path. Septic's quick reactions allow him to 'leapfrog' the other Hurricane, averting a costly disaster. However, this causes him to crash his replacement plane into the bungalow of Squadron Leader Barry Clinton (Cyril Raymond) at the end of the runway. This earns Septic the wrath of his new squadron leader, Bill Ponsford (Andrew Osborn), because he damaged his plane. The crash also injures the ligaments in Septic's neck, which he is able to self-diagnose, as he had been a medical student before the war. The next morning, Septic is told by Group Captain 'Tiger' Small (Jack Hawkins) that he will not be able to fly until his neck is healed, so he will instead serve in the operations room for the time being. Several days later, with the risk of a bombing attack on the airfield and all of Pimpernel Squadron's Hurricanes scrambled, Tiger orders all aircraft to take-off and fly out of harm's way until the raid is over. With Tiger quickly assembling all available pilots and finding aircraft to fly, Septic wins a foot race with Small to claim the last spare Hurricane for himself. He then proceeds to shoot down a Bf 110 from the attacking force. His delight is short lived however when he is admonished by Small and Squadron Leader Peter Moon (Michael Denison) for leaving his radio set to transmit, preventing the returning Hurricanes from being diverted to an undamaged airfield. A crestfallen Septic returns to his ground duties. Eventually a reinstated Septic joins in Pimpernel's operations, but he is mortally wounded while shooting down another enemy aircraft. His last words are heard over the Sector control room tannoy (public-address system), when he tells Small that their planned return foot race will have to be 'postponed indefinitely'. Small replies 'Your message received and understood. Out.' Septic then passes out and crashes to his death.

Wing Commander Arthur John Pelham Groom, who was also known for *Pretty Polly* (1967) died aged 72 on 6 April 1978 in Hong Kong.

The days of the lone fighter ace ended in the Kaiser's war and before the last war started the control of aircraft came from an Operations Room. I knew those

Operations Rooms well, for I was one of the sector Controllers at the time of my tale. The 'Hole,' as it was called at Biggin, was not one of the modern gin-palaces with a 400-ton ceiling, but a comparatively small brick building surrounded by a blast-proof wall. The centre of the Ops Room was occupied by a large outline map of South-east England with its guardian straits and channels, mounted on a 12 feet square plotting table. Around the table WAAF plotters, connected to various information centres, were busily recording the movements of all aircraft in the area. Identification plaques and brightly coloured plastic arrows were deftly manipulated with plotting sticks. Yellow plaques with black numbers on them indicated hostile or unidentified aircraft. Overlooking the plotting table was a dais, where sat the Controller, who directed the fighter aircraft on their sorties. He was flanked on one side by the 'Ops B' officer seated at a twenty-seven-line switchboard communicating with squadron dispersal points, Flying Control, satellite aerodromes, Observer Corps centres and adjacent Fighter Sectors. On the other side was 'Ops A' a head-phoned WAAF, permanently connected to Group HQ through which all operational orders were issued. Beyond 'Ops A' was the Army Gun Liaison Officer and his deputy, who controlled all antiaircraft defences in the sector. Facing the dais from across the plotting table was a frosted glass screen, on which were placed suckers indicating the position of airborne fighters and of the enemy aircraft which they were to intercept. Alongside, an indicator board showed the number and 'readiness' state of aircraft on the aerodrome. There were three squadrons at Biggin at that time, Nos. 32 and 79; regular squadrons equipped with Hurricanes and 610, an Auxiliary squadron flying Spitfires.

The 'Hole' had, besides the glass screen, which was unique in itself, something which was seldom to be seen in any Ops Room. It was a trophy, the magazine of a German machine-gun. Trophies could always be found in dispersal huts, but in an Ops Room it is seldom that any mark of conquest can be found, for the Controller is the planner; his job, by the information provided by radiolocation, and by the use of radio-telephones, is to move his fighters across the sky to intercept the incoming bombers.

Humphrey was responsible for that trophy. He came to the Operations Room, posted there as a Controller. He was young, athletic and a pilot and it was obvious from the start that there was nothing that he wanted more than to be with the pilots in pursuit of the Ju 88s. He was a good Controller, but took no satisfaction from his ability to gauge the speed and direction of the enemy and to place his fighters in such a position that battle could be joined. They were hectic days. Fighters took off, fought, landed, refuelled, came to readiness and took off again; and the strain was telling. But every day Humphrey was there on the dais, sending his friends out to a battle that he hated to be missing. We could all sense the frustration working in his mind. We understood how galling it must be for him, having achieved an interception, to be able to do no more. And even more galling was the knowledge that, although there were now gaps in the Squadrons, he was still confined to the 'Hole.' He became irritable and, although his work did not suffer, he became more and more critical of those around him.

One day the change came. He was seated on the terrace outside the mess overlooking the beautiful Kentish valley, waiting for his turn to go on duty, when a loudspeaker broke the summer silence: 'Attention, everybody. This is the Operations Room calling. Will the Stand-by Controller report to the Ops Room immediately. I will repeat that. Will the Stand-by Controller report to the Ops Room immediately. That is all.' The loudspeaker gave a final click and was silent. Humphrey, without any marked enthusiasm, walked to the Ops Room. In the 'Hole' the Duty Controller welcomed him with a smile and pointed to the French coast where a gaggle of hostile plaques was just being plotted.

'Trouble brewing,' said the Controller, and at that moment the WAAF on his left began to call out an order from Group HQ: 'Serial seventy-six, two squadrons patrol Ashford at fifteen thousand feet.'

Action was rapid but unhurried. The 'Ops B' on the other side of the Controller pushed two telephone keys forward on his switchboard. 'Thirty-two Dispersal? ... Good ... Stand by. Seventy-nine Dispersal? ... Order for both Squadrons... serial seventy-six... both Squadrons patrol Ashford at fifteen thousand. OK, Thirty-two? ... OK, Seventy-nine?'

Humphrey looked frankly bored, or perhaps tired, as he watched 'Ops B' push another key and call the Spitfire squadron to readiness. Three minutes later 'Ops B' announced that 32 Squadron had taken off and they were immediately followed by the Hurricanes of 79. Humphrey picked up the transmitter. 'Hello, Jacko leader, Jacko leader, Sapper calling. Let me know when you have reached angels one five. Sapper over to Jacko leader, over.'

Jacko leader, in other words the leader of 32 Squadron, replied that he would do just that, and he had been joined by the other squadron. A voice announced that the Spitfires were at readiness. A wave of raiders moved on across the board. Then Group came through with another signal. 'Serial eighty-three, 32 and 79 Squadrons intercept Raid 124... yes ... Serial eighty-four, 610 Squadron patrol Mayfield at seventeen thousand feet.'

This meant that all Biggin Hill's fighters were now airborne, and Raid 124 was Humphrey's special problem. The south-east corner of the board was already littered with raid plaques, and the 'Ops. B' was plainly impressed with the way in which Humphrey was manipulating his squadrons.

It was then that Raid 64 began to make its presence felt. Unmarked, it was steering a straight course from Thanet to Biggin Hill. The Group Controller came through and said that Hornchurch, another fighter sector, had failed to intercept, and although he was trying to get another squadron off he did not think that they would be in time. Humphrey picked up a microphone which was attached to the Station loudspeaker system: 'Attention, everybody. Action stations. Action stations. That is all.'

Raid 64 was uncomfortably close now. 'Attention, everybody. Operations Room calling. All personnel not engaged in operational duties take cover. Take cover. That is all.'

The tension in the Operations Room was now mounting. Everyone knew that there was nothing between them and what Raid 64 could give them, and that within a few minutes the enemy bombers would be plastering the aerodrome. Humphrey, with his hands behind his back, was biting his lip.

Suddenly he stopped and whispered in Bill's ear: 'You can manage alone now, can't you?'

The Controller nodded agreement, and in the next instant Humphrey had gone, edging his way through the blast-proof door as the Flight-Sergeant was about to close it. For a few moments no one realized that Humphrey was no longer in the Ops Room; they did not know where he had gone or why he had gone, they could not see him running towards practice flight, towards a solitary Hurricane, they could not see the airman wheel the starting battery into position, nor hear the cough as the Merlin engine came to life; but they did hear, a few moments later, a voice on the radiotelephone calling:

'Hello, Sapper, Sapper, Jacko Pink One calling. I am airborne, over.'

They heard nothing more from Humphrey for some time. Bombs began to fall, and the Ops Room shook, while Humphrey was carrying out his individual action against the enemy and doing his utmost to gain height in time to engage him. He was alone, alone over Biggin Hill, no one to guard his tail, no one to come to his assistance, just one Hurricane against an enemy raid. He met them head on, pressed his thumb down on the gun-button, and his eight Browning guns fired as one. This was a different Humphrey, a Humphrey who, although still calm, was giving vent to something which had been bottled up in him for some time, and then in the Ops Room the Controller heard three words: 'Got the bastard.'

" But you must remember that I outnumbered them by one to three."

Chapter 8

Five In A Day

David Masters

'What General Weygand called the Battle of France is over. I expect that the Battle of Britain is about to begin. Upon this battle depends our own British life and the long continuity of our institutions and our Empire. The whole fury and might of the enemy must very soon be turned on us. Hitler knows that he will have to break us in this island or lose the war. If we can stand up to him, all Europe may be free and the life of the world may move forward into broad, sunlit uplands. But if we fail, then the whole world, including the United States, including all that we have known and cared for, will sink into the abyss of a new dark age made more sinister and perhaps more protracted, by the lights of perverted science. Let us therefore brace ourselves to our duties and so bear ourselves that, if the British Empire and its Commonwealth last for a thousand years, men will still say: 'This was their finest hour'.'

Speech delivered by Winston Churchill, first to the House of Commons and then broadcast, 18 June 1940.

Future generations will want to know what manner of men were these young fighter pilots who saved the freedom of the world and what were their reactions in those stupendous days when all human progress depended upon their prowess. Such questions will not be easy to answer. Official accounts, cold and impersonal, lack the human touch. Yet although the fighter pilots in the air may be as young gods riding their thunderbolts to scourge the Nazis from the skies, on their return to earth they become human once more.

One of the names to assume prominence in the autumn of 1940 was that of Flight Lieutenant Harbourne Mackay Stephen, born in Elgin, Scotland on 18 April 1914. He came to London in 1931 to work with Allied Newspapers, joining the Evening Standard in 1936 and also the RAFVR in 1937. He was commissioned in April 1940 and posted to 605 Squadron in Scotland before transferring to 74 Squadron, seeing action over Dunkirk and during the Battle of Britain. On 27 August 1940 he was awarded a DFC for shooting down five enemy aircraft on 11 August in four successive fights with large enemy formations over the Thames Estuary, making his total up to twelve [sic].[55] On 15 November he added a Bar to his DFC by attacking single-handed four Messerschmitt 109s at 27,000 feet and shooting the tail off one before destroying another. And on 24 December he achieved the distinction of being the first fighter pilot to be awarded the first Immediate DSO of the war for the RAF.

Obviously a fighter pilot who succeeds in being awarded the DFC twice as well as the DSO within the space of five months must possess unusual qualities. Before his school days dawned he disclosed a stubborn will coupled with a fighting spirit, so no doubt he was able to take care of himself at school in Elgin and Edinburgh and Shrewsbury; but what his masters thought of him and what he thought of them remains unknown.

The roads from Scotland to London are well worn and he followed in the wake of many another Scot who has sought fame and fortune in the Capital of the British Empire. The English are rather tolerant and helpful to the Scots, the Irish and the Welsh, but whether these nations appreciate this fine quality in the English as much as the English appreciate and reward them for their valued services is an open question.

Young H. M. Stephen was lucky, inasmuch as work waited for him in London. His father happened to be a friend of Mr. William Will, of Allied Newspapers, who offered the boy a place in the office in Grays Inn Road, London. The pay was fifteen shillings a week and the job called neither for skill nor intelligence. He was just the 'copy' boy, a very humble cog in the machinery of a modern newspaper office. All he had to do was to take the 'copy' from the reporters and sub-editors up to the composing room where the linotype operators waited to set it up for the next edition of the paper. He learned a lot about newspaper offices and the writers who form public opinion and if he missed much of the glamour and romance with which the films have so generously endowed the profession, he could not fail to notice the perpetual work and rush inseparable from an endless race with the clock to put the paper to 'bed' in time for the newspaper trains.

A spell of some years on the staff of Allied Newspapers brought the opportunity to transfer to the advertising staff of the *Evening Standard*. Flying had long interested him and in 1937 he made up his mind to join the Volunteer Reserve of the Royal Air Force, which he did in April of that year, when he started his training at Maidenhead.

It was not always easy to get away from the office to carry out his course of instruction. But the difficulties were eased for him by Mr. J. G. Beaseley, one of the directors of the *Evening Standard*, of whom Flight Lieutenant Stephen has spoken in the warmest terms. 'I owe a lot to Mr. Beaseley. He encouraged me to keep on flying and used to smooth out difficulties about getting time off,' he remarked.

One of the good qualities of this brilliant fighter pilot is his appreciation of those who have helped him and his recognition of outstanding merit, particularly that of Wing Commander Malan under whom he fought so magnificently in the famous 74 Squadron. Stephen and his fellow enthusiasts who were anxious to fly on Tiger Moths at Maidenhead, used to give up their Saturdays and Sundays to the task. Instead of idling away the weekends, they devoted them to learning all they could about aviation.

His first thrill came when his instructor took him up and started to throw the Tiger Moth all over the sky. This experience, during which the earth appeared to rotate round the aircraft, gave some pupils a sickening feeling, but he weathered it without turning a hair.

After flying under dual control for nine hours with the instructor, he went up for his first solo flight. 'Were you nervous?' he was asked afterwards. 'Not at all. Either you can fly or you can't!' he said decisively.

From Tiger Moths he graduated to Hawker Harts and before the outbreak of war he was called up to join the Volunteer Reserve of the Royal Air Force as a sergeant pilot in order to take a course on Hurricanes. So his spare time hobby was to prove of invaluable service to the nation.

His first reaction to Hurricanes after Hawker Harts was that they were tremendously powerful.

'Were you scared of them?' someone inquired.

'No' came the calm reply.

It was simply a plain statement of fact. He has no fear. This young Scot with the dark, well-brushed hair, who is five feet nine inches tall, is cool, calculating. There is an appraising look in his dark eyes and flickering at the back of them is a glint of amusement as though he were enjoying a little joke all to himself, when he smiles, a dimple appears on his chubby, clean-shaven face.

'You wouldn't think he had shot down all those Germans - he doesn't look a bit like that!' a young lady once remarked. She was right. He is quiet, modest, with nothing swaggering about him despite the sudden fame and decorations. But still waters run deep and his opinions are clean-cut, swift and very decided.

When the war started, the routine of training swung automatically into top gear. Instead of working a few hours a day, those volunteer pilots began to work all day for seven days a week. They practised the most amazing evolutions in the air against the day when they would meet the enemy; they tackled the difficulties of interception, giving a section ten minutes start before setting forth to try to locate them. It was like playing hide and seek. When the clouds were about, the task was more difficult, so sometimes they succeeded and at others they failed, but successes and failures alike enlarged their knowledge and experience.

In April 1940 he received his commission as a Pilot Officer and went to cut his flying teeth in Scotland, where he helped to shoot down a Heinkel which they rounded up in those quarters.

It was being posted to 74 Squadron in the Home Counties which mellowed his experience and gave him the opportunity to shine. When the Germans began their thrust on 10 May 1940 this squadron of Spitfires became one of the British spearheads over the French coast. The British fighters were operating far from their base and their four patrols a day between dawn and dusk were arduous and exhausting. Theoretically the pilots knew all about air fighting, but their actual experience was extremely limited. Flight Lieutenant Stephen had the advantage of most, inasmuch as he had seen German aircraft in the air and had even played his part in helping to shoot one down. But many of the pilots had not seen an enemy aircraft in flight and none of them knew much about air fighting or how the theories would work out in practice. We know now that the theory and training were sound; that the pilots were superb and that everything worked out all right. In those days, however, it was unproved and the fighters of the Royal Air Force although they had gained their wings had yet to win their spurs.

Up and down between Ostend and Boulogne the Spitfires flew at heights which largely depended on the clouds. If the clouds were at 10,000 feet, they flew below them; if the sky were clear they flew at 20,000 feet. For days, not a Messerschmitt nor any other enemy aircraft came in sight, then the squadron came on fifteen German aircraft and got their first crack at them. In the dog fight, the British fighters shot down six or seven of the Germans, of which Flight Lieutenant Stephen destroyed one. In the ensuing May days when they joined issue with the Germans, they inflicted severe losses on them; their own losses in pilots were light, but their losses in aircraft were considerable. Continuous patrols from morning till evening coupled with the hard fighting told its tale on the pilots of 74 Squadron who grew exhausted and badly in need of a rest and refit, so on 27th May they were withdrawn for ten days, consequently they took no part in the evacuation of the British Army from Dunkirk.

'It was only by June or July that we began to learn the technique of air fighting and Wing Commander Malan was the greatest of leaders,' Flight Lieutenant Stephen once remarked.

His own big day of 11 August 1940, when he shot down five of the enemy was perfect in every way. Just after 6.30 in the morning he took off with the squadron to patrol over the Channel and climbed to 17,000 feet. About 6.45 am they sighted between twenty and thirty Messerschmitt 109s and in a minute or two they were all involved in a dog fight. 'I had a quick bang at one of the enemy and then at another' said Stephen. 'Then I happened to turn up sun and joined two aircraft that were climbing, when I discovered that I was following two Messerschmitt 109 fighters at only a few yards distance; in fact, I was formating on them. By the time I'd realised my mistake they had turned away from the sun and I opened fire on the leader. I came up behind him and gave him a burst and he dropped down into the Channel. When I gave the second one a burst he just exploded in mid-air.'

After the fight the squadron returned to the aerodrome and ordered coffee and toast to be sent to the hut at the dispersal point where the aircraft were being refuelled; but before they could take their coffee they were ordered up again. This time Stephen was out of luck, but the squadron landed with three more added to its total and one to the score of Wing Commander Malan. They were able to enjoy some fresh coffee and a cigarette.

'Stand by,' came the order to them at 10.30 am.

All climbed into their Spitfires, strapped themselves in and donned their oxygen masks ready to start up the engines and get away. Soon after taking off to guard a convoy in the Thames estuary, they were cheered by the sight of about forty bombers flying in groups of three spread out over a front about a mile wide. One of the flight commanders, thinking the bombers had already attacked the convoy and were retreating, was surprised to find himself in the middle of them before he knew it. The Germans were still more surprised, for they at once broke up their formation before the blazing guns of the leader and his section and moments' later aircraft were whirling all over the sky.

'The German aircraft were going round in steep turns. Imagine them, forty light bombers - very manoeuvrable and fast, the famous Messerschmitt Jaguar 110 fighter-bombers. We were chasing them and they were chasing us in and out of the clouds. In a few minutes they started to form one of their well-known defensive circles. By this time several Germans were lying smashed up in the water with the crews swimming round. The Spitfires were now diving in and out of the circle and never letting them complete it. I got my sights on one bomber and gave him a long burst and one of my tracer bullets must have hit his petrol tank, as in a few seconds he went down flaming into the sea. I climbed into the clouds just as another bomber darted at me and we passed each other so closely that I do not know how we avoided a smash. Turning on his tail, I silenced his rear gunner with a burst and as I closed the range the Messerschmitt rolled over and fell upside down in the sea.'

That was his fourth enemy aircraft in three sorties and by shooting down four in one morning, Flight Lieutenant Stephen accomplished a remarkable feat. Nor was his run of luck yet over, for when the squadron flew off after lunch they saw twenty Junker dive-bombers escorted by Messerschmitt fighters. They all turned tail at the sight of the Spitfires, but one was slow in getting away.

Flight Lieutenant Stephen sped after him and got in a burst of machine-gunfire. 'He dived and I followed him down, giving him another burst just before the pilot jumped out. He was so low that his parachute did not open and his aircraft crashed and burst into flames on the beach,' said Flight Lieutenant Stephen in summing up his record day.[56]

Over twenty of the enemy fell to his guns by December 1940, so he did his share in helping to win the Battle of Britain. Once he flew so high that he reached the very limit of the aircraft's climb and flopped about in the air like a pigeon with a broken wing. Another time when flying at 35,000 feet he saw two Messerschmitts flying 2,000 feet above him. 'I was jolly glad they didn't attack. I don't think they noticed me,' he commented.

His abiding impressions of those heroic days will probably be of simple things-the blazing sunshine which made it so hot in the cockpits that the pilots flew in their shirt-sleeves and helmets; the striking resemblance to a jigsaw puzzle of the clusters of islands in the north of Scotland when viewed from 20,000 feet; the ant-hill that was London seen from a height of about six miles, when the Thames was a tiny silver streak that could barely be seen and the high-flying balloons seemed no bigger than peapods.

One day while up with the squadron during the Battle of London he saw a black mass of about 200 bombers protected by fighters flying up the Thames estuary. Despite their overwhelming numbers, the Germans at the sight of the two squadrons of Spitfires turned tail - jettisoning their bombs around Tilbury as they were actually making their turn - and fled for their lives. No better proof of indiscriminate bombing by the Germans can be adduced than that, for it is impossible to aim at a target and hit it on a turn.

About that gigantic fire in September on Thameside which lit up the place like daylight, Flight Lieutenant Stephen was afterwards quite impersonal. 'We had to prepare our aircraft for next day and patch the bullet holes. We had our own job to do.'

And if they had failed to do that job, the Dark Ages would have shut down once more on Great Britain and the whole civilised world. Shooting down Germans needs courage and resource and a keen eye and a clear head. The pilot who can make his decisions coolly and instantaneously stands the better chance of vanquishing his opponent.

The British technique of dealing with the German masses which sometimes seemed to fill the sky was cleverly conceived and brilliantly executed. The Spitfires, which could climb higher than the Hurricanes, guarded the higher levels and dealt with the enemy fighters, while the Hurricanes at the lower levels concentrated on the bombers. Any enemy aircraft which managed to evade the first line of defenders were attacked by the squadrons posted further back. In those incredible air battles many a damaged Heinkel or Junkers turned and limped for home. It was the practice of the Spitfire pilots to conserve their ammunition as much as possible by firing short bursts at the German fighters, then directly the Messerschmitts were driven back the Spitfires could turn and use their remaining ammunition to help the Hurricanes finish off the damaged bombers.

At nightfall the Spitfires flew off from the station where they had been operating all day to a safer station around which the aircraft were dispersed to minimize losses in the event of a night attack. Here the pilots could generally get a good night's sleep to fit them for the morrow's fight. Before dawn the pilots rose and flew the Spitfires back to the station from which they were to operate during the day.

These were some of the methods by which the small numbers of the Royal Air Force dealt such a crushing defeat in the autumn of 1940 to the vast German Luftwaffe which was considered by Hitler and Goering to be invincible. [57]

Endnotes Chapter 8

55 Officially, his score on 11 August was, over Dover: 2 Bf 109Es unconfirmed; one Bf 109E damaged; 2 Bf 110s unconfirmed; one Bf 110 damaged and one Bf 109E confirmed. On 24 May he was awarded a half-share in a Hs 126 and a quarter-share in a Do 17 near Dunkirk. On 26 May his half-share in another Hs 126 at Bergues was unconfirmed, On 27 May he shot down a Bf 109E five miles from Dunkirk and was also awarded a half-share in a Do 17, 15 miles east of Boulogne. On 28 July he was awarded a Bf 109E damaged over Dover. *Aces High* by Christopher Shores and Clive Williams (Grub Street, London 1994).

56 Flight Lieutenant Harbourne Mackay Stephen, 74 Squadron, 11 August 1940. *'So Few: The Immortal Record of the Royal Air Force* by David Masters (1941).

57 In January 1941 Stephen was posted to 59 OTU at Turnhouse as CFI, promoted to Flight Lieutenant, but seconded to the RAE, Farnborough. In June he was posted to help form 130 Squadron. A month later he was given command of 234 Squadron, which he led until early 1942. His final score was 9 and 8 shared destroyed, 4 and 1 shared unconfirmed destroyed, 3 probables and 7 damaged. He was posted to India, becoming Wing Commander Flying at Dum Dum and later at Jessore. Later he commanded 166 Fighter Wing on the Burma front and then joined HQ. 224 Group, Fighter Operations. In 1945 he was Ops 'A' at Air Command, SEAC. On return to the UK, he joined Beaverbrook Newspapers, working on three Scottish newspapers until 1955. He also rejoined the Royal Auxiliary Air Force, commanding 602 Squadron (1950-52). He became General Manager of the *Sunday Express* and then the *Sunday Graphic*. In 1964 he joined Thompson Newspapers, becoming General Manager and then Managing Director of the *Daily Telegraph* and *Sunday Telegraph* until his retirement in 1986. *Aces High* by Christopher Shores and Clive Williams (Grub Street, London 1994).

Chapter 9

Winged Crusaders

David Masters

I was very concerned and very upset. I was annoyed at myself for having been shot down so decisively and I felt terribly isolated. I couldn't see or hear very well and so I couldn't recognise people. I felt so very sorry for myself, which is not a good situation for anybody. I felt so deflated, that half of my life had been taken and half wasn't worth bothering with. It was, I think, the worst period of my life.

There was one person in particular who put me on a much more even footing. He had been shot down by a Hurricane. He had sent a message to go and see him. I was on crutches at the time and I managed to get over to where he was with a hell of a lot of struggle and self-pity. As I opened the door in Ward 3, I saw what I can only describe now as the most horrifying thing I have ever seen in my life.

This chap had been really badly burned. His hair was burned off, his eyebrows and his eyelids. You could just see his staring eyes, with only two holes in his face. His nose and lips were also badly burned. Then I looked down and saw that his hands and feet were burned. I got through the door on my crutches with a struggle and then this chap started propelling a wheelchair down the ward. Halfway down, he picked up the back of a chair with his teeth - and it was then that I noticed how badly his lips were burned. Then he brought this chair down the ward and threw it alongside me and said, 'Have a seat, old boy.'

It was then that I cried - and I thought, 'What have I got to complain about?' From then on, everything fell into place.

Pilot Officer George Herman Bennions DFC. The badly burned pilot was Sergeant Ralph Carnall on 111 Squadron who was shot down in flames over Kent on 16 August. Carnall was born on 23 August 1913 and went to Longton School. He and Bennions were schoolfriends. Carnell recovered and later flew Mosquitoes in India. He stayed in the RAF and retired in 1963 as a squadron leader.

Each fighter pilot who took part in the Battle of London cherishes his own individual impressions and Pilot Officer G. H. Bennions DFC is no exception. 'We really began to earn our pay then,' he once remarked modestly -and posterity will not disagree with him.[58]

Hearing the call of the Royal Air Force as long ago as 1929 when he was a boy still under 16 years old, he learned so much about aero-engines in the following years that he could diagnose an unusual sound in an engine as easily and accurately as a heart specialist diagnoses a murmur in the heart.

But it was when he trained as a fighter pilot that his early dreams began to come true and the experience he gained over the Arabian coast, where the landing grounds were so small that the pilot who failed to drop in at 60 miles an hour with his nose well up was bound to find trouble by overshooting the boundaries - that experience confirmed his choice of a pilot's life. Step by step he gained promotion until he won his commission.

By the time his squadron was ordered on 3 September 1940, to take part in the defence of London he had already shot down two or three of the enemy. The first day they hurled themselves into the conflict against the Heinkels and Junkers and Messerschmitts was marked by the loss of their two leaders. They were very pre-occupied in the mess that night.

Next morning they were out at 6.30 on their first patrol and they set forth on their last patrol an hour before dusk. For day after day their normal routine was to get up at dawn, make three or four patrols of 90 minutes, attacking the enemy with more avidity than a well-trained terrier seizes a rat and grounding their Spitfires at night to repair them and prepare for the morrow, before; dropping into bed, dead tired, to be kept awake half the night by the battery of big guns just outside their windows.

As for food, they took it when they could. Often as not, when they sat down to a meal in the mess they would be called away to go up to fight the massed German formations. All the time they were in the mess, transport waited outside to rush them to their Spitfires at the dispersal point. The instant they were ordered up, the ground staff would start the engines to have the aircraft waiting ready for the pilots to take off directly they arrived from the mess. To save time, the pilots generally kept on their flying boots and left their other kit on the seat or wings of the aircraft, where they could grab it and don it quickly.

It says much for the fitness of the pilots that they endured those gruelling days for so long. Towards the end of September they began to show signs of getting a little stale. They displayed a lack of interest in anything on the ground. Men would fall asleep at odd moments during the day between patrols. One or two said they felt tired. They began to look up for a cloudy day that might give them a bit of a rest. Yet this lassitude vanished like magic and they became as keen as ever directly they went roaring up into the skies to meet the Germans.

They were hard days for the fighter pilots and grim days for Great Britain and humanity. Toward the end of September the German losses had so shaken the German command that the character of the air war hanged and instead of immense formations of bombers, the enemy began to send over high-flying fighters. This made the work of the fighter pilots much more difficult. It took longer for the Spitfires to climb and intercept. Sometimes they were dived upon by the Messerschmitts before they could reach the patrol line.

In spite of the big advance made in aircraft and engines, it is still a wearisome business to climb five miles and as the enemy began to send fighters over at 25,000 and 30,000 feet it was impossible to make contact with them at under five miles.

On one occasion Bennions climbed over seven miles to 37,500 feet - a long and arduous climb after two enemy fighters with the intention of engaging them. He could get no higher, although he kept the nose of his aircraft hard up in the air. Any little movement disturbed the balance and sent him flopping down 300 or 400 feet. The two enemy aircraft, which flew 1,000 feet above him, must have been fitted with two-stage superchargers to compress the rarefied air sufficiently to give the engines enough oxygen at the right pressure.

'They were leaving white trails in the air,' reported Bennions after he landed. 'I thought I would just get up behind them to shoot them out of the sky, but I couldn't. They kept diving at me, just putting their noses down and sweeping up to their old level again like a switchback; but they did not fire or come within 400 yards of me. Once I got into their slipstream and my perspex iced up instantly and I could not see anything at all. My screen became quite opaque and I had to open the hood to see where the two Huns had got to. I felt like a kite balloon being dived upon as my aircraft stood up at a ridiculous angle. In opening the hood I lost 1,000 feet, so I had to break off and come down without firing a shot. They were still patrolling when I went home.'

This explains some of the extraordinary difficulties of fighting on the verge of the stratosphere, so high in the sky that the aircraft are invisible to the naked eye.

On 1 October 1940, after fighting for a month in the greatest air battle the world has so far known, Bennions was due to go on leave for six days. His pass and railway warrant were made out all ready for him. During that nightmare month he had raised his victories to eleven and had probably destroyed five others.

'I thought I'd like to shoot down one more Hun before going for a rest,' he stated.

Accordingly he took off with his squadron and patrolled with them at 30,000 feet for go minutes, when the oxygen began to dwindle and they turned for home. On the way Bennions sighted some Hurricanes, with about 40 Messerschmitt logs above them. Calling up the leader, who acknowledged the message, he flew ahead to indicate the position of the enemy and the squadron split up into two formations. Turning right to take up a favourable position for attack, Bennions arrived at the Messerschmitts to find he was alone in the sky. His companions had seen the Hurricanes, but had not sighted the Messerschmitts, so they had just carried on and flown to base. It never entered his head to follow them. Undeterred by the odds, the lone English pilot turned to attack the rear of the pack. Singling out a Messerschmitt, he pressed the button twice and saw it fall away in smoke and flames, to bring his score to twelve. As it went a cannon shell exploded by the left side of his face. There was a short sharp pain in his eyes, he was momentarily blinded and the next thing he remembered was pulling his Spitfire out of a steep dive. Pains in his right arm and right leg suggested that they had been wounded.

'I cleared my other eye with my glove and found I was able to see vaguely,' he said when it was over. 'I could see that the hood and cockpit were shattered, so I decided to bail out. I undid the oxygen tube, disconnected the wireless plug, slid back the hood, opened the door, undid my strap and fell over the side.

I don't know what attitude the aircraft was in - I couldn't see. When I felt myself clear and falling through space, I put my left thumb through the ring of my ripcord and gave a slight pull. I felt a terrific jerk as my parachute opened. Then I lost consciousness. The next thing I remember is lying on the ground telling my name and squadron to someone attending me.'

It seems impossible that a man who was so terribly wounded as Pilot Officer Bennions could remain conscious and perform all those actions which enabled him to escape. His will-power was almost superhuman. His left eye was destroyed and there was a hole through which his brain was exposed. Within two hours Mr. A. H. McIndoe, the brilliant plastic surgeon and an eye specialist, were operating and doing their best to save him and repair the damage. For five weeks the wounded pilot was in hospital and Mr. McIndoe exercised the art of the plastic surgeon so skilfully that he prevented any disfigurement. Few people to-day would notice that the pilot has an artificial eye.

The miracles of healing which Sir Harold Gillies performed in the last war are being excelled in this. More than once Bennions has been heard to express his gratitude for the care and attention of the brilliant surgeon who saved him from disfigurement, but he feels sad at being grounded when he sees the Spitfires go roaring up into the blue.

Another young officer who is grateful to the doctors is Flight Lieutenant Douglas Hamilton Grice DFC[59], whose adventure started near Dover on 14 August 1940, when he with nine of his companions in arms sighted a big formation of German bombers north of Dover flying wing-tip to wing-tip. They numbered between thirty and forty, while above were as many Messerschmitts acting as escort. The British fighters although badly outnumbered, hurled themselves at the bombers and just managed to get in an attack as the Messerschmitts came diving down: in the fight which followed, Flight Lieutenant Grice's aircraft was badly hit and the cockpit soon became a mass of flames. He was then flying at 16,000 feet.

'I had either to get out or be frizzled to death,' he recorded. 'I was very nearly unconscious with the petrol fumes and heat, but I got the hood open and the Straps undone. I think the aircraft fell over and I fell out, for the next moment I knew I was in the fresh air. I held on for as long as I could without pulling the ripcord, until I started to turn head over heels, then I got so dizzy after I had dropped about 4,000 feet that I just had to pull it. I came down about five miles off Felixstowe between two trawlers steaming about 100 yards apart. I waved to them and although they saw me and one of the fishermen waved back to me, they just steamed on. Five minutes later, however, a launch appeared to pick me up.'

He had some bad moments when the rigging lines of his parachute got entangled round his legs and threatened to drown him, but luckily he was able to get free.

Echelon of Spitfires in flight shortly before the start of hostilities in WW2.

Pilots of 242 Squadron at RAF Coltishall, Norfolk in late September 1940. Standing left to right: Pilot Officer Denis W. Crowley-Milling, who remained with 242 Squadron until the spring of 1941, receiving a DFC on 11 April; Pilot Officer Hugh Tamblyn, a 23-year old ex-Defiant pilot who was decorated with the DFC by HM the King on 1 April 1941. Two days later he was shot down and killed; Pilot Officer 'Stan' Turner; Pilot Officer Norman Neil Campbell of St. Thomas, Ontario (KIA 17 October 1940); Squadron Leader Douglas Bader; Flight Lieutenant George Eric Ball; Pilot Officer Michael Giles Homer DFC (KIA 27 September 1940) and Pilot Officer Marvin Kitchener 'Ben' Brown (killed on a local flight on 21 February 1941). Ball received a bar to his DFC on 1 October 1940. At the end of January 1941 he was posted out to the Middle East, joining 73 Squadron as a flight commander in the Desert. On 12 April he flew into a sandstorm and was forced to land in Axis territory, spending the rest of the war as a PoW. On release in 1945 he joined 567 Squadron, an anti-aircraft co-operation unit, briefly, but in October was promoted Squadron Leader and given command of 222 Squadron on Meteor F.3 jets. He was killed in a flying accident on 1 February 1946, aged 27.

Behind Bader's right shoulder is Flight Lieutenant 'Willie' McKnight DFC. (KIA 12 January 1941 on a low level 'Rhubarb' operation). Sergeant John Ernest Savill sits on the wing with his left hand on the cockpit sill. Having joined the RAFVR in December 1937, Savill was called up on 1 September 1939 and he was with 151 Squadron at Martlesham Heath in July 1940, shooting a Dornier Do 17 down on 13 August. He was posted to 242 Squadron on 21 September, promoted Warrant Officer on 1 October and posted to 501 Squadron on the 12th. Early in 1941 Bader began leading squadrons of Hurricane IIs on offensive sweeps over France from North Weald. In March 1941 he was appointed Wing Commander Flying at Tangmere flying Spitfires on offensive sweeps over the continent. He had been awarded a DFC in January 1941 for ten victories and a bar to his DSO followed in July for 15 and a bar to his DFC came in September, for four more. On 9 August Bader was shot down over France on a fighter sweep and he spent the rest of the war in German prison camps until finally being released from Colditz Castle in April 1945. (IWM)

Fighter contrails over southern England in the summer of 1940.

Pilot Officers 'Red' Tobin, Vernon Charles 'Shorty' Keogh and 'Andy' Mamedoff, three of the first 'Eagles' who volunteered to fly with RAF Fighter Command during the Battle of Britain. All flew with 609 Squadron.

Group Captain Douglas Bader with Air Chief Marshal Sir Hugh 'Stuffy' Dowding, architect of the RAF victory in the Battle of Britain at the Battle of Britain commemorative flypast over London in September 1945.

Re-arming a 19 Squadron Spitfire at Duxford on 21 September 1940.

Pilots of 310 (Czech) Squadron wearing their Mae Wests and posing for the camera at Duxford in 1940. Centre, squatting, is the CO, Squadron Leader 'Bill' Blackwood, an old Etonian and an Edinburgh publisher in peacetime. To his left, arm on knee, is Flight Lieutenant Jerrard Jeffries one of the British flight commanders. On ground pointing finger at the map, cigarette in right hand, is Squadron Leader Alexander 'Sasha' Hess, one of the oldest pilots in the Battle of Britain having been born in 1899. On Blackwood's right, looking down at the map is Flight Lieutenant Gordon Leonard Sinclair, the other flight commander. (IWM)

'Eagle' pilots.

Gregory Augustus 'Gus' Daymond, born on 14 November 1920 at Great Falls, Montana. He joined the RAF and earned his wings on 15 October 1940. He was posted to 71 (Eagle) Squadron and scored 7 destroyed and 1 damaged flying Hurricane IIs and Spitfire Vbs in 1941 and 1942. He was awarded a DFC and bar. When the Eagle Squadrons transferred to the USAAF he was CO of 334th Fighter Squadron from 29 September 1942 to 3 March 1943 when he returned to the US.

James E. 'Goody' Goodson, who joined the RCAF in 1940 and in England was posted to 133 Eagle Squadron RAF before transferring to the 4th Fighter Group on 25 September 1942. Lieutenant Colonel James 'Goody' Goodson destroyed 14 enemy aircraft before being shot down by flak on 20 June 1944. He was taken prisoner.

Eagle pilot James Averill 'Jim' Clark Jr, born on 7 September 1920 in New York City marries Lady Bridget Elliott on 19 April 1944. Clark received his wings from the RAF on 20 November 1941. He joined 71 'Eagle' Squadron on 9 June 1942, which became the 334th Fighter Squadron on 15 September 1942. He was Squadron Operations Officer from 22 May 1943 and Squadron CO from 26 October 1943 to 15 March 1944. By war's end he had scored 10½ kills.

(Opposite) Famous wartime photo of Flight Lieutenant Robert Stanford Tuck (nearest to the camera) leading a formation of Spitfires of 65 Squadron. Behind are Flight Lieutenant C. Brian F. Kingcombe; Flying Officer George V. Proudman (KIA 7 July 1940); Flight Lieutenant Charles Gordon Chaloner Olive; Flying Officer John Beville Howard 'Nicky' Nicholas and Flight Sergeant Robert Reid McPherson (KIA 13 October 1941). (Charles E. Brown)

WAAF plotters and telegraphists at work in a Fighter Command Operations Room.

Feldwebel Heinz Friedrich, pilot (left) and Feldwebel George of 1/KG26 are marched away after their Heinkel 111H-3 was force landed at Burmarsh on Wednesday 11 September 1940 following an attack by Spitfire Is of 222 Squadron and anti aircraft fire near Hornchurch at about 1620 hours. The three other members of the crew were killed. The soldiers were billeted at Burmarsh Rectory nearby.

Pilots of 87 Squadron running to their Hurricanes at Vassingcourt, France during a 'Scramble'

Oberleutnant Karl Fisher of 7./27 who force-landed his damaged Bf 109E-1 'White 9' near Queen Anne's Gate in Windsor Great park on 30 September 1940 after combat with RAF fighters when escorting a bomber formation. His machine was later put on display in the local high street. Fisher was uninjured and taken prisoner.

Pilots on 19 and 616 Squadrons at Duxford. On the wing left to right: Squadron Leader Brian 'Sandy' Lane DFC 19 Squadron CO; Flight Sergeant George 'Grumpy' Unwin DFM and Flying Officer Francis Noel Brinsden, a 21-year old New Zealander from Auckland. Standing left to right: Sergeant Bernard Jennings; Flight Lieutenant Colin Hamilton Macfie on 616 Squadron; Squadron Leader Howard Frizelle 'Billy' Burton CO, 616 Squadron and Pilot Officer Phillip Howard 'Uncle Sam' Leckrone (or 'Zeke) on 616 Squadron. Leckrone, who was from Salem, Illinois was posted to 71 Squadron on 12 October 1940 to join other American volunteers in the first Eagle Squadron and was the first Eagle to be killed, on 5 January 1941 when he collided with pilot Officer Edwin 'Bud' Orbison, a 22-year old Californian, during a formation practice. (IWM)

Flight Lieutenant James Nicolson, a Hurricane pilot on 249 Squadron at Boscombe Down. He was awarded the first and only VC awarded to Fighter Command and later in the war was also decorated with the DFC.

Squadron Leader C. F. 'Bunny' Currant DFC*.

Wing Commander Mike Crossley.

On the set of *The First of the Few* shot at Ibsley in 1941 showing pilots of 118 Squadron. Left to right (standing) Squadron Leader Brian Kingcombe DFC; Flying Officer David Fulford DFC; Squadron Leader A. C. Bartley DFC (in doorway); Seated: Squadron Leader P. J. Howard-Williams DFC; Flight Lieutenant 'Jock' Gillan; Flight Lieutenant J. C. 'Robbie' Robson DFC; Wing Commander C. F. 'Bunny' Currant DFC*. In the background, two pilots from another squadron.

Flight Lieutenant Harbourne Mackay Stephen (in cockpit).

Fitters and riggers carrying out an inspection of John Simpson's Hurricane.

Members of 43 Squadron in the North of Scotland (left to right): Sergeant Buck; Pilot Officer Charles Anthony Woods-Scawen; Flight Lieutenant Caesar Hull; Flying Officer Wilkinson; Sergeant Garton.

Liam Burley Higgins, who on 14 September 1940 was killed in combat with Bf 109s. His Hurricane (P5184) crashed in flames at Swanton Bridge near Sittingbourne.

George Lott, who served on 41 Squadron in Iraq, 1935-38 and then with 11 Group, Fighter Command, until he took command of 43 Squadron in October 1939.

Heinkel 111 forced down south of Edinburgh on 28 October 1939. This was the first enemy aircraft brought down on British soil in the Second World War.

Squadron Leader Peter Townsend and Caesar Hull.

Richard Hugh Anthony 'Dickie' Lee DSO DFC, who on 18 August 1940 was last seen pursuing two Ju 88s after combat with Bf 109s north of Foulness Point and did not return.

John Simpson.

Pilot Officer Robert Laurie Lorimer was killed on 14 May 1940 at St Lupe-Terria, France, flying a Hurricane and Lieutenant H. J. 'George' Feeny, who was lost aboard the aircraft carrier *Glorious* which was returning from Norway, on 8 June 1940 while operating on 802 Squadron FAA.

Hurricanes of 85 Squadron on patrol.

Top: Spitfire pilot, Pilot Officer Eric Lock on 41 Squadron and Hurricane pilot Pilot Officer Tom Neil on 249 Squadron (left) who met in the sky over London on Sunday, 15th September 1940 and were interviewed shortly thereafter by RAF Intelligence officers.

Boulton Paul Defiants of 264 Squadron on patrol. The gallant pilots and air gunners who flew in Defiants during the Battle of Britain showed great heroism and fortitude against overwhelming odds. The rapidity with which the Luftwaffe found an answer to the Defiant was to prove the beginning of the end for the Defiant as a front-line day fighter.

Pilots of 264 Squadron after the success over Dunkirk on 29 May 1940. Pilot Officer Guy L. Hickman (KIA 31 May 1940); Flight Lieutenant 'Nick' Cooke; Squadron Leader Philip Algernon Hunter, the 27-year old Commanding Officer (KIA 24 August 1940); Pilot Officer Michael H. Young; Pilot Officer G. H. Hackwood; Pilot Officer Eric Gordon 'Dickie' Barwell; Pilot Officer Thomas; Pilot Officer David 'Bull' Whitley; Flight Sergeant Edward Rowland Thorne; Pilot Officer Desmond Haywood Sidley Kay (KIA on 9 October 1944 flying a Pathfinder Mosquito on 109 Squadron); Sergeant A. J. Lauder and Pilot Officer Richard William Stokes (killed on 29 May 1942).

Sergeant Edward Rowland Thorne and Sergeant Frederick F. James Barker of 264 Squadron.

Wing Commander (later AVM, Sir) Cecil Arthur 'Boy' Bouchier KBE CB DFC.

James Archibald Findlay 'one-arm Mac' McLachlan, who in 1941, flying Hurricane Is on 261 Squadron in Malta scored eight victories and a 'possible'. On 16 February, however, he was shot down by a 109E, bailing out with his left arm shattered by a cannon shell. His left forearm was amputated and was evacuated back to England where he had an artificial limb fitted at Roehampton. He was then posted to command 1 Squadron in November and he claimed five victories flying Night Intruder sorties over France. In June 1943 he scored the last of his 16 and 1 shared victories flying the Mustang 1A on the AFDU. He was shot down on 18 July and crash landed, critically injured. He died in a German Field Hospital on 31 July. The previous day the award of a second bar to his DFC had been announced.

One of the Italian B.R.20M bombers of 243° Squadriglia, 99° Gruppo of the Corpo Aereo Italiano shot down by 257 Squadron in the Armistice Day battle, 11 November 1940 which crashed into fir trees of Tangham Forest in Suffolk. Two of the crew were killed and four others taken prisoner. The insigne has been cut off the fins of the aircraft when this photograph was taken.

Wing Commander 'Bob' Stanford Tuck outside Buckingham Palace after receiving a second bar to his DFC, summer 1941.

A group of 257 Squadron pilots at Martlesham Heath, Suffolk in 1941. Bob Tuck is centre, wearing cap. The tousle-haired off on his right is his great friend Peter 'Cowboy' Blatchford.

Pilots on 257 Squadron posing for the camera with Italian booty taken from the downed aircraft they destroyed.

Wing Commander Gordon 'Peter' Panitz RAAF, who on 22 August 1944 was killed with his navigator, Flying Officer Williams attacking railway communications near Dijon when their Mosquito struck the side of a hill.

Pilots of 112 Squadron grouped around the nose of one of their Curtiss Tomahawks at LG 122, Egypt. Squadron Leader F. V. Morello, the CO, is fifth from left.

Russell 'Russ' Ewins and fellow pilots on 453 Squadron RAAF. Ewins was born on 18 March 1917 in Ballarat, Victoria. Before the war he trained as a mining engineer at the Ballarat School of Mines and was working at Mount Isa when he enlisted in the RAAF in 1941. He trained as a pilot in Canada under the Empire Air Training Scheme and was posted to 453 Squadron when it was re-formed at Drem, Scotland in 1942.

Wing Commander Donald George Andrews DFC of Southport, Queensland, CO, 453 Squadron RAAF (centre) with Squadron Leader E. A. R. Esau of Brisbane (left) and Squadron Leader C. W. Robertson of Jerilderie, NSW, CO of 451 Squadron RAAF, in the operations room of RAF Station Matlask in Norfolk on 14 April 1945 for one of the last aerial attacks on a V-2 site.

Pilot Officer J. P. Pfeiffer; Flight Lieutenant John Bernard William Humperson; Flight Lieutenant P. M. Gardner; Squadron Leader Michael N. Crossley; Flying Officer Douglas Hamilton 'Grubby' Grice DFC; Flying Officer A. F. Eckford; Pilot Officer Karol Pniak and Pilot Officer B. A. Wlasnowolski.

Pilots of the 334th Fighter Squadron, 4th Fighter Group at Deben in 1942. Lieutenant Colonel Chesley Peterson is in the cockpit of the Spitfire. All the pilots pictured in this photograph flew with 71 Squadron RAF.

Cleaning the cannon on a Spitfire.

Group Captain Alfred Basil 'Woody' Woodhall, fighter controller in the Battle of Britain and in Malta.

Wing Commander 'Laddie' Lucas CBE DSO* DFC. His total score was 1 and 2 shared destroyed, 1 probable, 8 and 1 shared damaged.

Wing Commander Donald George Andrews DFC of Southport, Queensland, CO, 453 Squadron RAAF.

Spitfire WX-R of 302 Polish Squadron over France.

'Johnnie' Johnson with 'Sally', his black Labrador on the cover of Illustrated magazine on 23 September 1944.

'Johnnie' Johnson in the cockpit of his Spitfire. At the end of the war, he was the RAF's officially-recognised top-scoring fighter pilot with 34 and 7 shared destroyed, 3 and 2 shared probables, 10 and 3 shared damaged, 1 shared destroyed on the ground in 515 sorties flown.Wing Commander Donald George Andrews DFC of Southport, Queensland, CO, 453 Squadron RAAF.

Spitfire Vb BM590 flown by Captain Don Willis who flew and fought with the Finns and Norwegians before joining 121 Squadron RAF and transferring with it to the 4th Fighter Group.

USAAF Spitfire V BN635 WZ-Y of the 67th Observation Group (in 309th Fighter Squadron markings) with an attendant Piper L-4 at Membury early in 1943.

Adolph Gysbert 'Sailor' Malan.

So badly burned were his face and wrists that he was in hospital a month; but he was not permitted to shave for two months, at the end of which time he possessed a most luxuriant black beard-as well as a new skin on his face which, thanks to the improved method of treating burns, was left unmarked.

Flight Lieutenant Grice, who has destroyed eight enemy aircraft; was shot down once before over France on 8 June 1940. The weather that afternoon was perfect, with brilliant sunshine and not a cloud to be seen as he turned about 4 o'clock to attack three Heinkel 111s, whose cross-fire punctured his radiator and oil system. Immediately the glycol from the radiator poured into his cockpit and nearly blinded him as he broke off the attack and turned south to land if possible behind the French lines. He glided fifteen miles before he came to earth in a little village ten miles from Rouen, to be met by a French peasant who insisted on shaking him by the hand.

Failing to find anyone in the village who could help him, he returned to his aircraft, to discover that some British gunners, who had just arrived, were willing to give him a lift to Rouen. Here he met another officer who helped himself to an abandoned car and together they drove from aerodrome to aerodrome until in two or three days they had made an adventurous passage of 400 miles across France.

At Dreux Flight Lieutenant Grice secured an aircraft in which he attempted to cross the English Channel, but the way was barred by an impenetrable fog of black smoke which had drifted from the burning oil tanks at Rouen. He was consequently compelled to change course and make a landing in Jersey, from which little island he flew to England next day to rejoin his squadron.

Endnotes Chapter 9

58 Born in 1913, George Harman Bennions came from Burslem, Stoke-on-Trent. He joined the RAF as a Halton Apprentice in 1929, graduating as an engine fitter and was subsequently recommended for the officer cadet college at Cranwell. Although he took basic flying training here, he did not become a cadet. He completed his training at 3 FTS, Grantham in 1935 and was posted to Kharmaksar, Aden as a Sergeant pilot, joining 41 Squadron flying Hawker Demons. The squadron returned to England in 1936, converting to Fury IIs and later to Spitfires. In November 1938 he was promoted Flight Sergeant. In April 1940 he was commissioned. He gained his first victories late in July 1940, but after claiming the second of these in 29 July, crashed on landing his damaged Spitfire at Manston. On 15 August he belly-landed at Rochford, slightly wounded in the heel. He was awarded a DFC on 1 October, when, after claiming his 12th and final victory [he was also credited with 5 probables and 5 damaged] he was shot down over Hatfield by Bf 109s and was badly wounded, being hit in the face and head, losing his left eye. Plastic surgery by Sir Archibald McIndoe at the Queen Victoria Hospital, East Grinstead, followed and he made a good recovery, but was thereafter only allowed to fly by day. Nicknamed 'Cyclops', he was posted to North Africa in 1943 as liaison officer with a US fighter group, but in October he was wounded again by shrapnel when a landing craft in which he was going ashore at Ajaccio, Corsica, was sunk. He left the RAF in 1946 and became a school teacher. *Aces High* by Christopher Shores and Clive Williams (Grub Street, London 1994).

59 'Grubby' Grice was born on 15 July 1919 in Wallasey Village, Cheshire. He served as a Private in the Artists Rifles, TA, before joining the RAF in November 1937 on a short service commission, being posted to 32 Squadron in August 1938. On 6 June 1940 he was shot down by return fire from a He 111 and force-landed near Rouen. He later reached the HQ of the Expeditionary Air Force at Dreux and eventually, was flown home in a Rapide to England. He received a DFC, the citation recording six victories. He was shot down by Bf 109s on 4 July and force-landed at Manston. On 15 August, having just claimed a Bf 109, he was shot down in flames, bailing out into the sea. Rescued by an MTB, he had on this occasion been burned and spent some weeks in hospital. In October he was posted back to Biggin Hill as a controller. By March 1942 he had become Senior Controller at North Weald and then in December 1943 at Tangmere. In December 1944 he moved to HQ, 11 Group, to a staff job and then in April 1945 to Fighter Command HQ. He left the RAF as a Wing Commander in April 1947, having been awarded an MBE. *Aces High* by Christopher Shores and Clive Williams (Grub Street, London 1994).

Chapter 10

'Red Knight'

Not a single sausage, score, flap or diversion of any description today. Amazing. Heavenly day too.

Squadron Leader M. N. Crossley DSO DFC, 17 August 1940.

'Michael Crossley was the CO of 32 Squadron, with its Hurricanes, when I was posted to it in 1940 after my rather miserable experiences in Poland and France. He was therefore the first CO I served under after reaching England. You could tell at once that he was a first-class officer and an excellent squadron commander, but he was also an exceptional character. He didn't have an easy job as 32 Squadron had become a very mixed lot. Apart from the unit's basic English core, which had been knocked about a bit in the fighting over France and Belgium in support of the withdrawing forces, there were seven Poles, two Czechs and a Belgian[60] *in it. Yet Michael had the personality and the leadership to blend us all together.*

'Everyone liked him both on and off duty and his good sense of humour proved a particular asset. On social occasions he was, in his quiet way, 'the life of the party' and one of his favourite sayings was, 'I don't believe in interfering with bad habits.'

'He used to drive an old Bentley and often when we were off duty he would bundle a load of pilots into the car and off we would go to see a film in nearby Andover. Not once that I can remember did we ever reach the cinema - there were too many pubs to call at along the way.

'When, eventually, Michael was promoted and had to leave us (we were then at Ibsley, another airfield in the same sector) the house where we had our Mess was renamed Crossley Towers in his honour. It was still called that years after World War II.

'Our Polish and Czech names presented quite a mouthful for the average Britisher, so Michael saw to it that each of us was given a nickname. Mine was 'Johns'. As my English happened to be a little better than the rest of my countrymen's by then I occasionally had to act as interpreter. When Michael was leading the whole squadron in the air he would give his instructions over the R/T in English. Then he would call me and say 'Johnsy, tell them' and I'd translate ...'

Michael Crossley, Etonian Diplomat by Wing Commander Karol Ranoszek[61]

To Squadron Leader Michael Nicholson Crossley DSO DFC a Hurricane pilot on 32 Squadron, the day of 8 June 1940 also brought its thrill for at that time he was a Flight Lieutenant just starting to shine over France, beginning to pile up the long list of triumphs which led him to become one of the honoured band of fighter pilots who have officially destroyed 22 enemy aircraft - not to mention at least seven others which he has damaged. Known on his squadron as 'Red

Knight', Michael Crossley was born in Halford, Warwickshire on 29 May 1912. He attended Eton College and the College of Aeronautical Engineering in Chelsea before joining the RAF in 1936 on a short service commission. He was posted to 32 Squadron on completion of training, becoming flight commander of 'Red Flight' just before the outbreak of war, hence his nickname. With the commencement of the 'Blitzkrieg' in May 1940 his unit was constantly in action, commencing on the 11th when a strafing attack on German troop-carrier aircraft at Ypenberg airfield, Holland, was undertaken. By the end of May he had claimed five victories and was awarded a DFC.[62]

'He is about 6 feet 3 inches tall' wrote David Masters, 'with the slim body of an athlete and the poise of an Etonian. Many a time he has gazed from the playing fields of Eton across the Thames to the venerable grey stones of Windsor Castle piling up in beauty on the opposite bank, but if the playing fields of Eton claim some of the credit for his victories, the College of Aeronautical Engineering which he attended at Chelsea may certainly claim more. With lightish hair, a fair clipped moustache and alert blue eyes, he has a clean-cut nose and nostril which give him an air of great keenness. Born in Warwickshire in 1912, he conceals a fearless fighting spirit under a delightful sense of humour that impels him to poke fun at himself, as some of his notes testify.

'Whoa! What a shock! Whole outfit up at 3.15 am. Going to France. Everyone amazed. Set off to France, land at Abbeville, refuel, hear dreadful stories, get very frightened, do a patrol, see nothing, feel better; do another, see nothing, feel much better; return home, feel grand.'

That is the amusing way in which this fighter pilot, who has helped to put the fear of the Royal Air Force into the Luftwaffe, jests about himself. He is one of those men whose actions speak louder than words, as many misguided Nazis have discovered.

Flying with his flight of Hurricanes to patrol between Ostend and Zeebrugge on 10 May 1940 when the Germans began their thrust into Holland and Belgium, he did not observe any of the invaders or their aircraft. And the general impression that anyone flying over the beaches of Dunkirk during the evacuation must have seen everything was not borne out by his own experiences, for he was twice sent with the squadron to Dunkirk and did not know that the beaches were crowded with men until afterwards. 'We were the top squadron and at 26,000 feet we saw nothing,' he reported when it was over. 'Of course we saw a lot of battles going on, but our job was to keep guard above and although we saw the beaches were black, we did not know what it was until after Monday June 3rd.'

To his chagrin, the first time he got a Heinkel 111 right in his sights, he discovered that his guns would not operate. But he made up for his disappointment next day on May 19th by shooting down two Messerschmitt 109s during a dog fight in which the squadron as a whole shot down seven of the enemy. On that occasion he had the strange experience, which has aroused the comment of so many fighters, of being in the midst of a mass of whirling aircraft at one minute and climbing up, after seeing his adversary crash in flames, to find the sky empty as though the previous air battle were a hallucination.

It is not easy when moving at speed among the clouds to identify the enemy in the brief glimpses that are sometimes afforded. He was once patrolling with a companion who was on guard higher up when he saw what he termed a 'big ship' going past and thought it was British. 'It's a Blenheim!' he shouted on the radio-telephone to his companion.

'Hell! It's a Junkers 88!' was the reply, as the other Hurricane dived on it, just too late to prevent it escaping into a cloud.

'Just after that another came across in the opposite direction,' commented Squadron Leader Crossley. 'I fixed him up all right. I gave him all I had. He tried to dive into the smoke coming up from Dunkirk, but it wasn't thick enough to hide him. Going in after him, I got him and saw him crash sideways into the sea in flames about a mile out east of Dunkirk.'

The great clash of his squadron came on June 8th when he was about to lead them home after their patrol. Flying at 18,000 feet, he detected what appeared to be a black mass moving toward them at a lower level. The squadron followed him down to make the attack from the stern on the back ranks of the enemy, who were stepped up in layers. He put a burst into a Heinkel 111 which flared and crashed in flames and as he broke away to climb again he found himself half way up a huge line of bombers. 'I just spotted one with a section of two and nipped in behind and gave it a clout. Its undercarriage came down and it broke out of line and went down to make a crash landing in a field. I didn't stop to see whether the crew got out. The enemy fighters were so far behind that we got the chance of attacking the bombers before they came up,' he explained.

In that battle the Hurricanes destroyed three Messerschmitt 109s and six Heinkel 111s. The two German bombers which fell before the guns of Squadron Leader Crossley brought his score to seven and led to the award of the DFC.

His experience when the Germans began to fire their first shells from the French coast over the Channel was not without its funny side. He was patrolling with 'A' flight to protect a convoy near Dover when all of a sudden he saw an enormous splash about a mile away. It was followed by three more immense white fountains which shot up out of the sea.

'Good heavens!' he thought. 'They're bombing the convoy and we're supposed to be looking after it.'

At once he bobbed up through the clouds, which were at 6,000 feet, to look for the bombers who were engaged in the dirty work. To his surprise he could see nothing at all. Very perplexed, he dived down below again to have another look for the enemy and get to grips with him. Still he could find nothing. Completely baffled, he called up Control.

'They're bombing the convoy,' he reported.

'Well, do something about it!' was the laconic reply. The Hurricanes hunted around like terriers that have lost a rat, but the rats had apparently bolted back to their holes. Squadron Leader Crossley was feeling completely mystified by the affair when Control got in touch with him. 'You can't do anything about it. They're shelling from Cape Gris Nez!' came the voice over the radio-telephone.

So the Hurricanes were obliged to sit aloft watching the gun flashes at Cape Gris Nez and marking the spots where the shells exploded just 61 seconds later. The German shells fell among the convoy, but they failed to damage a single ship.

Another day he was leading the squadron in to land at the base and actually had his landing wheels down, when he happened to look back in the direction of Dover and saw some ack-ack bursting right over the port. At once he whipped up his wheels and, shouting to the other pilots to reform, tore back to Dover.

The ships which they had so recently left were being subjected to an intense bombing attack by Junkers 87s and Messerschmitts 110s, otherwise Jaguars, which appeared to be diving down in all directions. The Hurricanes did the only thing possible; each selected an enemy and went for him. Squadron Leader Crossley singled out a Jaguar that was just starting its dive and, waiting until it was half way down, dived after it. A large black bomb dropped from the enemy and fell a hundred yards away from a ship, then the Jaguar pulled out of its dive about twenty feet from the surface and made off toward the French coast.

The squadron leader was about three-quarters of a mile behind, but with all the impetus of an 8,000 foot dive to help him he found himself steadily overtaking the Jaguar. They were travelling so fast that he dared not lose sight of the enemy for a moment to glance in the mirror to see if anyone happened to be chasing him. The slipstream of the Messerschmitt kept hitting the Hurricane and throwing it about and Squadron Leader Crossley, flying no more than ten feet from the surface, had such difficulty in keeping an even keel that he was afraid his wing might touch - which was not the sort of ending to the chase that he intended.

Gradually the Jaguar grew larger until it filled his sights. Then the eight guns of the Hurricane stuttered for three seconds and the rear-gunner of the enemy, who had opened fire from a distance of 800 yards never fired again.

As the Hurricane overhauled the enemy, the German pilot began to try to evade the pursuer by steering from side to side. As a matter of fact, instead of the German making it more difficult for the English fighter, he made it easier, for each time the Jaguar swerved it exposed a greater area and the British fighter simply sat still and pressed the button every time the jaguar crossed his sights.

Smoke began to pour out of the starboard engine of the Jaguar and suddenly it did a sharp climbing turn up to about fifty feet. As Squadron Leader Crossley was about to give him the final burst he heard another pilot yelling to him on the radio-telephone: 'Look out behind!'

Instinctively Squadron Leader Crossley nipped to the left for a few hundred yards and saw another jaguar coming up after him. As he flashed across the nose of the jaguar in turning, he heard an ominous bang. Then the jaguar roared past with the other Hurricane hard on its tail. For a moment Squadron Leader Crossley wondered what had happened to his own Jaguar and then he saw a large white circle of foaming water which slowly changed to an oily patch to mark the grave of the enemy. On landing he found that a bullet had punctured one of his tyres and missed his ankle by inches.

They were a happy set in his squadron, each of whom was known to the others by a 'trade' name, among them being; 'The Mandarin', 'Jackdaw', 'Grubby', Hector, Pete B,[63] 'Polly',[64] 'Humph', Jimmy, David, while they dubbed Squadron Leader Crossley the 'Red Knight'. They were a deadly team which exacted heavy penalties from the Luftwaffe every time they could get to grips and the notes of the leader were expressive. The 'Mandarin' was Squadron

Leader John Worrall, who was born on 9 April 1911. He entered RAF Cranwell on January 1930. On 19 July 1940 Worrall, seeing a number of Ju 87s dive-bombing Dover Harbour, led his squadron through the anti-aircraft barrage to the enemy aircraft which turned tail and fled. The Hurricanes were then set on by twelve Bf 109s and in the dogfight which followed one of the Hurricanes was shot down in flames. The pilot bailed out and admitted to Dover Hospital. On 20 July Worrall led eight Hurricanes on 32 Squadron straight through some 109s to shoot down two and cripple four dive-bombers below. One Hurricane flown by a FAA loan pilot was lost. Worrell made a forced landing near Hawkinge.

'Jackdaw' was Victor George Daw, who was born in Portsmouth, joining the RAF on a short service commission in November 1938. He was posted to 32 Squadron on completion of training, seeing action with this unit over France and Dunkirk during May and June 1940 and being awarded a DFC on 25 June, which he received from HM King George VI two days later. On 25 July he force-landed his Hurricane near Dover following combat with Bf 109s and was slightly injured. Later he was posted to 145 Squadron and then in July 1941 he went to 242 Squadron as a flight commander.[65]

'Grubby' was Flight Lieutenant Douglas Hamilton Grice, born at Wallasey, Cheshire on 15 June 1919 - the day on which Alcock and Brown made the first successful trans-Atlantic flight. Deprived by ill health of a formal education, young Douglas was tutored privately. Subsequently, after a spell as a machine-gunner in the Artists Rifles, he was granted a RAF short service commission in December 1937. On June 6 1940 he was crossing the French coast when he saw a gaggle of Heinkel 111 bombers. But before he could engage, he was attacked by four Me109's. 'I let them get within 500 yards or so' he said 'and then did an Immelman turn - a half loop and roll off the top - so that I could meet them head on'. After shaking off the fighters Grice attacked the German bombers until return fire badly damaged his Hurricane and wrecked his engine. After gliding 15 miles he belly-landed in a field near Rouen. He hitched a lift with a passing RAF padre to an airfield at Dreux, from where he was dispatched home, making a stopover on Jersey, as a passenger in a de Havilland Dragon Rapide. Back at Biggin he learned he had been awarded a DFC [66]

'Later we intercepted a large number of assorted Huns' wrote Crossley. 'The following tipped stuff into the Channel - Hector, Pete B, Sergeant Higgins,[67] 'Humph', 'Red Knight'. The 'Mandarin' converted three non-smoking Ju 87s into smoking 87s but earned the attention of at least four squadrons of 109s to such an extent he couldn't make the 'drome. He force-landed in a field and his aircraft was burnt out.'[68]

'Humph' was either Humphrey a'Beckett Russell, who claimed a Bf 110 on 18 August 1940 when a cannon shell exploded in his cockpit and he bailed out, seriously wounded in the leg (in April 1941 he took command of 32 Squadron, was shot down in May 1944 and became a PoW) or John Bernard William Humpherson, born in Enfield, Middlesex, who joined the RAF on a short service commission in October 1936, being posted to 32 Squadron in August 1937. In September 1939 he transferred to 607 Squadron which went to France, where in May 1940 he was to claim his first victory. On return to England he went back to 32 Squadron, being engaged over France again at once. On 23 August he was again posted to 607 Squadron, where he received a DFC on 30th and became a flight commander on 3 September. His total score stood at 5 destroyed, 2 probables and 3 damaged. On 7 May 1941 he was posted to 90 Squadron which was just forming with the first of the Boeing Fortress Is to be received by the RAF. On 22 June however, before operations had commenced, Fortress AN522 broke up in the air and crashed at Catterick Bridge, North Yorkshire. Humpherson, aged 24 at the time, was killed with his crew.

Of Monday 12 August Crossley wrote: 'Coo! What a blitz! Patrol base. All of a sudden we sight a cloud of Huns and move unwillingly towards them, but sight another cloud complete with mosquitoes a bit nearer; we move even more unwillingly towards them and attack. Everyone takes a swing at the fifty Dornier 215s and the Messerschmitt 109s. Hell of a lot of zigging. Very hectic. Day's bag nine 109s, three 215s.'

His subtle sense of humour was emphasized when he wrote that the fighter pilots who were spoiling all the time for a fight moved 'unwillingly' toward the enemy, although top speed was much too slow to please them. A squadron that slapped down 12 of the enemy when it was 'unwilling,' should give Goering a headache when it was 'willing'!

Once when they were caught in a bombing raid on one of the aerodromes a pilot dived into some hay for cover. He was proceeding to pull it carefully over him when he suddenly concluded that it did not offer much protection, so he made a dash for the shelter. His escapade amused the mess for many a day!

They were one of the squadrons which helped to make the Germans pay so dearly for their surprise attack on Croydon on Thursday 15 August 1940. If ever Squadron Leader Crossley and his fighter pilots touched the peak of excitement, it must have been that afternoon, which he afterwards referred to as 'a remarkable blitz afternoon.' Few will disagree with him. They started by chasing some Germans up to Harwich, where they had a mix-up with Messerschmitt 109s. Returning to their base to refuel, they were ordered down to Portsmouth to help beat off a very heavy attack by German bombers, after which they flew to base to refuel again. They were then sent away to patrol off Dover and had climbed to 10,000 feet in the neighbourhood of Maidstone when the Control called them up and told them an attack on Croydon was pending. They needed no second invitation. Up to then they had destroyed six German aircraft that day and were keen to add to their score.

'We turned round and beat it for Croydon as hard as we could. Sure enough when we approached I saw a large party in progress,' recorded Squadron Leader Crossley. 'Masses of Me 110s were dive bombing the place. As they did not appear to notice our approach, I steered straight past them, with the object of getting between them and the sun. This was successful and we charged at them. I put a long burst into the first one I saw and he promptly caught fire and went down in flames. Then I saw another detach itself and make off, so I made after it and gave it a long burst, at which the starboard engine caught fire. I broke away and the Mandarin gave it a long burst and it altered course inland as if looking for somewhere to land. I nipped in and gave it another bang and as I broke off I saw the starboard airscrew revolving slowly and then stop. Another burst from the 'Mandarin' and one of the crew bailed out and the aircraft crashed in flames in a wood near Sevenoaks.'[69]

In that running fight lasting no more than two minutes the antagonists covered about twelve miles.

That day the fighters led by Squadron Leader Crossley knocked down thirteen enemy aircraft out of the sky. It was an unlucky number - for the Germans.

Endnotes Chapter 10

60 Pilot Officer Count Rodolphe Ghislain Charles de Hemricourt de Grunne. Born in Brussels on 18 November 1911, de Hemricourt began his military service in the cavalry and he also obtained a civil pilot's licence. In December 1936 he attended the Escuela Tablada (Flying School) in Seville and fought on the Nationalist side in the Spanish Civil War flying the Fiat CR32 and scoring destroyed ten Nationalist aircraft by January 1939. He returned to Belgium and after being put in the infantry secured a transfer to flying duties, piloting Hurricanes. After the Belgian capitulation he withdrew to France and later left for England, on 20 June 1940. After training at 7 OTU he was posted to 32 Squadron flying Hurricanes. He claimed two victories but was shot down on 18 August and was seriously burned. On release from hospital in February 1941 he went to Portugal to recuperate. Returning to England he joined 609 Squadron on 28 April 1941. On 21 May he was shot down over the Channel. He bailed out over the Goodwin Sands but was not found. *Aces High* by Christopher Shores and Clive Williams (Grub Street, London 1994).

61 Quoted in *Thanks for the Memory; Unforgettable Characters In Air Warfare 1939-45* by Laddie Lucas (Stanley Paul & CO 1989).

62 *Aces High* by Christopher Shores and Clive Williams (Grub Street, London 1994).

63 'Pete B' was Peter Malam Brothers, born at Prestwich, Lancashire, on 30 September 1917. He learned to fly at the age of 16, joining the RAF in January 1936. After training, he joined 32 Squadron in October of that year, and had become a flight commander by late 1938. Active throughout the spring and mid summer of 1940 with this unit, he was posted to 257 Squadron on 9 September, having been awarded a DFC in August. He was rested in January 1941, becoming an instructor at 55 OTU, but in June was promoted Squadron Leader and formed 457 Squadron RAAF on Spitfires. A year later he was posted to command 602 Squadron, which was just about to withdraw to Scotland although it returned briefly to Biggin Hill in August for the Dieppe operation. In October he returned south to lead the Tangmere Wing, receiving a Bar to his DFC in June 1943. At the end of July he was posted to 61 OTU and then in November to HQ, 10 Group. He returned to operations at the head of the Exeter Wing in 1944, later leading the Culmhead Wing during the Normandy Invasion. His total score was 16 destroyed, 1 probable, 3 damaged.

64 'Polly', either Pilot Officer John L. 'Polly' Flinders or Sergeant Reginald James Parrott, who was killed aged 25, on 257 Squadron on 5 May 1941. (His parents, Herbert and Ethel Parrott were killed by enemy action on 14 January 1945). Flinders, born 3 August 1917 in Chesterfield, Derbyshire, joined the RAF in January 1936. As a Sergeant pilot was posted to 74 Squadron before being commissioned and posted to 32 Squadron in April 1940, serving with that unit until 3 March 1941. He was posted to 55 OTU as an instructor until August 1941. He later instructed in Canada, returning to England in March 1945. After retirement he emigrated to Canada in 1978 to be near his family in Ontario. He died there in 1998. *Aces High.*

65 Rested on 8 August, he did not return to operational flying. He was promoted Squadron Leader during July 1944 and in June 1945 was awarded an AFC. He remained in the RAF after the war as a Flight Lieutenant, again becoming a Squadron Leader in August 1947, but was killed in a flying accident on 24 March 1953.

66 On 15 August 1940, having already scored eight victories, Grice was flying 'tail-end Charlie' of ten Hurricanes, intercepting enemy raiders making for the port of Harwich. He had just reported a group of Bf 110s flying in a defensive circle overhead when an incendiary bullet flashed over his left wrist and into the instrument panel. Piercing the fuel tank behind the instrument panel, the

incendiary set the Hurricane on fire. Grice was engulfed in flames and, as the fighter turned over, fell out. Although Grice was unaware of it at the time, his prolonged dip in the sea was a boon: the 'briney' aided the healing process of the burns Grice had suffered to the face and the wrists. Sir Archibald McIndoe, the celebrated RAF consultant in plastic surgery, gave Grice the good news: 'You're a lucky chap, because you are going to look handsome again without any help from me. I won't need a piece of your bottom for skin grafting. Thanks to you and others rescued from the sea we have discovered that a brine bath is the best treatment for a bad burns case'.

Once operational again, Grice was briefed on the morning of 27 June to escort Bristol Blenheim bombers on an operation. On his return he and his fellow pilot Jimmy Davies (who would later be shot down and killed) were decorated by King George VI. On 4 July Grice was patrolling with 32 Squadron over Deal when he was attacked by three 109s. 'There was a loud bang and the controls suddenly felt slack. I switched off and belly-landed, not far from Sandwich golf course'. To his astonishment Grice was greeted by an Army officer who had served with him as a private in the Artists Rifles. After being shot down for the third time and recovery in hospital, Grice served briefly as a 'Jim Crow' at Gravesend. This entailed observing and reporting enemy formations. Finding that his nerve had deserted him, Grice was then invited by his namesake Group Captain Dickie Grice, Biggin Hill station commander, to return as an operations room controller. This enabled him to further his romance with Pam Beecroft, a Biggin WAAF cypher officer, whom he married in October 1941. Following further fighter controller and staff appointments, Grice, by then a wing commander, resigned his commission in 1947.

67 William Burley Higgins was born at Hodthorpe, Whitwell, Derbyshire in 1914 and educated at Brunts Grammar School, Mansfield. He trained as a teacher and taught at his old junior school at Whitwell. Higgins joined the RAFVR about October 1938 as an airman u/t pilot and carried out his elementary flying training at Tollerton. Called up on 1st September 1939, he completed his training at 5 FTS Sealand and joined 32 Squadron at Biggin Hill on 2 July 1940. Next day he shared a Do17; on the 20th destroyed a Bf 110 and on 12 and 24 August he shot down Bf 109s. On 9 September Higgins was posted to 253 Squadron at Kenley. He shot down a Bf 109 on the 11th. On the 14th he was killed in combat with Bf 109s. His Hurricane (P5184) crashed in flames at Swanton Bridge near Sittingbourne. He is buried in the family plot at St. Lawrence's churchyard, Whitwell. Also buried there is his brother Michael. On 6 October 1961 he was captain of Dakota G-AMSW of Derby Aviation en route from Gatwick to Perpignan in the south of France. In poor weather and probably off course it struck a mountain (Le Canigou) in the Pyrenees. All 34 passengers and crew were killed.

68 The diary did not reveal that Sub Lieutenant Geoffrey G. R. Bulmer, a naval pilot on loan to 32 Squadron had been killed on 20 July. He was shot down over Dover, bailed out into the sea but drowned. They were, as the Squadron diarist noted, 'blitzy days'.

69 The 'Mandarin' (Squadron Leader Worrall, who was awarded the DFC on 6 August) was awarded a half share in the Dornier Do 17Z-2 of 6./KG3 on 15 August. Leutnant Kringler and two of the crew were killed. Late that month Worrall went to the Control Room at RAF Biggin Hill. In March 1944 Wing Commander Worrall was SASO/HQ No.216 Group. In July 1945 he became Senior Personnel Staff Officer at HQ, Transport Command. He continued to serve in the RAF after the war, retiring on 1 January 1963. Air Vice Marshal John Worrall CB DFC died on 14 January 1988. Crossley was credited with two Ju 88s and a Do 217 on 15 August. During the Battle of Britain he was to claim 12 and one shared during five days of action between 12-25 August; receiving a DSO on 20 August. He was promoted to command the squadron on 16th, but two days later was shot down by Bf 109s, bailing out unharmed over the Herne Bay area. He was shot down again on the 24th, crashing at Lyminge after an engagement over Folkestone; again he escaped unhurt. Following the fighting on 25th, the squadron was withdrawn to the North to rest. His score stood at 20 and 2 shared destroyed, 1 unconfirmed destroyed and 1 damaged. He remained with the unit until April 1941, when he was sent to the USA to act as a test pilot for the British Air Commission there. On his return to the UK in 1943 he was sent to lead the Detling Wing, having been promoted Wing Commander in September 1942. Now however, he contracted tuberculosis which put an end to operational flying. He was awarded an OBE in 1946 and released from the RAF during that year. He died in September 1987.

Chapter 11

'Archie'[70]

David Masters

'He was the little Scots fighting man of the past, the Alan Breck build, with bonnet cocked against the world...'

A. B. Austin in *Fighter Command,* published in 1941.

As a boy, Archie McKellar had two ambitions - to become a plasterer and to fly. Born at Paisley in 1912, he was the only child of John McKellar who had himself served his apprenticeship' as a plasterer before launching into business as a contractor and Archie McKellar was determined to learn his father's trade and follow in his footsteps. No family could have been more united, but when Archie McKellar left Shawlands Academy his father was anxious for him to go on to the university to continue his education and adopt a professional career.

'I want to be a plasterer, Dad,' Archie said.

'But a good education will make life 'so much easier for you,' his father urged him. As a compromise the lad went into a stockbroker's office after leaving school, but he did not like it.

'I want to be a plasterer, Dad,' he repeated to his father.

'But it's very hard manual labour and if you join the trade you will have to serve your apprenticeship and get the same pay as any other boy;' his father insisted. 'If you go to the university, a good education will make life much easier for you.'

'Education is only knowing the world and its ways, Dad. I want to be a plasterer,' Archie pleaded, so at last his father gave way. Making out his indentures; Mr. McKellar bound his son to serve as an apprentice for five years, during which time Archie McKellar worked on the same terms as the other boys and neither received nor asked one special privilege from his father.

He was perfectly happy. It was never necessary to call him in the morning and not once was he late for work. Every day before dressing he spent half an hour doing physical exercises, with the result that although short in stature he developed great physical strength and endurance.

Wing Commander W. M. Churchill DSO DFC[71] who became his commanding officer when Archie McKellar transferred from 602 'City of Glasgow' Squadron to 605 'County of Warwick' Squadron, used to refer to him as the 'pocket Hercules' while other companions in the Royal Air Force called him the 'pocket battleship,' so compact and strong was he.

Keen on all forms of sport, he played rugby for his school, enjoyed a swim, liked a gallop on a horse, drove a good ball in a game of golf and displayed a keen eye and quick muscular reactions at tennis and squash. Many a time when he gazed out of the office window at the works during the lunch hour and saw the schoolboys playing cricket with three stumps chalked upon the wall to serve as the wicket, he would go out and show them how to bowl. The boys doted on him. He was so vital, so happy, so friendly that everyone liked him.

More than once his father noticed that he was immersed in books on flying, that he was very interested in the life stories of the great pilots of the last war, Ball and McCudden, Bishop, Mannock and the rest. After work was finished, Archie would often go out on the moors near Glasgow to watch with delight the gulls and peewits and other birds flying around. He studied their actions closely and used to tell his father how they zoomed and dived and banked, but it was all incomprehensible to his father.

Then one day Archie came in, his blue eyes sparkling with joy, his voice full of excitement. 'I can get into 602 Squadron!' he exclaimed. It was the City of Glasgow Auxiliary Squadron of the Royal Air Force. His father was horrified. 'It's a dangerous game, flying, I can't let you do it,' he replied.

'I want to learn to fly, Dad,' pleaded the son.

'It's too dangerous. I can't allow it.'

In vain Archie McKellar pleaded. 'All right, when I can afford to pay for lessons, I will learn to fly,' he said and for weeks refused to speak to his father, although they were so deeply attached.

During the last year of his apprenticeship he acted as working foreman for his father and had fifty men working under him, so he gained experience of handling men before he joined the Royal Air Force. Directly his apprenticeship was terminated, he remained in his father's business as working foreman and eventually became general foreman.

He kept his word. As soon as he could afford to pay for lessons, he secretly joined the Scottish Flying Club and in due course gained his pilot's certificate. They knew nothing about it at home and he was flying for some time before his father discovered it. But the bonds between them were so close that the fact did not disturb the happiness of their family life.

Every week-end when Archie McKellar went flying he flew over the house and waggled the wings of his aircraft in greeting to his mother. He dived so low that more than once it seemed that he would strike the chimneys. 'I'll have those chimney pots off yet, mother,' he used to say jokingly when he got home.

So far as I can gather, his entry into 602 'City of Glasgow' Squadron was due to the presence of the Duke of Hamilton at a meeting held by the Scottish Flying Club. Apparently the Duke of Hamilton, who was the Commanding Officer of 602 Squadron, was impressed with the skill and verve of Archie McKellar, who was granted a commission as Pilot Officer in 1936. He was promoted Flying Officer in 1938 and was at once called up for active service when war broke out.[72]

He proved himself after his course of training to be a superb pilot who could fly the Hurricane and Spitfire with equal confidence and zest. 'A Spitfire's just like a soft-mouthed, high-spirited thoroughbred, Dad!' he once told his father.

His hour of glorious life lasted from 3 September 1939 until 1 November 1940 and he enjoyed every moment of it. His father wrote of him: 'He had a happy and cheery word for everybody, rich or poor, young or old, he loved them all and they all loved him.' My experience confirms it, for I have never heard anyone spoken of with such deep affection as Archie McKellar by his friends and fellow officers in the Royal Air Force. He was a little man, about 5 feet 3 inches tall, but he possessed a great heart and unflinching courage.

The Scots have a reputation for being dour and taciturn and impassive. But Archie McKellar was the reverse of this. He was demonstrative and voluble. 'He would keep up a running commentary over the radio-telephone for miles from the time we first sighted the enemy until we made contact,' Wing Commander Churchill once remarked. As for his kindness, Squadron Leader Robert Findlay Boyd DFC and Bar who was with him in 602 Squadron, said: 'He would share his last ten shilling note with you.'[73]

He radiated cheerfulness, swept away depression. To be with him was as stimulating as a glass of champagne. His popularity is proved by the fact that everyone called him Archie. He had the happy knack of making friends. When the other apprentices in his early days took advantage of his small size, he promptly learned to box so that he could take care of himself.

Always he was immaculate. He looked after his body as carefully as an athlete and kept himself in the pink of condition. No matter what happened, he shaved and groomed himself every morning, even during the Battle of Britain, when many a fighter pilot in other squadrons went unshaved for two or three days. He insisted on his squadron following his example. 'If I have to die, I want to die clean,' he remarked to his colleague, Squadron Leader 'Bunny' Currant DFC.[74]

He was a connoisseur of good food and good wine who smoked a pipe and enjoyed a good cigar. 'You can tell Uncle Archie that I shall be looking for that box of cigars,' he wrote to his mother in a letter describing how he shot down three of the enemy in a raid on Newcastle.[75]

'Dearest Little Mother, I am very well and very pleased with myself. On Thursday at 12 o' clock I was sent off with my flight to patrol Newcastle at 20,000 feet. We all arrived safely and remained there until 1.30, when I saw seventy to eighty Nasties in one big formation followed by a second formation of twenty-to-thirty. They were approaching Newcastle from the south. I whipped into them with my flight. I got three down, with one possible and the rest of the boys got five down with seven possible - possible being when the Hun breaks away from the formation with engines out or flames coming, but is not seen to crash. By this time there was a lot more fighters, so everyone gave the Nasties the fright of their lives. I was very proud. The Air Vice-Marshal came along and congratulated the Flight on their good show. It really was, as the majority were all new and inexperienced. Two of the boys were shot down, but without damage to one and only scalp and head wounds to the other, so I reckon it was pretty good going. Unfortunately I caught my little gold bracelet on one of the clips of my aircraft during the show and broke it and it is lost, so if Dad is feeling pleased about this news I would like another one, please!!! All my love, Sonnie.'

He scored his initial success when he helped to destroy the first enemy to be brought down off the British coast, during a raid on Rosyth of which he wrote: 'Spitfires full out, 300 mph. 350, 380, 400 and there was the enemy. I picked mine and attacked. I saw him lurch, a flame from his engine which went out and then I saw his tracer bullets coming back at me and I broke away like mad. By this time George who had lost his in clouds joined me and we started to beat him up together. The Hun trying to dodge into the clouds all the time, but one of us always headed him off. At last the poor devil crashed into the water. As there was a destroyer near, I circled round them for a little. The pilot was saved, but all the other three had been shot dead.'

His sense of humour peeps out at the end of the letter.

'P.S. There is a lovely line in to-day's *Scottish Express* about a sheep farmer and a plasterer shooting down a Hun.'[76]

Many a time he went up to practise dog fighting with Wing Commander Douglas Farquhar, who exercised a good deal of tact in persuading Archie not to transfer to another squadron where the prospects of fighting seemed rosier. Those early months of enforced idleness when he was so anxious to get at the enemy were as irksome to Archie McKellar as to other fighter pilots. Fortunately he took the advice of Wing Commander Farquhar, who wrote: 'I am glad I was successful and that as a result of staying in 602 he was the first fighter pilot to fire at an enemy machine, took part in the destruction of the first enemy raiding bomber and led the attack on the first enemy bomber to be brought down on land - a magnificent record. He did an enormous amount of flying and his successes were due to careful preparation and thought.'[77]

The way he transferred to 605 Squadron discloses his agile brain and how swiftly he saw and seized a chance. When Wing Commander W. M. Churchill DSO DFC[78] went to Drem to reform 605 Squadron, he was rather gloomy at leaving his old squadron. Preoccupied by the task in hand, he strolled for the first time into the mess where he was promptly approached by a sprightly little man with a twinkle in his eye and every brown hair of his head most immaculately brushed into place. 'I'm sorry to hear that my services will not be required as your squadron leader,' the smiling Scot remarked in the friendliest manner. 'I understand you are waiting for another member of your old squadron. It was just the job I wanted.'

A telephone call to the Air Officer Commanding and Archie McKellar had got the job and started his friendship with Wing Commander Churchill as well as with another keen pilot, Gerry Edge.[79] 'From that day on began the most charming triangular friendship I have ever known,' the Wing Commander wrote. 'I used to think that I was a good Flight Commander, but those two boys were marvellous. They used to conspire together to think up new ideas for the squadron and to make things easy for me.'

Notwithstanding that Archie McKellar was highly-strung, he had wonderful self-control. Always he was thinking of the squadron, how to improve them and weld them into a finer team. In the end he achieved such a high degree of understanding that he had only to give a flick of his wings and the boys knew at once what he wanted and would automatically take up position.

One extraordinary thing which he did at Drem was considered by the technical experts to be impossible. 'He put a permanent wave into the wings of a Spitfire,' is the way Wing Commander Churchill described it.

Diving upside down out of a cloud at terrific speed and finding he could not get out of the dive in the normal manner, he managed to roll over out of the dive, placing such a strain on the aircraft that he actually bent the wings. The case was so remarkable that they had the test pilot up specially to examine it and see what the pilot had done.

For a small man, the fighter pilot had a loud voice and when he grew very excited his Glasgow accent became so broad that many of his English friends found it difficult to understand him. He was very loyal, very truthful and had intense likes and dislikes - there was no middle course for him. He was intuitive to a degree and had a pretty sense of humour. He sensed if anyone was a bit depressed and would do his best to cheer them.

'Let's go to Edinburgh for a dinner,' he would remark.

After one such party which he arranged for two of his superior officers, they found the police had let the air out of their motor tyres. The senior officer, who prided himself on his fitness, got out the pump. Archie, who had no intention of doing the work, at once volunteered as the officer started pumping. 'Oh, sir, do let me help,' he kept saying politely, while his senior went on pumping to show how fit he was. The sight of the senior exerting himself to blow up the tyres while the fighter pilot looked on has raised many a chuckle since.

There was one bombing raid which sent Squadron Leader Currant and three of his colleagues dropping to the floor to gain what protection they could from flying glass by pulling tub chairs over their backs. There they crouched, like dogs in kennels, while bombs exploded and shook the place. During a temporary lull the door suddenly opened and they looked up to observe the ashen face of a sergeant with a mop of red hair staring at them as though he could hardly believe his eyes. They looked at him, then at each other as they crouched on their hands and knees with the chairs over their backs and even the exploding bombs failed to stop their roars of laughter. Never had they seen anything so ridiculous as the figures they cut at that moment.

Once Archie McKellar received a bottle of very special whisky from

Edinburgh, which led him to expatiate upon it and promise his friend Bunny Currant the finest drop of whisky he had ever tasted in his life. That evening the whisky was brought out and his friends beamed in anticipation as they took their tumblers and raised them to their lips.

'It's grand stuff!' said Archie, helping himself.

'Jolly good,' said Squadron Leader Currant, looking curiously at his companion.

'Very!' agreed that gentleman with the utmost courtesy.

Then Archie took his drink and exploded.

Someone had purloined three-quarters of the whisky and filled the bottle with water.

He had a kind word for all ranks and would stick up for anything which he thought right. 'You've no business to tick off my flight sergeant like that,' he once said to Wing Commander Churchill after the latter had given the flight sergeant an admonishment which Archie considered was undeserved.

Strangely enough, although he was fond of shooting and had a lovely sporting gun, he generally missed his birds. Yet when it came to shooting down Huns he was deadly. In this respect he was rather like Squadron Leader Currant who received the DFC and Bar for shooting down so many Huns, yet when he goes up for a practise shoot at the drogue towed by another aircraft he can seldom hit it. More than once he has been made to feel an awful fool by a pupil who has riddled the drogue with bullets while he has been shooting into the blue, yet he has no difficulty in hitting the Germans when he is after them.

Keen as were the other pilots in the squadron, Archie McKellar was sometimes a little too keen for them, especially when they had been patrolling at 28,000 feet and were frozen stiff and anxious to get down. He always wanted to stay up a little longer in the hope of catching the enemy.

'Come on, pancake!' the Controller would remark over the radio-telephone.

'Can't we stay up another ten minutes?' Archie would inquire and generally got his way.

The sight of the blazing docks on the Thames, when the enemy managed to set an oil tank alight by day to serve as a beacon for them at night, filled him with fury. 'We must do something about it,' he insisted. Every night he would volunteer to go up. Once he went up without any lights at all and landed safely. But in the end he got his enemy at night. He had been flying around for an hour when he heard the voice of the Controller calling to him to land.

'I've got to get a Hun tonight. I'll give you a bottle of champagne if you put me on to one,' he replied.

'All right' came the voice of the Controller, 'I'll give you a vector.'

The Controller duly gave the Scot a vector; otherwise the course which he hoped would bring him into touch with an enemy. 'There's a Hun caught by the searchlights over there,' he remarked.

'Fine! I'll go over,' replied Archie.

He went and got his Hun.

The Controller got his bottle of champagne.

This phenomenal little fighter pilot shot down for certain twenty enemy aircraft, besides several others that were probably destroyed.[80] During the great air battles over London in September 1940 he shot down a German a day for eight days in succession.[81] His most extraordinary feat, however, was the destruction of three Heinkel 111s - 'great, fat, lazy bombers,' as he used to call them - in one long burst.

It was on 9 September 1940 that Wing Commander Churchill led his squadron [605] of fighters into the air from Croydon at 9.30 in the morning to come to grips with the enemy once more. It was a beautiful day, with some cloud at 4,000 feet and a clear sky above. Heading south, the Spitfires climbed steadily to intercept at 20,000 feet.

They had reached 15,000 feet when the voice of Archie McKellar came to his leader over the radio-telephone. 'Enemy ahead, sir,' shouted the Scotsman as he caught sight of a cloud of thirty Heinkel 111s with an escort of fifty Messerschmitt 109s about 4,000 feet above them and twenty Messerschmitt 110s to guard the flank.

At that distance Wing Commander Churchill could see no more than six Messerschmitt 109s and at once went in to draw them off with his section in order to give the other fighters a chance to get at the bombers which Archie McKellar told him were present. Directly he had drawn off the first batch of Messerschmitts and seen them go flashing past, he saw six more and as he was forcing them away a bullet grazed his leg and sent him spinning down out of the formation.

By the time he recovered, he had lost the bombers and his squadron, but he headed after them all out on the course they were following. To his amazement, he soon observed the Heinkels still flying in the same direction as though unaware of the British fighters who were stalking them.

As he flew to overtake them, he saw Archie McKellar's section of three turn up sun and swing round to the attack. At that very moment the Heinkels turned into the sun straight toward the Spitfires which were concealed by the glare. The Germans were, in the parlance of the fighters, 'a piece of cake.' No deflection was necessary at all. Archie McKellar, seeing the leading Heinkel in front of him, just pressed the button on his control column and squirted at it and Wing Commander Churchill watched it blow up in the air and knock the wing off the port Heinkel, which immediately went down just as the starboard Heinkel turned straight into Archie McKellar's stream of bullets and got what is known in the service as a 'gutser.' Black smoke began to pour from the engines, the nose of the bomber reared up for a moment and then the third Heinkel went down on its back.

'It was a most marvellous show,' said the commander, who saw it as though he had been sitting in the front seat of the stalls. When he got back to base, he found his pilots at the dispersal point chattering like a lot of magpies, with Archie McKellar, who had knocked down a Messerschmitt

109 on the way home, telling them all about it. To destroy four enemy aircraft in one sortie was indeed a triumph for the fighter pilot, a feat which cost him 1,200 rounds of ammunition. His leader was able to confirm the destruction of the three Heinkels in one burst of fire: But unhappily the triumph was marred by the loss of a friend during the fight and Archie McKellar never referred to it again.

'I'm sorry I made such a mess of it,' said Wing Commander Churchill apologetically.

'Your sight is no good. You are too old - you're an old man!' exclaimed Archie McKellar - which must have been rather a shock for a young man of thirty-two.

'I'm going on flying,' the commander replied.

'You'll simply be shot down,' was the Scotsman's blunt reply.[82]

'All right, I'll let you lead,' was the rejoinder and the next day and thereafter Archie McKellar led 605 Squadron most brilliantly. Keen sight to the fighter is as important as it is to the peregrine falcon. Without it, neither can detect their prey. The fighter risks being shot down and the falcon risks starvation, so defective sight threatens death to both. Archie McKellar knew this and used to lie upon his bed with pads of cotton wool, soaked in a special lotion, over his eyes in order to preserve his sight.

He refused to go on leave and as the strain mounted during the Battle of Britain he and Squadron Leader Currant[83] began to get on each other's nerves. 'You're due for a week's leave, Bunny,' said Archie to his friend. The latter protested, but the Scotsman had his way.

So Squadron Leader Currant went on leave and when it was over, on the morning of 1 November 1940 he returned to the station and found Archie shaving in the bathroom.

'Had a good time?' inquired Archie.

'Fine, thanks,' was the reply.

'What are you doing?' asked Archie. 'I'm going on patrol.'

'You can't go on patrol directly after leave. Wait here and I'll see you when I come back,' said the cheery Scotsman.

He went out and never returned. At half-past seven on that morning of November 1st, the day after the Battle of Britain was officially ended, he was killed.[84]

To the general public his name was unknown, but in the Royal Air Force he was recognized as one of the finest fighter pilots of them all, a kind and generous man who made friends wherever he went, one whose skill and valour were an inspiration to all who knew him.

Sir Archibald Sinclair, the Secretary of State for Air, will not soon forget the vivid personality of Archie McKellar, as he mentioned during his visit to Glasgow when Sir Patrick Dollan, the Lord Provost, welcomed him on 16 January 1941. 'How greatly are the achievements of your gallant, your magnificent 602 Squadron regarded by your comrades in the Royal Air Force!

Apart from those officers who remain with the squadron now, all the officers of this splendid squadron are now serving as squadron leaders or wing commanders in the Royal Air Force. It is a glorious record is the record of 602 Squadron... Not long ago I visited a fighter squadron which was taking part during the dark days in the battle of this island. That squadron had lost its leader in an air fight - and they felt the loss. He had been wounded in combat and had been withdrawn from service. I found in his place, taking the air with daring and resolve, proving himself a leader among leaders, a young Scot. His name was McKellar. He had come from the City of Glasgow Squadron to lift up this squadron in its dark hour and to carry it on to fresh victories and achievement by his spirit. It was quite apparent to me that he had the whole squadron with him. He was regarded with the greatest admiration and affection by his officers. I will never forget the impression he made upon me when I saw him.'

Archie McKellar was a true champion of Democracy, a man of the people who died for the people. In thirteen months his outstanding abilities lifted him to the foremost ranks of the fighter pilots of the Royal Air Force and won for him the DSO, the DFC and Bar. His straight shooting helped to defeat the Germans in the Battle of Britain and his influence will help to deal the Nazis the mortal blow that will save Mankind.

Endnotes Chapter 11

70 Squadron Leader Archibald Ashmore 'Archie' McKellar DSO DFC and Bar.

71 Walter Myers Churchill from Leamington, Warwickshire, was born in Amsterdam, Holland on 24 November 1907. He joined 605 Squadron, Auxiliary Air Force, in 1931 and was commissioned in January 1932. He went onto the Reserve in 1937, but was recalled when the unit was mobilized in August 1939 and in November was posted as a flight commander in 3 Squadron. On 10 May 1940 the unit was rushed out to France to join 63 Wing of the Air Component at the commencement of the 'Blitzkrieg' and he was given command of the squadron on the 16th when the existing commanding officer was lost in action. He was reported to have had poor eyesight, but when his unit was withdrawn to England he was awarded a DSO and DFC, the citation crediting him with seven victories (4 and 3 shared destroyed). Early in June 1940 he returned to 605 Squadron. On 29 September he left to help form the first 'Eagle' Squadron (71) with American volunteer pilots, of which he was to be the first commanding officer. However, severe sinus problems cut his post short on 23 January 1941 and he was promoted wing commander and given command of RAF Valley, Anglesey. He returned to flying in 1942 and went out to Malta aboard the carrier HMS *Furious* as part of the 'Pedestal' convoy, flying off to the island on 11 August 1942. Now a Group Captain, he took command of Takali airfield. Churchill was killed over Sicily on 4 September 1942 when his Spitfire suffered a direct hit from flak as he was leading the Takali Wing on a strafing attack on Axis airfields. *Aces High* by Christopher Shores and Clive Williams (Grub Street, London 1994).

72 There were four Douglas-Hamilton brothers in the RAF and all became squadron commanders. The eldest, 'Douglo', was captain of boxing at Oxford and only lost the

middleweight championship of England in the final fight. He learnt to fly privately, joined 602 'City of Glasgow' Squadron in the Auxiliary Air Force and thereafter commanded the squadron for ten years. (His brother Lord David Douglas-Hamilton commanded 603 Squadron.) In the early thirties was chief pilot of the high-altitude expedition to the Himalayas with David MacIntyre, another member of 602 Squadron offering invaluable support. When war broke out Douglo became an operations controller at 11 Group in Fighter Command. The following year he took over the Turnhouse (Edinburgh) Sector of 13 Group. It was while Hamilton was commanding the Turnhouse sector, on 10 May 1941 that Rudolf Hess, Hitler's deputy, made his dramatic flight from Augsburg, Germany, to Scotland and bailed out. Dressed in the uniform of an Oberleutnant in the Luftwaffe, he asked to be taken to the Duke, for whom he had a 'secret and vital message'. Douglo had met Albrecht Haushover, a fairly highly placed civil servant in the German Foreign Office before the war. The exact story may never be known but it is virtually certain that Haushover gave Hess Douglo's name and address. Hess correctly saw the need for Germany to bring peace in the West before attacking Russia. He also wished, no doubt, to do something to restore his own sagging prestige...' Hess, with a remarkably astute piece of solo navigation, overflew Dungavel House, Hamilton's residence in Lanarkshire and after some toing and froing, rolled his long range Messerschmitt 110 on to its back and, with difficulty, bailed out. Remarkably, Douglo was commanding the sector where the house was situated. He heard than aeroplane had crashed and assumed that one of his night fighters had made a successful interception. As he went to bed that night he got the message that the prisoner wished to see him. 'He can wait' he said 'until the morning.' Group Captain Lord George Douglas-Hamilton, later the 10th Earl of Selkirk, the second of the quartet and its only wartime survivor, writing in *Thanks for the Memory: Unforgettable Characters in Air Warfare 1939-45*, edited by Laddie Lucas (Stanley Paul & Co Ltd 1989.

73 Robert Finlay Boyd was born in East Kilbride, Scotland on 8 June 1916. Working as a mining engineer before the war, he joined the Auxiliary Air Force in 1935, serving on 602 Squadron. The unit saw its first action over Scotland during 1939-40. In August it moved south where Boyd, now a flight commander, was awarded a DFC on 24 September for nine victories and a Bar a month later for 12. In December 1940 he was posted to command 54 Squadron, which he led until July 1941. He then became an instructor at 58 OTU, Grangemouth until December, when he was appointed Wing Leader at Kenley. His final score was 14 and 7 shared destroyed, 3 probables, 7 damaged. In February 1942 he was out on an early sortie with the Station Commander, Group Captain Victor Beamish, when they saw the German capital ships Scharnhorst and Gneisenau heading up the English Channel, and returned to raise the alarm. A DSO followed in April 1942, after which he commanded Eglinton airfield for a period in 1943. Subsequently he was posted out to the Far East to AHQ, Bengal, from where he was posted to command 293 Wing on the Burma front at the start of April 1944. Rumours have circulated that he made many claims against Japanese aircraft while in the East, but no confirmation of this has been found. He left the RAF in 1945 as a Group Captain. He died in April 1975. *Aces High* by Christopher Shores and Clive Williams (Grub Street, London 1994).

74 Christopher Frederick Currant was born 14 December 1911 in Luton, Bedfordshire, 'Bunny' Currant obtained direct entry to the RAF in 1936, joining 46 Squadron the following year on completion of training, as a Sergeant pilot. He was posted to 151 Squadron later in the year, but moved to 605 Squadron in April 1940 when he received his commission. Operating over France from Hawkinge during May, he was shot down south of Arras on 22nd, and force-landed. His first successful engagement occurred on 15 August during Luftflotte 5's attack on North-East England. Thereafter his unit moved south and here he was to claim a further eight and four shared victories by the end of the year, receiving a DFC on 8 October and a Bar to this on 15 November. *Aces High* by Christopher Shores and Clive Williams (Grub Street, London 1994).

75 On 15 August 1940 when he was credited with three He 111 'probables' and a He 111 victory.

76 For the action on 16 October 1939 Squadron Leader Archie McKellar DSO DFC* and 30-year old Flight Lieutenant George Pinkerton both Spitfire I pilots on 602 Squadron were awarded half-shares in the destruction of a Heinkel 111, which was subsequently re-identified as a Ju 88A-1 of I/KG30. Pinkerton was a fruit farmer in Renfrewshire where his wife and 6 month

old daughter lived. A few minutes earlier Spitfires on 603 'City of Edinburgh' Squadron brought down a Heinkel He 111 in the sea about four miles south of Port Seton for the first aerial victory over the British Isles in WWII. The AOC-in-Chief, Fighter Command, Sir Hugh Dowding sent the following telegram: 'Well done. First blood to the Auxiliaries'. F. G. Nancarrow in *Glasgow's Fighter Squadron,* published in 1942, said of the forcing down by McKellar of the 1./KG26 Heinkel He 111 bomber: 'The German rear gunner, who had been fighting back, was suddenly silent ... The big plane shuddered, lost height, climbed again to clear the roof of a farm house and then slid on its belly up a sloping field. Once, almost as if it were trying to make the air again, the Heinkel soared, only to fall back mortally wounded. McKellar, triumphant, circled overhead'. The Heinkel, which had its nose shattered, its back strained and its starboard tailplane wrenched off, was riddled with bullets. Two of the crew were dead, pilot wounded and the observer unhurt but badly shaken. The exact spot was close to the Longyester-Humble road near Kidlaw Farm, Gifford, East Lothian in the Lammermuir Hills.

77 On Sunday 28 October McKellar was credited with another half share, in the destruction six miles south of Trament of a He 111 of Stab/KG26, which crashed south of Haddington. It was the first enemy aircraft since the First World War to be forced down on British soil.

78 Throughout his account David Masters continues to refer to him as 'Wing Commander' Churchill but he did not achieve this rank until January 1941.

79 Gerald Richmond Edge. Born on 24 September 1913 Edge served on 605 and 253 Squadrons in 1940 and claimed about twenty kills. By 1 January 1945 he was a Group Captain with a DFC and an OBE.

80 His total score stood at 17 and 3 shared destroyed, 5 probables and 3 damaged. On 15 August, an action five miles South-East of Newcastle resulted in him being credited with three probable He 111s and one He 111 confirmed. *Aces High* by Christopher Shores and Clive Williams (Grub Street, London 1994).

81 605 Squadron moved to Croydon on 7 September. McKellar actually shot down eight aircraft on four days, 9-16 September and was awarded a half share in a He 111 and a He 111 probable on 11 September. He was also awarded a He 111 probable on 15 September in addition to the confirmed victories of two Bf 109Es and a Do 17. *Aces High* by Christopher Shores and Clive Williams (Grub Street, London 1994).

82 On 29 September 1940 Churchill left to help form the first 'Eagle' squadron (71) with US volunteer pilots, of which he was to be the first commanding officer.

83 On 15 September 1940 Bunny Currant shot down two Do 17s, damaged three others and damaged a He 111 and destroyed a Bf 109. Walter Churchill DSO DFC, CO, 605 'County of Warwick' Squadron recalled: 'The 15th of September dawned bright and clear at Croydon. It never seemed to do anything else during those exciting weeks of August and September. But to us it was just another day. We weren't interested in Hitler's entry into London; most of us were wondering whether we should have time to finish breakfast before the first blitz started. We were lucky. It wasn't till 9.30 that the sirens started wailing and the order came through to rendezvous base at 20,000 feet. As we were climbing in a southerly direction at 15,000 feet we saw thirty Heinkels supported by fifty Me 109s 4,000 above them, and twenty 110s to a flank, approaching us from above. We turned and climbed, flying in the same direction as the bombers with the whole Squadron stringed out in echelon to port up sun, so that each man had a view of the enemy. 'A' flight timed their attack to perfection, coming down sun in a power dive on the enemy's left flank. As each was selecting his own man, the Me 110 escort roared in to intercept with cannons blazing at 1,000 yards range, but they were two seconds too late - too late to engage our fighters, but just in time to make them hesitate long enough to miss the bomber leader. Two Heinkels heeled out of the formation. Meanwhile the 110s had flashed out of sight, leaving the way clear for 'B' flight, as long as the 109s stayed above. 'B' Flight leader knew how to bide his time, but just as he was about to launch his attack the Heinkels did the unbelievable thing. They turned south; into the sun; and into him. With his first burst the leader destroyed the leading bomber which blew up with such force that it knocked a wing off the left-hand bomber. A little bank and a burst from his guns sent the right-hand Heinkel out of the formation with smoke pouring out of both engines. Before returning home he knocked down a 109. Four aircraft destroyed for an expenditure of 1,200

rounds was the best justification for our new tactics.'

84 It is probable that Squadron Leader Archie McKellar had been shot down by Hauptmann Helmut Lippert of II/JG27. 'Bunny' Currant became temporary commanding officer until Gerry Edge took over the unit, but in February 1941 he was posted to 52 OTU at Debden, becoming Chief Flying Instructor in July. On 14 August 1941 he commenced his second tour as commander of 501 Squadron, appearing briefly in the wartime film First of the Few whilst with this unit. On one occasion his aircraft was shot-up and pursued by three FW 190s, one bullet actually striking the back of his head. He escaped at low level and landed at Lympne, but here his aircraft turned over on its back due to the undercarriage tyres having been shot through. June 1942 he was promoted to lead the Ibsley Wing. On 7 July he was awarded a DSO. In August 1942 he moved to Zeals to form and command 122 Wing, which was to come under the control of the new 2nd Tactical Air Force, adding a Belgian Croix de Guerre to his decorations in April. He led this Wing during the D-Day landings in June 1944. He was then despatched to the US with Wing Commander P. J. Simpson to undertake a lecture tour of the Eastern States for four months. On return, he went to the 84 Group Control Centre in Holland, allocating targets until the end of the war. His final score stood at 10 and 5 shared destroyed, 2 probables and 12 damaged. *Aces High* by Christopher Shores and Clive Williams (Grub Street, London 1994).

Chapter 12

Combat Report

Hector Bolitho

The bomber pilot has the reticence and silent loyalties of a sailor. But the fighter pilot is as independent as an eagle and he is noisy. He leaps where the bomber pilot walks.

Hector Bolitho. He published *Combat Report* (Batsford, 1943) based upon John William Charles Simpson's regular letters to him.

Early in May 1936 23-year old John Simpson hired his first private aircraft and landed in a field beside (Henry) Hector Bolitho's house near Thaxted in Essex. Bolitho was a freelance journalist, 49 years old, a New Zealander of Cornish origin, born in Auckland on 28 May 1897, the son of Henry and Ethelred Frances Bolitho. A prolific author, novelist and biographer, in total, he had 59 books published. He travelled in the South Sea Islands in 1919 and then through New Zealand with the Prince of Wales in 1920, and Africa, Australia, Canada, America and Germany in 1923-1924. Bolitho had been to Egypt, Palestine and Transjordan each winter for three years and had come to know the pilots of the RAF who policed the desert.[85] Aboard the SS *Maloya* in the summer of 1934 he met John Simpson. Born in 1913 in Ramsay St. Mary's, Huntingdonshire, in the black, cold Fen country, Simpson went to Australia at the age of 21 to train as a jackeroo, as young management trainees on a sheep or cattle station are known, on a sheep station in the hungry stretches of the North-West, but the men he worked with had been as hard as hell; they reeked of old filth, they lived with aborigine women and they ate snakes, cooked on lids of biscuit-tins. It was not a life for a boy who had grown up on the subdued fens of East Anglia. Worn out, ill and his legs and arms covered in 68 boils which had been lanced without any anaesthetic, he soon decided to return to England. As they neared Suez Bolitho sent a wireless to some of the pilots who had since been posted to Ismailia. His first winter had been spent in Transjordan when he was living with the Amir Abdullah. The most startling pilot on the Air Force station, which was three miles away from the palace, was Richard Atcherley, the former Schneider Trophy pilot, who was known as 'Batchy' and who kept a lion cub as his pet.[86] They acted together in a touching production of *Journey's End*. Batchy was Stanhope, Eric Loverseed.[87]

When war came the friends Bolitho made during those winters became fewer and fewer. Rodney Wilkinson, who was with Sir Wilfred Freeman in Jerusalem, was killed in the summer of 1940. George Mooreby 'the dearest and most generous scapegoat who ever had an overdraft' crashed into Southampton Water. Kenneth F. Ferguson who once flew Bolitho so low over the Dead Sea that the 'blossoms on the oleander bushes met at eye level and 'who used to walk with him through the dusty streets of Amman' was lost over the North Sea flying a Whitley V on 10 Squadron on the raid on an oil plant at Merseburg on 13/14 November 1940. Wing Commander Ferguson was 29 years old. And dark, soft-voiced Philip Algernon Hunter, who once flew Bolitho 'upside down and inside out at Cranwell', was lost while leading 264 Squadron, soon after Dunkirk. Hunter, of Chesham, Buckinghamshire, was born in Frimley, Surrey in 1913 and was educated at King's School, Canterbury; Rosslyn House, Felixstowe and Bishops Stortford School. 'A grand type of pilot who had the essence of the RAF in his blood', he had joined the RAF on a short service commission in September 1931. He then joined 25 Squadron at Hawkinge on 29 August 1932 before being posted to Ismailia on 28 February to join 6 Squadron. Hunter was waiting at Ismailia for Bolitho and for the first time in his life, John Simpson ate breakfast in a RAF mess. 'You know, I think I'd like to fly' Simpson said. 'I can remember when I was a boy in Ramsey. I was about four. It was in the last war. We lived near an aerodrome and when the pilots were coming home, they'd circle round the house and if there was enough food my mother would spread a tablecloth on the tennis lawn to tell them that they could come to dinner. One of them used to hold me over his head, with both hands and run with me to give me the idea that I was flying.' Hunter felt that Simpson would be a good pilot. On return to England Simpson worked as Bolitho's secretary for a while at his farm and his house at Thaxted in Essex, which the author had bought to escape from the hurly burly and 'to rest a little' but his rest became a myth; and then Simpson joined the RAF on a short service commission in January 1936.

'There was a scar in the field all through that summer' recalled Bolitho. 'John brought his sister Ruth, in a Hornet Moth and landed like a bird. He stepped out of the aircraft and shook my hand with so much authority that I was almost shy. His hesitancy had gone and I was abashed by the definite way in which he talked. He chaffed me for my little bits of pomposity, which he had always accepted without demur. He no longer needed a guiding mind. When he took off again in the late afternoon, I walked back to the house with a pleasant sensation of pride. One more pilot had found himself in the character of the Royal Air Force.'

Simpson learned to fly at Ansty, four more miles or so from Coventry. The CO was Poppy Pope, 'who stood six feet two in his socks and who imprisoned the spirit of an imp in his gigantic frame'.[88] In 1932 he had commanded 54 Squadron at Debden and in 1939 Group Captain Poppy Pope became the Station Commander there. He had once given John Simpson's brother-in-law, the racing driver Bernard Rubin, a five hour blind flying course at Hamble after twenty-five hours' solo flying. Rubin then flew to Australia and back, alone, in a Leopard Moth. In May 1934 one of three de Havilland DH 88 Comet Racers was entered in the Mildenhall to Melbourne air race by Ruben. Predictably, Rubin's machine was in British Racing Green, with racing number 19.[89] At Ansty Simpson met others; Jack Roulston, a South African who worked in a gold mine on the Rand and 'was as tough as hell' and Dennis Collins, 'a baby faced artist in Chelsea'. Collins would be killed at Kenley in 1938 while teaching a pilot to fly at night. Simpson shared a room with three Canadians, Jack Sullivan, who had been a 'Mountie', Charlie Olsson and Lionel Manly Gaunce, all of whom had already flown solo in Canada. The Canadians had a guitar. They would sit on the side of their beds and play and sing *Coming Down the Mountain* before they turned in for the night. Sullivan would die at the beginning of the war, in France.

In October 1936 John joined 43 Squadron at Tangmere four miles from Chichester on Hawker Furies' continues Bolitho. 'In other parts of England, most of the Air Force stations were new. But Tangmere already had a small tradition. Its buildings were mature and its trees had settled into the earth. I Squadron and 43 Squadron had been there since 1926, each with its souvenirs of the last war. On guest nights the mess table shone with good silver. 43 held the trophy for gunnery and the Sassoon trophy for the annual pin-pointing competition. It was a silver bowl which held three bottles of champagne. On the walls of the mess were the propeller of a Hun shot down by I Squadron during the last war and the Squadron memorial of 43 - an enemy propeller with the names of past heroes beneath it. There was a spirit at Tangmere for John to take into himself, according to his talents and his sense of history.'

During the late thirties life on RAF stations was akin to living the dream in what was described as 'the greatest flying club in the world'. At Tangmere partying by the 'Fighting Cocks', as 43 Squadron were known, was usually followed by all sorts of games with their rivals on I Squadron, which usually involved rolling about the floor. Simpson wrote Bolitho that he could not do much 'cock-fighting' himself as he had only just had the plaster removed after breaking a wrist. The bravado was also evident in the air. 43 Squadron enjoyed a reputation throughout the Service for their formation flying and Caesar Hull and Prosser Hanks went one better, twice changing seats in the air (no-one believed them the first time) in a Hart. 'It was 'pretty hair-raising when you consider that they had to take their parachutes off to do it!' Simpson said.'[90]

'When John came home on leave' continues Bolitho 'the house was like a small Air Force mess. I think we enjoyed it because pilots are a clanny lot and they like the exciting round of their own shop.' Some of the pilots from Debden were John Simpson's friends and they took possession of Bolitho's house almost as soon as they arrived. No one talked much of war in those days, but the RAF was slowly capturing the countryside and five or six miles away, a pleasant old farm at Debden on the Essex-Suffolk border was being turned into an aerodrome. Bolitho and other local residents - John Gielgud and Gwen Ffengcon-Davies,[91] who lived for many years in the village of Stambourne - were soon shaken out of their rural peace.

'Gigantic hangars rose from the placid fields. A long weather-boarded hut was built for the officers' mess and the village girls walked out of a Sunday evening on the arms of the boys in blue. Noisy cars roared down our peaceful lanes and I was dragged from my remote little house and made the first honorary member of the mess. Some of the old ladies in their gardens did not welcome the change. They sat beneath their cedar trees and rattled their tea cups in protest as the aircraft swept low over their houses. They wrote to *The Times* and to the Member of Parliament because beauty was being chased out of England by the hell birds that screamed overhead, day and night. But they were happy days.'

'In the careless days of peace the pilots came to rest in the house when they were tired from flying and they brought their gramophone records to play on my radio gramophone. The house was always wide open. Every Sunday morning I threw a party. They came.' Dickie' Lee was to win his DSO and DFC before he was lost in August 1940.[92] We used to call him 'Dopey' in the old days because he always fell asleep if the conversation took a serious turn. He was already a hero and in most of the newspapers there had been photographs of him receiving his decorations from the King. The long hell in France[93] had left creases at the corner of his sleepy eyes.'

Richard Hugh Anthony 'Dickie' Lee was born in 19I7 and educated at Charterhouse. He entered the RAF College at Cranwell in September 1935, graduating in July 1937. The following year he was posted to 85 Squadron with which unit he was posted to France in September 1939 as a Flight Lieutenant. On 21 November he claimed the unit's first victory when in the Boulogne area he shot down a Heinkel 111 of Stab (Staff flight) KG4 which crashed in the sea ten miles north of Cap Gris Nez. In March 1940 was awarded a DFC. On 10 May he damaged a Ju 88, was awarded a half share in another Ju 88 and credited with the destruction of an Hs 126 north-west of St. Armand. Next day he claimed two enemy aircraft. On 19 May he was posted to 56 Squadron when 85 withdrew from France. He was shot down into the sea near Dunkirk on 27 May, but was picked up after an hour and on 31 May was awarded a DSO. He returned to 85 Squadron in June.[94] In a letter to Hector Bolitho, John Simpson said that he had heard that' Dickie' Lee had 'done wonders'. 'You see who were always looked upon as being the naughty ones, are doing so well. They needed a war to convince the old gentlemen in Whitehall. Do you remember that' Dickie' was almost given his bowler hat for low flying? That same low flying has apparently stood him in good stead.

'I met some of the chaps from Walter Churchill's squadron[95] and they were full of stories of Belgium. They all say' Dickie' did marvellously. In the first ten days of the German invasion of Belgium and Holland his squadron brought down between 60 and 70 Huns.' Dickie' was actually taken prisoner on the second day. On the first day he was wounded but he carried on. So like him. Next day he shot down two enemy aircraft and then he was caught by the German flak. He came down in a field and asked the way. The man told him to go so some tanks which were nearby and said that they were Belgians.' Dickie' was a bit of a sucker about this and, with a Belgian officer, he went towards the tanks, armed with a machine gun. The tanks turned out to be German so the machine gun was not much use.' Dickie' had on an overcoat and the Huns did not realise that he was one of us. They popped him into a barn with some refugees. There was a high window in the barn. 'Dickie' climbed up the wall to look out. Of course, he's a lucky blighter. There was a ladder beneath the window so he just climbed out and walked four miles, got a lift from some Belgians and he was back with the squadron to fight next day.'

'Dickie would have none of our attempts at war talk' continued Bolitho. 'He said that he had a date with a blonde in Saffron Walden and that he could not stay very long.' Dickie''s taste in blondes was not always reassuring to his friends, but he was obviously more concerned with his date than with our efforts to make him talk of how he had won the DFC and DSO on his tunic. I remember that when he stood up to go I noticed a hole in the leg of his trousers. It was where a bullet had gone through without touching his skin. I suppose that Peter and John and I were a bit pensive, being the older ones, so' Dickie' yawned and said, 'Well, I must get cracking.'

'He made one gesture to sentiment before he went. On the day that war was declared he had left his favourite pictures with me... before his squadron flew off to France. They were photographs of friends, of aircraft and one of a spaniel. He asked me for them, so I brought them down from the attic and he flew off to his blonde with them, piled before him on the screeching, violent motor bicycle.'

'Dear old Laurie Lorimer was also to do well in battle, before he went missing in May 1940. I must say that it would leave a gap in my life if I never heard his Irish laugh again. He used to cook sausages in the kitchen and yell, 'Heigh! The bangers are coming up like nobes (like nobody's business)![96] There was Bill Sykes[97], Rhys-Jones, George Feeny, who was posted missing while serving with the Fleet Air Arm in June 1940,[98] Eric Stapleton, now serving with the RAF in Rhodesia, dear old Boothby with his oily car. And Jeff [Gaunt]. We called him Social Type Jeff because he was something of a gallant, with the smartest blue suit on the Station. He was also to be killed in action.[99]

'When I felt rich, we drank champagne. When I was poor, we drank beer. When they came in a party they would be noisy and gay. When they came alone they would be quiet and eager to talk before the fire. For there was never a bore among them. They never read any of my books and I never talked to them of my work. Their life was mine. Sometimes, we would have somebody beautiful, like Dorothy Dickson, for them to meet. They adored her.

'The servants also fell under the spell of the pilots, who never bothered to tell me when they were hungry. Mitzi would cook sausages for them, or they would cook them themselves. They would help her wash the dishes and make their own beds if they wished to stay all night. This tide of young energy changed my life. The pilots came to me with their troubles: an angry bank manager, an impatient tailor, or even the indignant mother of a favourite blonde had to be pacified. I wrote their letters for them and I even interviewed their bank managers when I thought they were going a little too far with their demanding letters. The pilots would fly over the house and drop an evening newspaper for me because I could not have them delivered from the village.'

Simpson's Flight Commander was Peter Townsend,[100] who described the Squadron Adjutant as 'everybody's friend - he always flew with my flight and not even I could see that behind a shield of reticence lay uncommon skill and courage. John was half-Jewish - perhaps that partly accounted for the mixture of sensitiveness, steely resolution and gaiety which made him remarkable.'[101] In 1938 John Simpson wrote that 'Peter Townsend used to be rather aloof, going to his room at night and avoiding our games and parties. But we are bringing him out of his shell. He is very shy and has no idea of his own courage. He thinks he will hate war if it comes. Caesar moans because there is no war. He reads Winston Churchill by the hour and knows all the answers. Peter is a different type. Very English on the surface. His brothers are in the Navy and Army and he was in torpedo bombers in the Far East. He's the greatest gentleman I have ever met in the Service. He surrounds himself with armour, but I am slowly breaking through. We are becoming friends. You will like him when you know him more. He's got the sort of face you notice immediately he comes into a room.' Bolitho wrote that Townsend 'was tortured rather than exulted by his victories over the enemy and he was troubled as to what would come out of the war. 'The only way a man can qualify for leadership is through personal example and thus parliament is condemned' he said. The sentence may sound a little sententious standing alone. But it grew naturally out of our argument over the world as we would like it to be when the war is ended. I asked him then, 'But you who survive the war must be the leaders of the peace. If you believe in what you are fighting for, then you should go into parliament when it is over and see that the right kind of world is built.' Then he sighed and answered. 'It would cost £3,000 to become a member of parliament and none of the pilots who are left will have £3,000 when the war ends.'

'The victories of the Royal Air Force started Britain soon after the war began' wrote Bolitho. 'The numbers of the squadrons were kept out of the newspapers, but people in country towns began to talk of those stationed on nearby aerodromes with local pride, as if they were their own regiments. Few seemed to realize that some of them were old and already rich in history, with trophies on their walls recalling the victories of a quarter of a century before. The newspapers began to sing the praises of the pilots of 43 Squadron, although they were not then allowed to mention the Squadron's number. 43 brought down their first enemy aircraft in the war, over England in January 1940. We were all concerned with the battle in hand and there was no time to remember that 43 had been formed in 1916 and that it was rather a veteran. While the outside world discovered the Squadron as something new and exciting, there were many older pilots within the Service who saw in the valour of the young, merely a new chapter added to an old story. Captain Balfour, the Under Secretary of State for Air, had flown with

43 in 19I7. He watched its new life with fatherly interest: sometimes escaping from his desk at Whitehall to fly with the new aircraft that were so different from the machines he had used in France, twenty-five years before.

With the outbreak of war, now on Hurricanes John Simpson was involved in two early engagements in February 1940. On the 20th he crashed on landing and was injured. Recovered by May and promoted flight commander, he claimed the first Do 17 to be shot down off the English coast on 9 May and was then engaged over Dunkirk and in Normandy early in June, to where his flight moved to operate for a few days after the Dunkirk withdrawal. On 30 January 1940 'when the war in the air was still young, while the German pilots were still too careful to attack more than fishing smacks or lifeboats loaded with supplies' Caesar Hull brought down the first enemy aircraft for his squadron, off the East Coast.[102]

'Caesar was a South African' wrote Hector Bolitho 'but his energies were controlled by a tenderness of heart which might have emerged from an old, rather than a young civilization. His face was so lively with laughter and intelligence that one did not realize for a long time that it was a very average face as far as features go. He moved quickly as if, accustomed to flying, he was rather impatient with the slow tempo of his feet. Like most of the pilots who loved the Service in pre-war days he had little life beyond the Air Force. Girls were toys to be fondled in the back of a car, but forgotten. He was married to the RAF. Caesar was a boxer, but in the rough and tumble games which were played in the mess, his hands were never angry. In the quiet of his room, he read long serious books, mostly Winston Churchill. He was a strange mixture. At night he looked beneath his bed, imagining that somebody might be hiding there. He wore a scarf which had belonged to him since the day he first flew. He would not fly without it and one afternoon when his CO hid it, as a joke, Caesar refused to go near his aircraft.'

John Simpson told Bolitho the story in a letter.

'January 31, 1940.

'I am very tired. We have had three days of great activity, with some success. You know I told you yesterday that Caesar, with another pilot, intercepted and shot at a German bomber. During the attack a bullet hit his aircraft behind the cockpit and went through the aircraft, doing no damage. The German news claimed that Caesar had been shot down. Perhaps you heard it.

'Yesterday, Caesar and the same pilot, in the same aircraft - intercepted and shot down a bomber ten miles out to sea. There were no survivors. Don't you think that is good! The same pilots, in the same machines (one of which the Germans claim to have shot down) got their revenge for the one bullet (which did no damage) by shooting down a Heinkel 111 the next day. We are all as pleased as Punch.[103]

'Thirteen [sic] days later[104], the three friends, Peter Townsend, John and Caesar, came into their own as fighter pilots. They were the leaders of three formations that brought down three German aircraft off the East Coast, within the space of five minutes.

Simpson wrote to Bolitho:

'Birdie Saul has just telephoned the CO.[105] He was away, because his wife is having a baby. So I had to take the call, being Adjutant. Birdie Saul congratulated me and said that the Hun I claimed earlier in the day had been confirmed.

'The bodies of two of the crew were already on the way to us at Acklington for a military funeral. One German was picked up in the sea and one was washed ashore. The medical officer asked me if I would like to go and see the corpses when they arrived at the mortuary. But I said no.

'I'll begin at the beginning.

'Last night we slept at Dispersal Point for early morning readiness. We had cold kippers brought over for breakfast, cold and unpleasant because we are so far from the mess. These kippers are unique. One morning George Lott had just swallowed half his kipper when we suddenly scrambled. He was told to go up above all cloud. He couldn't climb above 29,500 feet: that was as high as the bloody thing would go. He says that it is the highest a kipper has ever flown in its life and how surprised its mother would be if she ever knew.[106] 'This morning was misty and damp with occasional showers and low clouds down to five hundred feet. You know how depressing this part of the country can be, with the slag heaps and the wind coming in from the North Sea.

'Peter and his section were ordered off and told to patrol South Shields. Shortly after, both Caesar's sections and mine were also ordered off, Caesar to the mouth of the Tyne and me to the Faroe Islands. We were warned that there were enemy aircraft about, presumably looking for our convoys. We flew around the Faroe Islands... they are quite small, with a lighthouse and millions of birds. There was enough rain to keep the windscreen misty and make flying unpleasant. We found a small convoy after about half an hour and we were circling it when I saw three white splashes in the water, to one side of the centre ship. It was a small ship, with a sail and one funnel... a fishing boat I suppose. I realized the splashes were from bombs and I looked up and saw an immense aircraft just below the clouds.

'But, it was the first Heinkel I had ever seen and I just hoped that it wasn't one of ours. The Heinkels look quite like Ansons from underneath. Several times we have taken Ansons for Heinkels and only just realized in time, much to the alarm of the Coastal Command pilots. But I was certain this time. It looked dark and ugly and I pulled up the nose of my Hurricane and pressed the tit. I hit him fair and square in the wings and fuselage. One of his engines stopped and bits of metal flew off. He then disappeared into some wisps of cloud. We circled round for a few seconds and my Number 2 (Eddie Edmonds[107]) said, 'I see the bastard.' He could see the crippled Heinkel in a gap in the clouds and he fired.

'The Hun was now flying towards the English coast. I caught up and finished all my ammunition on him. He was burning well when he disappeared into the mist above the sea. My ammunition tanks were empty so I called up Eddy and set course for base. All the troops were on the tarmac when we arrived.[108] 'I thought that they had come out because they could see that my guns had been fired.[109] For a moment I thought that I had drawn the first blood for the day. But Peter had gone in before me. He had already landed, having brought down his first over Whitby in Yorkshire. It was a Heinkel also and it had crashed near a farm. Peter was obviously very excited, but modest. He just said, 'Poor devils, I don't think they were all killed.' As we were talking, news came over the R/T that Caesar and Frank Carey[110] had shot down another near the mouth of the Tyne. They landed a few minutes later and Caesar was frightfully excited, saying, 'God! It was wizard. Frank and I did beam attacks from opposite directions and nearly collided.'

'The crew of Caesar's Heinkel stood on top of the fuselage when their aeroplane landed in the water. It was so like Caesar... he dived on them, but without firing, just to beat them up. They all jumped into the water and he was delighted. He kept all saying, 'It was wizard.'[111]

'152 Squadron are here also and they brought down one. They have only just farmed so it was a terrific show for them. They only have Gladiators. I was not absolutely certain of mine although we claimed it, until Birdie Saul rang through. I had given the position of the Hun over the R/T and one ship in the convoy had been diverted to look for the crew. Also a local lifeboat had put out. It was awfully hard luck on George Lott. We sent him a wire, telling him to listen to the six o'clock news. He was bloody annoyed at missing the Huns and he is coming back on the night train. He's so terribly keen I'm sorry he missed the show.

'152 are arranging a party for us to-night.

'*Later*

'The party was a great success. Peter and Caesar did their wonderful La Cachita dance to the gramophone record we brought from Tangmere. It is a cross between a rumba and an apache dance and they throw each other all over the room, crash, bang! They jump aver the tables and chairs while they are dancing. We drank eight battles of champagne.

'We then sang our old Air Force songs ...*My mother comes from Norfolk, My brother Silvest and Take the Piston Rings out of My Stomach*. Poor old Caesar tried to join in. Have you ever heard him sing? It is a horrible business. He simply cannot keep tune. We just stopped and looked at him and he went scarlet. He was always the same in the old days in the little church at Tangmere. I remember one Sunday when he was in front and we all began to sing *Abide with Me*. He couldn't resist it and he began to sing. He was so loud and out of tune that somebody leaned over and touched me on the shoulder and said, 'Tell Caesar to pipe down.' I poked him in the back and told him and he went red to the back of his ears.

'Caesar is slightly religious. He always says his prayers and I think he would like to sing hymns. But he has no idea of being in tune, which is extraordinary because he has such rhythm in his flying.

'I admire him so much about this side of him... I mean his saying his prayers. When we were at camp at Watchet, we shared a room. After he had done all his little fusses, like looking under the bed and in the cupboard, he just laughed and told me to look under mine. 'You never know, there might be some Feeneys about.' Then he knelt by the side of his bed and said his prayers.

'You know that Caesar has invented a La Cachita attack in the, air. He calls out La Cachita over the R/T to Peter and follows with a noise like a machine gun. Then Peter calls back, *Himmel, Himmel! Achtung! Schpitfeuer*. Then they make an astern attack in echelon with three aircraft. They each came down and take on their opposite number. It is wonderful listening to it over the R/T. Caesar makes it all sound very exciting with his La Cachita nonsense.

'Next day, John told me, Peter went to inspect the wreckage of the Heinkel at Whitby. Afterwards, he went to see his German prisoner in hospital and took him cigarettes. John added, 'We are contributing to buy wreaths for the dead ones.'

On 23 February 43 Squadron left Acklington and an hour later landed at Wick near the north-east tip of Scotland, John o'Groats. Across the sea from there, in the Orkneys, lay the naval base at Scapa Flow. 43 Squadron's job was to defend it. On 29 January the biggest bombing raid to date had been made by German aircraft on north-east coastal shipping. Five separate attacks were launched involving, it was estimated, about twenty aircraft. Eight lightship men were killed. On 10 February, after raiding shipping in the Firth of Forth, Heinkel 111 1H+EH of KG26 (Lowen-Geschwader) made a forced landing at North Berwick. Unteroffizier Helmut Meyer landed the Heinkel intact, ran parallel with a small hedge and after bursting both tyres, tipped gently on to its nose. One of the crew was killed. This Heinkel, minus its wings, was towed away and later test-flown by 1426 (Enemy Aircraft) Flight.[112] By March 43 Squadron (and the resident 602 and 603 Squadrons) had been joined at Wick by 111 and 605 Squadrons, all of them operating Hurricane Is and making a total of 39 aircraft widely dispersed around the aerodrome. On 16 March about a dozen enemy aircraft flew over Scapa Flow and attacked two naval ships, unsuccessfully, with incendiary bombs. They also dropped some incendiary bombs on land near Stromness on the largest of the Orkney Islands; a house was demolished and bombs killed a civilian on an airfield and seven more men in a village were wounded.[113]

On 8 April German raids were made on the FAA airfield at Hatston and Scapa Flow and 43 Squadron claimed three Heinkel He 111H-3s of 6/KG26 and damaged two others. Thirty miles east of Duncansby Head Peter Townsend shot down one of the Heinkels. Twenty minutes' later, as Townsend approached Wick, he saw not a flare path but a 'confusion of lights'. 'Don't land yet' called the controller. But Townsend's tanks were almost dry so he touched down clear of the lights and taxied across to them. In the middle of the airfield lay Heinkel 1H+DP of 6/KG26 piloted by Leutnant Weigel: wheels up; propellers bent. Under the cockpit was the lion emblem of KG26. This Heinkel was intercepted over the Pentland Firth by Sergeant pilot Jim Hallowes on 43 Squadron who noticed a pair of them flying east at 8,000 feet, heading for their base at Westerland, Sylt. Hallowes was descending to land at Wick and fired a one second burst from his eight

.303 machine guns at Weigel's Heinkel before his guns stopped firing because of a broken pneumatic pipe. Hallowes crippled one of the engines and fatally wounded the two rear gunners. Both Heinkels dived into rain clouds in the darkening sky. Hallowes then returned to Wick in the dark and landed on the flarepath, noticing a Heinkel following him in. On getting out of his Hurricane, the squadron's Intelligence Officer met Hallowes and told him that he had just 'shot down a Hudson'.[114]

Sometime later George Lott told Bolitho that he had listened in to the astonishing conversation over the R/T, one voice saying 'Heinkel passing over aerodrome at 200 feet.' And the other protesting 'Are you sure it is not a Hudson?' Then the bewilderment of the German crew who thought they were landing on the water at Scapa Flow and were so certain of this that they took off their boots and threw their rubber dinghy on to the ground. Rumour had it that they climbed into their dinghy and began rowing! Later they insisted that a Spitfire had attacked them. 'It was the first sign of 'Spitfire snobbery' wrote Peter Townsend. 'There were no Spitfires for miles.'[115]

The Intelligence Officer and Hallowes drove over to the Heinkel, where Weigel and his co-pilot Obergefreiter B. Rehbein had jumped out into the snow. Weigel had lived in Canada and spoke perfect English. He had been a boxer and showed the airmen pictures of his family. He had seen the landing flares but thought they were fishing boats on the water in Scapa Flow and had 'ditched' his Heinkel to try to get urgent medical attention for his gunners but Oberfeldwebels E. Rost and K. Geerdts were already dead. The two survivors were held at the guardroom for a few days and were well fed. Although the wreck of the Heinkel was guarded, all removable parts such as radios, instruments and even ordnance gradually disappeared and even parts of the aluminium skin were made into trinkets for girls in town. The photographic department at the airfield took pictures of the Heinkel and sold them for two shillings each! A day later there was a special parade in the camp and everyone's lockers were searched, but very few of the missing mementoes from the Heinkel were recovered![116]

'Even in the brief hours of his flight back to Scotland [on 10 April], John missed 'another party' wrote Hector Bolitho. In a telephone call from Caesar Hull he broke the news that 'the Huns' had sent ten aircraft to bomb the fleet at Scapa Flow. It was their first attempt at a big raid and it had failed. 43 Squadron intercepted the Heinkels ten miles off the Orkneys and 'gave them hell'. At least five were shot down. Both Caesar and Peter Townsend had got one each [sic] and judging by the shouting over the telephone, Caesar had found everything 'wizard as ever'.[117]

'The story must be told' wrote Bolitho 'for it reveals the spirit with which 43 was taking its place in the front line'. Peter Townsend wrote it down for him. 'It was the afternoon of a lovely day, April 10. The sky and sea were very blue. There were scattered clouds and isolated rain storms which would give very little cover to a snooper. Caesar's flight was released from duty and he and some others were playing tennis. My flight was at 30 minutes notice and was the last of five flights available for action. So I went into the town with Eddie, to do some shopping.

'The siren sounded, just as we were buying some things. We ran to the aerodrome which was a mile away and arrived at our Dispersal Hut, hot and flustered. George Lott was already there. He had been sitting in his office when he saw a lot of chaps rushing past the window. He had telephoned Ops, to see if there was anything doing. When they told him that there were some Huns about he said, 'Can we go?' Much to my annoyance we found that our flight ('B' Flight) had only three aircraft which were serviceable. Several had been damaged when we brought down the five Germans in the blitz off Scapa Flow.

'Then Caesar arrived, with some others in his flight (A Flight). They were still wearing their tennis kit, shirts, flannels and rubber shoes. There were only a few of their pilots as the others had gone off for the day. It was a case of my flight having the pilots and A Flight having the machines. There was a rather heated discussion and then we arranged a compromise.

'As we flew out towards the islands, we saw one Hun. We gave the Tallyho in one bellow, over the R/T. The Hun might have heard us; he turned so steeply away and made for a small bank of cloud. George Lott got there first and gave him a burst just before he got into the cloud. Then Caesar showed his independence. He opened the throttle full out and drew away from me. Then he tore into the Hun who was then dodging in and out of cloud. Now it was a matter of each man for himself. We jostled and dodged each other as we tore in behind the Heinkel and every now and then there would be a yell of 'Look out! For Christ's sake, you nearly hit me.' I can remember coming in with another Hurricane dangerously close above me. The rudder and fin of the Heinkel were wobbling and his whole fuselage was riddled. We told the boys not to fire anymore because we saw that he was finished and we wanted, if possible, to bring them back alive.

'Caesar and I flew in close to him, one on each side and I could see the horrible mess in the rear cockpit. It was a sad and beastly sight. But we were elated then and we did not see it that way. The riddled aircraft with its flapping empennage, three terrified figures in the front - the pilot, his fair hair blown by the slip stream which was coming through his shattered windscreen, leaning forward and trying to urge his powerless machine to fly, his two companions making hopeless signs of surrender and despair.[118] They began to swim backstroke, in that icy water, towards the coast. The seven of us circled round and some of us transmitted to get a wireless fix of our position, so that they might send out a launch to rescue the Huns. But none came. We resumed our formation and flew back. I can still see the agony and despair of the last minutes of those Huns. We were indifferent to it then, when we saw them. We knew quite well that many of us would have to endure just as much before the war finished.[119]

'On 9 May John brought down his second aircraft, over the sea, forty miles out. It was a Dornier Flying Pencil, the first of its type to be shot down off the British coast. He wrote to me two days afterwards: I did not have a minute to telephone you on Thursday after my success. It was most exciting and a new type, which was pleasing.

'Well, let me begin at the beginning. Caesar left us on Thursday morning to go with his squadron.[120] I can't tell you where but he won't have to go to the Frigidaire for his ice. I felt bloody browned off about his going. We have done everything together since I joined the squadron. He was excited of course and quite fearless and full of all his theories on how to turn out the Hun.

'Two hours after he left us, we had to take off. It was my first job as commander of the flight because I have taken Caesar's place. Also, you must remember that I had never flown with any of the chaps before, as it is 'A' Flight and I was with Peter [Ottewill] in 'B' Flight.[121] We were to patrol the aerodrome below cloud while another flight had to patrol above. The cloud was grey and thick. We were told that enemy aircraft were coming from the west and that they were nearing the aerodrome. We had just got up to 3,000 feet when I heard the other flight give a Tallyho! I rather thought we were out of it. One Hun was already being fired on by the six aircraft above us and it was no use my joining in. We flew on under the clouds out to sea and I felt a bit peeved at not being able to fire my guns. I was about to turn back to base when I saw another Hun, a long, slim, green aircraft, flying beneath a cloud, hugging it and just staying enough in the open to be able to see the water. We must have been about forty miles out to sea. It was beautifully calm. I was terribly lucky because I was in a perfect position to open fire with a full deflection shot, almost the moment I saw him. Unfortunately, I was out of range with my first burst and I think that I missed. He tried to climb back into cover of the cloud, but I got him with my next burst before he disappeared. It was terrific. I blew his nose right off. I must have killed the pilot. It burned furiously and dived into the sea and exploded. A terrible but a wonderful sight. Three people had jumped out of the rear gun position and I saw them fall from about 800 feet into the sea. I could not see the aircraft after it crashed into the water. Only a column of fire and black smoke. I saw one of the Germans in the water. I noted my position and flew back to base.[122]

'I honestly did not care a bit. I hate their guts now, after so many of my friends have been killed. I found that I took this one in my stride without a tremor. But I still feel quite sick when I am on the ground, before I take off. I suppose this is some kind of fear. Once I am in the air this vanishes and I become excited instead. But I am always pleased when I land.'

'So much had happened to him within himself and there was so much quiet authority in his voice as he spoke that I felt rather like a schoolboy listening to an old soldier. He had brought down two enemy aircraft at Dunkirk [on 1 June] without even mentioning it when he spoke to me on the telephone the evening before 43 Squadron had been ordered to help in the last days of the evacuation.

'On the first day of our Dunkirk patrol [on 1 June] we took off from Tangmere while it was still almost dark. I shall never forget the mass of balloons all down the Thames, from London. 'We saw them in the distance, glittering in the morning light. They were so thick that they seemed to form a line, like silver battleships in the clouds, following the curves of the river.

'We breakfasted at Manston and waited by our aircraft for the hour of our patrol. We were lying on the grass, reading the morning papers and I came upon the announcement that dear old George [Lott] had got his DFC. There he was, lying next to me. And I realized, I don't know - how a sort of instinct - that he had read it himself and had not said a word. I congratulated him and he said, 'Christ knows what I got it for.'

'I could not have been more pleased about any decoration. George is an extraordinary person and he deserves it. Behind that slow, quiet manner, there is a lot of courage and a good brain. What was so nice was that when we returned from our patrol and he asked his batman to buy a DFC ribbon for his tunic, the twizzet bought a DFM ribbon by mistake. George wore it without even noticing, until we told him.

'On that first morning we made our way across the Channel to Dunkirk. 43 flew 'above and be'ind.' We crossed the water above clouds and saw nothing of the evacuation which was going on below. But the smoke from the oil tanks at Dunkirk had reached us at Tangmere and we knew what to expect. We had smelled it in Sussex as we flew through it. You can fly from Brighton to Dunkirk on the smoke trail... just follow it and find Dunkirk at the other end.

'All the harbour at Dunkirk seemed to be on fire with the black smoke from the oil dumps. The destroyers moved out of the pall of smoke in a most uncanny way, deep in the water and heavily laden with troops. I was flying at about 1,000 feet above the beach and the sea. And there I could see the Brighton Belle and the paddle steamers and the sort of cheerful little boats you see calling at coastal towns on Sunday. Hundreds of boats! Fishing boats and motor boats and Thames river craft and strings of dinghies, being towed by bigger boats. All packed with troops and people standing in the water and awful bomb craters in the beach and lines of men and groups of people sitting down. Waiting, I suppose. And I could see rifles - stacked in threes. And destroyers going back into the black smoke. And wrecked ships on the beach: wrecked ships of all sizes, sticking out of the water. And a destroyer cut in halves by a bomb. I saw it! A Junkers 87 came low over the water and seemed to fly into the destroyer and drop its bomb. That was pretty terrible. It was shot down after, thank God. I saw the destroyer crack in two. And I saw parachutes coming down from wrecked aircraft, landing in the water and on the beach and on the land.

'The first day we were patrolling, there were nine of my squadron, flying in a sort of oval-shaped route over the coast, at between 10,000 and 20,000 feet. We flew two miles out to sea and then two miles inland. And suddenly I realized that there were more aircraft flying than had come with us across the Channel. That was a bit disturbing! A squadron of Messerschmitt 109s had joined us and they were sharing our patrol peacefully, waiting to take their chance in getting a straggler. It was a bit shaking. I signalled to my CO when I recognized them. We had only come on bombers when we were in the North. Before the CO had time to give the order to attack a lone Messerschmitt dived down on him. The battle was on then. We picked our opponents, while two squadrons of our fighters flew low to protect the shipping. After avoiding several on my tail, for what seemed to be ages, I got on to one and opened fire. We chased about and lost height rapidly, coming down to 5,000 feet above the land. When he was diving I got in a steady burst and he crumbled up as if he were made of cardboard. He crashed in flames on a golf course.

'I climbed up again and found that more German fighters, Messerschmitt 110s, also strangers to us, had joined in. I got on to the tail of one of them, which was firing at a Hurricane piloted by [Flying Officer Malcolm Keith] 'Crackers' [Carswell, a New Zealander].[123] I got so close that when I fired, his tail just blew off in mid air.'Crackers' was on fire too. But he bailed out and he was brought home by a destroyer two days afterwards.[124]

'Then I dived to the sea and made for home. I thought it was all right, but I made a silly mistake. In the heat of it all, I flew towards Calais instead of Dover. When I realized this, I turned and thought I was alone for the journey across the Channel. But I looked back and saw that I was being followed by an enemy aircraft. We weren't more than three or four feet above the water. I zig zagged to avoid his bullets. God was kind to me. We continued that mad, zig zagging journey, so low over the smooth water and he kept at me until I was eight miles or so from Dover. Then he turned and went home. It was our first combat with anything more than five aircraft... our first combat with any fighters. We got nine destroyed and six probable and we lost two.'

'He brought down his fifth, sixth and seventh enemy aircraft about the time when the German thrust was proceeding southwards [on 7 June]. He wrote and told me the story.

'It was a fine, clear summer day. Our squadron was ordered to patrol with nine aircraft on a line between Le Treport, Abbeville and Amiens. We flew straight from our base on the English coast and made our land-fall south of Le Treport. Along the whole of our patrol line were smouldering villages, columns of black smoke and burning forests. Others had been there before us. As we turned to make for Rouen, where we were to land for lunch, a squadron of Messerschmitt 109 fighters attacked us from out of the sun.

'In a second we had broken our formation and each one of us engaged an enemy in a dog fight. There were more of them than of us and it was difficult to fire at one without being attacked by two others at the same time. I finished my ammunition, having fired at three of them. But the battle was too hot for me to follow and see if they crashed. I dived to the ground and made my way over the tree tops to Rouen which I found by following the Seine. When I landed I found that six pilots of my squadron had arrived before me. We were two short. 'Dickie' Bain[125] the Station Commander would not allow us to stay. The aerodrome had been bombed that morning and they were all preparing to move south. So we had to take off again for an aerodrome thirty miles away. I had only ten minutes petrol left when we landed in a cut wheat field. While the ten men in the field refuelled our aircraft with only one petrol tanker between them, we climbed on to an American car and were driven at a hellish speed to a village. It seemed to be very peaceful, except for the motor cycles which flashed through on their way to Headquarters. There was a cart, with flowers and fruit and vegetables for sale. We were hot and thirsty. We talked of the combat, but not much of those who were missing. We just felt that they would turn up. We had a miserable lunch of cold sausage meat, brown bread and quantities of watered down cider. We had no French money and we had to pay the angry madame with an English pound note.

'We went back to the farm but the telephone wires had been cut. While the CO went back to the village to telegraph for orders, we stripped to the waist and lay in the sun, in the middle of the wheat field. We were seven, very white and clean, lying in the wheat. In one corner the Frenchmen were making a haystack and in the other corner some Cockney airmen were belting ammunition. We became thirsty again as we lay in the sun, but nothing could be done about it.

'The Germans had advanced many miles while we were lying there. Our orders came. We were to patrol the same line, but two miles into enemy territory. We seemed to be very small ... only seven ... taking off. We flew in peace for ten minutes after arriving on our line and then the sky was filled with black puffs of smoke, like hundreds of liver spots. We dived and climbed and none of us was hit. When we turned at the eastern end of our patrol line the sky was fantastic. The black puffs of smoke from the anti-aircraft guns had woven weird patterns in the sky.

'The guns stopped firing. We knew then that the German fighters were on their way. Coming towards us, in layers of twenty, were what seemed like a hundred of the enemy, looking like bees in the sky. Some were level with us. Some above. Some below. My CO climbed up with us to sixteen thousand feet and there, while we were being circled by all of those hungry fighters, he gave the order to break up and engage. Forty were bombers. They flew south: perhaps to bomb Rouen. I singled out a Messerschmitt 109 and had a very exciting combat with him. He was a good pilot and he hit me several times. We began to do aerobatics and while he was on his back, I got in a burst which set him on fire. He jumped out, but I did not see his parachute open. His machine was almost burned out before it hit the ground. There were scores of fighters about me, but I still had plenty of ammunition. I got on to the tail of another 109 and while I was firing at him two Messerschmitts 110 fired at me from either side. I continued to fire at the 109 which was badly winged. He suddenly stall turned sharply to the right, went into a spin and crashed straight into one of the other Messerschmitts which was firing at me.

'I couldn't resist following them down. It was a wonderful sight. They stuck together in a sort of embrace of flames, until they were a few hundred feet above the ground. Then they parted and crashed, less than twenty yards apart.

'I turned for home, flying as low as I could. Crossing the Channel seemed to take hours. I was wet through with sweat: I had been fighting at full throttle. The sea looked cool and it made me feel cooler. But I was afraid that I might be caught without ammunition and go into the sea. There were no boats to rescue me.

'Luck was with me for there was a mist above the sea. I flew in it for twenty minutes before I emerged into the sunlight again. I was lucky. The Germans had lost me. I could see nothing but the sea and the English coast.

'My wireless had been disabled so I could not inquire of my friends. At last I flew over land and very soon I was circling the aerodrome. I landed to find that I was the first home. My CO followed, having bagged two himself. We sat in the sun on the aerodrome for a long time, waiting for our other pilots. We searched the sky for them for what seemed an hour. But no more arrived. So we went to the Mess and we drank to ourselves and to them.

'A few days later the newspapers announced that John had been awarded the Distinguished Flying Cross. His own account of the day in France suffered from under-statement. I learned afterwards that he had done very well. In the words of the official announcement, he had shown 'a confident and offensive spirit' in the face of the enemy and it was for this that he was to be decorated by the King. [126]

'John went back to 43 Squadron to take his part in a problem which beset many other squadrons about this time. 43 as he had known it almost came to an end on the evening when he sat on the edge of the aerodrome with George Lott, waiting for the rest of the squadron, who did not come back. Some were prisoners, maybe. Others might come back by the devious ways that were already operating across the Channel. New pilots had to be trained into the code of 43 and Flight Lieutenant Tom Morgan was brought from the Air Ministry to take over 'B' Flight.[127] Flying Officer [Frank Reginald 'Chota' (because he was only 5 feet 3inches tall)] Carey, who had been a Sergeant Pilot with the squadron in the first months of the war, also came back, with the experience of war in France to add to his usefulness.

'There was one more disaster to harass the squadron before it resumed its place in the front line. One day [9 July] while John was in London, George Lott and his section were ordered off from Tangmere, in very bad weather, to investigate some plots approaching the aerodrome from the south. Almost as soon as they broke cloud, they saw six Messerschmitt 110s flying away from them. The enemy had the advantage and they turned back and opened fire with their cannon. George was flying John's aircraft. A cannon shell hit the windscreen which splintered and filled George's right eye with glass. He was bleeding badly. The wound was so terrible that he eventually lost his eye. But he said nothing. He took refuge in cloud while the Germans were engaged by the other two. George called them up and told them to return to base. He was almost blinded then and his difficulties were increased by the clouds which hung close to the ground. At last, George found Arundel Castle. While flying at 500 feet, he had to abandon his aircraft.

'John wrote to me two days later:

'I have just been to see George[128] at Haslar Hospital. He is in terrible pain. They have operated to try and save his eye, but it has failed. To-night they are taking his eye out. It will relieve the pain. His other eye will be OK.

'Hector, I think I admire him as much as any human being I know. He began in the Service as an AC2. I think he's been in the RAF something like eighteen years. I remember you saying to me once something about the RAF being a school for character. The phrase was something like that. If ever a great character emerged from the RAF, it is George. God, I do admire his guts. I am sorry if I did not make it clear about Tony.[129] George and I were having a lunch time drink in the hall when Tony walked in, wearing an army shirt and a tin hat. Under his arm was his same old parachute. On the 7th, when we lost him, he had bailed out over the German lines. He landed all right and hid in a ditch. After it was dark, he crept out and he walked twenty miles, still hanging on to his parachute. He found a British patrol with whom he was eventually evacuated.

'But I wish you could have seen him walk into the mess, his face covered with smiles. He said to George, 'I am sorry I am late, sir.' All George did was to call Macey and say, 'Bring us a drink.' George asked Tony why he had lugged his parachute all the way home with him and Tony said, 'Well, I know that this one works and I might have to use it again.'[130]

'The new boys are doing fine. Tom Morgan is first rate. He shot down his first Hun yesterday - a Heinkel.[131] There is a lot of activity now that the blitz has really begun. Caesar is out of hospital and on leave in Guildford. Carey and I are going up to London to have a party with him to-night.'

On 26 May Caesar Hull and two others were detached to a muddy airstrip at Bodø where he managed to take off and attack numbers of aircraft. He claimed two or three of the raiders but four actually fell. The state of the airstrip made further operations foolhardy but some of the troops were being withdrawn by sea during the night and the small RAF contingent at Bodø was determined to provide what support it could muster. All hands laid down more snow-boards until these covered almost all the airstrip but successive patrols that night by Caesar Hull and two other pilots proved fruitless. Next morning Caesar and Lieutenant Anthony Lydekker, a Fleet Air Arm armament officer with flying experience, had breakfast and were at readiness when the Luftwaffe attacked. Caesar Hull wrote up the events in his diary:

'Suddenly at 0800 hours the balloon went up. There were 110s and 87s all round us and the 87s started dive-bombing a jetty about 800 yards from the aerodrome. Tony's aircraft started at once and I waved him off, then after trying mine a bit longer got yellow and together with the fitter made a dive into a nearby barn. From there we watched the dive-bombing in terror until it seemed that they were not actually concentrating on the aerodrome. Got the Gladiator going and shot off without helmet or waiting to do anything up. Circled the 'drome climbing and pinned an 87 at the bottom of a dive. It made off slowly over the sea and just as I was turning away another 87 shot up past me and his shots went through my windscreen knocking me out for a while. Came to, and was thanking my lucky stars when I heard rat-tat behind me and felt my Gladiator hit. Went into right-hand turn and dive but could not get it out. Had given up hope at 200 feet when she centralized and I gave her a burst of engine to clear some large rocks. Further rat-tats from behind, so gave up hope and decided to get her down. Held off, and then crashed.'

Caesar was shot down by a Bf 110 flown by Leutnant Helmut Lent of I/ZG76, crashing with wounds to his head and knee. Lydekker was wounded and with his Gladiator badly shot up, he managed by skilful evasive action to get back to Bardufoss, where his aircraft was promptly classed as a complete 'write-off'. Caesar was evacuated from Norway in a Sunderland flying-boat and on 21 June was awarded a DFC which credited him with five victories in Norway.

'John's squadron were soon re-formed and back in the battle' wrote Hector Bolitho. 'Two weeks passed between the time of his leave and the day when he was to appear at Buckingham Palace, to receive his DFC and in this time he brought down two more Messerschmitts, both on the same day [19 July]. But his new glory ended rather sadly... he crashed into a villa at Worthing and landed in a cucumber frame, with a broken collar bone.

'I travelled to the South Coast in the late afternoon of the following day and found him propped up, with nurses to fuss over him and a view of the sea. By this time I was playing Tacitus to his Agricola so I sat down and wrote his story, as he told it to me.

'It was a lovely evening and the wind was warm about us as we passed through the slip-stream of our aircraft to our cockpits. We were to patrol the coast at 10,000 feet and we soon reached the patrol line at this height. I could see for miles. There was a thin layer of cloud one thousand feet above us and it shaded our eyes from the sun.

'We were flying east when three enemy aircraft were seen flying west in the clouds overhead. I told my leader that I would climb above the clouds with my flight and investigate. As I did this, no less than twelve Messerschmitt 109 fighters emerged from the clouds. Still climbing, I made for the sun and turned and gave the order for my flight to break up and attack. In a moment our battle began. Our six Hurricanes were against the enemy's twelve.

'The eighteen aircraft chased round and round in and out of the cloud. I chose my first opponent. He seemed to be dreaming and I quickly got on to his tail and gave him a short burst which damaged him. I flew in closer and gave him a second dose. It was enough. He dived, out of control and I followed him down to 6,000 feet. There I circled for a minute or two and watched him dive vertically into the calm sea. There was only the tell-tale patch of oil on the water to mark where he had disappeared.[132]

'I opened my hood for a breath of fresh air and looked about the sky. There was no sign of either the enemy or of my own flight. I was alone, so I climbed back into the cloud which was thin and misty. Three Messerschmitts; flying in line astern, crossed in front of me, so close that I could see the black crosses on their wings and fuselages. I opened fire on number three of the formation. We went round and round, in decreasing circles, as I fired. I was lucky again. I had the pleasure of seeing my bullets hit him. Pieces of his wings flew off and black smoke came from just behind his cockpit. He dived and I fired one more burst at him, directly from astern. We were doing a phenomenal speed. Then my ammunition gave out just as the other two Messerschmitts attacked me. The cloud was too thin to be of help. It was merely misty and you could see the blue of the sky throughout. So I had to rely on my aeroplane. I twisted and turned and dived towards the coast. I was flying at about 16,000 feet, eight miles or so out to sea. But they were too accurate. I could hear the deafening thud of their bullets hitting the armour plate behind my back and I could see great hunks being torn off my wings. There was a strong smell of glycol in the cockpit, so I knew that the radiator had been hit. What little wisps of cloud there were, were far beyond my reach and my engine was chugging badly. It was terribly hot.

'Then came a cold, stinging pain in my left foot. One of the Jerry bullets had found its mark. But it really did not hurt much. I tried to dive faster to the sea and make my escape, low down, when the control column became useless in my hand. Black smoke poured into the cockpit and I could not see.

'I knew that I must leave the aircraft. Everything after this was perfectly calm. I was now at about 10,000 feet, but still some miles out to sea. I lifted my seat, undid my harness and opened the hood.

'The wind was my ally. It felt like a hand lifting me from the cockpit, by my hair. But it was actually a combination of the wind and the slipstream catching under my helmet and pulling me free of the aircraft. It was a pleasant sensation. I found myself in mid-air, beautifully cool and dropping without any feeling of speed. It seemed hours before I reminded myself to pull my ripcord and open my parachute. This part was quite easy. The noise of the wind stopped and there was a terrific jerk. It seemed that my body was being pulled in every place at the same time. Then I began to swing like a pendulum. Then I vomited, just as I looked down and saw the coast and the sea near Worthing.

'I stopped swinging and settled down to look about me. Then I had a horrible fear. I felt terribly afraid of falling out of my harness into the sea. I put my hands up and held the straps above me. I was frightened of touching the quick release box on my tummy by mistake.

'I became calm and I was able to enjoy the full view of the world below. The beach was some miles away, with soldiers. And there were the long lines of villas in Worthing. There was no sensation of speed. I knew I was descending only because the ripples on the water became bigger and the soldiers on the beach seemed to grow.

'Then came a minute of anxiety. As I floated down one of the Messerschmitts appeared. The pilot circled around me and I was alarmed. He was near enough for me to see his face ... as much as I could see, with his helmet and goggles. I felt very much that he would shoot me. And I felt helpless. But he didn't shoot. He behaved very well. He flew so near the noise of his aircraft was terrific. He flew around me about one and a half times and then he suddenly opened a piece of his hood and waved to me. Then he dived towards the sea and made off across the Channel to France.

'I'd like to know why he let me get away. He could have got me as simply as anything, but he didn't try.

'When I recovered from my fear I found that the wind was still being friendly. It was carrying me in towards the beach. I took out my cigarettes and lit one with my lighter without any difficulty. Ages seemed to pass and I was quite happy. I had forgotten about my foot but I suppose that it had been bleeding all the time because I began to feel rather sleepy. I threw away my cigarette as I came nearer and nearer to the beach. I heard the 'All Clear' siren and as I passed over the beach and the houses on the sea front, I could see people coming out of their shelters-people looking up at me. I was then at about 1,000 feet.

'The changing temperature of the air at a low level seemed to affect my speed - and I began to sway a little. I could hear my parachute flapping like the sound of a sail in a small boat. The soldiers' faces became quite clear. I could see their rifles but they were not pointing at me. I must have looked English, even at a thousand feet. This was comforting.

'I became anxious again, for the first time since the enemy pilot circled around me. I was afraid that my escapade was to end by my being killed against the wall of a seaside villa. It did not seem possible that I could reach the fields beyond. It was all very quick after that. I seemed to rush ... and then I hit the roof, or the edge of the roof, of a house. I suppose my parachute crumpled then because the next thing I realized was that I was going through a garden fence backwards and then, bang into a cucumber frame.

'I lay still for a moment. Then I released my parachute. I don't know quite what happened. I was in pain. My collar bone was broken and I was pretty badly bruised from hitting the house and the fence. And my foot was still bleeding. But I remember that when I released my parachute and lay still, my brain was quite clear and I whimpered because I was so grateful for being alive.

'It was a little house and a little garden. The woman ran out and others came, 'because they had seen me coming down I suppose. The woman brought me tea and then a policeman came with a glass of whisky. He was in the street and he handed it over the garden wall. I drank the whisky and then the tea. There seemed to be about twenty people wanting to be kind to me. The woman who owned the garden brought me a blanket.

'My ankle and shoulder were bound up and an ambulance arrived.

'I was in awful pain, but my mind was quite clear. I remember that as I was being lifted into the ambulance, there were some men who had seen the battle and they seemed to know that I had brought down a Hun. One of them said, 'We saw what you did sir' and then a woman pushed a little boy forward and said, 'Ernie, give the gentleman those cigarettes.' And the little boy came running up to me and said, 'Good luck sir. When I grow up I'm going to be an airman too!'

In the first year of the war, 43 Squadron lost thirty-six pilots for the reward of ninety-seven German aircraft. John Vincent 'Tubby' Badger, who had been with 43 in the early days, came back as its third commanding officer since the war began.[133] On 8 August when a dozen Hurricanes on 43 Squadron advanced to meet the third raid, 82 Stukas and their Bf 109s were stepped up in tiers 'looking like an escalator on the Piccadilly Underground' as Tubby Badger put it. What Frank Carey saw was 'a raid so terrible and memorable it was like trying to stop a steam roller'. According to John Simpson, Tony Woods-Scawen, 'brave as a lion and blind as a bat (we called him Wombat) flew clean through the Stukas, firing as he went.'[134] Tony was the 'biggest and smoothest flirt' that I had yet come across. His room is surrounded with pictures of naked jobs much to the delight of Knockers North, a New Zealander after my own heart, with whom I could gossip about the beauties of the Southern Alps and the joy of New Zealand fish and butter. A frightfully brave little chap, he had been ill with his kidneys and he had been badly shot up in the Battle of Britain. His back and arms were riddled with pieces of shrapnel. He would pinch little points of steel out of his arm, like blackheads. His body was a perpetual distress to him. He had two rows of false teeth and a face that laughed all the time. He was only twenty-four, but his hair was grey and if his face had ever rested from smiling I think he would have looked very old. [135]

'All the key men fighting with 43 were shot down or killed within eight days' wrote Hector Bolitho. 'Tubby Badger was shot down on August 30 and was unable to fly again. Caesar Hull took over the command on 1 September, a fulfilment to his career which meant more to him than all his victories: He didn't live long enough to have the third stripe sewn on his sleeve. He led 43 through a succession of combats for only seven days. On 8 September he was found dead, beside his aircraft, in a field in Kent. He had been killed by a bullet during the Battle of the London Docks. The Huns had come over in continuous waves all day and Caesar had led the squadron in to attack a formation of Dornier bombers. Tony Woods-Scawen was killed on 2 September. Tony crashed near an aircraft of 85 Squadron which had also been shot down, in the same battle. Unknown to Tony, the aircraft was flown by his brother. They were killed within a few minutes of each other and fell side by side (sic).[136] Tom Morgan was shot down on September 6.[137] On September 7 Flight Lieutenant Richard Carew 'Dickie' Reynell, one of the finest pilots in the country, was shot down and killed.'

The Australian, who was born at Reynella, South Australia, where his family owned large winery estates, arrived in Britain in 1929 to study at Oxford and he became a Hawker Test Pilot. Reynell had been attached to 43 for only two weeks to gain combat experience with a Hurricane and he had destroyed a Bf 109 on 2 September. On the morning of the 7th he was called back to Hawkers because of the death of another test pilot, but he opted to finish out the day with the squadron. In the afternoon 43 Squadron was scrambled to meet the first big raid on London. The squadron had 12 Hurricanes against well over 100 enemy aircraft. Reynell was shot down and killed by a Bf 109 over the Thames Estuary. [138]

'The ranks of 43 were sadly thin' wrote Hector Bolitho 'when the squadron was posted to Usworth on 9 September to recover itself and reform for fresh battles.'

John Simpson was resting his ankle and shoulder in Cornwall during the battles of August and September. He wrote to Hector Bolitho on 4

September:

'For two days I have been thinking of Caesar. I loved him as I would a brother. He was more than a rare person in the RAF and there can never be anyone to replace him in character, charm and kindliness. We came to 43 together and grew up in it together. We knew each other from A to Z and it was a privilege no one else could share.

'This hell cannot go on forever. And reassure yourself with the feeling and knowledge that we do the same to them. I was glad I was here, in a quiet, calm place when the news came. I swim and fish with the wonderful old fishermen and I walk miles into the woods every day. They are full of giant hydrangeas and wild orchids...

'Your letter about Caesar. I don't know what to say. I thought I was quite used by now to people dying. Do you realize that there are only three of us who were with the squadron when the war began... still alive and serving with the squadron? But Caesar was like a brother. I went for a long walk in the woods when the news came and I cried for the first time since I was little.

'Poor 43. But we can take it. We will have to begin all over again. New CO. New pilots. But the squadron spirit is safe. Dear old Caesar. He commanded the squadron he began in as a pilot officer. I would have loved to fly with him as my CO. It seems funny to think that I shall never see him shaking that left foot of his as he used to do when he was excited. And how he used to rub his nose between his thumb and forefinger when he was nervous. And that laugh! He had a good life and I think that he loved every minute of it. I never heard anybody say an unkind thing about Caesar and I never heard him say an unkind thing about anybody else. One can't say more than that.'

The countryside seemed very empty when John and I snatched three days of leave in Essex, before he went back to his squadron. There was nobody we knew at Duxford or at Debden. The Battle of Britain had taken still more of our friends. Rodney Wilkinson, with whom I used to drink bitter coffee in Jerusalem and who shared a house with me in London for a few months at the beginning of the war, had been killed almost as soon as he went back to operational flying. [139] He was one of my oldest flying friends and when he was at Duxford, long before the war, he used to come to see John and myself and go into huddles of pilot talk. Once when he stayed for the week-end, he left at crack of dawn with my shaving brush. He flew over the house an hour after and dropped the brush, tied to a multi-coloured message streamer. Somebody in the village reported us to the police and the story grew into a scandal. My name ended with a vowel, so I was obviously Italian. And the aircraft that flew low over my house was obviously dropping messages from Mussolini.

'The Royal Air Force was faced by a romantic but formidable problem at the end of the first year of the war. The service had to absorb the hundreds of European pilots who came to Britain when their own countries fell before the German invaders. In the early months, Polish and Czech pilots had crossed Europe to join what previously had been an essentially British service. Then came Norwegian, Dutch, Danish and French pilots who escaped to continue their fight in Britain. The migration of these warriors was overshadowed at the time by reports of battle and disaster. Some day their story will be gathered together and told in all its majesty.

'One morning a French boy of eighteen years came into my office at the Air Ministry. He had gathered petrol together in secret, gallon by gallon, until he had enough to dare to fly to England so that he could fight for France. He had prepared his shaky old aircraft for the flight in the shelter of a wood. And he had flown across, knowing that he would be arrested and more or less certain that he would be fired upon by our anti-aircraft guns. He had never flown beyond the French, coast before. Yet he came because he believed that the freedom of his country could be recovered from this island.

'One watched the advent of these pilots in amazement. They came, from broken Poland and Czechoslovakia, from unhappy France and from Holland. It was not easy for the RAF to absorb all of them, with their multitude of tongues. Many squadron and flight commanders in the Air Force found themselves in command of pilots who could not speak a word of English. This was one of John's problems when he went back to his squadron near Newcastle in September, 1940. For the moment, fighting in the air was his second consideration. Czechs and Poles had arrived to be trained into the discipline of 43. Tom Morgan was in command [140] and John, with an old friend, John Kilmartin [141] were the flight commanders. They had to reform 43, bringing in new young British pilots and adapting themselves to the temperament of the Czechs and Poles. John's letters during the next few months show how his startled Englishness over the advent of the exiles was slowly broken down and turned to affectionate respect. In his first letter after going back to his squadron, he wrote:

'I am as tired as I was two months ago. None of the pilots here are operational. Czechs and Poles for the most part, who cannot speak English and who understand very little.

'A week or so later, he wrote: 'I was wrong about the Czechs and Poles. I suppose I was a bit depressed, finding so many new people. It did not seem like the old 43. I miss Caesar and the others terribly. Thank God for Killie. He is like Laurie in many ways. Nice, unreasonable Irish. He knows all the old jokes add slang and the songs we used to sing. So we are like a couple of old veterans, sighing for the old days and snorting at the young. But I took your lecture to heart. It is very good for all of us having to work and fly with the Czechs and Poles. Their flying is wizard and they are grand.

'Killy has three Poles in 'A' Flight and I have two Czechs in mine. They are Sergeants [Jaroslev] Sika and [Josef] Pipa. Nice names, don't you think! Sika and Pipa. They are grand pilots and very keen to go south and have a smack at the Hun.

'You were right. The Poles are the most amazing people. They hate so passionately. One of them has a very sad face. Sometimes I see him sitting in the mess and he runs his hands over his face and sighs. And what my two Czechs have been through! I'd like to feel that every Englishman would face the same for his country. These boys went through all that happened in Czechoslovakia, then to fight in France and then escaped and made their way to this country. It shakes one to the core ... seeing patriotism like that. They both wear the Czech war cross and the French Croix de Guerre. Sika, who flies with me as my No. 2, is a charmer, but very naughty. Now that we can talk easily I find their sense of humour not so very different from ours. We laugh at the same things.

'I am teaching him to sing some of the Air Force songs. You should see his face when he tries to sing:

We are the fighting 43
Up from Sussex by the sea...

'His English is now quite good. The Czechs seem to pick it up very quickly. I am going to the Sergeant's mess to drink with them to-night. I'm told that they drink spirits neat.

'It has been interesting to see the way everybody now likes them. I suppose we are a lot of stodgy Englishmen, imagining that foreigners are difficult. Now everybody likes the Czechs and the Poles and the ground crew are wonderful with them. All out to help. It is good to see the fitters leap to it and treat Sika and Pipa with just a little more kindness because they are strangers. As Killy says, 'It's a good thing.'

'The Poles are very intelligent. Tom Morgan, Killy and I took them to the local last night and by the end of the evening they had taken possession of the pub.

'We were given bacon and eggs and beer with the owner and his wife. And they were both so charming to the Poles. They were very touched and the quiet one, who sits in the mess alone, was obviously moved. They kept saying, 'Sank you' and one of them bowed over the pub lady's hand when he said, 'Good night.'

'Now that we are all settling down, the spirit of the squadron is incredible. After all those knocks! Killy and I feel very pleased about it. The 43 spirit can never die; however much it is mauled.

'At the end of November John brought down his tenth enemy aircraft. He wrote the story to me some time afterwards:

'Our work here is local defence and the defence of the coastal areas where occasional Huns might snoop about, hoping to tell their Headquarters the position of our convoys. By catching them in time, before they can transmit the good news, we may ward off a big attack. Sometimes in bad weather, a sneak raider will come in under cover of the cloud and drop a stick of bombs on a shipyard. We are here for all these things and to rest while we are pulling ourselves together again.

'Now I'll tell you what happened. I was at readiness with my flight in the early afternoon. The weather was lousy, low cloud at 200 feet and visibility the width of the aerodrome. It did not seem likely that anything would happen so we were not at instant readiness. We were sitting in the dispersal hut, rather cold, browned off and hating life. I was asked for on the telephone. There was a report of one aircraft off the coast near Newcastle. I was asked if I could send off two aircraft to have a look for it.

I did not like the look of the weather so I decided to go alone. The little Czech Sergeant, Sika, was very fussed. He is my No. 2 and I find that now we are getting over the language difficulty I understand him much better. He is very keen and his eyes sparkled and then went sad when I said he could not come with me.

'I took off through the mist and cloud. It was filthy. I flew out to sea and at about five thousand feet I emerged into bright sunlight, above the clouds. The surface of the clouds below me was perfectly level. I am told that this has something to do with atmospheric conditions near big industrial areas, but that is all too clever for me. Well, I did not know where I was. I was told over the R/T where to go and after about fifteen minutes I saw an aircraft. It was also flying over the top of the clouds, going east. I felt that it must be a Hun. As I closed on him I recognized it as a Ju 88. I was about a quarter of a mile away and above him. Apparently he had not seen me. I closed in, fired and hit his starboard motor. He dived for the clouds, but I fired again from closer quarters. This stopped his starboard engine and pieces fell from his port wing root. He waffled in the air, banked over and dived steeply into the clouds. It was too risky in that weather to follow him. So I fixed my position over the R/T and returned with some difficulty. I could only claim a 'probable' but I hoped that that dive was his last. Fortunately for me, the Hun had crashed through the cloud into the sea, near to a trawler. The captain reported that a Ju 88 had crashed nearby and as the time was the same, my 'probable' became a' destroyed.' [142]

'About this time there was a complaint in some of the newspapers that the ground crews of the Royal Air Force were not being sufficiently honoured. I do not think the question ever arose among the older squadrons of the Service. I went to stay with 43 for a few days late in the winter of 1940 and I realized, as well as anybody bent over a desk in the Air Ministry can realize, the pride and faith that held the flying personnel and the ground crews together.

'The word party has a special meaning for older members of the Royal Air Force. It does not necessarily call for invitations, lights and many people. Seven or eight pilots sitting in a room, tippling and talking and singing, may have a party, if the spirit that is with them is right. The number of pilots in 43 who could have a party in, the old sense of the word, had become very few. When I went to stay with the squadron, now and then, I felt that an age of time had fallen upon them in little more than a year.

'One evening I spent with 43 is clear in my memory. There were only Tom Morgan, Kilmartin and John left of the older ones. And there was Knockers North, who also came into the picture because he had been with the squadron almost a year.

'Tom Morgan, Killy, Knockers, John and I stood before the fire, laughing and sighing over what had been. It seemed to me that the whole pattern of the changed Air Force was spread in that room, with its dilapidated armchairs, its ubiquitous RAF carpet and the mantelpiece upon which we rested our glasses.

'Tom Morgan was English to the core: modest, fiercely proud of the

Service, devoted to his wife and certain of his own ideas. His was the Englishness that cannot boast. He commanded 43 and kept its spirit high, through terrible vicissitudes. [143]

'Next to the typical Englishman was John, not so typically English ... but more English than anything else. A man who had killed the enemy without losing the gentleness of his own spirit.

'And Kilmartin! I don't think one can say anything about Killy except that he is Irish. That implies charm, casualness, courage and a loyalty to his friends which is a form of religion.'

'...Death followed quickly on the days of fun.

'On May 10, 1941 the London Gazette announced that John had been awarded a bar to his DFC because he had 'displayed great skill and initiative both as a squadron commander and as an individual fighter.' The notice added, 'He has destroyed twelve enemy aircraft of which two have been shot down at night.'

'On fine days, the King stands in the courtyard of Buckingham Palace to decorate the sailors, the soldiers and pilots. July 6 was a coldish day and the ceremony was in the entrance hall where the walls awaken scenes of one hundred years ago, with early Winterhalter portraits of the old Duchess of Kent, the young Queen and her husband.

'A band played but otherwise, there was no sign that this was a special day. The King walked on to a low dais and pinned the medals on the heroes, one after the other, in the long procession. There was not a glimmer of pomp. One felt that he had simply asked them into his house to thank them for what they had done.

'Mothers, wives and sisters had come to look on; old mothers in spick and span black dresses, with faces and hands that told the story of work. Young wives with children. Fathers from the countryside in gleaming white collars and Sunday suits. It was a domestic and unpretentious scene rather than a ceremony. A year before when he appeared before the King to receive his DFC, John's arm had been in a sling. The royal memory did not fail. The King asked him, 'How many have you destroyed?'

'John replied, 'Thirteen, sir.'

'Then the King asked, 'When did you get your DFC?'

'John told him that it was in June of the previous year. The King asked, 'Wasn't your arm in a sling?' John walked out of the Palace, beneath the balcony from which Queen Victoria waved farewell to the soldiers leaving for the Crimea. It seemed that he was taking his place in an old and splendid company.

'That afternoon John went into the nursing home. About four days afterwards a nurse walked into his bedroom and said, 'There's a telephone message just come for you. Somebody has told the King that you are ill and he has sent a message to say that he hopes you will soon be better.' [144]

Endnotes Chapter 12

85 He undertook the first of several lecture tours of America, in 1938-39 and he settled in Britain. At the start of WWII he joined the RAFVR as an intelligence officer with the rank of squadron leader, editing the *RAF Weekly Bulletin*, which in 1941 became the *RAF Journal*. In 1942 he was appointed editor of the *Coastal Command Intelligence Review*.

86 Group Captain (later Air Marshal Sir) Richard Llewellyn Roger Atcherley KBE CB AFC* was one or a pair of twins born on 12 January 1904 serving in the RAF. His brother was Air Vice Marshal David Francis William Atcherley CB CBE DSO DFC who destroyed three aircraft flying Beaufighters on 25 Squadron and was killed in a crash in a Meteor jet fighter in the Mediterranean area on 8 June 1952. Air Marshal Sir Richard Atcherley died on 18 April 1970 aged 66.

87 John Eric Loverseed was born on 4 December 1910 in Downham in Norfolk, the son of Liberal politician and former MP for Sudbury, John Frederick Loverseed. He flew with Republican forces in the Spanish Civil War in 1937/38 and was injured in January 1937. He rejoined the RAF in November 1939, as a non-commissioned officer. After a refresher flying course, he was posted to No.1 Anti-Aircraft Co-operation Unit (AACU) on 20 May 1940. The AACU towed targets for anti-aircraft practice. On 21 May he joined 501 Squadron as a sergeant pilot. 501 had been deployed to airfields in France as part of the Advanced Air Striking Force (AASF) providing air support for the British Expeditionary Force. He was injured when his Hawker Hurricane crash-landed on 31 May and was evacuated to a hospital in England. By the time he recovered and returned to his unit on 19 July, 501 Squadron had also returned to England following the Fall of France. He took part in six operational sorties in the Battle of Britain before being posted back to 1 AACU on 19 August 1940. He had been promoted to the rank of Warrant Officer by the time he was awarded the AFC on 1 January 1943. That same year he was elected as a wartime MP for the Common Wealth Party. He was later a co-founder of the pacifist Fellowship Party. Loverseed left the Common Wealth Party in November 1944, becoming an independent and then joining the Labour Party in May 1945. He was expelled from the Labour Party in July 1945. In May 1955 he stood against Herbert Morrison unsuccessfully for South Lewisham as an Independent Pacifist. In June 1955 he was a co-founder of the pacifist Fellowship Party, which claimed to be the oldest environmentalist party in Britain. John Eric Loverseed married five times. He died in 1962. His son, Raymond Eric William Loverseed was born on an RAF base in Egypt in 1932. Bill joined the RAF in 1952 and flew with the Red Arrows in their first year, 1965, and also in 1970. He took command of the Red Arrows in 1971 after the previous leader, Dennis Hazell, broke his leg after ejecting due to an engine failure in practice in November 1970. Four Red Arrows' pilots were killed in an accident at RAF Kemble in January 1971, when two planes carrying two men each collided in mid-air. Bill Loverseed was promoted to Squadron Leader in July 1971 but resigned his commission in May 1972. He married four times. He flew a Buffalo transport plane that crash-landed at the Farnborough Air Show in 1984 and a Piper Cherokee that suffered severe icing and crashed in Newfoundland in 1987. He died in 1998 on a Dash 7 that he was piloting on a test flight over Devon.

88 Air Commodore Sydney Leo Gregory 'Poppy' Pope CBE MC DFC AFC MiD, born Dublin, Ireland 27 March 1898 - died 5 November 1980, was a WWI flying ace with six aerial victories. He made the RAF his career, retiring in 1946. Pope joined the Inns of Court Army Officer Training Corps as a lance corporal in 1916 and was commissioned a second lieutenant in May 1916. He was assigned to 60 Squadron in Bloody April 1917 where he originally flew a Nieuport fighter. Pope scored twice with a Nieuport, on 8 and 20 June 1917. Flying a Royal Aircraft Factory SE5 he destroyed an Albatros D.III on 16 September. Flying the SE5a, he destroyed two reconnaissance planes on 8 November and a D.III on the 11th. One week later, he was wounded and forced to land near Saint Julien. He ended the war with a Military Cross. He served in Iraq and Egypt

89 This Comet was flown by Owen Cathcart-Jones and Kenneth Waller. They arrived in Melbourne on 25 October and were placed fourth in the Speed Race.

90 Caesar Barraud Hull was born in Shangani, Southern Rhodesia, but was brought up in South Africa, becoming a cadet in the SAAF Reserve. In 1935 he was accepted for a short service commission in the RAF and on completion of training joined 43 Squadron at Tangmere in August 1936. Peter Prosser Hanks, from York, was born on 29 July 1917 and joined the RAF late in 1935, being posted to I Squadron, with whom he scored eight victories on Hurricane Is in 1940. He rounded off a long and distinguished career, retiring in June 1964 with the rank of Group Captain

DSO AFC. His score stands at 13 destroyed, 1 and 3 shared probable, 6 damaged and 2 probably destroyed on the ground. *Aces High* by Christopher Shores and Clive Williams (Grub Street, London 1994).

91 Dame Gwen Lucy Ffrangcon-Davies OBE (25 January 1891-27 January 1992) was a British actress and centenarian who died aged 101. She was born in London of a Welsh family; the name 'Ffrangcon' originates from a valley in Snowdonia. She made her stage debut in 1911 as a singer as well as an actress and received encouragement in her career from Ellen Terry. In 1924 she played Juliet opposite John Gielgud as Romeo and Gielgud was grateful to her for the rest of his life for the kindness she showed him, casting her as *Queen Anne in Richard of Bordeaux* in 1934. In 1938 she appeared with Ivor Novello in a production of *Henry V* at Drury Lane, and as Mrs. Manningham in the first production of *Gas Light*. She played Lady Macbeth for almost an entire year in 1942 opposite John Gielgud's *Macbeth*. She won the *Evening Standard Award* in 1958 for her performance as Mary Tyrone in *Long Day's Journey Into night*. She retired from the stage in 1970, but continued to appear on radio and television. In the 1980s, well into her 90s, she appeared on Wogan, in which she recited, word for word, the famous death scene of Juliet. She made her final acting appearance in a teleplay of the Sherlock Holmes mystery *The Master Blackmailer* at the age of 100. Her films included *The Witches* (1966) and *The Devil Rides Out* (1968), both for Hammer Films.

92 On 18 August he was last seen pursuing two Ju 88s after combat with Bf 109s north of Foulness Point and did not return.

93 On the first day of the 'Blitzkrieg', 10 May 1940 he was slightly wounded and next day was shot down by flak and taken prisoner. He managed to escape and return to his unit. *Aces High* by Christopher Shores and Clive Williams (Grub Street, London 1994).

94 *Aces High* by Christopher Shores and Clive Williams (Grub Street, London 1994).

95 3 Squadron, commanded by Flight Lieutenant Walter Churchill.

96 Pilot Officer Robert Laurie Lorimer was killed on 14 May 1940 at Ste Lupe-Terria, France, flying a Hurricane.

97 Flying Officer Harold Hugo 'Bill' Sykes, who was born on 8 August 1918 at Alexandria, Egypt, was KIA on 28 November 1940 on 80 Squadron when his Gladiator II collided with a Fiat CR.42 on the Greek-Albanian border. Both aircraft went down.

98 Lieutenant H. J. 'George' Feeny was lost aboard the aircraft carrier Glorious which was returning from Norway, on 8 June 1940 while operating on 802 Squadron FAA.

99 Pilot Officer Geoffrey N. Gaunt, a Spitfire pilot during the Battle of Britain, serving on 609 Squadron, was from a well-known textile family and screen star James Mason was a cousin. Gaunt was KIA on Sunday 15 September 1940. His friend 'Red' Tobin, an American pilot, saw 'a Spitfire... spinning down on fire'. 'I sure hope it wasn't Jeff and if it was - well from now on he'll be flying in clearer sky.' It was Gaunt's Spitfire. *Duel of Eagles* by Peter Townsend (Weidenfeld & Nicolson, 1970).

100 Peter Wooldridge Townsend was born in Rangoon, Burma, on 22 November 1914, being brought to England as a child to be raised in Devon. After attending Haileybury School he entered the RAF College, Cranwell, in September 1933, graduating top of his entry two years later and being posted to 1 Squadron. In January 1936 he was sent out to Singapore where he flew Vildebeest torpedo-bombers with 36 Squadron. In 1937 he was sent back to England due to a nervously-induced skin condition and he joined 43 Squadron, returning to fighters. Claimed by Coastal Command because of his Vildebeest experience, he was sent to the School of Navigation and then posted to 217 Squadron. Claiming that this brought a resumption of his skin condition, he obtained a return to 43 Squadron. *Aces High* by Christopher Shores and Clive Williams (Grub Street, London 1994).

101 *Duel of Eagles* by Peter Townsend (Weidenfeld & Nicolson, 1970).

102 Early in May 1940 he was posted to 263 Squadron as a flight commander as the unit prepared for its second sojourn in Norway, the unit's Gladiator IIs being flown off HMS *Furious* to Bardufoss in the far north. On 26 May Hull and two others were detached to a muddy airstrip at Bodø. He managed to get off the ground to engage numbers of aircraft; claiming two or three of these as shot down though four actually fell. Next day he shot down a Ju 87, but was then hit by another and shot down by a Bf 110 flown by Leutnant Helmut Lent of I/ZG76, crashing with wounds to the head and knee. He was evacuated back to the UK in a Sunderland flying boat. On

21 June he was awarded a DFC and credited him with five victories in Norway. On 31 August he was posted back to 43 Squadron as CO. On 7 September he was last seen diving to attack bombers, failing to return. It was believed that the 27 year old Rhodesian had been shot down by Bf 109s. His score was 4 and 4 shared destroyed, 1 unconfirmed destroyed, 2 and 1 shared probable, 2 damaged. *Aces High* by Christopher Shores and Clive Williams (Grub Street, London 1994).

103 On 30 January Caesar Hull's and Frank Carey's claims each for a half share was for He 111H-2 1H+KM of 4./KG26 which went down 10 miles east of Coquet Isle. *Aces High* by Christopher Shores and Clive Williams (Grub Street, London 1994).

104 It was on 3 February and Peter Townsend was awarded a third share with 'Tiger' Folkes and Sergeant Hallowes in the destruction of Heinkel 111 1H+FM of 4/KG 26 five miles south of Whitby. It was the first German aircraft to crash on English soil in WWII. Folkes - 'outwardly Timid but a tiger at heart' was killed a few weeks' later.

105 Air Vice-Marshal R. E. Saul CB DFC who was then in command of 13 Group.

106 George Lott was born in Portsmouth on 28 October 1906. Rejected by the Royal Navy he entered the RAF as an apprentice. Learning to fly, he went to 19 Squadron in 1927 as an NCO and was commissioned in 1933. He served on 41 Squadron in Iraq, 1935-38 and then with 11 Group, Fighter Command, until he took command of 43 Squadron in October 1939. *Aces High* by Christopher Shores and Clive Williams (Grub Street, London 1994).

107 Flying Officer J. D. Edmonds.

108 Originally claimed as probably destroyed and believed to be He 111 of II/KG26 which force-landed at base 40% damaged. However, the crew of a Ju 88 of I/KG30 were picked up from the sea (dead) and confirmation followed. It is believed that the latter aircraft had fallen to ships' gunners, rather than the Hurricane's however.

109 The gun ports on an aircraft are covered with fabric which is naturally blown away when the first shot is fired.

110 Now Wing Commander F. R. Carey DFM DFC and two bars. He rose from the rank of Sergeant Pilot to Wing Commander in two years.

111 Caesar Hull and Frank Carey each received a half share for the destruction of Heinkel 111H-2 1H+GM of 2/KG26 which went down 15 miles off Tynemouth.

112 This Heinkel, re-coded AW177 and which featured in Combat America in July 1943, crashed at Polebrook on 10 November 1943 while attempting to avoid a Ju 88 of the Flight, killing seven of the eleven men on board.

113 The British Government ordered Bomber Command to carry out a reprisal raid on one of the German seaplane bases but only where there was no civilian housing nearby. On the night of 19/20 March the seaplane base at Hörnum on the southernmost tip of the island of Sylt was the target for thirty Whitleys and twenty Hampdens and 41 crews claimed to have got their bombs away accurately. This was the biggest bombing operation of the war so far and the first raid on a German land target. *Bomber Command War Diaries* by Martin Middlebrook and Chris Everitt (Midland Publishing Ltd 1985, 1990, 1995).

114 Herbert James Lempriere 'Darkie' Hallowes was born in Lambeth, London on 17 April 1912. He lived for three years in the Falkland Islands as a boy, where his father was a medical officer. In January 1929 he joined the RAF Apprentice Scheme, training at Halton as a metal rigger, passing out in 1932. In 1934 he volunteered for pilot training, becoming a sergeant pilot in August 1936 and being posted to 43 Squadron. During the fighting over the French coastal area on 7 June his Hurricane was set on fire by an attacking Bf 109E. This overshot as he was about to bail out and he remained in his cockpit long enough to claim its destruction, before bailing out and suffering a dislocated shoulder. Soldiers who picked him up confirmed having seen the 109 crash. He was awarded a DFM and Bar on 6 September and was commissioned that month. In November he was posted to 65 Squadron as a flight commander, but was rested soon afterwards. Early in 1942 he began a second tour as a flight commander in 122 Squadron. In July he was given command of 222 Squadron. A month later he began leading 165 Squadron, with which unit he made his final claims. His total score stands at 17 and 2 shared destroyed, 4 probables, 8 damaged. He was awarded a DFC in June 1943. He had been rested again in March, but in October 1943 commenced a fourth tour, leading 504 Squadron until March 1944. He was then promoted Acting Wing Commander and became airfield commander at RAF Dunsfold. He remained in the RAF after the war, retiring in July 1956 as Wing Commander. *Aces High* by Christopher Shores and Clive

Williams (Grub Street, London 1994).

115 *Duel of Eagles* by Peter Townsend. The third Heinkel was shot down by Flying Officer J. D. 'Eddie' Edmonds. He was killed on 7 June 1940.

116 *Airfields of Caithness* Focus (GMS).

117 Caesar Hull and Peter Townsend were among six pilots who shared in the destruction of the Heinkel of 3(F)/Obdl. *Aces High* by Christopher Shores and Clive Williams (Grub Street, London 1994).

118 In his book, *Duel of Eagles,* Townsend wrote that 'four more of Goering's airmen' perished in the sea 'after a skirmish with 43 Squadron. 'With seven of us lining up for a crack at that pitiful target the attack was a shambles. As I came in I could see the tail unit was already wobbling and the engines streaming vapour. I turned aside and as the Heinkel glided down I flew in very close alongside it. Caesar Hull stationed himself on the other side. The rear cockpit bore the signs of a charnel house, with the gunner slumped inside it mutilated beyond recognition. His fair hair streaming through in the slipstream which rushed through the shattered windscreen, the young pilot bent over the controls trying to urge his stricken machine to fly. Through the window panels the two other members of the crew regarded me in silent despair.'

119 Peter Townsend was awarded a DFC on 30 April 1940. On 23 May he was posted to command 85 Squadron. On 11 July he was shot down into the sea by return fire, but was rescued unharmed by SS *Cap Finisterre*. He was shot down again on 31 August, bailing out, wounded in one foot. Awarded a Bar to his DFC on 6 September, he returned to the unit in mid-September and the squadron then began conversion to night fighting, exchanging its Hurricanes for Havocs. Promoted Wing Commander, he was awarded a DSO on 3 May 1941. In June was posted as Wing Commander, Night Ops at HQ, 12 Group. April 1942 saw him commanding Drem airfield. In June he took command of 605 Squadron. He left in October to attend the RAF Staff College and then in January 1943 commanded West Malling. Subsequently he commanded 23 ITW, then attending 2 FIS on an instructors' course. In February 1944 he was appointed Equerry to King George VI. He was to remain a member of the Royal Household for eight years. He retired from the RAF in November 1956, having been made a CVO. His total score stands at 9 and 2 shared destroyed, 2 probables, 4 damaged. *Aces High* by Christopher Shores and Clive Williams (Grub Street, London 1994).

120 Caesar Hull went with the first Gladiator squadron to Norway. The story of his brilliant service was told in a series of articles by Victor McClure in *Blackwoods* and in his book *Gladiators over Norway*.

121 Peter G. Ottewill was born on 5 November 1915. He was a pre-war NCO pilot who was serving on 43 Squadron on the outbreak of war. On 7 June he was shot down, bailing out but suffering severe burns. Falling into German-held territory, he was hidden by French civilians who managed to smuggle him through to the British lines for evacuation home. He was too badly injured to return to operational flying and it was to be June 1941 before he received confirmation for his second victory of the day. Commissioned at that time, he later served as flight commander of a gunnery training unit in 1943. He remained in the RAF after the war, commanding 253 Squadron on reconnaissance Spitfires August 1946-May 1947. Promoted Group Captain in July 1960, he retired in November 1965 with a George Medal and an AFC. His total score stands at 4 and 2 shared destroyed, 1 unconfirmed destroyed or damaged. *Aces High* by Christopher Shores and Clive Williams (Grub Street, London 1994).

122 Do 17Z of Wekusta ObdL; This may already have been attacked and claimed by pilots on 605 Squadron; it may have been credited as shared with Sergeant P. Ottewill. *Aces High* by Christopher Shores and Clive Williams (Grub Street, London 1994).

123 Malcolm Keith Carswell was born in Invercargill on the South Island of New Zealand on 25 July 1915 and educated at Southland Boys High School. He was apprenticed to a chemist and began a course in pharmacy. In 1936 he began having flying lessons at the Invercargill Flying Club and in June his instructor arranged for him to have an interview for a short service commission. There were no immediate vacancies so Carswell made his own way to the UK in early 1937. He applied on arrival and was provisionally accepted. On 30th March he began his flying training at 12 E&RFTS Prestwick and in June was posted to 6 FTS Netheravon. After completing the course he joined 43 Squadron at Tangmere in January 1938. On 9 February 1940 Carswell was one of a section chasing a He111 which was attacking a cargo ship off the coast between Acklington and

Rosyth. His engine suddenly failed and, being too low to bail out, he decided to ditch his Hurricane L1744 close to the ship. The aircraft went straight down but Carswell managed to extricate himself. He could not inflate his life jacket and tried to swim through the freezing choppy sea to the ship, which was about a mile away. He passed out and came to in the ship, now docked at Rosyth. His life had been saved by the crew giving him artificial respiration. Carswell was off flying for three months but arrived back just in time to fly south to Tangmere on 31 May.

124 Carswell was shot down in flames over Dunkirk in Hurricane N2584. He landed very near the front line and after convincing French soldiers that he was an ally he was taken to an emergency hospital in Dunkirk where he boarded a destroyer under Stuka attack and finally reached England where he was taken to hospital, arriving there in the evening of the same day he had taken off from Tangmere. Recovered, Carswell returned to 43. On 2 September, in a combat over Ashford, Carswell's Hurricane (P3786) was hit and caught fire. He bailed out, burned on legs, arms, hands and face and with cannon shell splinters in his chest and thigh. After leaving hospital Carswell was grounded for medical reasons and took up fighter control duties. In October 1940 he went to Exeter as a Fighter Controller, moving in November to the Orkneys and serving in the defence of Scapa Flow. In March 1941 he went to Peterhead as Chief Fighter Controller and in May 1942 moved to Biggin Hill. He had a number of postings as Controller over the next three years. Carswell transferred to the RNZAF in January 1944. He regained his flying category in April 1945 and went to 17 SFTS for a combined refresher and twin-engined conversion course for night fighters. Carswell was released on 26 January 1946 and he settled in Rome where he worked in the film and theatre field. He later founded the Intercontinental Club there, a cultural exchange forum. He later retired to Australia where he died on 7 July 2003.

125 Later Wing Commander R. E. Bain. He commanded 43 Squadron before George Lott.

126 On 7 June Simpson hit a Bf 109 and he reported that it turned and collided with one of two Bf 110s which were attacking him. On 19 July he claimed one Bf 109 destroyed before he was shot down in flames and wounded in one leg, bailing out and breaking his collar bone on landing. His DFC was gazetted at this time, the citation recording seven victories. He received his DFC from the King with his arm still in a sling.

127 Thomas Frederick Dalton-Morgan was born on 23 March 1917 in Cardiff. He joined the RAF on a short service commission in August 1935. In November 1936, on conclusion of his training, he was posted to 22 Squadron on Vildebeeste torpedo-bombers. At the end of May 1939 he joined the staff of the Directorate of Training at the Air Ministry, working on a committee planning the handover of equipment to the new Fleet Air Arm and took part in the initial flying training of Naval personnel.

128 On 9 July Lott led an attack on a staffel of Bf 110s of III/ZG26, sharing in shooting down two before he was hit and forced to bail out with glass splinters in his right eye. His total score stood at 2 and 3 shared destroyed, 1 unconfirmed destroyed. Group Captain Lott took command of RAF Hornchurch in May 1942. In January 1943 he went to the USA to supervise the training of RAF pilots. He remained in the RAF after the war, becoming chief instructor at the RAF Flying College at Manby in 1950-52. He retired with the rank of Air Vice-Marshal DSO DFC CB CBE in 1959. He died in January 1990. *Aces High* by Christopher Shores and Clive Williams (Grub Street, London 1994).

129 Anthony Woods-Scawen, who had been shot down on the day when 43 Squadron suffered so severely while over France.

130 He was shot down and saved by his parachute no less than six times. The seventh time he was shot down he was killed.

131 Morgan shared the claim for a He 111 destroyed North of Fort Nelson, Portsmouth on 12 July.

132 This aircraft was not witnessed. Simpson also indicates that he may have shot down the second aircraft before he was shot down himself. Combats and Casualties show only the single Bf 109 unconfirmed. *Aces High* by Christopher Shores and Clive Williams (Grub Street, London 1994).

133 Badger was born in Lambeth in 1912, attending the RAF College at Cranwell from 1931, graduating as Sword of Honour for 1933. He was then posted to 43 Squadron on Hawker Furies. In 1934 he attended the School of Naval Co-operation, after which he went to sea on HMS *Courageous* with 821 Squadron in 1935. 1937 saw him at the Marine Aircraft Establishment in

Felixstowe, where he remained until June 1940, when he rejoined 43 Squadron as a supernumerary squadron leader. When George Lott was shot down later that month he became CO where he claimed at least six victories during August alone. On 30 August his Hurricane was shot down by Bf 109s and he bailed out, but impaled himself on a tree branch which injured him very seriously. He was taken to Ashford Hospital, but died on 30 June 1941. The award of a DFC was gazetted on 6 September 1940 and he was mentioned in Dispatches. His total score stands at 8 and 2 shared destroyed, 1 probable, 2 damaged. *Aces High* by Christopher Shores and Clive Williams (Grub Street, London 1994).

134 *Duel of Eagles.* Charles Anthony Woods-Scawen was the younger of two brothers who served as fighter pilots in the RAF at the same time. Patrick Philip was born in Karachi, India on 29 June 1916 and Tony was born there on 18 February 1918. The boys' father was an ex-purser in a shipping line who had become shore-based. Both boys were taken home to England in 1924 due to their mother's ill-health and were brought up in South Farnborough, Hampshire. Pat joined the RAF in 1937 on a short service commission, joining 85 Squadron in August 1938. Tony was determined to follow but his eyesight was very poor, due it was believed to tuberculosis from which he suffered as a boy. He learned the vision chart by heart and was able to bluff his way through his medical, allowing him enter the RAF on a short service commission in March 1938. He at once had special lenses made for his goggles so that he was able to see adequately in the air. On completion of training in December 1938 he joined 43 Squadron, seeing service with this unit over Scotland and the north-east of England early in the war. He made his first claims over Dunkirk late in May 1940, but on 31st his Hurricane was damaged by Bf 109s and he crash-landed at Tangmere on return. After the conclusion of the Dunkirk operations, his flight was sent on detachment to south-western France and here on 7 June his aircraft was again hit and he had to bail out near Dieppe. Landing in German-occupied territory, he evaded capture and made his way twenty miles to the French-held area, rejoining his unit after being missing for eight days. On 8 August he claimed a Bf 110 shot down, attacked fifty Stukas, reporting strikes on three of these, but was then himself hit by another Bf 110 and slightly wounded in the legs. Five days later, after claiming two Ju 88s, he had to bail out again, as he did on the 16th, falling to a Bf 109 over Sussex on this occasion.

135 Harold Leslie North was born in Dunedin on 31 October 1919. He gained a short service commission in the RAF in 1938, qualifying as a pilot in September 1939 and joining 43 Squadron in November. He achieved his first victories during the Battle of Britain but on 26 August he was shot down, bailing out of his Hurricane with shell splinter wounds in his arm and shoulder. He returned to the unit in September. By June 1941 Flight Lieutenant North was flying on 457 Squadron as a flight commander. On 1 May 1942, whilst on a bomber escort sortie over Marquise, France he was last being seen going after an enemy aircraft. A DFC was gazetted on 15 June, the citation crediting him with 'at least five victories'. *Aces High* by Christopher Shores and Clive Williams (Grub Street, London 1994).

136 The 2nd of September was the fifth time that Tony Woods-Scawen had bailed out, but he was too low and was killed. The previous day his brother Patrick had been reported missing. Posted to France with the unit as part of the Air Component in 1939, Pat Woods-Scawen was to achieve some success during the heavy fighting of May 1940 although on 19 May he was shot down, bailing out with slight wounds after having claimed two Bf 109Es shot down out of a large formation. In June he was awarded a DFC. Promoted Flying Officer after the unit had been withdrawn to England, he found that his new CO, Peter Townsend, had come from 43 Squadron where Tony, was serving. On 1 September Pat was shot down again by Bf 109s, bailing out near Caterham, Kent but his parachute failed to open and he fell to his death. His body was not found for four days. Tony Woods-Scawen's award of a DFC was gazetted on 6 September. *Aces High* by Christopher Shores and Clive Williams (Grub Street, London 1994).

137 Morgan, who had bailed out of his Hurricane with slight wounds on 13 August, having been hit by crossfire from He 111s had recovered and was soon back in action, but on 6 September he was wounded in the knee during combat with Bf 109s. He was obliged to crash-land at Tangmere. He was awarded a DFC. *Aces High* by Christopher Shores and Clive Williams (Grub Street, London 1994).

138 *Battle Over Britain* by Francis K. Mason (McWhirter Twins Ltd, 1969).

139 Squadron Leader Rodney L. Wilkinson assumed command of 266 Squadron on 6 July 1940.

He claimed a Do 17 on 12 August and a Ju 88 on the 15th. He was shot down near Deal the next day. He was found dead at Estrey. *Battle Over Britain* by Francis K. Mason (McWhirter Twins Ltd, 1969).

140 He had taken command of 43 on the death of Caesar Hull, on 16 September.

141 John Ignatius 'Killy' Kilmartin was born in Dundalk, Eire on 8 July 1913, son of a forester and one of eight children. His father died when he was 9 years old and he was sent to Australia under a scheme known as 'Big Brother'. As soon as he was old enough, he obtained a job on a cattle station in New South Wales, where he remained for nearly five years during the Great Depression of the Thirties, then joining an aunt in Shanghai, China where he worked as a clerk in the accounts department of the Shanghai Gas Works for over two years. In 1936 he saw an advertisement for short service commission applicants in the RAF. He applied and was accepted and set out on the Trans-Siberian railway in company with a group of Japanese sumo wrestlers heading for the Berlin Olympics. He was taught to fly at a civilian school in Perthshire, Scotland and was then accepted by the RAF in February 1937 and joining 43 Squadron late in the year. Appointed adjutant at the outbreak of war, he took the opportunity to join 1 Squadron in France at the start of November 1939. On return to the UK, he was posted as an instructor to 5 OTU until August, when he returned to 43 Squadron as a flight commander, receiving the award of a DFC on 8 October. In April 1941 he was posted to command 602 Squadron, but went as a supernumerary to help form 313 Czech fighter squadron. In June he was posted to West Africa to command 128 Squadron. He returned to the UK late that year and was posted as a supernumerary to 504 Squadron, becoming CO in January 1943. At the end of March he was promoted to Wing Commander and led the Hornchurch Wing during May. He then returned to 5 OTU for a spell of instructing, before going to HQ, 84 Group, in the new 2nd TAF as Wing Commander Ops. During 1944 he was given command of 136 Wing, which was equipped with Typhoons. When the Wing was disbanded later in June, he went to HQ, 2nd TAF, as Wing Commander Fighter Operations, where he remained until the end of the European war. In June 1945 he was sent to Burma as Wing Leader, 910 Wing on Thunderbolts until the end of the Far Eastern War. He retired from the service in July 1958. His score stands at 12 or 13 and 2 shared destroyed, 1 damaged. *Aces High* by Christopher Shores and Clive Williams (Grub Street, London 1994).

142 It is believed to have been a Ju 88 of II/KG30, which crash-landed at Gilze-Rijen. Simpson was posted the following month to command 245 Squadron in Northern Ireland, where he claimed two victories at night, on 7/8 April 1941 (believed to be an He 111 of III/KG26) and 5/6 May 1941 (believed to be an He 111 of III/KG40), On 10 May 1941 he was awarded a Bar to his DFC. On 13 May, as he flew low over the Irish Sea to collect some spare parts from England, he intercepted a low-flying Dornier 17 15 miles NW of Stranraer, which he claimed as his 13th victory.

143 Flying Hurricane IIb's he gained 6½ night victories off the Northumbrian coast during the first half of 1941 to take his score to 13½. He received a Bar to his DFC on 30 May. After sharing in the destruction of a Ju 88 on 24 July, his engine failed and he came down in the sea, losing two front teeth against the gun-sight in doing so. He was picked up by HMS Ludlow. His total score stands at 14 and 3 shared destroyed, 1 probable and 4 damaged. He left 43 Squadron in January 1942 to become a controller at Turnhouse until November, when he was promoted and became Wing Commander Operations at 13 Group. He subsequently became Wing Leader at Middle Wallop, which was then expanded to become the Ibsley Wing. On 25 May 1943 he was awarded a DSO. He left the RAF in November 1952 to join the British-Australian Joint Project, testing missiles and other scientific projects at the Woomera Ranges in Australia, remaining until his retirement in 1982. *Aces High* by Christopher Shores and Clive Williams (Grub Street, London 1994).

144 Simpson left 245 for a staff post in June 1941 but was taken ill, an abdominal abscess on the point of bursting being diagnosed and he was hospitalized for operative treatment. In November 1942 he was at Gibraltar as a Wing Commander during the North African landings and by January 1943 he had been promoted to Group Captain. Simpson remained in the RAF after the war, but died on 12 August 1949 as a Wing Commander. *Aces High* by Christopher Shores and Clive Williams (Grub Street, London 1994).

Chapter 13

Two Pilots

The other day two fighter pilots met for the first time. They met in the sky, high above the Thames Estuary. One was in a Spitfire and the other was in a Hurricane and they had become separated from their squadrons. Finding themselves together, they formed a little team. Between them they 'beat up' six German raiders. They know that they destroyed three of them-two Dorniers and a Messerschmitt - and they don't think the others were likely to get home. Having finished that job they flew back to the coast, waved to each other and went their different ways. Ten days later they met again, this time on land. The Hurricane pilot flew across to the Spitfire pilot's aerodrome and they went over the battle together. To-night they are going to talk it over again for your benefit. They found that they were both about the same age (the Spitfire pilot is twenty-one, the Hurricane pilot twenty), that they both had the DFC; that they had joined the RAF Volunteer Reserve at the same time - February, 1938 and that they had each won their commission since war broke out. The Spitfire pilot was a farmer in Shropshire before the war. The Hurricane pilot was a Manchester bank clerk. Perhaps he'd like to begin the conversation.

Winged Words; Our Airmen Speak for Themselves (1941). **The Spitfire pilot was Pilot Officer Eric Lock on 41 Squadron[145] and the Hurricane pilot was Pilot Officer Tom Neil on 249 Squadron.[146] They met in the sky over London on Sunday, 15th September 1940 and were interviewed shortly thereafter by RAF Intelligence officers. In October Eric Lock and Tom Neil recorded events for the BBC.**

In spite of the day's happenings, Tom Neil's letter home that evening contained no mention of combat or flying, concentrating instead on a different subject. 'Two intelligence officers had arrived at dispersal during the afternoon, one a squadron leader. After consulting John Grandy, [147] they called me across. Was I the fellow who had shot down the Dornier over the convoy on 15 September? I said that I was and there were nods all round. A Pilot Officer Eric Lock, flying a Spitfire of 41 Squadron from Hornchurch, had been full of the encounter, it seemed, reporting that a Hurricane pilot had not only joined him in the destruction of a Dornier I7 out to sea but, immediately prior to that, had knocked down two Me 109s before his surprised and admiring eyes. Could they have my account of the ole affair? I was happy to oblige. They spent more than an hour writing copious notes then informed me that the event had enormous publicity value and was a subject suitable for a world-wide broadcast. If I agreed, they would arrange a meeting between Lock and myself and produce a script. I was quite stunned by all the fuss but also gratified and flattered by the attention I was receiving. Of course I would take part! I would await developments. The intelligence officers departed and my parental letter was written only after I had tried unsuccessfully to telephone. If the Huns only knew what a mess they were making of our telephone system!

'For the next several days, the weather was marginal and the Huns soporific - except at night. A bevy of press photographers arrived; to roam about with their cameras asking us to pose and making everyone feel self-conscious. Not all of us were in dispersal at the time but those present were rounded up like sheep and made to walk from our aircraft in groups. These photographs were later to achieve world-wide circulation even among our opponents, the German fighter squadrons. Our smiles were probably more of derision than good humour. Not permitted to take photographs ourselves, supposedly for security reasons, here were all these civilian nonentities snapping everything in sight! A silly arrangement in my opinion.

'In the evening of 24 September I drove down to Hornchurch and met the two intelligence officers who had interviewed me a week or so earlier and also Pilot Officer Lock. 'Sawn-off' Lock was a bouncy, dark-haired little chap who hailed from Shropshire, an area well known to me. Full of quips and high spirits, he had a tremendous reputation in 41 Squadron and quite embarrassed me with his version of our combat on 15 September, describing my contribution in terms I could scarcely have improved on myself. I warmed to him immediately; a couple more trips with him and I was destined for stardom!

'Suitably fortified with grog, we retold our story at length and a script emerged. Finally, when all was completed, Eric Lock and I hung on each other's necks - insofar as that was possible, he being all of 5ft 4in - and over innumerable whiskies and ginger-ales, continued to fight the war to our complete satisfaction, becoming positively lyrical by the time I left towards midnight. [148]

When the interview was broadcast on the BBC in October Tom Neil and Eric Lock were simply referred to throughout as 'Hurricane pilot' and 'Spitfire pilot'. Tom Neil began the broadcast:

'I'd like to go through that day again. When I first saw you come alongside in your Spitfire I thought you were a Messerschmitt. Then, you remember, I pointed at the Dornier about a mile in front and saw you go away from me, because a Spitfire certainly has the legs of a Hurricane at that height. When you'd made your first attack, I caught up with him and we took our time finishing him off. As a matter of fact, I ran out of ammunition towards the end, when he was down to fifty feet. I made several dummy attacks on him before I saw you send him into the sea.'

Lock: 'And I thought you were playing the little gentleman. It just seemed that you were saying: 'Look, you have this one, it's your turn.'

Announcer: 'Now you are getting on too fast. Let's start again with the Spitfire.'

Lock: 'What happened to me was this: Our Spitfire squadron was over London when the battle began and pretty soon we were all split up into a series of dog-fights. When you are tearing about the sky you don't see much and you sometimes find yourself alone when you do get a chance to look round. That was what happened to me. I could see no sign of my squadron or of the enemy formation. There were plenty of clouds about, remember. I looked around and saw, about 2,000 feet above me and away to the north-east of London, three Dorniers and three Messerschmitts being dogged by a Hurricane. I decided to go up and give whatever help I could, but before I could get up there the Hurricane was milling around with the Messerschmitts and two of them were walloping down through the clouds absolutely done for, in my opinion. When I got up there I shot down the odd Messerschmitt, Then I saw you blaze away at a Dornier. He did a somersault - a couple of somersaults. As he whirled over, bits of his wings fell off and he went crashing down through the clouds. After that I drew alongside your Hurricane and you pointed forward. I looked where you were pointing and saw a Dornier about a mile ahead, heading off for the sea. I opened up and drew away from you, made an attack and the Dornier went down through the clouds. We both followed him through and took it in turns to attack him. By the time he had reached the coast he was at 1,000 feet, still going down steadily. He was only at fifty feet when we passed down the middle of a convoy. We were below the tops of the masts all the way between the ships. Then, about forty miles off Clacton-on-Sea, I gave the Dornier a final burst and in he went. He alighted on the water tail first, quite comfortably, you might say. Then a wing cracked off, his back broke and down he sank.'

Announcer: 'What does the Hurricane say to that?'

Neil: 'I really didn't notice your Spitfire until you flew alongside when the chase of the final Dornier began. I remember cracking one Dornier down and attacking another and then being set on by three Messerschmitts 109. And after the milling around with the Messerschmitts I started after the Dornier. I know I hit at least two of the 109s, but I didn't see them go down. I was too busy. I remember, though, attacking a Dornier earlier on. Maybe two. It's hard to say.'

Lock: 'I saw you do it. The first one was lovely. And the other went straight down through the clouds in a vertical dive.'

Neil: 'The main thing is that we beat them up, isn't it? What I liked was when you shot off in front of me chasing that last Dornier. When you caught him up and started squirting at him I was about half a mile behind you. He dived through the clouds, so I dived through after him. I came out below the clouds and the Dornier came out a short distance away. I think he was a bit of a nit-wit, don't you? If he had stayed in those clouds he might have been safe.'

Lock: 'You're right. But, mind you, he had a lot of my bullets inside him even then and maybe he wanted to stay in the clouds and couldn't. It was easy after that, wasn't it? Those quarter attacks we made on him, in turn. First you from the right, swinging across his tail, then me going at him from the left. We just criss-crossed as he flew on a straight course, though losing height all the time. I should say he was about 1,000 feet when we reached the coast and he got down to fifty feet before we finished him off.'

Neil: 'Before YOU finished him off you mean. I liked the way we both flew back to the coast, grinning at each other. I thought once of coming along with you to your aerodrome so that we could discuss the battle together. Then I thought I'd better get back. I only had a few gallons of petrol left when I landed.'

Lock: 'So had I'.

Announcer: 'Well, your story certainly shows that it doesn't really matter - to the Germans, I mean -whether a Spitfire or a Hurricane attacks them.'

Neil: 'There's no doubt about that at all. Nevertheless, I'm used to the Hurricane, so give me a Hurricane every time.'

Lock: 'And give me a Spitfire. By the way, a Spitfire is a lot easier to handle than some of the trainer aircraft I learned in. I do hope that my old instructor is listening in to this, for he always said I was the world's worst pupil in any kind of aircraft.'

Neill: 'That's funny. That's what my old instructor used to tell me.'

Announcer: 'Perhaps that's part of the instruction.' [149]

Endnotes Chapter 13

145 Eric Lock was born in Bayston Hill, Shrewsbury, in 1920, joining his father's farming and quarrying business on leaving Prestfelde School. Lock in fact joined the RAFVR in February 1939, and was called up on the outbreak of war, being posted to 41 Squadron in August 1940, shortly after having married a former 'Miss Shrewsbury'. His first claim was on 15 August. He was awarded a DFC on 1 October for nine victories, eight in one week.

146 Born on 14 July 1920 in Bootle, Lancashire, Tom Neil (also to become known in the RAF as 'Ginger'), joined the RAFVR in October 1938 and was called up on 2 September 1939. He joined 249 Squadron in May 1940. He saw his first action in July. He was credited with seven and two shared victories during three weeks in September. He was awarded a DFC on 8 October. *Aces High* by Christopher Shores and Clive Williams (Grub Street, London 1994).

147 John Grandy was born at Northwood, Middlesex on 8 February 1913. On 14 April 1940 he was given command of 219 Squadron. On 16 May he took command of 249 Squadron. He was shot down in combat over Maidstone on 6 September 1940 and admitted to Maidstone Hospital. He left the squadron in December 1940. Marshal of the RAF Sir John Grandy CB KBE KCB GCB GCVO retired on 1 April 1971.

148 Tom Neil drove back to North Weald 'in a haze of good spirits, convinced that next to 249, 41 was absolutely the greatest squadron ever created.' *Gun Button to Fire* by Tom Neil (William Kimber, 1987, Amberley 2010). On 7 November, after claiming three victories over the North Sea off the Essex coast, a Hurricane flown by Wing Commander Victor Beamish collided with Tom Neil's aircraft, cutting off the tail and he to bail out. He received a Bar to his DFC on 26 November. On 13 December he was promoted flight commander. The squadron was posted to Malta in May 1941, flying off HMS *Ark Royal* on 21st. He claimed one further victory on 12 June to take his final score to 12 and 4 shared destroyed, 2 probables, 1 damaged. On 7 October he led a fighter-bomber attack on Gela station, Sicily. He departed the island in December 1941, returning to the UK, finally arriving in March 1942. He capped a very long and distinguished career in the RAF when he retired with the tank of Wing Commander with an AFC in 1964. *Aces High* by Christopher Shores and Clive Williams (Grub Street, London 1994).

149 Eric Lock was awarded a Bar to his DFC on 22 October for 15 victories in 16 days. On 17 November he made his 23rd claim, but he was 'jumped' by a Bf I09 of JG54 and wounded in his right arm and both legs, crash-landing on Martlesham Heath. He was trapped in his aircraft for two hours until rescued by two soldiers, who carried him for two miles on a makeshift stretcher. Awarded a DSO on 17 December, he was to remain in hospital until May 1941, undergoing 15 operations for the removal of cannon shell splinters. On recovery in June he was sent on a refresher flying course. Early in July he became a flight commander on 611 Squadron and he claimed three more victories. On 3 August 1941 he spotted some German soldiers on a road near Calais and dived down to strafe them, not being seen again. His final score stood at 26 destroyed, 8 probables. *Aces High* by Christopher Shores and Clive Williams (Grub Street, London 1994).

Chapter 14

They Flew Defiants

Although the Defiant failed by day and was by no means a brilliant night fighting machine compared with the Beaufighter and Mosquito it filled a vital gap in Britain's defences. Unlike the Spitfire and Hurricane of Battle of Britain fame, the Defiant never became a household name yet in its own way achieved far more than most experts ever envisaged, for this Bolton Paul machine was as outdated as the biplane at the start of hostilities.

Philip Burden, writing in *RAF Flying Review*, August 1963.

On the beaches around Dunkirk the remnants of the British Expeditionary Force waited to be evacuated back to England. It was 29 May 1940 and the order of the day for the RAF was to prevent the Luftwaffe attacking the troop-laden beaches at all costs. One of the squadrons entrusted with this unenviable task was 264 equipped with Bolton Paul Defiants and they patrolled the area with three squadrons of Hurricanes. The Defiants had been assigned the task of searching for bombers while the Hurricanes scouted for enemy fighters. This was the plan - but in a short while it was the slow Defiants who were taking on Messerschmitt Bf 109s and 110s for the Hurricanes had completely missed the German fighter aircraft! The tranquillity of the patrol was broken when six Bf 109s pounced out of the sun on the twelve Defiants but they were shaken off for the concentrated fire from the batteries of four Browning 0.303 machine guns in each of the RAF fighters' power operated gun turrets proved decisive and two German machines were destroyed. Moments later 264 Squadron faced a much tougher task - or so their pilots thought - when 21 of the Luftwaffe's much-vaunted Bf 110s attacked. There followed a terrific air battle in which the Defiants, although devoid of any forward firing guns, proved vastly superior and fifteen twin-engine 'Destroyers' plus a stray Junkers Ju 87 that had somehow become mixed up in the melee, crashed to the ground. When the squadron landed back at Manston, Kent Squadron Leader Philip Algernon Hunter, the 27-year old Commanding Officer discovered that only one aircraft - that of Pilot Officer Desmond Haywood Sidley Kay with 31-year old LAC Evan J. Jones RAFVR as air gunner - had been badly damaged. Kay, of Thurlstone, Devon was born in London on 14 February 1919 and educated at Sedburgh School. He ordered Jones to bail out after the turret was hit by fire from a Bf 109 but he was drowned. His body was washed up on the French coast and he is buried in Dunkirk. Despite extensive damage Kay flew his Defiant home and made a successful landing. He was awarded the DFC on 14 June and later converted to Mosquitoes. He was killed on 9 October 1944 flying a Pathfinder Mosquito on 109 Squadron.

In the evening of 29 May there was a second patrol and this time the squadron engaged 40 Ju 87s and three Ju 88s bombing Dunkirk. Eighteen of the dive bombers were accounted for, plus one Ju 88. This tremendous success brought a message of congratulations from the AOC 11 Group on the shooting down of more than 30 enemy aircraft without losing a single aircraft. One of the reasons given by Squadron Leader Hunter, in the official squadron records, for destroying such a large number of aircraft was that 'the enemy mistook us for Hurricanes.' If this is what happened then the Luftwaffe did not make the same mistake again. This proved to be the peak 264 Squadron reached as a day fighter unit - although official German records showed that on this day only fourteen aircraft were lost - and those who had predicted a great future for this turret fighter had their dreams shattered during the Battle of Britain for Defiant squadrons, particularly 264, took such a mauling from the Luftwaffe that they had to be withdrawn from the battle and relegated to the night fighter role. The gallant pilots and air gunners who flew in Defiants during the Battle of Britain showed great heroism and fortitude against overwhelming odds. The rapidity with which the Luftwaffe found an answer to the Defiant was to prove the beginning of the end for the Defiant as a front-line day fighter.

Brainchild of the Bolton Paul design team headed by J. D. North, this aircraft was born at a time between the wars when views on fighter armament were undergoing radical changes. There were those in favour of the single-engine single-seat machine with a battery of wing guns who were later to be proved tactically correct, while others favoured the single-engine two-seat fighter with all its armament concentrated in a power operated turret such as the Defiant. It failed as a day fighter... but this was due to no fault of the design team. No designer in the world could have produced a fighter handicapped by the weight and drag of a bulky turret which could match the agility and speed of other contemporary single-engine machines with more conventional armament. But this was not the most serious drawback, however, for the biggest shortcoming undoubtedly lay in the division of responsibility between the pilot and air gunner. With no forward firing guns the pilot had to continually think of the gunner's likely line of fire and it was easy for an enemy fighter to creep up under the blind spot beneath the tail and deliver the knock-out punch. Although it possessed these drawbacks the Defiant, flown for the first time on 11 August 1937, was undoubtedly an excellent flying machine and had very few vices except for a tendency to swing to port during take-off. Otherwise pilots found it possessed excellent handling characteristics and as well as being pleasant to fly proved extremely sturdy under operational conditions. Powered by a Rolls-Royce Merlin 111 twelve-cylinder Vee liquid cooled engine, the Defiant Mk.I entered RAF service with 264 Squadron in December 1939.

Being the first Squadron to be equipped with these new aircraft, 'teething' troubles were numerous, difficulties being experienced with items such as the four gun electro-hydraulic turret and the undercarriage system. Tactics for operating the Defiant, the only fighter with a turret and no forward firing guns, took a considerable amount of working out and the great success of these when employed was largely due to the skill and inspiration of Squadron Leader Hunter who assumed command in March 1940. A few convoy patrols were flown in March and April, but partly because the war was still in its 'phoney' stage 264 Squadron were not deemed operational until 8 May when the Allies were being driven back in France. During the usual training period and working up at Martlesham the Defiant was grounded owing to a number of minor faults and also due to some malfunctioning of the hydraulics. But these were soon corrected. On 20 March 1940 the squadron had six aircraft ready for operational duties and next day these went to Wittering.

On 10 May 264 Squadron was suddenly moved to Duxford, when the Low Countries were being invaded and two days later gained their first 'blood.' 'A' Fight flew to Horsham St. Faith near Norwich and after refuelling linked up with six Spitfires of 'B' Flight on 66 Squadron for a swoop over Holland, hoping to catch German Troop carrying aircraft. They flew direct to the Dutch coast to patrol an area near The Hague. Unfortunately the Squadron was a day late as a large number of Ju 52s had already discharged their cargoes on the beach and also on the airfield at The Hague, which had been captured by paratroopers. Red section was led by Squadron Leader Hunter with 24-year old LAC Frederick Harry King manning the turret. King, of Leicester, had joined the RAF in 1935 as an Aircraft Hand and re-mustered as an Airman under training-air gunner. The others in Red section were 24-year old Pilot Officer Edward H. Whitehouse and Sergeant Smalley and 20-year old Pilot Officer Michael Hugh Young and 37-year old LAC Stanley B. Johnson RAFVR. Young, who had joined the RAF on a short service commission in February 1939, would claim four and six shared victories in five days. Yellow section consisted of 26-year old Flight Lieutenant Nicholas G. Cooke and Corporal Albert Lippett, Pilot Officer Eric Gordon Barwell and Pilot Officer J. E. M. Williams, 21-year old Pilot Officer David 'Bull' Whitley and LAC Robert Charles Turner. Whitley and Turner returned to base soon after take-off with a fault.

Each section flew behind a Spitfire section and soon after commencing their patrol a Ju 88 was spotted. The bomber dropped a bomb near three destroyers and then tried to make its escape by diving low. Red section cut off its escape and an overtaking attack was started, each Defiant making a 'cross over' attack in turn. The Ju 88 was repeatedly hit and smoke started pouring from both engines. Seconds later it crashed in a field. Meanwhile Yellow section, accompanied by a section of Spitfires, spotted a Heinkel He 111 at 3,000 feet which promptly dived to ground level. While three Spitfires attacked from behind Flight Lieutenant Nick Cooke with 37-year old Corporal Albert Lippett carried out a 'cross over' attack from the starboard side. Smoke belched from the bomber's engines. Twenty-six year old Pilot Officer Eric Barwell and Pilot Officer J. E. M. Williams were positioning themselves to make a similar attack from the port side when the enemy machine crashed in another field ending up against a hedge. Barwell, younger brother of P. R. 'Dickie' Barwell who was station commander of Biggin Hill during the early war years, was from Clare in Suffolk. Educated at Wellingborough School, he worked in the family rubber manufacturing and engineering business near Cambridge and in July 1938 joined the RAFVR and doing his elementary training at Marshall's airfield, Cambridge. He had joined 264 on 5 February 1940.

On the evening of 12 May the RAF planned a strafing mission of six Defiants of 264 Squadron and six Spitfires of 66 Squadron to attack German troop transports along the Dutch coast. At dawn the next day, the Defiants of 'B' Flight took off from Martlesham Heath again with a flight of Spitfires from 66 Squadron. The patrol was a complete failure. Over Ijmuiden intense Dutch antiaircraft fire caused the sections to turn about and later more flak, this time German, was met over Maassluis. Soon afterwards the Spitfires turned sharply inland diving from 6,000 feet on a number of enemy aircraft. The Defiants followed close behind and attacked seven Ju 87s of 12./LG1 diving towards Dutch positions at Alblasserdam, south-east of Rotterdam before they were pounced upon by 24 to 27 Bf 109s of JG26. Two 109s were claimed destroyed but all of the Defiants, with the exception of Pilot Officer Desmond Kay and Leading Aircraftman Evan Jones were shot down. The Defiant flown by Pilot Officer P. Greenhouse and Sergeant F. Greenhalgh crashed near Dordrecht and both men were taken prisoner. Pilot Officer E. McLeod and LAC Walter Edward Cox also crashed near Dordrecht. They returned by boat to England. Flight Lieutenant George F. A. Skelton and his Canadian gunner, 28-year old Pilot Officer Jack E. Hatfield managed to bail out. Pilot Officer S. Thomas also bailed out after his gunner Leading Aircraftman John S. M. Bromley had been killed. Thomas, Skelton and Hatfield returned by boat to England. Hatfield saw an aircraft explode and this was assumed to be that of 20-year old Pilot Officer Gordon E. Chandler with 20-year old Leading Aircraftman Douglas L. McLeish. Pilot Officer Kay landed at Knocke, refuelled and reached Duxford in the evening. The Defiants claimed four Ju 87s and one Bf 109 - but at an exceptionally high price. This was to prove a foretaste of what 264 and other Defiant squadrons were to experience during the Battle of Britain.

On 14 May 'A' Flight having taken off from Martlesham Heath for a further show over Holland, were recalled as they crossed the Suffolk coast because the Dutch had capitulated. The squadron moved to Manston on 23 May and during the next few days maintained regular patrols over the Dunkirk-Calais-Boulogne area. On 24 May a Bf 110 was claimed shot down by Flight Lieutenant Edward H. Whitehouse and 33-year old Pilot Officer Horace Scott RAFVR. 'Bull' Whitley and Robert Turner were awarded a half share in the destruction of a Bf 110. On 27 May 264 Squadron added two Bf 109s and three He 111s to their tally without loss but a day later three Defiants were lost in a dog fight with 27 Bf 109s of 6./JG51 led by the Staffelkapitän, Oberleutnant Josef 'Pips' Priller over the Channel north-west of Dunkirk around mid-day. Whitehouse and Scott and Pilot Officer Alexander McLeod (24) and Jack E. Hatfield did not return. Also, Sergeant Lionel C. W. Daisley RAFVR and LAC Harold Revill were shot down, possibly by Leutnant Herbert Huppertz. [150]

The squadron claimed six enemy aircraft destroyed. Sergeant Edward Rowland Thorn and LAC Frederick James Barker returned with damage to the Defiant's wings and tail after a combat with Unteroffizier Haase. Thorn was born in Portsmouth in 1913, joining the RAF to become an NCO pilot. Fred Barker was born in Bow, London, on 16 March 1918 and he went to Old Palace School and Coopers' School, joining the RAFVR in April 1939. He was called up on 1 September. The pair would claim seven and one shared victories within three days, beginning on 28 May with a claim for three Bf 109s destroyed ten miles north of Dunkirk. On 29 May they claimed two Stukas, a Bf 110 and were awarded a half share in a He 111. 264 Squadron flew two missions this day. On the first mission, in the morning, it was attacked from behind by six 109s and 21 Bf 110s. The Squadron claimed 17 enemy aircraft destroyed. One of the Bf 109Es and the two Stukas were claimed by Pilot Officer Eric Barwell and Pilot Officer J. E. M. Williams. On the second mission, in the evening, 264 Squadron intercepted 40 Ju 87s and Ju 88s. Of these at least 19 were claimed by the Squadron. The Defiant flown by Pilot Officer Michael Young and Sergeant Stanley Johnson collided with the Defiant flown by Pilot Officer David Whitley and Young bailed out. Johnson went down into the sea with the aircraft. The Defiant flown by Pilot Officer Richard William Stokes, of Acton, London and Leading Aircraftman Fairbrother was damaged in combat and Fairbrother bailed out. Stokes crash landed the aircraft at Manston airfield. In 1942 he was a flying instructor at 23 SFTS, Southern Rhodesia. He was killed on 29 May aged 21.

Two days' later, on 31 May, Pilot Officer Eric Barwell and Pilot Officer J. E. M. Williams claimed another Bf 109E and, during the second sortie, a Heinkel 111. The Defiant was hit by return fire from the Heinkel and Barwell turned for home but he was unable to maintain height and came down on the sea between two destroyers five miles from Dover. The aircraft broke up and Barwell and Williams, who had been knocked unconscious in the crash, were thrown into the sea. Barwell held Williams upright until they were rescued.[151] Ted Thorn and Fred Barker claimed a He 111 and damaged two others. Nineteen-year old Pilot Officer Guy L. Hickman and 27-year old Leading Aircraftman Alfred Fidler RAFVR were shot down and killed. Flight Lieutenant Nick Cooke DFC and Corporal Albert Lippett DFM were also killed. Ted Thorn and Fred Barker both received the DFM on 14 June and Barker was made up to sergeant. At the end of the month the total of enemy machines claimed as 'destroyed' was 65 for the loss of fourteen Defiants. During June and July, 264 was brought up to full strength in readiness for the Battle of Britain.

On Friday 19 July, among the fighters that were moved forward during the morning of what promised to be a hot summer's day, were twelve Defiants of 141 Squadron, ordered from West Malling to Hawkinge at 08.45 hours. No. 141 Squadron was as yet untried in battle, having only arrived in the South about a week earlier with aircraft, many of which had lacked essential modifications. In order to improve the performance of the Defiants, constant speed propellers had been fitted during the last week, but this spell on the ground by the aircraft (although staggered) had deprived the crews of much-needed flying practice. The Squadron had flown a few uneventful patrols during the previous days at Section or Flight strength and generally lacked practice in manoeuvring with larger numbers. At 12.23 hours twelve Defiants were ordered off from

Hawkinge to patrol twenty miles south of Folkestone at 5,000 feet. In the event, three pilots could not take off owing to engine trouble so that nine crews, led by Squadron Leader William Richardson, were left to continue to the patrol line.

Punctually at 13.00 hours Hauptmann Hannes Trautloft, leading III/JG 51 made rendezvous with Hauptmann Rubensdorffer's Erp Gr. 210 over St Inglevert. In perfect visibility, fighter-bombers and escort climbed north toward the English coast in search of the target, an armed trawler north-east to Dover. They could see it miles off, already zigzagging and, as the Zerstörers [destroyers] dived, Trautloft could see it 'firing furiously from all 'button-holes'.' Then the ship disappeared in a mountain of spray. Trautloft's Gruppe escorted the Bf 110s back to the French coast then decided to return for a Frei-jagd ('free-hunt', or 'sweep'). A voice - Leutnant Wehnelt's - yelled over the radio: 'On the right, below, several aircraft.' Suddenly, and apparently without warning from the Controller, the sky was filled with German fighters but it was not until half a mile away that Trautloft noticed a turret behind the Defiant pilot. 'The sun was behind me ... I made sure there were no Hurricanes or Spitfires about.' Trautloft checked his watch: 'It was 13.43 hours. Then he dived with his stab Schwann. 'I aimed at the right Defiant... the rear gunner's tracers streamed towards me. Suddenly... a violent blow somewhere on my Bf 109. But the enemy had to go down... my guns fired ... pieces of the Defiant... broke off and came hurtling towards me... I saw a thin trail of smoke...and then suddenly just a fiery ball.' Trautloft turned back quickly for France with a juddering engine and strong smell of burnt oil in his nostrils. A few minutes later he crawled in low over Cap Blanc Nez to crash land at St. Inglevert.[152]

In less than sixty seconds the Defiants of Pilot Officers' John Kemp, Richard Howley, Rudal Kidson and John Gard'ner were shot down in flames. All of the gunners died in their aircraft; of the pilots only Gard'ner was rescued, wounded, from the sea. Flight Lieutenant Ian Donald's aircraft was set ablaze and the gunner, Pilot Officer Arthur Charles Hamilton, left the aircraft but was never found; Donald had left himself insufficient time to abandon his cockpit before the aircraft crashed and blew up at Dover.

As the pilots of 141 Squadron had sought to extricate themselves from combat, twelve Hurricanes of 111 Squadron, led by Squadron Leader John Thompson, were flying to their rescue at top speed from Hawkinge. There is no doubt that but for their arrival in the nick of time the entire Defiant squadron would have been destroyed. As it was, Pilot Officer Peter Simpson destroyed one of the Messerschmitts - the pilot of which was rescued, wounded, from the sea. A destroyer, which later searched the area for survivors, was promptly attacked by German bombers, but was not hit.

At length four Defiants straggled into the circuit at Hawkinge, two in obvious difficulties. As three touched down on the airfield, the engine of the fourth cut out and Flight Lieutenant Malcolm J. Loudon crashed on the outskirts of Hawkinge village; on being severely hit, Loudon had ordered Pilot Officer Eric Farnes to bail out and this gunner was the only one to be picked up alive after abandoning his aircraft. Of the three that landed on Hawkinge airfield, 20-year old Pilot Officer Ian Neil MacDougall's Defiant was so badly damaged that it was promptly written off charge. MacDougall recalled that as the Messerschmitts pressed home their attacks, he had seen their tracer streaking through the British formation 'like small bright glow-worms'. He had watched as first one and then another Defiant dropped away, pouring smoke and flames. One had plunged into the sea, leaving a widening ring of foam; close to him, another was going down while two parachutes floated above it. Suddenly, bullets slammed into his own Defiant. The engine stopped and the cockpit filled with smoke. MacDougall dived, undoing his harness and calling to his air gunner, Sergeant John Francis Wise to bail out. There was no reply, so he kept shouting, 'Sergeant, are you all right, are you all right?' Then the sea was coming up at him and as he levelled out the engine spluttered into life. A few minutes later Ian MacDougall crash-landed at Hawkinge. His gunner was never to be seen again.

With the loss of twelve pilots and crew members and seven aircraft, 141 Squadron was no longer a fighting unit. During the next few days the survivors were withdrawn to Prestwick while Fighter Command considered whether the Defiant should again be committed to the risk of facing combat with enemy single-seat fighters.[153] In September 1940 a detachment was sent to southern England for night patrols, the whole squadron moving there in October. In April 1941 the Squadron returned to Scotland where it converted to Beaufighters for the defence of central Scotland and north-east England.

In the meantime, 264 Squadron had begun night patrols from Kirton-in-Lindsey, but it was not until Thursday 15 August that an enemy aircraft was engaged during one of these patrols. 'Bull' Whitley, on a routine patrol, succeeded in intercepting a He 111 two miles south of North Coates but as he closed in, came under heavy fire. This did not deter him and he got close enough for Robert Turner to fire a number of short bursts before the bomber escaped under cloud cover. There was little further night action at this time and the squadron was still primarily a front line day fighter unit. On Wednesday 21 August the Squadron went south to Hornchurch for what was to be its final spell of day fighting. On the evening of Friday 23 August 264 were told that they would move to the forward airfield at Manston the next morning. One of the youngest pilots on the squadron, James Richard Abe Bailey, born in England on 23 October 1919, third son of the South African tycoon, Sir Abe Bailey, and yet to fly a sortie, dared ask Squadron Leader Hunter what was the sense in sending Defiants forward to Manston? Hunter said quietly, 'we are in the place of honour and we must accept it.'[154]

Clashes with fictitious He 113s were reported during August and one of these occasions was on Saturday 24 August. At 0830 hours there was a routine patrol from Manston. 'Our vulnerability' recalls Pilot Officer Frederick Desmond Hughes 'was well illustrated by the occasion when the 'B' Flight commander [Flight Lieutenant Ernest William Campbell-Colquhoun, who had only just been posted to the squadron] had difficulty in starting his engine. It took him a couple of minutes to get it going and, as he took off, he saw his faithful Nos.1 and 2 waiting for him on the circuit. He flew in front of them and waggled his wings - only to be shot down because they were 109s!' Hughes, who came from Donaglidee, County Down although he was born in

Belfast on 6 June 1919, had joined the Cambridge University Air Squadron in 1938 while reading law at Pembroke College. Campbell-Colquhoun's Defiant received a cannon shell in the fuselage which ignited the Very cartridges. He took evasive action and returned to base where he reported being attacked by 'a number of He 113s.'

Later the same day, at 1255 hours, Manston was attacked by twenty Ju 88s escorted by a large number of Bf 109Es. The enemy bombers dived out of the sun and caught seven Defiants on the ground refuelling. Somehow, the Defiants took off despite the falling bombs which left the airfield a shambles of wrecked and burning hangars, bomb craters and unexploded bombs. Flight Lieutenant Arthur John Banham and Sergeant Barrie Baker and 25-year old Pilot Officer Harold Ingham Goodall and Sergeant Robert Bett Mirk Young combined in damaging a Ju 88 south of Manston. Banham and Baker were awarded a Ju 88 'destroyed'; it was piloted by the Geschwader Kommandeur, Major Moricke of Stab II/KG76. Oberleutnant Schulle and two other crew were also killed. 'Bull' Whitley and Robert Turner shot down a Ju 88 of 4/KG76 south of Manston at about 13.05 hours killing Leutnant Grell and his three crew. Whitley's Defiant was severely damaged in the tail by return fire from a Ju 88 he was attacking over Manston but he and Turner returned safely. Ted Thorn and Fred Barker also claimed to have destroyed a Ju 88 at Ramsgate at the same hour. Another Ju 88 was claimed as 'damaged' by Pilot Officer William Rodney Alexander Knocker.[155] Pilot Officer Eric Barwell and Sergeant A. Martin shot down a Bf 109E which they identified as a He 113. Three Defiants were lost in this action. At 1315 hours 21-year old Pilot Officer Joseph Trevor Jones and 30-year old Pilot Officer William Alan Ponting, who was from Whetstone, Middlesex were shot down and killed, possibly by Major Günther Lützow of JG3. (Lützow was killed on 24 April 1945 by P-47s while attempting to attack B-26 Marauders. He had 110 victories in over 200 sorties).

Five minutes' later, Squadron Leader Hunter, who had been awarded the DSO on 14 June and Pilot Officer Fred King, who was awarded the DFM the same day, were last seen by the other pilots of Red section chasing a Ju 88 at full throttle south east of Manston. They were not heard from again. Peter Townsend had talked with Philip Hunter at Martlesham and described him as the 'gentle, parfit knight, a man of quiet and selfless courage.'[156] At 13.25 hours Flying Officer Ian Garston Shaw and Sergeant Alan Berry, who was from Longsight, Manchester, were shot down and killed, possibly by Major Lützow of JG3, east of Manston.

At 15.40 hours Manston was again attacked, this time by a large formation of Ju 88s of KG76 and He 111s, escorted by Bf 109s. Two Defiants collided prior to the 'scramble'. Both crews were unhurt. Squadron Leader George Desmond Garvin, 23, and 31-year old Flight Lieutenant Robert Clifford Vacy Ash, the senior ranking Defiant gunner, attacked the main formation and shot down two Ju 88s. Pilot Officer Terence Deane Welsh and LAC Lawrence Hamilton Hayden destroyed a straggler in a 'cross over' attack. He also managed to damage a Bf 109 which attacked him with two others. The victory took the pilot's score to 5½, having shared in a He 111 victory on 27 May and claiming a Bf 109, a Bf 110 and two Stukas on the 29th.[157] Pilot Officer Michael Young, separated from the main formation, found a solitary He 111 which he and his gunner, Sergeant Leslie P. Russell, a New Zealander, claimed shot down in an overtaking attack.[158] Pilot Officer Richard Stuart Gaskell, just recently turned 21, who put up a terrific fight against half a dozen Bf 109s of JG51 before being shot down over Hornchurch at 1610 hours. His 20-year old air gunner, Sergeant William Howard Machin of Handsworth, Birmingham, died from the wounds he sustained in this action while Gaskell was lucky and lived to fight again.

There was more action for the squadron on Monday 26 August. Led by Flight Lieutenant Arthur Banham they were ordered to intercept a large formation of Dornier Do 17s near Herne Bay. Just as they were getting ready to perform their complicated cross-over attacks on the Dorniers the lone Defiants were set upon by two Gruppen of Bf 109s - more than fifty fighters! Banham was one of the first to be shot down. After destroying a Do 17 his aircraft was set on fire by an explosive shell in the cockpit. He rolled on his back and told Barrie Baker to bail out and then bailed out himself. Banham finished up in the Channel and remained in the water for over an hour and a half before being rescued. Baker, who was 27 years old and from Kings Norton, Birmingham, was never found. Banham, who was educated at Perse School, Cambridge, had been a pre-war regular and had joined 19 Squadron at Duxford on 24 August 1936. He was promoted on 6 September 1940 and given command of 229 Squadron.[159]

Pilot Officer Goodall and Sergeant Robert Young were attacked by a Bf 109 and after beating off the attack made an overtaking attack on a Do 17. Goodall's last glimpse of the bomber was a ball of fire rapidly losing height with two parachutes floating near to it.[160] This was a tough day for all the squadron and even the most inexperienced fighter pilot soon became a hardened veteran. One such was Pilot Officer Desmond Hughes who, in his first air engagement, with Sergeant Fred Gash as his gunner, distinguished himself by destroying two Do 17s by converging attacks. Flight Lieutenant Ernest Campbell-Colquhoun, after attacking a Do 17 which dived, smoking from both engines, was attacked by a Bf 109 and was unable to confirm the destruction of the Dornier. Flying Officer Ian Raitt Stephenson's Defiant was set on fire by a Bf 109; the pilot bailed out and was picked up from the sea and later taken to Canterbury Hospital with minor injuries. His gunner, 23-year old Sergeant Walter Maxwell, who was from Moels, Cheshire, was killed. Stephenson, who was born in 1917 was the son of the Reverend H. Stephenson and was a member of the London University Squadron in 1936-37. He was educated at King's College School, Wimbledon and the Royal College of Science, South Kensington. He later commanded 406 'Lynx' Squadron RCAF at Valley in 1943 and took command of 153 Squadron at Reghaia, Italy that September. He was killed on 26 November, aged 26.

At the height of the battle Ted Thorn and Fred Barker claimed two Dornier Do 17s destroyed but soon afterwards they were themselves attacked by a Bf 109E. Their aircraft was hit and developed oil and glycol leaks. Thorn took evasive action and spun away hoping to make a crash landing somewhere near Herne Bay - but the German pilot was not prepared to let his prey escape and closed in for the kill at 500 feet. He scored numerous hits and it seemed as if the Defiant was doomed to a watery grave. But showing great determination Thorn managed to keep his stricken machine in the air and succeeded in making a wheels-up landing in a field near Herne Bay. Just before the Defiant crashed Barker fired his remaining rounds and had the satisfaction of seeing the Bf 109E crash. Luck was with the RAF crew for their aircraft finished a mass of twisted metal but neither sustained serious injuries. Both men were promoted to flight sergeant shortly afterwards and were awarded bars to their DFMs on 11 February 1941. The squadron then went over to night fighting and Thorn and Barker were able to claim one further victory in this role - He 111 G1+DN of 5/KG55 at Brooklands, which crashed in flames at Burbridge near Godalming - to become the most successful Defiant team of the war.[161]

Despite continuing to fight with great tenacity and showing outstanding courage against overwhelming odds, the squadron's numbers slowly dwindled and, at one time, only had three serviceable aircraft. At Manston on the morning of 28 August Jim Bailey, educated at Winchester College and Christ Church College, Oxford where he read Philosophy, Politics and Economics, at last got his chance to fight. 'I had a great deal more confidence in my ability than my ability warranted' he said. What he and his fellow pilots did not know was that Spanish Civil War veteran Major Adolf 'Dolfo' Galland[162] and his Bf 109Es of III/JG 26 'Schlageter' were on their way from Caffiers in the Pas de Calais to take on the Defiants in what would prove an unequal struggle.

The Defiants were at 17,000 feet when a 'flock of Heinkels' came in over Folkestone heading for the airfield at Eastchurch. Far above, like 'black dots in the empyrean' the top cover of Messerschmitts was already fighting back against the high-flying Spitfires. The Defiants climbed up beneath the enemy bombers. 'The Heinkels looked as big as elephants,' said Jim Bailey. Sergeant Oswald Hardy, his air gunner, was firing into the belly of one of them which then fell out with an engine on fire. Galland's 109s dived and pulled up under the unwary Defiants. The battle was over in minutes. Jim Bailey heard strikes on his aircraft and a voice, 'I'm wounded.' Flicking over he went for the ground in a steep spiral. It was most likely his Defiant that Galland came diving at, but he overshot when Bailey throttled back his engine. Bailey's luck still held as he glided beneath some high tension cables and crashed through a hedge to make a forced landing at Court Lodge Farm, Petham. Hardy was out in a flash. 'I thought you said you were wounded?' said Bailey, squinting down a cut nose. 'No, I said turn to starboard,' replied Hardy.

Adolf Galland found himself flying alongside a 'lonely, weaving' Defiant, which was immediately shot down by tracer bullets fired by Oberleutnant Walter Horten for his first victory. The Defiant 'burst into flames over its entire wingspan and fell away as a burning torch' he later recalled.[163] After overshooting Bailey's Defiant, Galland dived after a third, opening fire from 100 yards and closing to twenty. His cannon ammunition was gone; only his two light machine guns were firing. Squadron Leader George Garvin and Robert Ash went down, their fuel tank bursting into flames. Ash managed to hole the 109 four times but it was not enough. He and Garvin bailed out but Ash hit the Defiant's tail and his parachute streamed and he was killed.[164] The

Defiant crashed at Luddenham Marsh, Faversham. Garvin, who had taken over command on the death of Hunter, landed with minor injuries and was flown back to Hornchurch in a transport aircraft with one other passenger - Flight Lieutenant Al Deere, who had been shot down by a Spitfire! 'Bull' Whitley and Robert Turner were shot down and killed by a Bf 109E over Thanet. The Defiant crashed at Kingswood in Challock Forest.[165] Twenty-one year old Pilot Officer Peter Lewis Kenner and his gunner, 34-year old Pilot Officer Charles Edward Johnson were shot down by a Bf 109E. The crew did not bail out and were killed in the crash at Sillibourne Farm, Hinxhill. Both men had been educated at Brentwood School. Kenner had gone on to Queen Mary College, London where he read engineering. Johnson, who later lived in Nottingham, went to tailoring college and was later employed as a travelling cutter and fitter before he and his younger brother Louis volunteered for aircrew. [166]

Four Defiants lost; five others damaged, five aircrew dead. Adolf Galland could only wonder; 'How can they put such planes into the sky?'

'We were hushed all the next day, quietly subdued in the mess,' wrote Jim Bailey. [167] In four days they had lost eleven aircraft; fourteen air crew.

Although the RAF had discovered that the Defiant was unsuitable for day operations there were large numbers coming off the production line and so 264 along with 141 Squadron who had also fared none too well during the Battle of Britain, were assigned the night interception role. Flame damper exhausts were fitted and the mid-crew perspex panels deleted. Both squadrons participated in the development of night fighting techniques and with the start of the Luftwaffe's night offensive against London were transferred to bases from which they could operate in the defence of London. No. 307 Squadron, which had started to form as a day fighter unit in September, was the only new night fighter squadron with the Defiant operating at the start of the New Year. But later more Defiant night fighter squadrons came into being[168].

There was plenty of night action for 264 Squadron towards the end of 1940. Pilot Officer Desmond Hughes and Sergeant Fred Gash, who had destroyed two Do 17s on 26 August, were at the forefront. On 15/16 October, Hughes and Gash destroyed Heinkel 111H-3 1H+DN of II/KG26 at Brentwood. All the crew were killed. A few days' earlier, on the evening of 8 October, Harold Goodall and Robert Young were patrolling from Halton to Maidenhead at 10,000 feet. At 2120 hours Goodall reported that he was going to investigate a suspected enemy aircraft. Nothing more was heard and at 2140 hours his Defiant came down at Marlow. Young was a New Zealander, born Palmerston North on 1 August 1918. He had worked as a bank clerk before arriving in England.

On the night of 23/24 November a solitary searchlight probed the night sky over Braintree in Essex and suddenly its thin beam of light illuminated the distinctive shape of a twin-engined bomber. It was a Heinkel He111 but seconds later the aircraft disappeared into the protective cover of the clouds. The searchlight crew at Braintree, Essex, resigned themselves to the fact that yet another German bomber would reach London, adding more weight to the Luftwaffe's night 'Blitz' of the capital. Fate, however, determined that this bomber would not get through, for unknown to the searchlight team, the pilot of a Defiant had also caught a glimpse of the machine silhouetted against the night sky. Pilot Officer Desmond Hughes recognised the aircraft as a He 111 and, after alerting Sergeant Fred Gash in the gun turret, chased after the bomber at full throttle. Slowly the Defiant crept up on its prey and soon Hughes had his machine in a position that enabled Gash to fire a two seconds burst which destroyed one of the He 111's engines. Hughes closed in for the kill. At this moment, however, the night fighter's gun turret jammed and Gash was unable to either rotate or elevate his guns. Then, to make the situation even worse, three searchlights mistook the dark outline of the Defiant for a raider and focused their beams on it. Undeterred, Hughes pressed home the attack. He instructed his gunner to keep firing while he manoeuvred the Defiant into a position where the bullets would hit. This almost resulted in a collision as the RAF night fighter was only a matter of feet away from the He 111 on several occasions. Although the enemy aircraft evaded the continuous stream of fire it was forced off course and slowly dropped lower and lower. Finally it turned for the coast with the Defiant in pursuit. Elated at having achieved so much under such difficult conditions Hughes shadowed the bomber to the coast and then turned for home base at Rochford as he was low on fuel. His last sight of the He 111 left no doubt in his mind that it would crash into the sea, but as he was unable to furnish positive proof of its destruction he did not claim it as destroyed. This pursuit later led to Hughes being awarded the DFC while Fred Gash received the DFM.

A month later, on 22 December, a 141 Squadron machine piloted by Pilot Officer James Ghillies Benson with Pilot Officer Blain as air gunner attacked a He 111 and after firing three bursts from 75 yards it crashed in flames at Underwoods House, Etchingham. On the night of 12/13 March 1941 Desmond Hughes and Fred Gash destroyed another Heinkel 111 - it was G1+GN of 2/KG55 and they followed this with a probable night victory on 8/9 April south-east of Biggin Hill. Two nights' later they shot down He 111 6N+HL of KGr100. South of the Isle of Wight.[169] Off Beachey Head that same night Pilot Officer Eric Barwell DFC and Sergeant A. Martin claimed He 111 1H+1D of III/KG26 and a probable He 111 (likely to have been a He 111 of I/KG55 which was lost and is believed to have been attacked by a 604 Squadron aircraft). [170]

It was not long before 307 (Polish) Squadron earned themselves a great reputation as a night fighting unit. The squadron's first confirmed 'kill ' came on 12 April 1941 when a Defiant flown by Sergeant Jankowiak with Sergeant Lipinski as gunner shot down a He 111. Having taken off from Colerne they intercepted a He 111 at 13,500 feet. Lipinski opened fire into the nose of the enemy bomber from a distance of 40 yards firing one short burst then a long one. He saw several small explosions and pieces began to fall off the aircraft. It dived steeply and disappeared into cloud. Several minutes after the combat the Observer Corps reported a crashed He 111. On 16 April Flying Officer Lewandowski with Sergeant Zakrocki, on patrol at 12,000 feet, spotted a He 111 about 300 yards ahead and 150 feet below, flying in the same direction. Zakrocki opened fire from about fifty yards and 75 feet below and the bomber immediately returned the fire, but did not hit the night fighter. The Defiant scored many hits and the German machine dropped to 5,000 feet with the Defiant sticking to it and firing continuously, first from port and then from starboard. Finally, having exhausted all its ammunition, the night fighter broke off the action, leaving the bomber plunging towards the ground with smoke pouring from its port engine.

In the autumn of 1941 radar equipped Defiant IAs began to appear, 264 Squadron being the first to employ these operationally. The Defiant 1A was equipped with the early AI Mk. 4 radar with 'Arrow head' type aerial on the starboard wing and 'H' type aerials on the fuselage sides. The Mk. IA was also delivered to Nos. 96, 125, 256 and 410 Squadrons.

Of those who flew this unusual fighter it will perhaps, suffice to say that they deservedly gained themselves an honoured place in RAF history due to sheer guts, determination and heroism. [171]

Endnotes Chapter 14

150 Huppertz was born on 3 June 1919 at Rheydt in Rhineland. He joined the Luftwaffe in autumn 1937. In autumn 1939 he was posted to 6./JG51. He gained his first victory during the French campaign on 28 May 1940 when he shot down a Spitfire fighter near Dunkirk. He gained four victories in the aerial battles over England. In spring 1941 Huppertz was transferred to 12./JG51 operating over the Eastern front. On 30 December 1942 Huppertz recorded his 60th victory. On the first day of the Allied invasion in Normandy, Huppertz claimed five victories over Allied fighters shot down (73-77). On 8 June Huppertz was shot down and killed in FW 190A-8 (W.Nr. 730 440) by US fighters near Cintheaux in the Caen area. He was posthumously awarded the Eichenlaub and promoted to the rank of Major. He recorded 33 victories over the Eastern front. Of the 45 victories recorded over the Western front, 17 were '4-mots'.

151 *Men of the Battle of Britain* by Kenneth G. Wynn. (CCB Associates 1999).

152 *Duel of Eagles* by Peter Townsend (Weidenfeld and Nicolson, 1970).

153 *Battle Over Britain* by Francis K. Mason (McWhirter Twins Ltd, 1969).

154 *Duel of Eagles* by Peter Townsend (Weidenfeld and Nicolson, 1970).

155 Knocker was flying Defiant N1547 on 15 November 1940 when it caught fire. On an emergency approach he hit a tree and crashed and burned out on Rochford Golf Course. He was unhurt but his gunner, Pilot Officer Frank Albert Toombs was badly burned and died of his injuries. In May 1941 Knocker was shot down over London but bailed out safely. *Men of the Battle of Britain* by Kenneth G. Wynn. (CCB Associates 1999).

156 *Duel of Eagles* by Peter Townsend (Weidenfeld & Nicolson, 1970).

157 He and Hayden destroyed a He 111 South of Hastings on the night of 12/13 March 1941. *Aces High* by Christopher Shores and Clive Williams (Grub Street, London 1994).

158 Young was awarded a DFC on 11 February 1941 and on 8/9 May he claimed a Bf 110 at Merville airfield on a night intruder with Russell for his seventh confirmed victory of the war (plus 6 shared destroyed). He claimed three enemy aircraft damaged flying Hurricanes in Africa in 1942 when he commanded 213 Squadron. Russell meanwhile became a rear gunner on Halifax bombers on 35 Squadron and was KIA on 19/20 May 1942 on the raid on Mannheim. Young left the service in January 1946 and later became a brewer. He died in January 1998.

159 On 15 October he was shot down in flames in a Hurricane. He bailed out, badly burned and the aircraft crashed on to farm buildings at Stockbury. Banham underwent plastic surgery by Archibald McIndoe at Queen Victoria Cottage Hospital, East Grinstead. He eventually returned to flying duties and commanded units in Malta and Italy. *Men of the Battle of Britain* by Kenneth G. Wynn. (CCB Associates 1999).

160 This is possibly the same Dornier Do 17Z that was raised from the Goodwin Sands on 10 and 11 June 2013 and taken to the RAF Museum, Cosford. Of the four man crew, Feldwebel Willi Effmert and Feldwebel Hermann Ritzel survived to serve out the war as PoWs in Canada whilst 21-year old Gefreiter Heinz Huhn and Gefreiter Helmut Reinhardt perished in the crash. Huhn is buried in the Germany Cemetery at Cannock Chase.

161 In October 1941 Ted Thorn was promoted to Warrant Officer and posted to 32 Squadron, where he was soon commissioned and was promoted to command the unit in April 1942, leading it until September when he received a DFC. After a rest from operations he joined 169 Squadron as a night-fighter, commanding a flight and adding a Bar to his DFC in December 1944. On 12 February 1946 he was killed in a flying accident in a Meteor at Rectory Farm, Milton, Cambridgeshire. Fred Barker had remained on 264 Squadron until 1943 when he was posted to the Middle East as an air gunnery instructor. He was commissioned in April 1944 but left the service in 1946 with the rank of Flying Officer. *Aces High* by Christopher Shores and Clive Williams (Grub Street, London 1994).

162 On 1 August Galland was awarded the Knight's Cross for his 17 victories. By 15 August he had increased his own score to 22. On 22 August he replaced Gotthard Handrick as Geschwaderkommodore of JG 26.

163 *JG 26: Top Guns of the Luftwaffe* by Donald L. Caldwell (Ivy Books New York, 1991).

164 Ash had been granted a permanent commission in the Stores Branch of the RAF in January 1935 and had also served in Iraq in Supplies Branch before he transferred to General Duties Branch on 30 October 1939, having volunteered for aircrew duties. He was posted to 149 Squadron at Mildenhall as Gunnery Leader but had requested a transfer to Defiants. He had joined 264 on 20 June. *Men of the Battle of Britain* by Kenneth G. Wynn. (CCB Associates 1999).

165 Turner, who was 25 years old, was born in Reading on 26 December 1914 and was educated at Christ's Hospital, Horsham. He joined the RAFVR about May 1939 and was called up on 1 September 1939.

166 *Men of the Battle of Britain* by Kenneth G. Wynn. (CCB Associates 1999).

167 Jim Bailey later flew Beaufighter VIFs on 125 Squadron and later on 600 Squadron in Italy and was credited with six victories. After the war he returned to Oxford, getting a BA in 1947 and a MA in 1949. Oswald Anthony Hardy broke both his legs bailing out over London in 1941 after being shot down by AA fire. He bailed out twice using the same 'Parasuit', a special chute for Defiant gunners. *Men of the Battle of Britain* by Kenneth G. Wynn. (CCB Associates 1999)/ *Aces High* by Christopher Shores and Clive Williams (Grub Street, London 1994).

168 These were Nos. 96, 151, 255, 256, 85, 125, 153, 409, 410 and 456.

169 Hughes converted to the Beaufighter and later the Mosquito. His total score was 18 and one shared destroyed, 1 probable and one damaged. He rose to the rank of Air Vice Marshal Hughes CB CBE DSO DFC*. *Aces High* by Christopher Shores and Clive Williams (Grub Street, London 1994).

170 This took Barwell's score to seven. Flying Mosquito XVIIs on 125 Squadron with Flight Lieutenant D. A. Haigh as radar operator, he destroyed two Ju 88s and a V-1 in 1944 to take his overall score to nine, 1 probable and 1 damaged (a Do 217 while flying a Beaufighter II on 125 Squadron on 1/2 July 1942). He retired from the RAF as a Wing Commander with a DFC and bar in April 1945 and returned to his family business. Aces High by Christopher Shores and Clive Williams (Grub Street, London 1994).

171 Adapted from *They Flew Defiants* by Philip Burden *RAF Flying Review* August 1963.

Chapter 15

A Station Commander Looks Back

Wing Commander (later Air Vice Marshal Sir Cecil Arthur Bouchier KBE CB DFC*) 'Boy' Bouchier, Station Commander of Hornchurch, in 11 Group, who wrote this wartime article, was known as 'Daddy' to his pilots.Born on 14 October 1895, he served with the British Army, Royal Flying Corps, Indian Air Force and Royal Air Force from 1915 to 1953. He was Air Officer Commanding (BCAIR), British Commonwealth Occupation Force in Japan during 1946-48. Bouchier was married to Dorothy Britton, who translated a number of Japanese books into English. He died on 15 June 1979.*

'I have been asked to tell you something of what goes on at a Fighter Station. I'll try to do this by 'looking back' over the war in so far as my station was concerned. We all knew, of course, it was going to be an Air War and you can imagine, therefore, our intense excitement when war was actually declared. But how different those first seven or eight months turned out to be. There was no immediate 'blitz' and my pilots spent their time incessantly chasing the odd elusive Hun far out over the North Sea, with only here and there a success. I remember in those early days, the shrieks of almost childish joy with which the very sight of an enemy aeroplane was hailed by our boys in the air and the tears of anguish when one got away by diving into clouds after a long chase, far out over the North Sea. Little did we know then that the Hun was progressively to switch the whole weight of his Air Force on to a single objective... and our turn was not yet. Little did we know then of the intensive air fighting that was so soon to come.

And then came a red-letter day. May 16th, saw the first Spitfire Squadron leave my station to make an offensive sweep over the Continent. Two hours later the squadron returned, having patrolled as far north as Ostend. The enemy had not been engaged, but throughout the whole station there was a feeling of satisfaction and anticipation - that at last things were beginning to move; and a few days later, on a similar patrol, a Junkers 88 was shot down in a smother of sand near Flushing... I remember the high excited voice, the breathless excitement of the youngster as he 'hared' home to report in person. His little dance of joy on the aerodrome as I met him - bright-eyed - indescribably happy.

Less than a week later was to see the great Battle of Dunkirk and the evacuation of our Army in the face of the whole might of the German Air Force. How can I begin to describe those momentous days? What a target those beaches were-right on his own door-step... crowded with the flower of the

British Army - and the sea between these shores and the Dunkirk jetty - stiff with troops in every conceivable kind of boat, barge, tug and paddle-steamer -until the way home looked for all the world, as one of my pilots described it to me, 'like Piccadilly in the rush-hour'. What a task our fighter squadrons had to keep the bombers away from those beaches - from the ships loading up - from the long procession home. I wish I could give you the picture as I saw it. How heroically they fought-from the dark of four in the morning to the dark of eleven at night, out and back, out and back, facing the whole might of the German Air Force - protecting a target such as the Hun must have dreamed about.

For eleven days, hour after hour, my squadrons fought him away from those beaches and from dropping his bombs... fought him - heavily outnumbered. Load after load of bombs were jettisoned harmlessly in the sea as our Fighters went into the attack and many a bomber fell with them - whilst the unarmoured Messerschmitt fighter of those days were 'easy meat' - and the 'bags' obtained were terrific. On one day alone my station destroyed thirty-one enemy aircraft and during those eleven days my squadron alone destroyed one hundred and twenty and a further seventy-five so badly damaged that they probably never reached their home bases. Nice work that, when one remembers that we were fighting with every tactical disadvantage, fighting over enemy territory and against odds of often seven and even ten to one and yet our losses were less then one-tenth of the confirmed casualties inflicted on the enemy. But what a strain it was - a strain that could be seen in the faces of my boys, as towards the end of those eleven days, they went into action dizzy with fatigue - but well knowing in their young hearts how much depended upon them.

But they came out of it - as they went into it, with a light heart and a smile - and there was never a day so grim that my pilots failed to make it less grim, by their spontaneous humour - often spoken to themselves in the air... What a joy it was to me, directing their efforts in my Operations Room, to hear - in the middle of a dog-fight-the radio silence broken with a 'Oh! Boy, look at that so-and-so going down', or the solicitude for each other: 'Look out, George, there's a 109 on your tail' and the calm, unhurried: 'OK Pal,' of the reply.

With the 4th June, the Dunkirk days were over. What a difference the complete collapse of France which followed meant to us. Now we were faced with the enemy a few miles across the water and rapidly occupying aerodromes all along the French and Belgian coasts. From these bases - from June to the beginning of August - he concentrated his attacks on our shipping. Often my squadrons were engaging odds of anything up to ten to one and rarely less than five to one, but in six weeks, fighters from my station added a further 135 enemy aircraft destroyed, together with another sixty probables to their 'bag'.

I remember during this period that one of our squadrons, which was in four engagements on one day, destroyed twenty enemy aircraft, for a loss of only two of their own pilots. One pilot 'wrote-off' five Huns all in a row on the same day. Another two lads between them got six 109s and shot up a German E-boat in the Channel for good measure.

And then suddenly in mid-August, the Hun switched his offensive against our shipping and for about a month launched a bitter and relentless attack against our fighter aerodromes, admitting by this change of tactics, that our fighters were getting the upper hand of him and that his only hope was to smash them and break their morale.

By sheer weight of numbers he hoped to do this and to blot out the 'hornet's nests', which alone stood between him and the daylight annihilation of London. Hundreds of bombers, supported by high flying fighters, came over day after day - but more and more of the all-important bombers fell to my squadrons and still we stayed on top. Steadily we took our toll, until in the end even the Hun couldn't take any more. During this short period we added another one hundred and twenty-five destroyed and from the air the Thames Estuary and Kent could be seen strewn with his wreckage.

I hope I'm not giving you the impression that all this was 'just too easy' - it wasn't ... here and there, we had to 'take a bit' ourselves. I well remember the days when his bombers got through ... and fairly blew blazes out of my station-on one occasion twice in one day, until the whole place was rocking. I remember thinking after each attack how incredible it was that so many bombs could fall all together - produce such an inferno of noise - blot out the station and aerodrome with their black and yellow smoke, in so short a space of time ... and yet, when the smoke cleared, do so little real damage. But then, we were always a lucky station. I remember every man and woman 'turning to' and filling in the hundreds of craters, rushing round in circles organizing the labour-'rounding up' steam-rollers from near and far. I remember also the fabulous bills that came in to me afterwards for free beer which I had promised... but it was well worth it - we were never out of action for a single day.

And then, about the 7th September, the Hun ceased his attacks on our fighter aerodromes. From then on throughout September he threw the whole weight of his attacking forces against London. Over came the same large formations in broad daylight, but now, with a single objective - London.

What a party that was! And what a beating was administered to his Luftwaffe! Do you remember such days as the 11th, 15th and 27th of September, when our fighter squadrons shot down well over three hundred enemy aircraft on those three days? And that total does not include those who managed to limp home with a packet of trouble on board, or failed and fell in the sea.

When October broke, the Hun had had enough of daylight raiding and from then onwards took to the night bombing of London and elsewhere; contenting himself by day with swarming over Kent with enormous numbers of his high flying fighters - some of which carried bombs. These 'tip-and-run' raids, mostly at 30,000 feet and over, were designed to wear out our pilots and were more difficult to deal with. These two months were, comparatively speaking, bad ones for my station, but somehow we managed to chalk up another eighty-two destroyed and thirty probables. This 'falling off' in our batting average was relieved, however, by one or two amusing features. The 'Eyeties' showed themselves. One day they ventured too near the Thames

Estuary and I swung one of my squadrons on to them. I asked the squadron leader afterwards why there was such complete radio silence once he had sighted the enemy. His reply was: 'Well, sir, when I saw who they were, I was quite speechless with surprise - and before you could say 'Jack Robinson' we'd got seven of them.'

This same squadron a few days later was on patrol in the Maidstone area when the Naval Authorities at Dover rang up and said that there was a solitary German bomber 'inconveniencing' our shipping in the Thames Estuary. 'Could we deal with it?' they asked. We said we would be delighted to and as there was nothing else German about, the whole squadron was sent to intercept him - and a 'free for all' followed as he raced for home. But he was too late and was shot down in the sea.

I heard about his fate by radio from the squadron leader and rang up Dover to inform them that we had disposed of their 'inconvenient' bomber - a Dornier 17. I asked that a boat should be sent out to pick up the crew - before the Germans, themselves, rescued them to fly again. 'All right,' came the reply, 'but is this the Hun I phoned you about a few minutes ago?' On my replying 'Yes' he rang off with a 'What service!' And so I come to the end of my story and, as I look back, what a glorious fifteen months these have been. Little did I dream when I took over my station of the history that would be made there. Eight hundred enemy aircraft accounted for - five hundred and twenty odd destroyed and nearly three hundred probables.

As I look back - what memories come crowding in and of this cherished shore - what are the things I like most to remember?

First of all I like to remember with a grateful heart, what a privilege it has been to serve and live amongst the people of my station. Of the happy spirit that permeates my station - and all those unsung airmen and airwomen who have worked so unceasingly - so uncomplainingly, day and night to keep the airscrews turning. Their loyalty and confidence in me, which has made my work such a joy.

I like to remember and, if I may, to thank all those kind people who, anonymously, have sent cigarettes, sweets and other comforts for my pilots and my people. So many came from the East-end of London - surely no better tribute to my pilots. Of them I like to remember their simple modesty and the way they could always raise a laugh, as over their half cans of beer at the end of each interminable day's fighting in the summer - they swopped experiences - tired to death but unconquerable of spirit.

Do you remember those understanding, inspiring and surely immortal words of Mr. Winston Churchill: 'Never in the field of human conflict was so much owed by so many to so few.' I do, for I have seen the valour of their ways.

Chapter 16

Hanged By The Neck

Gerald Bowman

The thing I feel most about it is the way we just asked for trouble in those days. We flew such clottishly close formation - nearly everyone was watching everyone else instead of keeping their eyes open all around them. Before we learned to fly a more open formation we were just bound to get jumped by the Hun in the sun.'

Sergeant pilot Frederick Stanley Perkin, born in 1920; he joined the RAFVR in April 1939. On 15 September 1940 he was posted to 73 Squadron.

On Monday 23 September 1940, Sergeant pilot Frederick Stanley Perkin was a member of the famous 73 Squadron based at Castle Camps, Essex. At that time this satellite of Debden aerodrome was nothing much more than a few fields thrown into one, with a bunch of Nissen huts and a marquee for general accommodation. Perkin who had, up until this time, done two operational sorties on the Hurricane, was feeling somewhat relaxed and luxurious, since the Squadron had not been ordered to be at 'readiness' until 9 am. For the first time after many days of having to scramble out before dawn, Perkin and his friends lay slothfully in bed until 7.30 and thereafter took their time over dressing and breakfast. Then they lunged about in their hut listening to a 'bind' on the forthcoming day's work, the formation to be adopted and kindred matters. While this was in progress the telephone rang and the man nearest to it, having listened for a moment, slammed it back on its rest.

'Scramble - Thames Estuary - Angels 20,' he said briefly.

But almost before he had finished speaking, the hut was filled with plunging bodies, as men grabbed for their gloves, helmets and gear and went streaming out of the door and across the airfield. In ordinary English, their telephone orders were to get off the ground forthwith and climb to a height of 20,000 feet over the estuary of the River Thames, there to take on any enemy aircraft which might appear, or to act under further radio orders from the Control Room. Perkin, getting a move on with the rest, was annoyed to find that someone had swiped his gloves. He bellowed at a rigger to get him another pair as he clambered up into the cockpit of his Hurricane and started buckling up and plugging in his gear. By the time the rigger got back to hand up a pair of gloves, Perkin was fuming with impatience because he could already see the leading Hurricane trundling off to start their take-off run. He wrenched his gloves on and reached up for his canopy to slam it shut, but the rigger, outside, held it back.

'Better do your leg straps up, Sarge' he said.

Perkin glanced down at his own lap and saw that in his impatience he had forgotten to fasten the all-important leg straps of his parachute to the centre harness and buckle. If the rigger had not noticed it, the end of this story would have been different; tragically so. Perkin nodded his thanks as he attached the straps. It was the first - and the last - time in his flying career that he ever made such a mistake.

A few minutes later he was away off the ground, feeling the satisfying clicks as his undercarriage wheels retracted and locked. He climbed to catch up with the rest of the Squadron, finally taking up his place just behind the right wing of his Squadron Leader as they orbited over base. Behind him were the rest of the Squadron, finally taking up his place just behind his Squadron Leader as they orbited over base. Behind him were the rest of 73 Squadron, many of whose names became famous in Fighter Command as the war went on; 'one-arm Mac' McLachlan,[172] who later in the war had a claw at the end of a steel mechanism with which he worked the engine controls in place of his missing right arm and did his shooting with his left hand; the big, cheerful, stuttering Jas Storrar;[173] the handsome and witty Mike Beytagh, who was afterwards to fight through the desert campaign and command 602 City of Glasgow Squadron in the closing stages of the war, to name only a few.[174]

In tight formation 73 Squadron climbed to 20,000 feet above the river estuary in the bright sunshine of mid-morning. Then the controller's voice came over the radio: 'Twenty escorted bandits approaching Burnham.'

The Squadron turned obediently, but before they had Burnham beneath them, radioed orders came through again: 'Fifty Ju 88s approaching Clacton at Angels 5.'

Unnecessary natter (talk) over the R/T was officially discouraged, but there were those who offered an opinion about the controller as the Squadron Leader altered course again and led his followers in a dive to 5,000 feet. As they went, everyone strained their eyes ahead and around, but there was nothing to be seen in the vast blue bowl of the sunlit sky.

Clacton appeared unmistakably on the coastline far below... at which point the controller suddenly came through and ordered them back to 20,000 feet where a large force of enemy fighters were reported to be milling around.

Perkin was amused to hear Jas Storrar's famous stutter: 'O-oh, bub-bub-blast!' but he immediately opened up again and started the long climb back in to the heights, steadily in his place on the Squadron Leader's right wing. Nothing could be seen in the brilliant glare of the sun.

Still the formation was kept very tight, flying in three vics of three aircraft each with two 'weaving' in the rear. These two swung from side to side as they flew, so that they could get a wider range of view all round and would be able to spot unexpected attack and warn their comrades ahead. At least that was the general idea at the time. Different tactics were adopted later 0n, especially in conditions of brilliant sunlight. It was this factor which beat the weavers on this occasion. Neither they nor any other pilot in the Squadron caught a glimpse of the enemy attack which was, even then, coming down at them out of the blinding glare of the sun.

At that moment Perkin had his eye on the coastline below. He had just checked height at around 22,000 feet on the altimeter and was marking the town of Colchester. Then he was startled by what seemed to be an explosion in his Merlin engine immediately in front of him. In actual fact that 'explosion' was the impact of a burst of cannon shells from an enemy fighter which had dived directly upon him from out of the sun. In the next moment Perkin's cockpit was filled with flames. The enemy cannon shell had hit his reserve tank and the petrol had 'gone up'.

The attack was so sudden and unexpected that he had no chance of either taking evasive action or fighting back. At one moment he was checking position; at the next, his cockpit was on fire and he could feel the flames at work on the skin of his hands and face. There was only one thing he could do - get out, fast.

Perkin reached up, slammed his canopy back and jerked out the hart pin which secured his Sutton harness. With the straps sliding over his shoulders he heaved up to get himself out of the blast of the fire and over the side of the Hurricane. But something stuck. What it was he had no idea at the time. He pushed and kicked his legs to free them of whatever had got tangled. When at last he got clear and went over the side, he had the unpleasant impression that he had managed to kick his parachute off as well in the general upheaval. 'Something seems to happen to your mind at a moment like that' he said quietly. 'I know I didn't care whether I'd got a parachute on or not. I only wanted to get away from the damned fire.'

Perkin got away, but only by a matter of feet. He had no sooner tumbled over the side than he was pulled up with a tremendous jerk which seemed as though it had dislocated his neck. In his scramble to get himself out of the fire he had not had time to undo his oxygen and R/T leads, the ends of which were firmly plugged inside the burning cockpit, while the other ends were still connected to the helmet which was strapped round his head. For the next few seconds he hung by his helmet anchored to the burning Hurricane, which went diving down the sky in an uncontrolled spin, leaving a whirling trail of flame and smoke behind it. He was completely helpless. At the speed at which he was being dragged he could not get his hands up with enough strength to unbuckle the helmet strap. Fortunately, however, the helmet had not been designed to withstand strains of that order. The strap suddenly broke and then Perkin performed a spirited somersault head over heels over the burning Hurricane's tail... which he felt was hardly a text-book departure.

As he went down the sky, still turning head over heels, his first clear sensation was that of deep relief in the cool draught against the skin of his face and hands. When the daze of his neck-wrenching wore off he realized that he had better find out if his parachute had really been kicked off. With some relief he found that it hadn't. He grabbed the release ring, gave it a hearty wrench and found that the handle came away in his hand trailing about a yard of cord. This seemed to indicate that his parachute pack had either been shot away or burnt to uselessness by the fire. Perkin tensed himself to face one of the more unpleasant methods of departing this life. Then he heard a thudding crack from above, felt a violent jerk on his body harness and glanced up to see the white parachute canopy fully opened above with its shroud lines supporting him with comforting strength.

When he discovered that providence had given him at least an extension of life, Perkin allowed himself to relax and look around. He found that he wasn't alone. A Hurricane was making steep turns all around his parachute and he recognised 'Scotty', a comrade. [Alfred Enoch Scott came from Nottingham]. 'Scotty's occupation became obvious as Perkin again grew conscious of the roar and drone of aircraft close at hand. He looked up to see the sky above still filled with Hurricanes and Bf 109s diving and climbing and rolling all around in a general uproar of open exhausts and thudding armaments. Scotty meanwhile, was playing guard to his helpless comrade, circling round the drifting parachute ready to discourage German pilots from their light-hearted habit of shooting down men who had to bail out.

Perkin waved his thanks for the protection offered. Then he felt a bit queer and, as he hung in his parachute harness, he was suddenly and shatteringly sick. In the moments of giddy nausea that followed he became sharply conscious of the smell of burnt flying-suit and skin, which hung about him like an aura. By the time he recovered himself, he found he was in an empty sky and that the uproar of exhausts and machine guns had died away. The effect of speed was such that the sky could be full of a howling dog fight one minute and apparently clear at the next.

Perkin however, realized that he now had only a few hundred feet of height left and that he was coming down squarely in the middle of the Thames Estuary, with about five or six miles of water stretching on either side of him to the shores of Kent or Essex. There was no shipping of any kind in sight and the prospect looked distinctly unpleasant until he saw that there was a strip of sandbank not far away. He marked its position carefully as he drifted down. Then the shining surface of the water seemed to make a sudden rush upwards - and with a heavy splash he was in it.

He remembered his parachute drill clearly enough. He clapped undone the harness release as soon as he struck the surface. He was clear of it when he came up again and to his relief still had the sandbank in sight. But as he struck out and started swimming towards it his mind was occupied with thoughts about quicksands. When at last his feet touched bottom and he staggered forward still breast high in the water, he found to his relief that the sand was firm. Soon he had managed to wade out on the shallow top of the bank and then once again he heard a Merlin engine. Looking up he saw the faithful Scotty circling around him again, flying at only about ten feet as slowly as possible with wheels and flaps down. Once again Perkin waved, this time to show that he was alive with no bones broken and the reassured 'Scotty' forthwith opened up and flew off shoreward to give his position [at Hasty Ferry near Sittingbourne] and organize rescue.

For the next twenty minutes Perkin sat on his sandbank and hoped that what he had heard of the curative qualities of salt water as applied to burns was true. During that time he saw another parachute drift down on to the Isle of Sheppey and afterwards learned that it was his comrade Sergeant Maurice Equity 'Jim' Leng (who had been shot down on 25 August by British anti-aircraft defences whilst on a night patrol and had bailed out, unhurt). Meanwhile, Perkin had been spotted from the shore and before the rescue organized by Scotty had time to get to him, a couple of fishermen came rowing up in a boat to take him on board. [175]

In all, 73 Squadron had four pilots shot down by Bf 109s on 23 September. Pilot Officer Neville Charles Langham-Hobart ditched his Hurricane (L2036) near Lightship 93 after being shot down over the Thames Estuary. Born in Newcastle, he went to the Royal Grammar School there. On 7 September he had claimed a Bf 110 destroyed. After his ditching on 23 September, severely burned, he was rescued from the sea by the Navy and was also admitted to Chatham Hospital.[176] So too was Pilot Officer Douglas Steele Kinder, who crashed his Hurricane (P3226) near Lightship 93 after the attack by the Bf 109s and was badly burned too.[177] Twenty-seven year old Sergeant Maurice Equity 'Jim' Leng, who was wounded when his Hurricane (P8812) was shot down by Bf 109s over Sheppey, crashing at Ludgate, Lynstead near Rodmersham, was also admitted to the Royal Naval Hospital Chatham. It was not the first time that Leng had been shot down. On 25 August British anti-aircraft defences shot down his Hurricane (P3758, which crashed west of Beverley, Yorkshire) whilst on a night patrol and he bailed out, unhurt.

73 Squadron was posted to the Middle East in November 1940. It embarked on HMS *Furious* on the 10th and flew off to Takoradi on the 29th. It then flew in easy stages to Heliopolis, via Lagos, Accra, Kano, Maidugari, Khartoum, Wadi Haifa and Abu Sueir. The pilots were attached to 274 Squadron in the Western Desert in December. Early in January 1941 73 Squadron began to operate on its own account. 'Jim' Leng was shot down on 30 September 1942 in Spitfire BR411 near Tympaki, Crete on a shipping reconnaissance and captured. He was held in captivity at Stalag Luft III, Sagan from 20 October 1942 to 2 May 1945. [178]

Endnotes Chapter 16

172 James Archibald Findlay MacLachlan was born at Styal in Cheshire in 1919. In 1941, flying Hurricane Is on 261 Squadron in Malta he scored eight victories and a 'possible'. On 16 February, however, he was shot down by a 109E, bailing out with his left arm shattered by a cannon shell. His left forearm was amputated and was evacuated back to England where he had an artificial limb fitted at Roehampton. He was then posted to command 1 Squadron in November and he claimed five victories flying night intruder sorties over France. In June 1943 he scored the last of his 16 and 1 shared victories flying the Mustang 1A on the AFDU, destroying two Hs 126s and a Ju 88 and a half share in another Ju 88 destroyed. He was shot down on 18 July and crash landed, critically injured. He died in a German Field Hospital on 31 July. The previous day the award of a second bar to his DFC had been announced. *Aces High* by Christopher Shores and Clive Williams (Grub Street 1994).

173 James Eric Storrar was born in Ormskirk, Lancashire on 24 July 1921. In 1940 he destroyed In May 1940 he destroyed four aircraft during the fighting in France with 145 Squadron. During the Battle of Britain he scored four more and notched several unconfirmed and, damaged and probable kills. In August he was awarded the DFC. He ended the war with a total of twelve and

two shared destroyed, 1 unconfirmed destroyed, 2 and 1 shared probables, 3 damaged and 1 and 8 shared destroyed on the ground. *Aces High* by Christopher Shores and Clive Williams (Grub Street 1994).

174 Michael Leo Brench Beytagh was born in Shanghai in 1916, the son of a prosperous Irish businessman. When his parents divorced he and his brother and sister were looked after by Miss Esylt Newbery, their guardian. When Michael was 13 he was adopted by a Mr Morton, a wealthy American and taken to the United States. They did not get on and after a few years he returned to Miss Newbery. After working in a Maidstone Insurance law firm he joined the RAF in June 1936. On 7 September Beytagh claimed a Bf 110 and a Bf 110 'damaged' on 11 September. He died on 12 August 1952. *Men of the Battle of Britain* by Kenneth G. Wynn. (CCB Associates 1999).

175 Perkin's Hurricane crashed in the Swale, Elmley. He died in 1988. Alfred E. Scott was commissioned in February 1942. He was KIA on 19 August 1945 on 245 Squadron. *Men of the Battle of Britain* by Kenneth G. Wynn. (CCB Associates 1999).

176 Langham-Hobart later moved to the Queen Victoria Hospital, East Grinstead where he had skin grafts on face and legs, becoming a Guinea Pig. In 1941 he was posted to the Ministry of Aircraft Production and visited munition factories, speaking to the workers. He later went to Canada, where, after doing a specialist navigation course at Goderich, Ontario, he instructed at Charlottetown, Prince Edward Island. Back in the UK Langham-Hobart went to the Air Ministry and later moved to HQ 13 Group Newcastle as Navigation Officer. He went to HQ Cairo and given the job of setting up mobile light beacons between Tripoli and Algiers. With this task completed, he was appointed CGI at Abu Sueir. Langham-Hobart returned to England, did an intensive course on radar systems at RAF Shawbury and then returned to Air HQ Cairo. His final posting was as CO of RAF Port Reitz at Mombasa. He returned to the UK and was released from the RAF in September 1945 as a Squadron Leader. He died in Newcastle in September 1994.

177 Kinder had joined the RAF on a short service commission in July 1939, completed his training and joined 103 Squadron, operating Fairey Battles. Kinder volunteered to transfer to Fighter Command in August 1940 and he was posted to 615 Squadron at Prestwick on 9 September, moving to 73 Squadron at Castle Camps on the 15th. His subsequent service is currently undocumented but he must have returned to Bomber Command as on 7 December 1943 he was awarded the DFC as a Flight Lieutenant on 166 Squadron, operating Lancasters from Kirmington, Lincolnshire. Kinder was released from the RAF in 1947 as a Flight Lieutenant. He died in October 1993. *Men of the Battle of Britain* by Kenneth G. Wynn. (CCB Associates 1999).

178 He was released from the RAF in March 1946 and joined the RAFVR in September 1947. Leng retired in September 1962 as a Flight Lieutenant. He died in 1995.

Chapter 17

An Italian Interlude

'One Nazi plane which crashed and burst into flames on Sunday morning is believed by residents to be a Heinkel 111. One of the crew was found to be dead. His three companions got away but were soon captured by police officers, who took them to a police station before handing them over to the Military. One of the crew was wearing a decoration...Another plane, a Junkers 88, crashed and burst in flames some miles away...'

***Eastern Daily Press* Monday 5 May 1941.**

The first raid by the Corpo Aereo Italiano on Great Britain on 11 November 1940 was an event keenly awaited by the fighter pilots of the Royal Air Force. The luck of the draw fell to the Hurricane pilots on 257 'Burma' Squadron at Martlesham Heath. When about a dozen Fiat CR.42 biplane fighters of 18° Gruppo CT and twelve twin-engined BR.20 medium monoplane bombers of 43° Gruppo BT came over that day, Squadron Leader Robert Stanford Tuck DSO DFC **, the CO, much to his annoyance, was having a day off on the MO's advice having wakened during the night with a painful eardrum caused through flying while suffering from a head cold. The Squadron was led into combat by Howard Peter 'Cowboy' Blatchford DFC [179] a popular flight commander, born in Edmonton, Alberta on 25 February 1912. He had joined the RAF in February 1936.

'Cowboy' Blatchford had been posted to 257 'Burma' Squadron in answer to a request from Bob Stanford Tuck for 'a thoroughly experienced flight commander'. 'Blatchford, tall as a candle, was cheery-faced, chunky and chuckle-voiced' wrote Tuck's biographer, Larry Forrester, 'with an extraordinarily large backside that made him waddle and roll like an overfed puppy. The slowness of his movements and mannerisms proved wholly deceptive - his mind was rapier-swift, his reflexes instantaneous. He was a brilliant shot, never got excited - all told, a 'natural'. From the start 'Cowboy' and Tuck only had to look at one another and they were overtaken by a tremendous sense of fun. Even their grimmest and most urgent tasks were planned and executed in a spirit of banter and ribaldry. 'Cowboy' was the only member of the squadron who, in the middle of a battle, could tell the owner of that flat, curt voice to 'get stuffed' and get away with it - maybe even earn a long, loud and friendly raspberry in reply.

'In presence of the other pilots he addressed Tuck as 'boss', hardly ever said 'sir'. In private it soon became plain 'Bobbie', or 'Tommy'. Sometimes it was 'Beaky' - a dig at Tuck's long, thin nose. Tuck called him Cowboy most of the time, pronouncing the word with an exaggerated nasal accent and pushing it out of the corner of his mouth like a squirt of tobacco juice. At other times it was Pete or Peter, occasionally 'Fat Arse'. But though they never ceased to tease one another, somehow Blatchford always showed sincere respect for his leader. It was impossible to be with the pair of them for more than a few minutes and fail to see the affection they shared. Apart from flying and beer, they had practically nothing in common. 'Cowboy' had two absorbing interests: Hill-Billy music (which probably helped to earn his nickname) and girls. the Canadian got Tuck to listen to and even join in with, a host of twangy, corny records of 'mountain music' and traditional songs of the Wild West and once or twice even persuaded him to make up a foursome in Ipswich or London with 'my popsie's pal - real cute she is, honest ....'

By early 1941 by which time 257 Squadron's Hurricanes had moved to RAF Coltishall on the edge of the Norfolk Broads, Bob Tuck had become engaged to Joyce, whom he had met recently in the upstairs bar of the 'King's Arms' in North Walsham. Joyce lived with her parents in a large house a mile or two from Coltishall airfield. That spring Britain was forced to endure the Luftwaffe 'Blitz' on its towns and cities as almost nightly German bombers blasted residential areas, docks and industrial targets from East Anglia to London and the Midlands to Merseyside. East Anglia had many air raids and Norwich and several Norfolk villages suffered death and devastation by German 'tip and run' raiders in broad daylight. The beautiful Broadland village of Horning seems an unlikely target but when war broke out in 1939 the firm of H. C. Banham Ltd started Admiralty work on 27-foot whalers. Then they co-operated for war production with the Percival firm and joined in the construction of motor launches, motor torpedo boats and invasion craft generally until the end of 1944 when the building of the larger ships was drawing to a close. The Fairmile Marine Company delivered 1,500 tons of ships of war fully equipped for action, mainly for the Navy but also for the Royal Air Force. One of the RAF's favourite drinking haunts was the 'Ferry Inn' at Horning, which stood quite on its own in open country. Pilots from all the Coltishall squadrons nearby were in there three or four evenings a week.

On a dark moonless night, Saturday 26 April 1941 Bob Tuck and his fiancée and other regulars were in the bar of the pub when Tuck, all at once, quite unaccountably, grew feverishly restless. He drained his glass and said: 'Come on, everybody, let's whip into Norwich!' Flight Lieutenant Brian van Mentz, a South African pilot who on 25 October 1940 had been awarded the DFC[180] looked up at the bar clock and shook his head. On 28 January he and Bob Tuck had received their DFCs which were presented by HM King George VI at an investiture ceremony held at the Coastal Command station at Bircham Newton. 'Not worth it' he said. 'We'd never get there before closing time.' The others murmured in agreement.[181] Tuck and Joyce and their large and lazy bloodhound 'Shuffles' jumped into this car and sped off. At the next crossroads Tuck turned off the road to Norwich for Coltishall. Next morning as he was shaving, 'Cowboy' Blatchford told him in his measured drawl, 'Drinking will be the death of you, Bobbie.'

'Meaning what?'

'You were at the 'Ferry' last night - that so?' Tuck nodded, watching him in the mirror. 'Well, for once you must have left before closing time, because just as the bell rang for last orders a bloody Hun came over and scored a direct hit with a five hundred pounder. Bloody grim show.'

At a quarter to ten o'clock a Junkers Ju 88 flying at 500 feet had dropped 15 bombs in the vicinity of the inn. The bulk of them fell aimlessly on the surrounding marshland. Of the four which fell on the 'Ferry Inn' property one dropped on the pontoon ferry-boat, ten on the Woodbastwick side of the river and one in the river itself. The second of the series of bombs hit the 'Ferry' killing 21 people and injuring several more. Of six members of the family of Mr. Henry Sutton, a well-known figure in the Yarmouth fishing trade, five were killed including Mr. Sutton himself. The landlord, Albert Stringer and about half a dozen others had been dug out alive, though most of them were seriously injured. [182] Among the RAF dead were Van Metz, 222 Squadron's Adjutant, Flying Officer Robinson and Flight Lieutenant Attwell, the Coltishall Station Medical Officer.

Did Tuck have a premonition of disaster? Throughout the war 'Tuck's Luck' served him to an almost supernatural degree. On the Monday, the *Eastern Daily Press* carried a carefully censored half column story of the raid without disclosing the exact locality. It was just another tragedy in East Anglia. A month later a photograph of the ruins was published.[183]

'Well, we started with the usual afternoon blitz, just like any other day during the past three months and we were ordered up on patrol out to sea [east of Harwich]. Our job was to join up with another Hurricane squadron [17 and 46 Squadrons at North Weald took part] as their bodyguard. When we were about 12,000 feet up I saw nine planes of a type I had never seen before coming along. They were in tight 'V' formation. I didn't like to rush in bald-headed until I knew what they were so the squadron went up above them to have a good look at them. Then I realised that at any rate they were not British and that was good enough for me. So we went into attack starting with the rear starboard bomber and crossing over to attack the port wing of the formation.

'I must say that the Italians as they turned out to be, stood up to it very well. They kept their tight formation and were making for the thick cloud cover at 20,000 feet, but our tactics were to break them up before they could do that and we succeeded. I singled out one of the enemy and gave him a burst. Immediately he went straight up into a loop. I thought he was foxing me as I had never seen a bomber do that sort of thing before. So I followed him when he suddenly went down in a vertical dive. I still followed, waiting for him to pull out. Then I saw a black dot move away from him and a puff like a white mushroom - someone bailing out. The next second the bomber seemed to start crumpling up and it suddenly burst into hundreds of small pieces. They fell down to the sea like a snowstorm. I must have killed the pilot. I think he fell back, pulling the stick with him - that's what caused the loop. Then he probably slumped forward, putting the plane into an uncontrollable dive. But what usually happens then is that the wing or the tail falls off and it was a surprising sight to see the plane just burst into small pieces.

'Then I started to climb again and I saw another two of the bombers in the sky. They were mixed up in a fight and were both streaming smoke. At that moment another one shot past me flaming like a torch and plunged into the sea. After seeing that I thought the battle was over and I could go home, but just as I turned to do so I saw a dog-fight going on up above with another type of aeroplane I had never seen before. They were Fiat fighter biplanes. There must have been about twenty of them milling round with the Hurricanes. I went up to join in the party, but the fighter I singled out saw me coming and went into a quick turn with me on his tail. His plane was very manoeuvrable, but so was the Hurricane and we stuck closely enough together while I got in two or three bursts. It was a long dog-fight, as dog-fights go. We did tight turns, climbing turns and half-rolls till it seemed we would never stop. Neither of us was getting anywhere until one of my bursts seemed to hit him and he started waffling. For a moment he looked completely out of control and then he came in at me and we started all this merry-go-round business over again. I got in two or three more bursts and then ran out of ammunition. That put me in a bit of a fix and I didn't know what to do next. I was afraid if I left his tail he would get on to mine. Then he straightened up - he was just thirty yards ahead and I was a few feet above. At that moment I decided that as I could not shoot him down I would try and knock him out of the sky with my aeroplane. I went kind of hay-wire. It suddenly occurred to me what a good idea it would be to scare the living daylight out of him. I aimed for the centre of his top main plane, did a quick dive and pulled out just before crashing into him. I felt a very slight bump, but I never saw him again and somehow I don't think he got back.

'By now the scene had changed a bit. Another squadron of Hurricanes was chasing the Italians all over the sky. I did not know at the time, but I found when I got down that their squadron leader [Squadron Leader Lionel Manley Gaunce] was a great friend of mine from my home town of Edmonton, Alberta[184].

'He bagged a couple in that fight.[185]

'And now I thought its home for me, but the day wasn't over yet. As I was flying back, keeping a good look-out behind, I saw a Hurricane below me, having the same kind of affair with a Fiat as I had just had. I went down and did a dummy head-on attack on the Italian. At 200 yards he turned away and headed out to sea. I thought: 'Good, I really can get home this time,' but just before I got to the coast, still keeping a good look-out behind, I saw another Hurricane, with three Fiats close together worrying him. So down I went again, feinting another head-on attack and again when I was about 200 yards away the Italians broke off and headed for home. That really was the end of the battle. I was a bit worried because my plane had started to vibrate badly, but I managed to land all right. Just as I had got out of my Hurricane and was walking away my fitter and rigger ran after me saying that I had six inches missing from one of my propeller blades and nine inches from another. All the same, it certainly was a grand day for the squadron.' [186]

Tuck was waiting at the airfield when the Hurricanes came roaring home, in twos and threes, their broken gun-ports whistling, wings rocking a little as though tired, some of the engines sounding rough and breathless. 'Cowboy' and Pilot Officer Karol Pniak were the first to touch down[187] Pniak had attacked one Fiat BR.20M bomber that began to smoke and burn and then turned onto its back before it dived into the sea ten miles east of Harwich after one man had bailed out. He then attacked another, which glided in towards the coast, trailing smoke. 'Cowboy' bobbed out of his cockpit and came over the grass at a frantic, waddling run, waving his arms and emitting a mating-moose howl.

'Hey boss - guess what? A mob of bloody Eyeties! - yeah, Musso's boys! Jeez, what a helluva day for you to be sick!' He caught Tuck's arm and led him towards the parked little Hillman. 'Quick, boss - in you get. One of them pancaked just a few miles away - over by Woodbridge. Let's take a look at it!'

Pniak joined them in time to dive into the back seat. On the way, between directions, 'Cowboy' gave a full account of the action. Karol, who spoke very little English, lay back and appeared to go to sleep in an instant.[188]

Can't be far now - turn left at the next crossroads and we ought to be there ... Hey Karol, wakey-wakey!'

A few minutes later they found the Italian, crumpled against a thicket of firs not far from the road. Tuck - who took his aircraft recognition seriously and hadn't confined his studies to German machines like most of the others - identified it as a B.R. 20. It was riddled with bullet holes and badly smashed up.

Some local people and two policemen were already on the scene and had brought out most of the crew. Three of the Italians were conscious, but seriously injured. One of them had his right forearm almost completely severed and was bleeding copiously. 'Cowboy' grabbed one of the constables. 'What's the matter with you, man? Get a tourniquet on him, quick!' The policeman looked dazed and sick, but he nodded and went to work. As the tourniquet was tightened the Italian made no sound, but the pain and the fear shrieked in his eyes. Then he turned his head and caught sight of the three air force uniforms. His grey lips moved feebly once or twice and they caught the word Pilota. Then he passed out.

'Cowboy' led the way to the wreck, not looking at the other still forms stretched out on the grass. The side door of the bomber was huge - it seemed you could have driven a car through it. As he approached it 'Cowboy' trod on what looked like an old piece of hessian lying on the ground. His foot sank into something soft, one end of the hessian rose about a foot and there was a loud, vulgar noise - unmistakably - a belch! 'Cowboy' sprang back; his body arched like a cat's and cannoned into Carol and Tuck. Now, on closer inspection, they could make out the vague hump of a body under the hessian.

'Christ - it sat up! The poor bastard's still alive!'

'No,' Tuck said quickly. 'You must have stood on his stomach, that's all. Gases, you know....' And then he gave a short, hard laugh, because it seemed the only thing to do. 'Cowboy' shook himself, grinned sheepishly, then picked his way round the obstacle and clambered into the aircraft.

Just inside the door the top-gunner was still in his harness, swinging gently; full of bullets. The harness creaked faintly and the floor beneath him was slippery. They had to flatten themselves against the side of the fuselage and wriggle past. On the way Tuck looked up and saw a holster at the gunner's waist. He reached up, extracted a Brevetta automatic and stuck it in his pocket. Since ten years of age he'd been a keen collector of firearms, he still couldn't resist a chance to augment his private armoury...

In the waist they found two hampers, large as laundry baskets. One was stuffed with a variety of foods - whole cheeses, salami, huge loaves, cake, sausages and several kinds of fruit. The other held still more food and over a dozen straw-jacketed bottles - Chianti.

'Cowboy' whistled softly. 'They sure do it in style. What d'you think, boss? Pity if all this went to waste - rotting in some cubby-hole at Air Ministry.' Tuck nodded and between them they carried the hampers to the car. One of the policemen watched them, frowning, but Tuck went to him and explained in a purposely off-hand manner: 'I'm the commanding officer of 257 Squadron, North Weald. My chaps shot this one down. We're taking a few souvenirs - that's an unwritten law in the RAF. If anybody raises any objections, refer them to me.' The constable rubbed his collection of chins, but said nothing.

They went back to the wreck and picked up several steel helmets and bayonets. (Why such things should be carried in a bomber was beyond them.) Finally, just before the troops and the recovery trucks arrived, they took the bayonets, climbed up on to the twin tail unit and cut from the tip of each fin the beautifully hand-painted crests: they'd look splendid behind the bar at the mess.

Back at the airfield, a flurry of photographers greeted them. The 'Burma' boys posed with their trophies and the Chianti bottles circulated merrily.

Next day the papers blazed with highly-coloured reports of the battle. It was with difficulty that the 257 pilots sifted out the few hard facts. Mussolini, it seemed, had stated in a broadcast that he had asked his friend Adolf Hitler for the 'privilege' of participating in the air-war against Great Britain and had received consent for a few crack squadrons of the Regia Aeronautica to use Nazi bases in France and operate 'side by side with the Luftwaffe'. But the Germans had kept well clear of their slower, inexperienced allies. While the Italian mixed formation headed for the Thames Estuary, a German fighter wing had attacked a number of towns along the south-east coast. Other British squadrons had opposed this 'diversion', destroying twelve of them for the loss of two.

The Italian force was estimated to have consisted of nine B.R. 20 bombers, with an escort of between thirty and forty of the nimble Fiat C.R. 42 fighters. The Regia Aeronautica had lost at least twelve machines - of which 257 bagged five, or perhaps six - without destroying a single British fighter and entirely failed in its mission, which was to bomb shipping in the Thames. (They appeared over Britain only once more - on 23 November - when they received an equally severe mauling. But on that occasion 257 were not involved.)

The newspapers made fun of the Italians, making out that they'd fled at first sight of opposition. This greatly annoyed the North Weald pilots, who thought the Eyeties had displayed plenty of courage - especially in view of the inferior performance and speed of their machines.

Tuck was shocked to find that in several newspapers he was named as the leader of the victorious Hurricane wing. There were pictures of him captioned 'the man who smashed the Italians' and such like.

Shortly after this, there appeared in The People a rather lurid article by Arthur Helliwell, headed *'Chianti Tuck'-Terror Of The Wops.* Excellent propaganda, no doubt, but with no basis in fact. Tuck squirmed as he read: 'For weeks he and his men had been waiting for just such an opportunity. They descended upon the Macaroni airmen like avenging furies and played swift havoc among these ancient planes from ancient Rome... 'They were easy,' he [Tuck] said, 'Just dead meat of the skies.' '

Furious and determined to get the truth printed, he tried to contact Helliwell by 'phone. For five days he kept ringing *The People* office and also the London Press Club, but always the columnist had 'Just left'. [189]

On 22 November the Corpo Aereo Italiano carried out their second raid on Britain. Squadron Leader George Denholm, the Commanding Officer of 603 (City of Edinburgh) Auxiliary Squadron, who had been awarded a DFC on 22 October, led his pilots into action.[190]

'In this particular battle I was largely in the position of a spectator, so I can tell you all about it. I was leading the squadron when my engine began to misfire and splutter. So I called up one of my flight-commanders and told him to lead while I broke away and tried to clear my engine. By diving and roaring the engine, I managed to make it run smoothly again and then took up position at the rear of the squadron. We had taken off at about eleven-forty that morning. It was a sunny day with a slight ground haze which developed into mist from 18,000 feet up to about 26,000 feet. We were on a routine patrol with another squadron and after patrolling for forty or fifty minutes we were ordered to go here and there to investigate various raids which were reported over land and near the coast. While we were climbing through some cloud we lost touch with the other squadron.

'We carried on alone and were on a southerly course approaching Dover, when we were warned to look out for a formation of Italian aircraft. Every man was immediately on the alert. By this time I was at the back of the squadron and I heard the formation leader suddenly report aircraft dead ahead of us. At the same time someone else reported unidentified aircraft to the east, but the leader wisely held our course to fly towards the aircraft he had already seen. After a couple of minutes we saw the enemy aircraft flying south-west down the Channel. They were still some distance away and were 1,000 feet below us. They were Italian fighters - CR.42s - and were well over the sea flying at about 20,000 feet. When I first had a good look at them they gave me the impression of a party out on a quiet little jaunt. There were about twenty of them, flying along quite happily in good formation.

'When the leader gave the order to attack and told us to sweep round and down on their tails, we were in a very advantageous position. Our machines must be about 100 mph faster than the Italian fighters and it was dead easy to overtake them and blaze away. They were flying in a sort of wide fan-like formation and when we went to attack each of our pilots selected his particular target. You can imagine how effective the first few dives were when I tell you that one of our pilots at one time saw six Italian fighters either on fire or spinning down towards the sea. The Italians looked quite toy-like in their brightly-coloured camouflage and I remember thinking that it seemed almost a shame to shoot down such pretty machines. I must have been wrong, for the pilot who saw six going down at the same time said afterwards that it was a glorious sight. But I must say this about the Eye-Ties: they showed fight in a way the Germans have never done with our squadron. It is true though that they seemed amateurish in their reactions. By that I mean they were slow to realise that we were anywhere near them until it was too late. Another thing, they kept their formation very well, but it didn't save them.

'After a short while the Italians were dodging this way and that to escape our aircraft as best they could. One of them broke formation and turned towards France. I chased him and fired at him several times. I believe I hit him, too and would have finished him off if my engine hadn't begun to splutter again when I was half-way across the Channel. So I left him to limp home while I turned towards the English coast to find the rest of the battle. It had vanished by this time, so I came home. The whole fight lasted only ten or fifteen minutes.'

Endnotes Chapter 17

179 Robert Roland Stanford 'Bob' Tuck was born in Catford, South London, on 1 July 1916. A very keen shot from an early age, he won the Sherwood Trophy at Bisley whilst in the rifle team of St. Dunstan's College, Catford. On leaving school, he joined the Merchant Navy in 1932, spending two and half years on the SS Marconi, before joining the RAF on a short service commission in September 1935. Posted to 65 Squadron in May 1936, he collided with Flying Officer Bicknell whilst doing aerobatics in their Gladiators during April 1938, both bailing out, although Tuck suffered a severe cut to his face from a loose flying wire which scarred him permanently and led to his growing a slim moustache to draw attention away from the scar. Already converted to Spitfires by the outbreak of war, he was posted to 92 Squadron as a flight commander on I May 1940, seeing much action over Dunkirk later in the month. He was awarded a DFC on 11 June. On 8 August he was shot down by return fire from a Ju 88, bailing out over Horsmonden. On 25 August, his Spitfire was badly damaged whilst he was attacking a Do 17 and he was obliged to force-land after gliding fifteen miles with a dead engine. On 11 September he was posted to command 257 Squadron on Hurricanes, being awarded a Bar to his DFC on 25 October and a DSO on 7 January 1941. This was followed by a Second Bar to his DFC in April 1941.

180 Van Mentz was born in Johannesburg in 1916. He was commissioned into the RADF in 1938 after a year with the South African Reserve. At the time of his death, van Mentz, who was 24 years old, had flown 75 operational sorties and had shot down seven and one shared destroyed, 1 unconfirmed destroyed, 2 and 1 shared probable, 9 damaged.

181 *Fly For Your Life* by Larry Forrester (Frederick Muller Ltd, 1956).

182 Rescue squads came from Aylsham and Sprowston and their efforts were supplemented by troops stationed locally. On the Sunday 'Lord Haw-Haw' gloated on the wireless over this triumph for the German war machine and gleefully announced that an establishment on the Broads for building warships had been successfully raided from the air.

183 'Cowboy' Blatchford took command of 257 Squadron in July 1941. Two months later he was promoted to lead the Digby Wing. He was rested from April 1942 until February 1943, when he became Wing Leader at Coltishall, but on 3 May 1943 when leading the Wing medium bombers

to the Royal Dutch Steel works at Ijmuiden, Holland, he was hit by a II/JG1, FW 190 flown by Unteroffizier Hans Ehlers and ditched off Mundesley on the Norfolk coast at about 1815 hours. His body was never found. His total score stood at 5 and 3 shared destroyed, 3 probables, 4 and 1 shared damaged. On 21 June 1941 Bob Stanford Tuck was shot down into the Channel after claiming two Bf 109s shot down, but was picked up shortly afterwards by a coal barge from Gravesend. In July he was promoted to lead the Duxford Wing, but in October was sent with several other notable pilots on a lecture and liaison trip to the USA, joining in the USAAF manoeuvres and flying P-43 Lancers with the 1st Pursuit Group. Back in England in December brought a return to Spitfires, with a posting as Wing Leader at Biggin Hill. On 28 January 1942 he flew a low level strafing sortie over France, but his Spitfire was hit by flak and he crash-landed, becoming a PoW. His total score stood at 27 and 2 shared destroyed, 1 and 1 shared unconfirmed destroyed, 6 probables, 6 and I shared damaged. Bob Tuck died on 5 May 1987.

184 Born in Lethbridge, Alberta, the son of a Pacific Railway station agent, 'Elmer' Gaunce grew up in Edmonton and in England he took a wife who lived in Catherham, Surrey. He took command of 'A' Flight on 615 Squadron on 16 May 1940 and his coolness and leadership resulted in the award of a DFC on 23 August. His Citation said: 'His Flight took part in the Battle of Dover on July 14th when three of our aircraft were attacked by 40 Junkers 87s of which two were definitely shot down and one probably destroyed. Flight Lieutenant Gaunce has personally shot down three enemy aircraft since returning to England quite apart from taking part in numerous patrols whilst in France.' Gaunce received his decoration at the same time as Flying Officer Petrus Hendrik 'Dutch' Hugo, a 22-year old Afrikaner from Pampoenpoort, Cape Province South Africa, who flew with him. After being notified of the award the pair went aloft on 12 August and shot down three German aircraft to celebrate. ('Dutch' or 'Piet' Hugo completed a distinguished career in the RAF, being credited with 17 and 3 shared destroyed, 2 unconfirmed destroyed, 3 probables and 7 damaged. He left the RAF with the rank of Group Captain, in February 1950). On 18 August Gaunce was shot down by Bf 109s and he bailed out, slightly wounded. On 26 August he was shot down again, this time in flames, bailing out and suffering from shock. At tyhe end of October he was posted to command 46 Squadron. *Aces High* by Christopher Shores and Clive Williams (Grub Street, London 1994).

185 Gaunce was awarded a half share in the destruction of a BR.20M and a CR.42 and a CR.42 probable. Later that month he was taken to hospital, seriously ill of a duodenal ulcer. In July 1941 he returned to active service as CO of 41 Squadron. On 26 January 1942 the Royal Canadian Air Force's 154th official casualty list brought to 1,240 the number of air force dead and missing reported officially since the war started. The Canadian half of the famous team of 'Elmer and Dutch' was broken up with the loss of Gaunce (26) who was listed last November 22 as 'missing, believed killed in action. *Aces High* by Christopher Shores and Clive Williams (Grub Street, London 1994).

186 'Cowboy' Blatchford was awarded a BR.20 destroyed and a quarter share in the destruction of another and with damaging two CR.42s. in all 257 Squadron claimed 8 and 1 shared enemy victories.

187 Pniak had joined 32 Squadron on 8 August 1940 prior to being posted to 257 Squadron in October. He destroyed a Bf 109 on 12 August and two more Bf 109s on the 18th. He was shot down by a Bf 109 and slightly injured in the knee and ankle on 24 August. *Battle Over Britain* by Francis Mason.

188 Pilot Officer Pniak then transferred to 306 Squadron, serving from November 1940 to November 1941. Two months at the AFDU followed, before a return to 306 until January 1943. Pniak then served for five months in North Africa with the Polish Fighting Team. A spell at OTU in a training role (September 1943-November 1944) then saw Pniak serve as commander of 308 'City of Kraków' Squadron from 29 November 1944 until 30 June 1945. Pniak's final tally was 7 aircraft claimed destroyed, 2 shared destroyed, 2 probables, 1 damaged, with 2 shared damaged. In July 1945 he was assigned to HQ Polish Air Force and the Polish 131 Wing in November 1945. In August 1946 he returned to 308 Squadron as a supernumerary commander, receiving a Bar to his Polish Cross of Valour and the Dutch DFC. He left active service in 1947 and returned to Poland, where he died in 1980.

189 *Fly For Your Life* by Larry Forrester. Frederick Muller Ltd, 1956.

190 From Bo'ness, West Lothian, Scotland, George Denholm was born on 20 December 1908.

He joined the Auxiliary Air Force in 1933, serving with 603 'City of Edinburgh' Squadron for six years until the unit was mobilised in August 1939, by which time he had become a flight commander. He took part in the first successful engagement with a Luftwaffe bomber over the British mainland on 16 October 1939. He took command of 603 on 4 June 1940 and led it to the south in August. On 30 August he was shot down by Bf 110s over Deal, Kent, bailing out of his Spitfire. On 15 September he claimed a Bf 109 shot down and two DO 17s damaged, but return fire from the latter hit his Spitfire and again he had to bail out. Aces High by Christopher Shores and Clive Williams (Grub Street, London 1994).

191 Denholm's pilots claimed seven aircraft destroyed. Denholm was rested at the start of April 1941. His total score stood at 3 and 3 shared destroyed, I unconfirmed destroyed, 3 and I shared probables, 6 damaged. In December 1941 he formed 1460 Flight on Turbinlite Havocs, commanding this unit until March 1942, when he was promoted Wing Commander and posted to command 605 Squadron, flying Havocs on night intruder sorties. In February 1943 605 converted to Mosquitoes. He retired from the RAF in 1945 as an Acting Group Captain. *Aces High* by Christopher Shores and Clive Williams (Grub Street, London 1994).

Chapter 18

RAAF

More than 6,000 RAAF men were killed while on active service in theatres of war other than the Pacific, more than 2,000 were reported missing and about 1,500 became prisoners of war. When the Germans surrendered, Australia's eighteen squadrons then in action were flying Sunderlands, Lancasters, Halifaxes, Beaufighters, Mosquito night fighters and fighter bombers, Spitfires, Mustangs, Kittyhawks, Baltimores and Wellingtons. These were the aircraft whose units were flying in the last months of the war, but in the five years that Australia's flying men were abroad many changes took place, both in aircraft flown and in the squadrons themselves. Squadrons came to Britain, 13,000 miles from home, fought awhile, went elsewhere. Others stayed on through the years.

First Australians to fly operationally in the European theatre in this war were those who were already serving in the RAF in the task of meeting the enemy in combat, bombing his armies and patrolling the shores of Britain and France with equipment that in quantity seems pitiable today against the known strength of Germany at that time.

The 'phoney war' - as many people on both sides of the Atlantic called the conflict in its early stages - kept both sides busier, particularly in the air, than was apparent to the newspaper readers of those days. Whitleys carried out the first leaflet raids of the war over Hamburg, Bremen and the Ruhr on 3 and 4 September 1939; bombs weighing 500lb were dropped on the Von Scheer at Wilhelmshaven on September 4; the main body of the first echelon of the Advanced Air Striking Force crossed to France on September 10 and 11; and on October 10 the then Secretary of State for War (Sir Kingsley Wood) told England that in the first four weeks of the war, Coastal Command had completed its first million miles on reconnaissance, anti-submarine and convoy patrol, attacking submarines on thirty-four occasions.

From April to June came the Battles of Norway and France. An Australian flight commander in a Britain-based RAF fighter squadron doing coastal patrol work during the late stages of the Battle of France was one of those who saw from the air the German breakthrough into the Low Countries which began on 10 May 1940, with the landing of paratroops at 4 am, at Waalhaven airfield, the airport of Rotterdam. He was Wing Commander C. G. C. Olive DFC who later transferred to the RAAF in Europe. [192]

Working along the coast near Boulogne in his Hurricane on 10 May, he saw the German tanks coming in masses along the roads towards Abbeville after their breakthrough, while British warships shelled the roads inland. RAF squadrons on coastal patrols were taking it in turns to do two-hour patrols. When Olive went back for his next patrol about two hours later, he saw most of the warships lying on the bottom, with projecting parts on fire. A couple of others, still afloat, were carrying on the shelling. The previous patrol had run into a batch of the Stukas which had sunk the British ships and had shot down several of them.

A week later, Olive and his colleagues watched the beginning of the evacuation of Dunkirk. The town was well alight, with flames reaching skywards in long fierce tongues from the blazing petrol dumps. All along the French coast they could see an enormous storm cloud, a bank of silvery white cumulus. Over Dunkirk, in startling contrast, hung a great cloud of dirty grey smoke, below which, winding and twisting upward, came a black column from the heart of the flames.

In the days of June and July that followed the German blitzkrieg in 1940, Olive saw evidence from the air, during his patrols, of the amazing speed with which the enemy capitalized their gains. Down below one day there would be a bombed airfield. Next day it would be swarming with German workers. A little later there would be fifty or sixty enemy aircraft operating from it; then - almost next day it seemed the number of aircraft had grown to 1,000. And this seemed to be the case at airfields all round the French coast as the Battle of Britain loomed ahead, while on the rivers and at the ports the invasion barges began to accumulate.

These events in France of which Olive saw the first symptoms were disasters the approach of which, in the general confusion of swiftly-moving events, was unsuspected by the flying men whose task it was to fight the Luftwaffe and to co-operate with the land forces in the territory on which the Battle of France was being fought out. They were the men of the British Air Forces in France, or BAFF and the pilots of Britain-based fighter squadrons which, in the later stages, were detailed to extend their patrols across the Channel to give aid in France.

The BAFF comprised two main sections. One was the Air Component with GHQ at Amiens and operating over northern France, from the coast down to Le Havre and to the Belgian frontier near Lille. Its main task was Army co-operation. The other was the Advanced Air Striking Force (AASF), with headquarters at Rheims and operating variously along the Belgian and Luxembourg frontiers and the German frontier between Luxembourg and Lauterburg. Its principal duty was to co-operate with the French Army and Air Force.

When the Germans broke through, the Air Component comprised four Hurricane, four Gladiator, four Blenheim and four Lysander squadrons. The AASF was composed of ten Fairey Battle bomber squadrons and two Hurricane fighter squadrons.

Scattered through the units of the BAFF and the Britain-based fighter squadrons engaged on coastal patrols near the end of the Battle of France were the Australians and other men from the Dominions who had either entered the RAF years earlier, or who had joined on short-service commissions when war broke out.

Among Australia's representatives in the Battle of France was a South

Australian mechanic who had enlisted in 1935 as a cadet in the RAAF at RAAF Station Point Cook, Australia, and had gone to Britain on a short-service RAF commission in 1937. He was Leslie R. Clisby, [193] whose name was to become a byword for flying fearlessness. He was a Flying Officer, twenty-five years old, when he was sent to France with 1 Fighter Squadron AASF, as one of the crack peace-time pilots who held off the Luftwaffe during the tragic period in which France and the Low Countries tried to keep back the German tide. He was stationed near the Maginot Line, not far from where the late 'Cobber' Kain, the New Zealand ace of 73 Squadron AASF was operating.

The story of Clisby comes to a sudden end on 14 May 1940, four days after the German breakthrough into the Low Countries. On that day his Hurricane was seen going down in flames near Rheims and he was never heard of again. In that brief fighting career he shot down fourteen enemy aircraft. The citation to his DFC, announced a few weeks after the crash at Rheims, gives a glimpse of his vivid career:

'One day in April 1940 this officer was the pilot of one of the three Hurricanes which attacked nine Messerschmitt 109s, one of which he shot down. On the following day he destroyed another Messerschmitt 109. In May 1940, this officer was engaged in six combats against the enemy, in which he shot down eight enemy aircraft...'

Three days before Clisby crashed his Hurricane's rudder was shot away in a rear attack by a Messerschmitt after he had shot down three other Me's. As he came down, Clisby saw a Heinkel in front of him and fired a burst at it. Hurricane and Heinkel landed close together, the occupants of both aircraft unhurt. Clisby emerged from his damaged Hurricane, drew his revolver and pursued the German crew over the rough fields, firing as he gained on them. The Germans pulled up, their hands raised and Clisby marched them away to a nearby village, handed them over to the French and made his way unconcernedly back to his squadron.

Throughout his career in France, Leslie Clisby clung to his tattered RAAF blue uniform. 'It will see me through,' he told a war correspondent who was among his closest friends. He was still wearing it that last day at Rheims.

In 1938 Clisby had attended a gunnery school at Sutton Bridge, England and there he and another man from RAAF Station, Point Cook, Flight Lieutenant H. N. Fowler, were known to all as 'The Diggers'. Both then wore the RAAF blue, which regulations permitted them to wear until their uniforms wore out, when they were replaced by the lighter blue of the RAF.

While the younger Leslie Clisby who was to become one of Australia's outstanding fighter aces of the war was growing up at McLaren Vale, South Australia, another lad of the same age who, like Clisby, was to make his name in the war in the air, was playing at Fullerton, twenty-four miles away. Both were born in 1914, at the beginning of the First World War; both began their operational flying careers at the beginning of the Second World War.

The second youngster was Robert W. Bungey, who joined the RAAF as a cadet in 1936. He went to England and was commissioned in the RAF in 1937. Bungey became famous as a fighter ace, but long before he climbed into a fighter's cockpit he was a bomber man. He went to France when the war began, flying Fairey Battle bombers. He carried the atmosphere of Australia with him, like the other Australians of the period. In the chill of the French winter of 1940, he symbolized his link with his warm homeland by painted kangaroos ranged along the fuselage of his aircraft and a toy koala bear that dangled from his rear gun-sight. As the citation to his DFC award set out, Bungey was almost continually engaged on operations against the enemy from the beginning of the war. During operations in France he carried out many bombing and reconnaissance missions, some of which were associated with the attack on the Maastricht bridges which had kept Fowler and the other fighter pilots so busy from 10 May onwards. With the fall of France he went to England and converted to Hurricanes.

Out of the pages of history comes the name of another early Australian bomber pilot - Flying Officer W. M. Blom, an RAAF cadet who was given a short-service commission in the RAF from August 1937. He died on active service in France before the war was a year old. Blom was awarded the DFC on 24 May. Eleven other officers and men were listed for decoration that day, but not all had survived to receive them. They were the men of the bomber group of the AASF which had already dropped thousands of tons of bombs on enemy lines of communication and other military objectives, flying day after day and night after night, often with only a few hours' rest.

A few days before the awards were made [on 10 May] Blom had been detailed to lead a half-section of aircraft in a low-level bombing attack on an enemy motorized column advancing along a road in Luxembourg. Before he reached his objective, machine gun fire pierced his petrol tank, drenching him and almost blinding him. But he pushed on. His smarting eyes could not find the target, but he found another German column. From the column came up a heavy fire and his aircraft was almost wrecked in the air. But he pressed home the attack and then flew on to his base [at Ecury-sur-Coole] ninety miles away, in an aircraft which was later officially declared 'beyond repair.' [194]

Similar feats of endurance, tenacity and courage were being performed everywhere in Western Europe in those days. Not all could be officially recorded and not all earned awards... There were men like Squadron Leader Harold G. Lee DFC AFC, one of the first pilots in the AASF to undertake long operational flights at night in a type of aircraft which was not ideal for the task. During the intensive night and day operations before the evacuation of France he took part in a number of outstanding attacks on difficult targets, on one of which, because of engine failure, he had to abandon his aircraft and landing heavily, broke his leg. There were others, like Flying Officer Richard L. Glyde DFC who accounted for four enemy aircraft.[195]

The Battle of Britain, it is officially recorded, began on 8 August 1940 when Germany opened with attacks on shipping and coastal towns. There had, of course, been bombing raids long before that; the first bomb had fallen on British soil on November 13 the previous year. It was in those earliest days of the war that the foundation was laid for the successful defence of Britain. Part of that foundation were the coastal patrols instituted to counter marauding enemy aircraft.

In these early coastal patrols, as in almost every other phase of the war,

Australian flyers took part. One was Wing Commander Olive. When the Battle of Britain began, Olive was stationed at an airfield on the tip of Kent. August 8, the day the Germans raised the curtain on the first phase of the battle, was a vivid day in his life, as in the lives of other airmen. Of this day it is recorded that 300 enemy aircraft, operating in waves, attacked a convoy off the east coast of England and that British fighters destroyed sixty-one of them.

Warning that something was brewing had reached Olive's fighter squadron and that morning, on the airfield, the Australian and his English comrades were on 'pins and needles' awaiting the word to go. Then, suddenly, came the patter of running footsteps down a passage and the crews were told to get into the air as fast as they could. They were taxiing across the airfield to turn into the wind when, out of nowhere it seemed, a bomb landed. There was a terrific explosion and the hangar went skywards at the side of the parked aircraft. Two more enormous explosions occurred nearby; and looking up, the pilots saw no fewer than 300 enemy aircraft above, with detachments descending on them, their ominous black crosses showing clearly. They were a mixture of Dorniers and Me 110s.

Although the enemy machine-gunned the ground and dropped 160 bombs - the squadron counted the holes later - all the aircraft got off safely. When the Germans saw them airborne they made for the clouds. The fighters in Kent got only a glimpse of them with a line of AA smoke puffs following them, before they disappeared. It was impossible to chase them through the cloud, but three of them were shot down before they got away.

In the mess that night, pilots listened in to 'Lord Haw-Haw's *'Jairmany calling'* as usual, but when they heard him claim that the Luftwaffe had attacked their airfield, had caught twelve Spitfires taking off and had destroyed six in the air and six on the ground, that was the last time they ever listened to the man whom, five years later, the Allies arrested in conquered Germany in May 1945.

On 15 August, the day the first bombs fell in central London, Olive and his fellow fighters ran into a formation of about 200 enemy bombers escorted by 100 twin-engined fighters of the Me 110 class. The British airmen were fortunately placed up-sun, but even so they were amazed to see this great crowd of fighters, attacked by a mere fifteen Spitfires, form up into defensive circles, with thirty or forty aircraft in each circle. The Spitfires re-formed to attack, going up-sun for the purpose. They decided to delay the attack to save ammunition and to adopt tactics that would keep the enemy flying in the defensive circles so that the bombers would have to go on without escort. So the Spitfires remained up-sun and every time the Hun fighters broke their circles they made feint attacks, whereupon the German fighters re-formed and resumed their merry-go-round. The Spitfire men were playing on German psychology; it was evident that the enemy believed they were menaced by a large force and could not conceive that so small a number of Spitfires would attack without heavy support near at hand.

This went on until the enemy bombers were about twenty miles away on their course to their target without their escorting fighters. The Spitfire pilots could still see them, far off, looking like a black cloud of bees. Then, on the flanks of this swarm of black dots they saw many smaller dots and knew the

Hurricanes had got the unescorted bombers. It was an incredible spectacle, set against a great mass of brilliant white cloud. On this back-ground appeared elongated black columns of smoke, looking like question marks, as bomber after bomber fell to the Hurricanes.

Meanwhile, the German fighter escort was still circling twenty miles or so behind the bomber force. Then; apparently, they decided they had done the wrong thing and they split up and made for home. The Spitfires immediately pounced on the tail-end fighter of the line and then tackled the others in turn. They shot down several before the enemy reached cloud cover.

A month later, Olive, with five 'kills,' was awarded the DFC. He went on later to become first CO of 456, the Australian night fighter squadron.

There was sometimes a lighter side to the grim story of the Battle of Britain. Olive was leading a flight over south-eastern England when his oxygen apparatus 'blew up,' wrecking the cockpit. He parachuted down into a potato field, badly winded. Before he could get up, half a dozen land girls came running up with pitchforks, a spade and a hoe. He called out and seeing that he was not a German they dropped their weapons and asked whether they could get a car or an ambulance. Suddenly they dived for their forks and spades again, yelling: 'Hold off! Hold off!' and Olive looked around to see them running at a Home Guard who was stalking him, 200 yards away, with a rifle at his shoulder. Saved again, Olive breathed a sigh of relief and, when the ambulance came thought he was really safe. But within half a mile it took a bend too fast and turned over. He scrambled out with a few more bruises and was then picked up by a fire engine that was dashing to where his Spitfire was burning itself out. The fire engine, too, ended up a minute later in the ditch. After that, Olive decided to walk.

Wing Commander Desmond Sheen DFC*[196] an Australian member of the RAF who, in the early coastal patrols of the war had figured as one of Fighter Command's first casualties, fought throughout the Battle of Britain. He destroyed three enemy aircraft in the battle and had to bail out twice. The first occasion was on September 1, when a formation of 200 came in over Canterbury and headed for London. The Australian attacked a Me 109, his aircraft was riddled and he was forced to jump. He landed without injury. Three days later Sheen bailed out again after he had been wounded by shrapnel in the hand, leg and face. It was over Canterbury again. The attacking aircraft, an Me 109, shot away practically all Sheen's controls and damaged his oxygen supply. He was at 25,000 feet when his oxygen supply failed and when he came to he found his Spitfire diving to the ground at something like 400 miles an hour. The control column was useless. As soon as he undid his harness the suction lifted him out of the cockpit, but his feet caught under the windscreen. He had given up hope when his feet suddenly became free and he managed to pull the ripcord of his parachute. He was only about 800 feet up, but he fell into a wood near Canterbury and plunged through the boughs of a tree which slowed his descent and he landed safely.

Three Australian Battle of Britain DFC recipients, who between them brought down at least twenty-one of the enemy - seven apiece - were Flying Officer Howard Clive Mayers, a Sydney man who was commissioned in the RAFVR in

March, 1940; Flying Officer John R. Cock, a South Australia, who was commissioned in the RAF in 1938; and Pilot Officer John Curchin, a Melbourne lad who entered the RAF as a pupil pilot in June, 1939 and was granted a short service RAF commission in August that year. [197]

Behind each award lies a brief but vivid glimpse of the Battle of Britain. During one of Mayer's many engagements, a cannon shell passed through the port wing of his aircraft, making a hole four feet in diameter, but he succeeded in bringing his aircraft safely to base. In August, when in action against a large formation of the enemy, Cock attacked and destroyed a Ju 88 while being attacked from below. His aircraft caught fire and he was wounded, but he escaped by parachute, fell into the sea and swam ashore... [198] Of Curchin it is written that once he pursued an enemy aircraft thirty miles out to sea and finally destroyed it. In the Libyan Desert later, Mayers was to add a Bar to his DFC and to win the DSO as well, before he was killed in action. [199]

A collision with the wreckage of an enemy aircraft ended the career of another Battle of Britain Australian - Flight Lieutenant Paterson Clarence 'Pat' Hughes, who joined 234 Squadron when it was formed in November 1939. He had destroyed fifteen enemy aircraft at the time of his death on 7 September 1940. Eight of these he had destroyed in eight days of August 1940. During his last engagement, in which the squadron took off to intercept a large formation of enemy aircraft between London and Brighton, Hughes shot down a Dornier 17, flew into the wreckage and was himself brought down.[200]

Defeated in their attempts to bomb Britain out of the war by day, the Germans, after October, 1940 - the official end of the Battle of Britain - turned to night raids and the British night fighters came into their own. There was at that time no Australian night fighter squadron, but several Australians were meeting the Luftwaffe in the night skies as members of RAF units. Desmond Sheen, the Australian who had destroyed three enemy aircraft in the Battle of Britain, became one of them that October. His squadron, 72, fought at night through the air blitzes on Canterbury, Norwich, Sunderland, Newcastle and Glasgow.

One of his first engagements was over Canterbury one brilliant moonlit night soon after his squadron had joined the night fighters. The conditions were ideal for night fighting in a Spitfire. When Sheen first saw his enemy, a raiding Junkers 88, the German was about 1,000 feet above him. Sheen decreased the margin between them until he was about 100 yards below and behind. Then he opened fire and watched his tracer bullets hose-piping into the Junkers and soon black smoke poured from the raider. With it was oil, which sprayed Sheen's windshield and forced him to break away. When he turned for his next attack he saw that one of the Ju's engines was beginning to burn, but to make sure of the kill he pumped more bullets into it; then, suddenly, had to dive to avoid ramming the crippled aircraft. When Sheen pulled out of the dive, he had lost sight of the Ju, but members of the Royal Observer Corps, the famous British organization of sky watchers, had been following the fight in the moonlight sky above them and they told later how the Ju's wing had burst into flames and the raider had gone down like a flaring torch into the sea, where a mighty explosion indicated its end.

In March 1941 Sheen took command of 72 Squadron and led it for eight months, mostly on fighter sweeps, from its base at Biggin Hill, Kent. He added a Bar to his 1939 DFC in October 1941. When he was posted from 72 Squadron in November 1941 he had flown 260 operational hours and had destroyed six enemy aircraft, probably destroyed two and damaged five.[201] Sheen, of course, was only one of many Australians in the RAF who did outstanding work in attacks on enemy communications, bases and supplies and in intruder and night fighting. His story is typical of the many Australian members of the RAF who were making the Commonwealth's name known as new RAAF squadrons began to form in Britain. Out of the stream of Empire Air Scheme trainees that came from Australia, four Australian fighter squadrons were formed, three in quick succession in 1941, the fourth in 1942. They were 452, formed at Kirton Lindsey, Lincolnshire, in April, 1941; 457, formed at Baginton, Warwickshire in June, 1941; 456, formed at Valley, Anglesey also in June, 1941 and 453, formerly in the Far East, re-formed at Drem, Scotland, in June 1942.

Squadron Leader R. G. Dutton DFC took temporary command of 452 Squadron on April 12 and on the same day there arrived at the station a keen-faced, dark, Irishman of twenty - already a Battle of Britain veteran - who was to play a big part in leading the new Australian squadron on to fighting fame. He was Flight Lieutenant (later Wing Commander) E. B. 'Paddy' Finucane, who became one of Britain's greatest air aces.[202] Finucane was given command of 'A' Flight and the Irishman swiftly became to the Australians as much an Australian as Squadron Leader Bungey, who took command on 10 June 1941, or the late Squadron Leader Keith 'Bluey' Truscott, who took command of the squadron in its latter days in Britain.[203]

With the veteran Bungey as his CO, Finucane - joined later by Truscott as leader of 'B' Flight - bent to the task of welding 452 Squadron into a fine striking force, the efficiency of which was to be reflected later in a score of sixty-two enemy aircraft shot down, seven 'probables' and seventeen 'damaged' in the nine months the squadron operated in Britain. In four of those months the squadron led or shared the leadership of British fighter squadrons in the destruction of enemy aircraft, establishing a reputation as one of the most brilliant combat units in the history of air warfare.

It was on July 11 that the squadron first met the Hun in combat, when fourteen of its aircraft took part in a sweep over France. Finucane destroyed the first Me 109 and the squadron suffered its first casualty when Sergeant A. C. Roberts was brought down. Roberts survived, escaped from France and rejoined his unit later.

Very few days passed without operations over enemy-occupied territory during the ensuing months. Among days that stand out boldly in the squadron's annals is 16 August 1941 when it shot down six Messerschmitt fighters in six minutes while returning from a sweep over northern France. The only damage to the Spitfires was one bullet hole. The squadron had been escorting Blenheim bombers to a target inland and was crossing the coast on the way back when eight grey Messerschmitts dived on their tails. Whipping round to meet the attack, the Australians quickly turned the tables. Two of the Huns were destroyed by Finucane, bringing his score to three for the day - he had been out with the squadron in the morning and had shot down an enemy fighter then. In addition to Finucane's two in this combat, Sergeant K. B. Chisholm (a subsequent MC and DFM recipient) [204] got two and Truscott and Sergeants Stuart and Tainton one apiece. The fight, which began many thousands of feet above the sea, ended at sea level and the squadron - with one bullet hole in one aircraft - went home just above the wave tops.

September was the second month in succession that the Australian squadron topped Fighter Command's score sheet. It destroyed eighteen German aircraft in the month, twelve of them in two days. Finucane's September score was five, Truscott's four, Chisholm's three.

In October, when the Australian squadron moved to Redhill, Surrey, its run of success was maintained. On the 13th seven Me 109Fs were destroyed and three damaged when the squadron escorted four Blenheims through heavy flak to an attack on an important shipping installation in enemy-occupied territory. Of the enemy aircraft bagged that day Finucane destroyed two and damaged another, Truscott shot down two and Pilot Officer Raymond Edward Thorold Smith, who was later to succeed Truscott as the squadron's CO, destroyed one and damaged another.[205] Sergeant Jack Emery destroyed one and damaged a second and Sergeant E. H. Shraeder filled out the 'bag' with another. This put the Australian squadron's tally over the half-century mark and once again 452 headed the month's United Kingdom tally with ten kills.

November's weather curtailed operations, but the squadron kept at the top of the list, running level with two other squadrons during that month. Truscott claimed three during the month, Bungey and Thorold Smith one each. The tally for the four months was: August, twenty-two; September, eighteen; October, ten and November, five.

Because of adverse weather, operations were almost at a standstill during that December. On 25 January 1942 a few days after the squadron had moved back to Kenley, Bungey was posted to Shoreham and Finucane to 602 Squadron. Truscott was appointed CO.

Bungey and Finucane had 'made' the Australian squadron by their drive and energy. Truscott carried on the work. He was twenty-four when he took command. In Australia, where he had been widely known to Australian football followers for his resolute forward play with the Melbourne club, they had called him 'Bluey' - with the Australian propensity for inversion in nicknames - because he had red hair. The name stuck to him in England and to the end.

Three weeks after he left 452 Squadron, Finucane was in the news again and with him, an Australian, Flying Officer R. L. Lewis, a fellow member of 602 Squadron. The two Spitfire pilots had attacked a ship near Dunkirk on 20 February 1942 when they were engaged in a head-on attack by two Focke-Wulf 190s. The squadron leader was wounded in the leg and thigh. By radio telephone he ordered the Australian home, but Lewis, knowing that Finucane had been wounded, took up a safeguarding post a little behind and below. The German pilots, realizing that one Spitfire had been hit, gave chase. At least six times during the journey back Lewis turned to beat off attacks and he had the satisfaction of seeing one of the enemy crashing into the sea.

Twice Finucane turned to rejoin the fight and by the time they reached the English coast he was feeling very weak from his wounds. Base had been told of the fight and an ambulance was waiting, but he made a perfect landing before he blacked out. It was established later that Finucane had damaged the other FW before he was wounded.

A spell of warm sunshine early in March, 1942, marked the opening of a series of bitter air combats between crack British and Allied squadrons and the Luftwaffe, both using the then latest thing in cannon firing aircraft. In these fierce skirmishes Australian pilots played a conspicuous role, destroying at least ten enemy aircraft and probably destroying many others. German losses to the RAF at this period included five Messerschmitts, four Focke-Wulfs and a Heinkel.

On 17 March Truscott and others were posted to Australia. Thorold Smith assumed command and on March 23 the squadron moved to the Isle of Man, where it carried out patrols and training until it was returned to the mainland preparatory to moving to Australia. Thorold Smith, the new CO, had fought well in Britain and he was to fight on with the squadron when it went to Australia in July 1942 with 457 Squadron, to bolster the Commonwealth's defence against the Japanese. But there are sequels to record... the death of Finucane; a Christmas message from Finucane's parents in England to 'Bluey' Truscott, the dead ace's friend in Australia; the death of Truscott himself and of Bungey; and the posting of Thorold Smith among the missing.

All four leaders were honoured by the King with the DFC, Truscott and Finucane adding Bars to theirs and Finucane the DSO, during the Australian squadron's nine months in England. Finucane was the first of 452's pioneer leaders to go. A million-to-one chance shot from a German machine gun on the beach near Points de Touquet, France on 17 July 1942, caused his death. He was twenty-two when he died, newly a Wing Commander, with thirty-two German aircraft to his credit. He was leading his wing during the heaviest mass attack to that date by fighter pilots on enemy targets in France when he died. As he flew low over a machine gun post the gunner got in a lucky shot in the Spitfire's radiator. The engine temperature began to climb dangerously and Finucane, having carried on to attack his ground target, turned for home. He was too low to bail out and his engine was turning too slowly for him to gain height. He opened his cockpit hood, took off his helmet and tried to make a crash-landing on the sea. The Spitfire sank like a stone, carrying Finucane with it. His comrades circled the sea for long afterwards, but all they saw was a slowly widening streak of oil on the waters of the Channel.

While Finucane was leading his wing out to attack, his station commander was listening-in on the radio telephone to the radio conversations between his Spitfire pilots. He heard Finucane give his last message: 'This is it, chaps.'

Six months later, from England, three days before Christmas, came the voice of Finucane's father on the radio to Australia... 'Especially do we remember and send our sincere wishes for a happy landing to Squadron Leader 'Bluey' Truscott, who, before he left this country, led the immortal band of fighter pilots who formed the first Australian Spitfire squadron...' And then, in Gaelic, 'God's blessing be with you.'

But there were to be few more happy landings for Truscott. Three months later, in March, 1943, in the same month that Thorold Smith went missing on air operations 'somewhere in Australia,' Truscott met his death while instructing

Australian pilots in the finer points of air fighting. It was a mock attack by Kittyhawks on Kittyhawks. In the deceptive visibility of that day, Truscott went too low while making a low-level pass, stalled and dived into the sea.

The death of Bungey occurred at Adelaide on 6 June 1943. When 452, the squadron he and Finucane and Truscott had helped to make famous, moved from the front line, its place was taken by 457 Squadron, the second RAAF Spitfire squadron to be formed in Britain.

Seldom in the history of air warfare has a squadron experienced a fiercer baptism of fire than this unit did in the third week of March 1942 when the great air offensive of that April was looming. The pilots escorted Bostons and Hurri-bombers in daylight raids on Le Havre, St. Omer, Dunkirk, Abbeville, Desvres, Rouen and Lille and other targets such as railway yards, docks, airfields and factories and made many fighter sweeps.

The day after the new Australian squadron moved in to take up 452's cudgels, the pilots had their first 'scramble,' and two days later, on 26 March, when escorting RAF bombers raiding Le Havre, they encountered enemy fighters in strength and the CO, Squadron Leader P. M. Brothers DFC, one of the squadron's few non-Australians, bagged its first Hun, a Messerschmitt 109E.

King George VI was listening-in in the operations room on the afternoon of 29 April 1942 when 457 Squadron became involved over Cap Griz Nez with what were officially recorded as 'hosts' of enemy aircraft. Twelve to fifteen FW 190s were engaged at between 17,000 and 23,000 feet. The squadron became broken up during the engagement and there were many individual combats. Squadron Leader Brothers attacked one FW 190 from astern and saw his fire strike fuselage and cockpit. The enemy aircraft turned on its back and dived, turning into a right-hand spin, apparently with a dead pilot at the controls. The King was waiting to shake hands when the Australian Spitfire pilots came back an hour later.

On 31 May 457 Squadron was withdrawn from the line for a rest period. In June 1942 the third Australian Spitfire squadron to be formed in Britain - 453, which originally operated in the Far East - was re-formed under the command of Squadron Leader F. V. Morello. The new squadron was moved into the front line at Hornchurch, Essex in September 1942, a few days after Dieppe, and had its first brush with the enemy when large numbers of German fighters and fighter bombers arrived to bomb Canterbury on 31 October. For a long time late that autumn afternoon the squadron fought alone. Three sections of the squadron were on convoy patrol when its first warning came; a yell from one of the pilots, reverberating through the radio telephones of the rest:

'There are hundreds of the --'s coming; for God's sake send somebody out!'

A fourth section took off at once and joined the fray. Most of the enemy had the advantage of height, but the Spitfires set on one formation. Nine enemy aircraft were destroyed by British fighters in that engagement and many more damaged in half an hour. Anti-aircraft guns shared in the destruction.

Next day the squadron was taken over, because of Squadron Leader Morello's ill-health, by Squadron Leader John Richard Ratten. He became CO of the wing on 11 May, the first Australian JATP pilot to lead a Britain-based fighter wing. In January 1943 he relinquished command [206] of the Australian squadron to Squadron Leader K. M. Barclay DFC, a former flight commander and Barclay handed over on 28 September 1943 to Squadron Leader Donald George Andrews RAAF. Andrews had had a vivid career as a member of 453 Squadron. Six weeks before he became CO he had perhaps the most vivid experience of all. It happened during a sweep off the coasts of Holland and Belgium on 15 August. When the enemy aircraft were sighted Andrews was at the rear of the formation. There were five in the first bunch of FW190s, which dived out of the sun at 16,000 feet and came on the Spitfires from dead astern. Andrews warned the rest of the formation and broke away.

Then he noticed more enemy aircraft coming out of the sun. Instead of attacking the squadron, they concentrated on his aircraft. He called for help, but evidently his comrades did not receive the message and from then on he was attacked by twelve of the enemy, which circled around him making attacks from various angles. Encircled, Andrews could make no headway and he lost height gradually to nil feet about two miles north-west of Walcheren, the ground defences joining in the firing as he descended. By this time his Spitfire had been hit in numerous places. Then the number of enemy aircraft decreased gradually until there were only two attacking.

Andrews made several miles' progress for home before the next attack occurred, ten miles west of Walcheren. Then he found an opportunity to reply and made a head-on attack on a FW 190, allowing it to fly through his fire. The second Focke Wulf attacked and Andrews broke away, noting as he did so an explosion in the first FW, followed by a tremendous splash in the sea as the aircraft crashed in. The remaining Focke-Wulf immediately made off at full speed and Andrews flew his badly damaged Spitfire ninety miles to a base in England.

Four days before Andrews became CO he was awarded the DFC. Six weeks later, he led a formation of his squadron's Spitfires which shot down five of eight Me 110s during a patrol off the coast of England on 8 October. Two each were destroyed by Flying Officer P. V. McDade and Pilot Officer C. R. Leith and the fifth by Flying Officer Russell Herbert Sydney Ewins. Soon afterward, engine trouble forced Ewins to bail out over the sea. On the water he inflated his dinghy and climbed in as eight Me 110s flew low over him. They disappeared; then, about an hour later, two Spitfires appeared and flew round about five miles to the south. Eight Me 110s pounced on them and Ewins watched the battle. He saw a Me 110 shot down by a Spitfire and watched a German bail out from it while the machine belly-landed on the water half a mile away. Soon after that Ewins was picked up by a destroyer and taken to England.[207]

While the RAAF fighter squadrons were at grips with the enemy, individual Australians were busy, too, as members of many RAF fighter squadrons. One was Squadron Leader Hugo Armstrong, who, at twenty-six, became the first Australian JATP trainee to command a RAF squadron in Britain. At the end of May 1942 Armstrong was awarded the DFC after destroying at least five enemy aircraft and damaging a further two. In July 1942 he was one of three pilots who simultaneously shot down three separate enemy aircraft.

One of the three kills - which one it was could not be decided - made the 900th success scored by England's most famous RAF fighter station, Biggin Hill.

He added a Bar to his DFC in January 1943 and was posted missing in the same year. He had destroyed a further four enemy aircraft, making his total at least nine and had probably destroyed others.

456 Squadron, the Australian night fighter squadron formed in June 1941, was a unit subjected to many changes of aircraft and location. From Defiants it was re-armed with Beaufighters; Mosquitoes were its next aircraft. These changes involved considerable and continuous training and this, together with the marked disinclination of the Germans to visit the sector in which the Australians' squadron was located, reduced operational activities considerably.

Intruder operations - that is, the dispatch of one, or a few, aircraft to penetrate into enemy occupied territory and attack a particular target, with their movements controlled throughout by their base - had become so successful that early in 1943 the authorities decided to extend these tactics. Accordingly, a type of operation called 'Ranger' patrols was instituted. 'Rangers' did not work under control and this often enabled them to make deep penetration into hostile territory. They operated by night or by day if weather conditions were suitable. Aircraft used were Mosquitoes or Beaufighters from night fighter or intruder squadrons, or Mustangs from Army co-operation squadrons attached to Fighter Command groups for operations. Several squadrons, of which the Australian 456 Squadron was one, were allocated to this task.

'Ranger' work involved special training. Its principal object was to harass the enemy, to attack bomber, training and communications aircraft, to disorganize flying training and to destroy transport. 456 Squadron had already had a taste of 'Intruder' work. When the ranger patrols were begun one of the most successful was that carried out on 6 May 1943 when Wing Commander Gordon 'Peter' Panitz, with Flight Lieutenant Richard Sutton Williams of Patonga Beach, New South Wales as his observer, damaged six goods trains in six minutes on the Paris-Brest railway. It was their first daylight 'op.' Gordon Panitz, known as 'Peter' to most of his family and friends, was born on 21 September 1915 in Boonah, Queensland. His family ran a bakery for several years in Boonah and later moved to Southport on the Gold Coast, where Peter attended school. He was widely engaged with sporting teams and musical groups, playing the drums in the Southport State School orchestra. Following in his father's footsteps, Peter was a master baker for six years. On 6 December 1940 he enlisted in the RAAF at the age of 25. Panitz carried out his training at Archerfield and Amberley as a part of the Empire Air Training Scheme. He was awarded his flying badge in May and left Australia in August that year to continue further training in Canada and Britain.

A single engine was on the line, leaving Combourg, when the Australian Mosquito came over that afternoon. The Mosquito made a dummy run, the engine came to a standstill and the fireman and the driver emerged and hurried into the woods. Twice again the Mosquito attacked, using cannon and machine gun fire and steam rose from the perforated engine boiler to a height of more than 100 feet. Panitz and Williams returned to Combourg and set course for the Montfort railway. After following the main railway, they sighted a goods train on a branch line at St. Meen and this they twice attacked with cannon and machine gun. Steam was rising from the engine when the Mosquito turned in the direction of the main railway. A goods train was found stationary outside Caulnes Station. Machine gun bullets struck the boiler and the Mosquito moved on. A moving goods train was found on the line about two miles southeast of Dolo and it, too, was left severely damaged. The fifth attack was made on a train about five miles east of Lamballe, where a few minutes later, in a railway yard, three goods trains were also seen. One was hit in the firebox; a thick column of steam and smoke arose and the train stopped. Panitz and Williams were awarded the DFC on 29 October 1943, when the citation to Panitz's award gave the pair's tally as thirteen trains, as well as enemy installations of various kinds. Soon afterwards the famous combination was split by the exigencies of war and they were posted to different duties. [208]

456 Squadron recorded its first Mosquito night fighter engagement with the enemy on the night of 7 May 1943 when the late Squadron Leader A. G. Oxlade, with Flying Officer D. M. Shanks as observer, got on to the track of a night raider over England, dived on it and drove it down until an explosion below indicated that the raider had flown right into the ground.

Spitfires, Whirlwinds, Hurri-bombers and other types of single-engined aircraft also played a big part in Ranger attacks on enemy communications and installations on the nearer parts of enemy occupied Europe and in these attacks Australians in various RAF squadrons were well 'in the picture.' Some of them found strange targets. Three windmills in Belgium were the target on the morning of 12 March 1942 for Pilot Officer R. A. Mitchell and Sergeant G. F. Inkster, two Australians serving on a RAF squadron. They had taken off from Hornchurch in two of 64 Squadron's Spitfires to attack the barges on the Bruges-Ghent Canal. They found no traffic on the canal, but they saw the whirling arms of three windmills and like Don Quixote, attacked. At one of them the low-flying Spitfire pilots saw a gun emplacement and out of the windmill tumbled a number of running men. A body lay across the gun, which was camouflaged grey and green to match the colour of the windmill. The fighters swept on and the Australians shot up a locomotive and a truck which were being shunted on the outskirts of Ostend. They saw the driver jump out and watched the train crash into a buffer.

Three miles out to sea on the homeward journey, black puffs of smoke gave the fighters warning of following anti-aircraft fire, but it was very wide and the two marauders flew on safely.

Not all those who fought in the air across the Channel got home safely. In the Battle of Britain and the years that followed, thousands of aircrew men were rescued from the sea after they had been brought down by mishap or by enemy fire. In this work, soon after the war began, the Air Sea Rescue organization played an important part. The Air Sea Rescue organization, with its "Jim Crow' spotters, Walrus amphibians and rescue launches, included many Australians. One of them, Flying Officer T. Hilton DFC, once carried out a rescue in a minefield, hurdling the mines in his Walrus to effect a take-off. The 'Jim Crows' had located the pilot of a Whirlwind which had been pounced on by enemy fighters on the afternoon of 31 October 1942 and had to bail out of his damaged fighter a few miles from the French coast.

Hilton took with him as his gunner, on his rescue mission, Flight Sergeant

'Dizzy' Seals, who was widely known in Australia before the war as a dirt track rider. They found the stranded airman in his dinghy in the midst of a minefield and alighted between the parallel strings of high explosive with only about six feet clearance between it and the nearest mine. After much manoeuvring among the mines, Seals went to the rear of the Walrus and threw the airman a rope. Hilton had to leave the controls to assist with the rope. They had just got the airman up to the aircraft when the Walrus began to drift on to a mine. Hilton hurriedly let the rope go and took the controls again. They got through the mines safely, dragging the airman and his dinghy after them until Hilton could help again. It took much hauling to get the man, weak but unwounded, on board. His harness and parachute had to be cut away from him.

Hilton had just got up almost enough speed for the take-off when he saw a mine right in front of the Walrus. He pulled back on the stick and hoped for the best. The aircraft responded and leaped out of the water to about fifteen feet. But it had not quite reached flying speed and it came down again, bouncing six or seven times before finally Hilton got it off safely, to bring home yet another pilot to fight another day.

In the same month, Pilot Officer G. G. Galway of Ravenshoe, Queensland who was among the members of 453 Squadron helping to fend off the German bombers attacking Canterbury on the 31st, was shot down over the Channel, but managed to bail out and clamber into his aircraft's collapsible dinghy. One paddle went overboard while he was adjusting the apron of the dinghy, but although gripped with the cold, he used the other as much as possible and kept up vigorous toe exercises. But he could not warm his body and he suffered severely from seasickness. Some time after dark there was a heavy crash near him and a light which may have been shown by an enemy pilot who had been shot down in the darkness.

About 5 am, guided by another light, he reached a buoy, secured his dinghy to it and turned his attention to the important matter of getting warm. Finding that merely jumping up and down was of little use he began to Charleston and got some warmth back. On top of the buoy was a red light which flashed intermittently and Galway tried unsuccessfully to attract attention by obscuring it at intervals. Through the remaining hours a fog horn roared from somewhere close at hand. An Air Sea Rescue launch picked him up at first light and he was given dry clothes and taken to an RAF station.

Flying Officer F. E. Wilson (later DFC) was among the RAAF men who in 1943 took part in one of the greatest air sea rescue operations of the war, when he helped save ten British and American airmen in the North Sea. The first incident occurred on July 27 when an RCAF squadron leader who had had to bail out over the Somme estuary was rescued near Cayaux. Guided by the squadron leader's No.2, an Air Sea Rescue Walrus amphibian, in which Wilson was front gunner, came down on the sea in the haze of the last light of the evening and found the Canadian paddling his rubber dinghy. His only worry, it seemed, was that the sea was carrying him towards enemy shore, He kept saying: 'Can't believe it; it's too good to be true,' all the way back.

Next day Wilson helped rescue five Americans whose Fortress had been hit by flak while crossing the French coast and had been forced to ditch near the

English coast. It was the quickest rescue by his flight up to that time. The rescue aircraft were airborne before the Fortress had ditched - Spitfires had reported it the moment the Fortress was seen to be coming down. A third rescue that day occurred when Wilson was flying with Squadron Leader A. Grace of Adelaide. Helped by two Spitfires circling the spot, Grace located two dinghies containing four commandos. The Walrus returned safely with four very hungry men.

Launches were frequently attacked by enemy aircraft while on their way to a rescue. An attack of this kind occurred in the English Channel in July 1942, when several launches went out to rescue Sergeant Arthur Clayton, an Australian pilot who had to bail out from his Spitfire after an encounter with two FW 190s. After three hours in the Spitfire's dinghy, he was spotted by pilots of his own squadron and they guided the rescue launches to the spot. But the enemy was watching and one launch drove off fourteen separate attacks by enemy aircraft before it went down riddled with holes. Another damaged a FW 190 which was last seen making for the French coast losing height with smoke pouring from its tail. The battle continued for four hours, but the rescue of the Australian and other pilots shot down that day went on.

The Commando raid on Dieppe, in the early hours of 19 August 1942 was a 'blueprint' for the invasions of 1943-44. Australia was well represented in the operation. The raid had been highly planned and every aspect of it had been intensively practised. There were secret landings on the coast of England and navigation at night was perfected. The timing of the air support was carried out to the half-minute. The enemy was taken unprepared and only a few fighters appeared at first to meet the Allied air fleet. Allied aircraft were flying at great strength over a substantial part of enemy territory for five of the early hours of 19 August, before, at 10 am, the first enemy bombers appeared. Flight Lieutenant D. G. Andrews (then of 175 Squadron), who was later to lead the Australian Spitfires of 453 Squadron, was one of the first and last Hurri-bomber pilots on the scene that day. Andrews led a flight when his squadron made an attack on the shore batteries in the early morning and was over the battle area again at 11 am, when the withdrawal began. The Hurri-bombers went in the first time just as the troops were drawing in to the shore, as the anti-aircraft fire was rising to its greatest intensity. Andrews dived on to the gun position and dropped two 500lb bombs directly on the target. Meanwhile the Commandos had landed on the western sector of the town. The Hurri-bombers returned to refuel and reload, then went back to attack a strong gun post east of the town which was firing on the naval forces. Final order to the pilots was: 'You must get those guns.' The Hurri-bombers went in at zero feet with guns blazing and bombed the post out of existence. Then they turned sharply and fired on some enemy troops and transport. Sergeant Richard Vernon Beckwith Dulhunty RAAF attacked a transport travelling along a road behind Dieppe, saw it blow up in flames and blew five cows out of a cowshed he had mistaken for a military hut.

One of the many other Australian fighter pilots engaged was Pilot Officer B. E. Gale, a later DFC recipient. Gale made two sorties that day. His squadron arrived first over Dieppe at 4.40 am, about the time the first wave of 'Hurri-bombers began its attack on the coast batteries. It was quite dark, but Dieppe was well awake. It looked like a fireworks display as they went in with flak and tracer criss-crossing over the sky as the enemy searchlights tried to pick them up. As the squadron withdrew, the first invasion barges were about five miles off the coast, with the German shore guns firing on them. They took off on the second sortie at 1 pm. Just over the French coast, at 5,000 feet, Gale spotted a FW 190 at 2,000 feet, jumped on it as it crossed the French coast and put in three long bursts at gradually closing range. When Gale last saw it, the FW was going east of Dieppe at 300 feet belching smoke.

Almost at once Gale spotted a Dornier 217 bombing the ships. It had just dived on a destroyer and scored a hit. Gale chased the Dornier and got in a burst, but his ammunition ran out and the enemy got away into cloud. Dorniers were going in in waves over the ships every five minutes, but as soon as they began to bomb they were jumped on by the Spitfires and in most cases had to jettison their bombs and make for cloud cover.

Near the end of the operation, two low-flying Focke-Wulf fighters swooped down under the air cover over the control ship and dropped bombs and sprayed it with cannon fire. On board the control ship, Air Vice-Marshal A. T. Cole CBE DSO MC DFC RAAF was among those wounded.

The names of many other Australians appear in the records of the varied tasks carried out that day by the many types of aircraft engaged, such as the Blenheims that laid the smoke screens which were an important feature of the operation and the Spitfires that covered the Hurricanes engaged in ground strafing. Enemy aircraft shot down were conservatively totalled at ninety-one. Another estimate was 176.

The first invasion of Europe was two years distant then. In those intervening years, intense behind-the-scenes effort went into the implementation of the grand strategy.

When the landing in Normandy began, the Australian Spitfires of 453 Squadron flew forty-seven sorties to provide low cover for the troops; on the night of June 6 1944 the Australian Mosquito night fighters of 456 Squadron destroyed four enemy aircraft and the Australian Mosquito fighter bombers of 464 Squadron made twenty-seven sorties to attack road and rail junctions and bomb enemy troop concentrations in advance of the land forces. The enemy made repeated efforts to attack the Allied invasion shipping from the air and 456, led by Wing Commander Keith Macdermott Hampshire DSO DFC was among the defenders in the air. Hampshire was born on 10 September 1914 at Port Macquarie, New South Wales, second son of Percy George Hampshire, dairy inspector and his wife Gladys May, both born in New South Wales. After the family moved to Perth, Keith attended Scotch College, where he obtained his junior certificate. He called himself a grazier when he joined the RAAF as a cadet on 18 January 1937 and entered No.1 Flying Training School, Point Cook, Victoria. Six feet tall and strongly built, he had represented Western Australia in surfing.[209] In England in December 1943 he took command of 456 Squadron RAAF on night fighters. 456 Squadron had had a remarkable run of 'kills' against the Luftwaffe earlier in the year and it went on to add more after 'D-Day'. After the four enemy aircraft destroyed on the night of 'D-Day', it went on to shoot down three more next night and then singles on the nights of 9, 10, 12, 13 and 14 June and four again on the night of July 5, bringing its tally to thirty-seven enemy aircraft destroyed since formation on June 30 1941. It was a run of successes which brought the squadron several awards, among them a Bar to the DSO for Hampshire, who had a personal score of seven enemy aircraft destroyed when the award was made and a DFC to his observer, Flight Lieutenant T. Condon. The squadron ended the war with a tally of forty-one enemy aircraft destroyed and many others damaged or probably destroyed. Hampshire led 456 until November 1944. Flying with Flight Lieutenant T. Condon as his radar operator, he claimed seven victories and a probable, receiving a Bar to his DSO in February 1945. He was also awarded a DFC.

The Australians of 453 Spitfire Squadron had begun in 1944 under the Air Defence of Great Britain command, later re-named Fighter Command, but were transferred before D-Day to 2nd TAF, under the command of Squadron Leader D. H. Smith DFC, an Australian veteran of the Battle of Malta and recipient of the Soviet Medal for Valour.[210] The unit's first assignment with 2nd TAF was escorting US Marauders, Fortresses, Liberators and Mitchells over many parts of enemy occupied Europe and Germany, work which enabled the Australians to study daylight bombing technique before carrying out dive bombing and strafing. With the approach of D-Day, all types of targets were bombed and strafed - railway marshalling areas, headquarters buildings, road transport, railways, radar stations and West-Wall installations - targets of paramount importance in the invasion plan. Strong air opposition was expected on Invasion Day and when the squadron's aircraft were painted with the black and white Allied invasion stripes, pilots and ground crews alike shared in the excitement of anticipated battle. But when D-Day arrived and the Australians were ordered to patrol the beach head to protect the Allied landings, not one German aircraft was sighted from dawn to dusk.

For a time before operating from a permanent base in France, 453 Squadron flew from a temporary base in the invasion area. Their arrival on their first such visit attracted many peasants from a village nearby, who greeted them with hand-shakes and flowers. Some of the pilots were given German helmets and belts as souvenirs. The Australians spent the first night sharing slit trenches, blankets, stew and tea with the British Royal Engineers who were constructing the airstrip, while enemy shells whistled overhead. The airstrips were cut in cornfields and the dust rose in great suffocating clouds as aircraft took off or landed.

The Spitfire men's first post-invasion success came on 16 June. Patrolling the Caen area, they saw twelve Me 109s break through the clouds. A terrific dog fight took place at 2,000 feet in which the Australians destroyed two enemy aircraft and damaged others without loss.

The move to France was completed by 25 June. Thirty-five sorties were flown that day and forty-six the next.

German aircraft were still hard to find. It was accepted that the Luftwaffe would fight only when it had overwhelming numerical superiority and the advantage of height and cloud cover and it was almost ignored as 2nd TAF relentlessly pursued its work of smashing the enemy's road transport, starving him of supplies and ammunition, forcing him to use back roads and tracks and to travel during the dark hours. MET (mechanical enemy transport) became the priority target for 2nd TAF squadrons and the RAAF men quickly became adept at low-level strafing. Once, when a crucial battle was raging in the Caen sector, a section of Australian Spitfires spotted a convoy of nine tankers. With a whoop the Spit pilots dived to attack. They left seven tankers in flames and two damaged and went so low to press home their attack that when one man returned to base the wings of his aircraft were stained with smoke from the flaming wagons. Next evening the squadron received a message from 2nd Army Headquarters that the destruction of the oil wagons had been a big factor in the British tank victory that day.

The squadron's best bag of MET was the destruction of eighteen German trucks and the damaging of ten others before breakfast on July 29. It meant the complete annihilation of a convoy. The squadron had been on an armed convoy hunt at daybreak, half the aircraft carrying a 1,000lb bomb load for the first time. The Spitfire's bombs, cannon and machine guns destroyed or damaged every vehicle.

Rain and cloud after D-Day favoured the enemy. On such a day a formation of twelve Australian Spitfires on armed reconnaissance had been in the air about fifteen minutes when the squadron commander nonchalantly remarked on the radio telephone: 'Look up above boys and you will see something very interesting.' The other eleven pilots saw fifty FW 190s above them. Some of them had yellow noses and it is thought they were led by the crack German fighter ace, Walter Matoni.[211] The Australians manoeuvred quickly to receive the 'bounce' that was coming with as little disadvantage as possible. With the advantage of height and numbers, the Germans dived to attack. The Australian formation went up to meet them, weaving from side to side and firing frequent bursts. The manoeuvre surprised the enemy and forced them to split formation and lose their positional advantage. This threw them into such confusion that they immediately called off the fight and raced for home, with the Australians hard on their tails. The pursuers destroyed four of them, probably destroyed another and damaged five.

In the first month of operations from the squadron's Continental airstrip, rain fell on twenty-one days and only one day was passed by the weather men as suitable for flying. Despite the weather, the Australians flew 750 sorties that month, accounting for fifteen enemy aircraft destroyed and many others probably destroyed or damaged and more than 100 mechanical enemy transport destroyed or damaged.

After the break through in Normandy, the Australian Spitfires moved swiftly northward to successive airfields. When they reached their last airfield, near Antwerp they began operating within a few minutes of arrival, then spent a disturbed night under German shell fire. There were no casualties from the shell fire and when rocket Typhoons operating from the same airfield sought out the guns it soon ceased.

The Spitfire men found that the people of Belgium had not forgotten the Australian soldiers of the last war. On leave in the cities, they were quickly recognized and the exclamation, 'Australien' was heard continually as they passed through the crowds that were still celebrating liberation. Three Australian ground staff men, Flight Sergeant A. B. Aitkenhead, Sergeant Seth Parker and

LAC M. D. Hood, were entertained by a Belgian man and his wife at the Hotel Metropole, Brussels and were shown a picture of the graves of two RAF men which had been tended faithfully by the Belgians throughout the war years. The Belgian had fought with the Allies in the last war. Passing through a Belgian village, other men of the squadron saw an Australian flag in a window. The owner of the house was Mr. Maurice Pyke, Australian wool buyer. His two daughters had begun to make the flag during the German occupation in anticipation of the day of liberation.

Typhoon units and many other fighter bomber squadrons of the Allied Air Forces on the Continent had followed the bomb line forward from Normandy to Holland and in their ranks were many Australians. 464, the Australian Mosquito fighter bomber unit, completed its chief pre-invasion task of smashing up French airfields and went on to attack enemy-held bridges, road and rail junctions and transport. This non-stop blitz on transport meant stiff work for the ground crews. In the first fortnight after D-Day the ground staff of a Mosquito fighter bomber wing of 2nd TAF had 97.5 per cent of the available aircraft ready for operations every night. It meant long hours for these men, who included Australians, New Zealanders and Canadians, but whenever it was humanly possible no aircraft was held back from supporting the invasion because it required repairs. The wing, which included Australian and New Zealand squadrons and pilots, was able to break records in the number of sorties flown, weight of bombs dropped and number of cannon shells fired because their aircraft were always ready for the next night's operations. The officer-in-charge of the repair and inspection section was Flight Lieutenant A. C. Dibbs RAAF.

464 had begun its career in Britain in Bomber Command, using Ventura light bombers and became operational in December 1942 when it took part in the famous daylight raid by 100 light bombers on the Philips radio valve factory at Eindhoven, Holland. Wing Commander Robert Wilson Iredale DFC became its CO at the close of 1943. The squadron converted to Mosquito fighter bombers late in 1943. In July 1944 Peter Panitz DFC, the train buster whose highly regarded leadership skills saw him promoted to wing commander, was also awarded a DFC at Buckingham Palace later that month for his 'skill on numerous operational sorties on enemy' and his consistent display of 'fine leadership, skill and devotion to duty'. Wing Commander Panitz took over 464 from Iredale and led his men for the first time on 3 July 1944 when, in brilliant moonlight, they bombed and strafed trains and motor transport deep in France. Next night, supporting American troops in their attacks along the Cherbourg Peninsula, he reopened his list of wrecked enemy locomotives by shooting up his eighteenth on a railway south of Paris. He left the train at a standstill, its engine enveloped in steam and went on to attack a road convoy and bomb the mouth of a tunnel.

With Flight Lieutenant Williams DFC his friend and customary observer, Panitz did not return from an attack on rail communications in central France on 22 August. When the war ended and it was possible to intensify official investigations into the fate of missing personnel, their graves were found in a cemetery in France.[212]

On 31 October 1944 the squadron sent eight aircraft with the force which carried out the famous daylight low-level attack on Gestapo Headquarters at Aarhus, in Denmark. Two months later it moved to a base at Rosieres, near Amiens, an area rich in associations with the First Australian Imperial Forces in the First World War and not far from the Australian last war memorial at Villers-Bretonneux. The squadron was to end the war with twenty-four tanks and twenty-eight trains destroyed, 328 trains attacked and having inflicted general damage beyond estimation. It had fired 368,270 cannon shells and 267,291 machine gun bullets and dropped 1,547 tons of bombs during its two and a half years' operations.

The third invasion of Europe came on 15 August 1944 when the south of France was entered by the Allies. On the day before the landings the Australian Spitfire fighter-bomber squadron, 451, operating from Corsica, helped provide air cover for the big convoys on their way to the French coast and on invasion day itself Australians from this squadron and in many RAF squadrons were in the air from dawn till dusk, first helping protect the initial landings, then patrolling over the beaches ready to deal with any opposition the enemy might put into the air. The Wellingtons of 458 Squadron carried out Leigh Light anti-submarine patrols.

451 Squadron carried out five operations on the first day. The first section for duty was called in inky blackness at 4 am. By the light of the flarepath, pilots took off at 5.40, their job to patrol a lane off the French coast used by the hundreds of big transport planes and their gliders which dropped thousands of paratroops miles inland from the beaches. The Australians saw the transport planes - many with Australians in their crews - dropping their paratroops and they watched the bombers streaming in, in an endless procession, interspersed sometimes with fighter bombers, while the Navy put up a terrific bombardment.

The first flying bombs buzzed like aerial motorcycles over southern England on the night of June 13 1944, seven days after the Normandy beachhead was established. But before the official announcement of their arrival was made a few days later, people in London and the southern counties had already seen the glow of their exhausts moving through the night skies, heard the ominous sudden stopping of their engines, the fearful ensuing pause and the thunderous blast that marked the end of their downward glide.

Some watchers on the ground in those June days caught glimpses of V-1 as it sped on its way, but none saw the new weapon in more stark detail than the airmen of Britain and the Dominions who joined with the men and women of Balloon and AA Commands and other services in the 'Battle of the Robots'. Of these, none, perhaps, had a closer view of V-1 than the Flying Officer Ken Collier, an Australian Spitfire pilot on 91 Squadron RAF on 23 June.

The first flying bomb fell at Bethnal Green, London, on 13 June; Collier and his colleagues of 91 Squadron first heard of the robot bombs one dawn soon afterward. They were scheduled that morning for patrol and were having an early breakfast when one of the night fighter men, just back from a night sortie, rushed into the mess and said: 'The rocket jobs are coming over!' He went on: 'We're not allowed to touch them yet, because they're not sure what'll happen when we hit them. All we can see is a big flame.'

Gradually Collier and his colleagues found out things about the jet (not rocket-) propelled bombs. They found that it was not safe to fire from closer than 300 yards; if the bomb exploded in the air there was a great risk of being caught by the terrific blast. They found, too, that it was of no use to take off when they heard one coming. The bombs were too fast and by the time the fighters were airborne they were gone. 'Standing Patrols' were instituted and a technique worked out for dealing with the bombs. Britain had set up four lines of defence. Fighters attacked the bombs first over the Channel; bombs which got past the fighters came to a belt of AA fire along the coast; after this there were more fighters; and then there were the balloons and their cables. Collier's squadron could see the bombs coming through the flak on the coast and were often in the right position to destroy one when suddenly ground fire would blow it up before they had their chance.

On the evening of June 23, after an uneventful spell of duty on flying bomb patrol, Collier was about to land when he saw a 'doodlebug' coming over the coast. He chased it and one of several bursts he fired at it must have hit it, for it slowed and Collier caught up with it fairly easily. By this time, to his chagrin, he had used all his ammunition. He came alongside it, flying parallel, only a few feet from its stubby sixteen feet wing and cigar-shaped body. The 'stove pipe' on top of it was white hot and the flame shooting out through its rear vent was bright and eerie in the dusk. Collier was close enough to see the German letters on the side. There were no other markings - no swastikas or black crosses. The top of the bomb was a bronze colour, the underside pale blue - both probably camouflage tints. Collier could hear no noise from it above the sound of his own aircraft.

The two small elevators on its tailplane kept moving under the impulsion of the flying bomb's inner robot gyro pilot. It seemed to move with a shuddering effect, probably, Collier thought, caused by the crude explosions in the propulsion unit. It gave the Australian a feeling of powerlessness to watch the bomb travel towards London, its nose filled with a ton of high explosive and to sit there in his Spitfire unable to do anything to stop it. He could not see where his bullets had hit it. He looked the bomb over carefully as he kept pace with it and considered how he could attack. Then he thought of trying to upset the gyro mechanism and divert the bomb from its course. He 'took a jab' at one of the bomb's elevators with his wing, but got uncomfortably close to the flame and hastily moved out a little. He decided he could do little that way and tried instead to manoeuvre his wing under that of the bomb. Suddenly he saw that the bomb's wing had gone red and moved out again quickly. Then he realized that it was the reflection of his own red navigation light. He manoeuvred into position again and this time got the bomb's wing resting on his. He tipped his wing up gradually until the wing of the bomb slipped off his own and the 'doodle bug' went downward and underneath him. That startled Collier and he hauled back his stick and moved upward sharply. Then seeing that the explosion he feared had not happened and the bomb was flying on again, he decided that he had not tipped the bomb far enough to upset the gyro and he tried again. Again flying side by side with the bomb as miles of English countryside slipped away beneath this grim drama, he got his wing under its wing, but this time a little farther under, to get better leverage. Again he tilted it slowly, - then gave it a final 'push,' and moved hastily away to see what happened. To his delight it rolled over on its back and spiralled down. The flame went out before it reached the ground and Collier saw it explode with a brilliant flash in a field near a town, rings of blast waves spreading out around it and leaving a pall of black smoke that looked, to the watching Australian, 'like one of the old Moreton Bay fig trees in the Sydney Domain.' It takes time to tell, but the macabre battle in the air between man and robot all happened in the space of minutes.

Collier later received letters of thanks from residents of the town from which he had diverted the bomb. One came from the local branch of the National Union of Railwaymen; it promised that railwaymen would do all they could to hasten the end of the war so the Australian could return to his 'folk across the seas.'

'It is the unanimous wish of my members that I convey our most heartfelt thanks to you for all you did recently when an enemy 'jitter bug' was brought down in our neighbourhood,' wrote the secretary. 'We should like you to know that we are aware that it was the courage and initiative of yourself that resulted in so many lives and so much property being saved from total destruction.'

Collier did not come back from a sortie on 5 December 1944 in which his squadron provided withdrawal support for bombers attacking Hamm. Just before the rendezvous with the bombers, two large formations of enemy fighters were seen below to starboard of the Spitfires and 91 Squadron made a head-on attack, each pilot making an individual attack from the sun. Collier was last seen entering the mêlée.

Nine flying bombs were shot down by Flight Lieutenant Keith Alexander Roediger, a Mosquito pilot on 456 Squadron, whose observer was Flight Lieutenant R. J. H. Dobson. They were top scorers for the RAAF. 456 opened its flying bomb account on the night of 24 June, when Flight Lieutenant G. R. Houston, with Flying Officer L. Engberg as his navigator, got some strikes on one and claimed it as a 'probable.' The squadron destroyed twenty-four flying bombs in the succeeding fifty days and many others were destroyed by Australian airmen serving in RAF squadrons - eight each, for instance, being destroyed by Flight Sergeants Donald John Mackerras and H. J. Bailey, who flew with 3 Squadron, the RAF's top scoring anti-flying bomb Tempest squadron.

The flying bomb - the 'buzz bomb' or 'doodlebug'- was in Hitler's plans not only a tactical weapon, but a weapon which was to sway the course of the entire war. In Whitehall they knew a good deal about it long before the man in the street began to talk about it.

Although it was almost a year before the world knew of it, the attack by 597 Lancasters, Halifaxes and Stirlings on the V-weapon research station tucked away in a forest behind the beach of the Baltic Sea at Peenemunde, sixty miles north-west of Stettin, on the night of 17 August 1943 was a decisive factor in preventing the Germans developing fully their terrible robot plans. Forty-one aircraft failed to return from the attack, including two of the thirty-four Australian Lancasters which took part in the 1,400 miles' round trip, but the attackers' bombs killed thousands of Germany's leading scientists and technical men, wrecked forty important buildings and detonated their stores of explosives and set the Nazi V-weapon programme back a very long way.

The dam busting Lancaster squadron, 617 and Mosquito, Mitchell and Boston medium bombers of 2nd TAF made the ominous installations along the French western coast their especial target from late 1943 onwards. Australian Lancasters, Halifaxes and Mosquito bombers joined in the attack early in 1944. The RAAF heavies bombed forty-two installations and sites between January and March, the Mosquitoes twenty-four.

In the end, it was the land operations which stopped the V-1 menace. The khaki tide rolled up the map of Europe and when the northernmost V-1 sites in Holland were captured, the Germans began launching flying bombs from pick-a-back aircraft against England and Allied concentrations on the Continent. But the end of V-I was at hand and the last of them fell on 29 March 1945 at Sittingbourne, in Kent.

Then a new menace appeared - the rocket bomb, V-2. It became the turn of the Australian Spitfires to help in the attack on Germany's latest secret weapon.

In the wooded park in the city of The Hague, administrative centre of Holland, one day in December 1944, men in field grey worked busily about a cleared space. Three hundred yards away stood an ancient building, built in 1645 as a palace for the Consort of the Prince of Orange. The Dutch knew it as the Huis den Bosch - the 'House in the Wood' - and they treasured it as part of the glorious history of their past. In 1899 the first International Peace Conference was held there but the 'House in the Wood' had seen many changes in international consciences since then.

Suddenly, on that December day - the 6th - the enemy air raid sirens sounded and the roar of approaching fighters came nearer. The AA guns surrounding the area came into action and in another minute RAF and Australian Spitfire bombers - the latter led by Flight Lieutenant W. R. Bennett, of Queensland - were screaming down through the flak in a power-dive precision attack on the site.

Every bomb fell in the target area without apparent damage - save perhaps some broken windows - to the historic building so perilously close. The smoke and dust from the bombs and wreckage of the site had scarcely settled before more Spitfires appeared, this time from a South African squadron and more bombs crashed into the V-weapon buildings.

Chosen in the hope that fear of causing civilian damage and casualties would prevent a British attack, the 'House in the Wood' was typical of the sites the Germans used in Holland to launch and store the rockets and the liquid oxygen with which they were filled. Sites like these presented the Empire air forces with the problem of helping save England from the new menace without taking Dutch lives or destroying valuable or historic Dutch property.

The advent of V-2 was an open secret in southern England soon after the first of them fell at Epping, in Essex, on 8 September 1945. Unlike the slower flying bombs, whose coming could be heralded by the sirens and could be heard in passage, the first knowledge that a V-2 had arrived came with the sudden streak of vivid flame, the almost instantaneous explosion and the ensuing minutes of rumbling thunder as the sound waves 'caught up' with the rocket's arrival.

Against V-2 the balloon barrage, the AA batteries and the fighters were useless on the British side of the Channel. Defence lay in finding the heavily defended, elusive and extremely mobile, cunningly and easily camouflaged launching platforms in Holland and strangling the launching centres by cutting the roads and railways along which V-2s were transported to Holland from Germany.

To seek and destroy Germany's V-2 sites, therefore, was the task set the fighters and it was the Australian Spitfire squadron, 453, under the command of Squadron Leader E. Esau DFC, which made the first reconnaissance flights and the first attacks. Late in the anti-V-2 campaign 451 Squadron RAAF joined these operations after four years' duty in the Western Desert, Palestine, Syria, Cyprus, Egypt, Corsica and the south of France. Equipped with the latest Spitfire fighter bombers, these units were given the task of locating the well-hidden targets pin-pointed by Air Ministry Intelligence, making precision power-dive bomb attacks on them and strafing the surrounding areas. Strafing was especially important, because the V-2 crews who were stationed in the target areas had received special training and the killing of such specialists would be a serious loss to the enemy's V-2 programme.

The success of the operation hung upon the effectiveness of the Spitfire when used in a power dive and it was held that even greater accuracy could be obtained on 'pin-point' targets than with high-level precision bombing. And accuracy was of prime importance, with launching platforms often sited only a few yards from a hospital, an historic palace or a museum. The pilots practised at a bombing range near their station, where, as far as possible, the actual conditions under which the attacks would be made were duplicated.

The first attacks from the anti-V-2 wing were carried out by 453 Squadron on 21 November. The Spitfires met intense flak over the target area (a rocket storage dump at The Hague), but the pilots went in, power diving from 8,000 feet. Esau's bombs fell 'dead on' the target, a happy beginning for the squadron. The other aircraft followed their leader in and after they had bombed, sprayed the target area with cannon fire. They scored hits on something which may have been a V-2 standing near the edge of the clearing, but it did not explode, perhaps because - if it was a V-2 - it was not filled with its charge.

The CO of 451 Squadron (Squadron Leader C. W. Robertson DFC RAAF) saw a V-2 launched while he was on patrol over The Hague. The Spitfires had just finished bombing and were reforming when he glimpsed a flash on the ground and saw the rocket rise at what seemed no more than three or four miles an hour. It was wobbling as though about to fall over; then it gained speed and shot up. It passed 500 feet out from the Spitfire formation and the blast of gases from its tail rocked Robertson's aircraft. Its vapour trail disappeared from sight at 50,000 feet, still going up.

At first the Spitfires operated only from England, carrying long-range tanks to enable them to cross 140 miles of water and return and two 250lb bombs. Then bases became available on the Continent and the pilots could take off with one 500lb and two 250lb bombs, cross from England to The Hague, bomb and strafe V-2 sites; and land in Belgium. There they would refuel and re-arm, take on another 1,000lb of bombs and repeat the attack on their way back to England. The large number of sorties put a big strain on the ground staff, who frequently had to work through the night to get the aircraft ready for dawn next day.

The two Australian squadrons made 1,328 sorties over Holland, bombing and strafing launching sites, storage buildings, workshops and transport, cutting railways leading to the firing sites and dropping 2,309 bombs - 500 and 250 pounders - on V-2 targets.

Many other Australians flew with 2nd TAF, whose bombing of V-2 supply lines running through Apeldoorn to The Hague was so effective that the Germans were forced to keep a permanent base of the Todt organization near Apeldoorn. Every time the Germans ordered workers to repair the lines they hid and only a few could be conscripted. In desperation the Germans resorted to press gang methods for obtaining civilian labour. When they knew most people were in their homes, the SS blocked roads, threw a cordon round the area, forced their way into houses and carried off workers. But the Dutchmen deliberately slowed repair work and finally men from the Todt labour corps had to be brought in from building fortifications on the Western Front to clear the lines. Cuts on railways often produced delays of forty-eight hours and never less than twenty-four hours.

Australian pilots on quick dashes to London on leave knew first hand of the city's ordeal. Two of them - Pilot Officer R. Lyall and Warrant Officer N. A. Stewart - were blasted out of their beds when a V-2 landed 150 yards from their hotel. To spur their comrades on they went to a post office and sent this cryptic telegram to the wing: 'Pull your hooks out, chaps. They nearly whoofed us last night.'

The last rocket bomb fell at Orpington, Kent, on 27 March 1945.

While civilians awaited Mr. Churchill's VE-Day speech on 8 May, some Australian aircraft were still in the bright morning skies around the British Isles, but for the most part RAAF squadrons marked the day with a general forty-eight hours' stand down. Members of 464, the only Australian squadron in Belgium, were playing cricket when news was brought of the general German capitulation. The game continued as though nothing unusual had happened (the 'erks' beating the aircrew by ten wickets), but there was a party that night. The squadron's last operation - an anti-transport sweep in the German pocket round Hamburg - had occurred on the night of 2 May, two days before the German armies opposing Montgomery's 21st Army Group surrendered. Next night bad weather prevented operations. Crews were being briefed for a night intruder mission when the end of organized resistance in north-west Germany was announced and the mission was called off.

In London, the Church of St. Dunstan-in-the-West, in Fleet Street, was filled by Service and civilian members of the staff of RAAF. Overseas Headquarters on 10 May, when a service of thanksgiving for the end of the war in Europe was held. At the same time Mass was celebrated in the Church of St. Anselm and St. Cecilia, Kingsway.

Endnotes Chapter 18

192 Charles Gordon Chaloner Olive was born in Bardon, Queensland on 3 July 1916, joining the RAAF in 1935 as a regular officer. He transferred to the RAF in February 1937 and was posted to 65 Squadron. By 1940 he had become a flight commander, seeing action over Dunkirk and during the Battle of Britain. He was awarded a DFC in September. In June 1941 he formed and commanded 456 Squadron RAAF as a night fighter unit, but in March 1942 he returned to Australia, becoming Wing Commander at Air Defence, Sydney, in 1944 and then at HQ, Morotai, in 1945. His total score was 5 destroyed, 3 unconfirmed destroyed, 3 probables, 1 and 1 shared damaged. He died in Australia in 1987.

193 Leslie Redford Clisby was born in McLaren Vale, South Australia, on 26 June 1914. He lived in Walkerville, Adelaide, until joining the RAAF as a cadet at the age of 21. Despite having to bail out of a Gypsy Moth trainer on one occasion, he passed out from Point Cook on 29June 1937, obtaining a Permanent Commission. The following month he departed with other graduates for the UK to take up a short service commission in the RAF, Australia having no modern air force at this time. After a period as instruction at I FTS, Leuchars, he was posted to I Squadron. In September 1939 the squadron moved to France. Here he was engaged in several actions over the frontier in April 1940, during which he claimed two victories. With the commencement of the 'Blitzkrieg', he was constantly in action from the 10th to 15th May. On the latter date five of the unit's Hurricanes pursued a formation of Bf 110s, seven of which were claimed to have been shot down, two of them by Clisby, for the loss of three of their own number. Clisby was one of the two pilots killed. In the period of six days it was estimated that he had destroyed of the order of 15 or 16 aircraft.

194 Flying Officer W. M. Blom DFC was killed when his Fairey Battle I (L5528) exploded at RAF Newton on 27 July 1940. Also killed in the explosion were his two crew and four ground crew personnel.

195 Richard Lindsay 'Dick' Glyde was born in Perth, Western Australia on 29 January 1914. He joined the RAF on a short service commission in June 1937. He saw service on 87 Squadron in France in May 1940 and then during the Battle of Britain. He was awarded a DFC early in June; the citation recording that he had claimed four victories in France, details of one of which are not available. On 13 August 1940 he was shot down by return fire whilst attacking a He 111 with other members of his unit and his Hurricane crashed into the sea south of Selsey Bill; he did not survive. His score stood at 2 and 3 shared destroyed, plus I probable, I damaged.

196 Desmond Frederick Burt Sheen was born in Sydney on 2 October 1917. Living in Canberra, he joined the RAAF in January 1936 before transferring to the RAF in February 1937 and he joined 72 Squadron in June that same year. He was involved in one of the early engagements of the war in October 1939 when a formation of He 115 floatplanes were intercepted off the north-east coast of England. He joined 212 Squadron in April 1940 for service in France as a photo-reconnaissance pilot. He was awarded a DFC on 7 May 1940. After the fall of France, he rejoined 72 Squadron. On 1 September he was shot down and again on the 5th, bailing out both times. He returned to the unit as a flight commander on recovery and in April 1941 was given command of the unit, which he led until October, when he received a Bar to his DFC. In November 1942 he took command of RAF Manston until April 1943. His total score was 4 and 1 shared destroyed, 2 probables and 2 damaged.

197 Although born in Hawthorne, Victoria, in Australia on 20 January 1918, John Curchin's family were resident in Grange Park, London, when he joined the RAF on a short service commission in June 1939. Initially he was posted to 600 Squadron on completing his training at 5 OTU but on 11 June 1940 he was moved to 609 Squadron, seeing action that summer, and spring of 1941. He was awarded a DFC on 18 October 1940 and promoted flight commander in April 1941. On 4 June 1941 the squadron was despatched to search for Flight Lieutenant George Gribble of 54 Squadron, missing on an earlier operation. They were attacked by Bf' 109s of JG53 and Curchin FTR, probably shot down by Oberfeldwebel Stefan Litjens. Curchin's score stood at 8 and 4 shared destroyed, 1 shared u/c damaged, 1 probable, 1 damaged.

198 John Reynolds Cock, a native of Grange, South Australia, was born on 3 March 1918. He travelled to England early in 1938 to take a short service commission in the RAF. Posted to 87 Squadron in December, he went with his unit to France in 1939 as part of the Air Component. He

claimed his first victory on 10 April 1940 whilst based at Le Touquet, departing for England on 20 May after ten days in action. He was shot down by fighters over Portland Bill on 11 August, bailing out with slight injuries and being fired on as he fell. On 24 October he collided with Pilot Officer D. T. Jay's aircraft and both Hurricanes went down, Jay crashing to his death, but Cock force-landing safely. Next day the award of a DFC was announced. By now he had claimed over ten victories. He became an instructor before joining the new 453 Squadron RAAF as a flight commander and after a short spell with the US 81st Fighter Group and 222 Squadron in Scotland, at the end of November 1943 he departed for Australia. In 1944 he returned to the UK and flew Tempests. His score stood at 10 and 1 shared destroyed, 1 u/c destroyed, 4 probables, 5 damaged.

199 Mayers was born in Sydney, New South Wales, on 9 January 1910. He was resident in London before the war, having attended Cambridge University, where he joined the University Air Squadron. He became Managing Director of a company, but was called up into the RAF on the outbreak of war and after training, joined 601 Squadron on 3 August 1940. Ten days later he was shot down by fighters, bailing out of his Hurricane into the sea with slight wounds. He was rescued by an MTB. By late September had claimed seven victories, being awarded a DFC on 1 October. Once again on 7th he was shot down, this time by Bf 110s and force-landed near Portland, suffering slight injuries. He left the squadron in May 1941 and was posted out to the Middle East, where in July he was given command of 94 Squadron in Egypt. On 25 December, whilst strafing an enemy column, he saw one of his pilots shot down, and at once landed alongside. With Axis vehicles heading towards them, he got the pilot into the cockpit, sat on his knees and took off again, flying back to base. He was awarded a Bar to his DFC for this on 13 February 1942. Promoted to lead a Hurricane Wing in January 1942, he moved to 239 Wing in April where he gained several more victories. On 20 July he had just been seen to shoot down an MC202, when he was shot down himself, force-landing in the Qattara Depression. Searching Spitfire pilots later spotted his Kittyhawk with the cockpit open but he was never seen again. It is believed that he had been captured, but was lost when a ship carrying prisoners to Sicily was sunk in the Mediterranean by British fighters. His DSO was subsequently gazetted on 28 July 1942. His score stood at 11 and 1 shared destroyed, 3 and 1 shared probables, 6 damaged.

200 Hughes was born in Cooma, NSW, Australia, on 19 September 1917. He lived in Haberfield in the same state. He joined the RAAF in 1935 as a cadet, receiving his commission and completing his training. He then travelled to England early in 1937 and was posted to 64 Squadron but in October 1939 was sent as a flight commander to the new 234 Squadron. The award of a DFC for his first seven victories was gazetted late in October, after he had been killed. On 7 September 1940 he had shot down a Do 17 but had either flown into the wreckage, which caused him to crash to his death, or he was shot down by Bf 109s on this date. His score stood at 14 and 3 shared destroyed, 1 shared destroyed u/c, 1 probable.

201 Group Captain Desmond Sheen died aged 83 on 3 July 2001.

202 Brendan Eamonn Fergus 'Paddy' Finucane was born in Dublin on 16 October 1920. Educated at O'Connell's Irish Christian Brothers School in Dublin, he was a devout Roman Catholic, who reportedly took himself very seriously. After working briefly as a ledger clerk, he joined the RAF in May 1938 and after training was posted to 65 Squadron. During the summer of 1940 and spring of 1941 he claimed five and one shared victories, receiving a DFC on 13 May 1941. Meanwhile in mid-April he had been posted as a flight commander to 452 Squadron, which was just forming as the first RAAF fighter unit in the UK. He claimed this unit's first victory on 11 June, adding 17 and two shared by mid-October, receiving two Bars to his DFC during September and a DSO the following month. He then broke an ankle whilst jumping over a low wall in the blackout, and was off operations until January 1942, when he was posted to command 602 Squadron. On 20 February his aircraft was hit by an FW 190 and he was wounded in the leg, but again recovery was rapid, and he was back in action on 13 March. In another period of rapid claiming, he had added five and three shared to his total by the end of May. On 27 June he was appointed Wing Leader of the Hornchurch Wing. On 15 July, whilst leading a formation exiting France at the end of a sweep, machine gun fire from a gun position on the coast hit the radiator of his Spitfire. His wingman, Alan Aikman of 154 Squadron, dived down to strafe this, but as Finucane headed out over the Channel, his engine seized due to coolant loss and the aircraft was seen to sink instantly on hitting the water, taking him down to his death. His total score stood at 26 and 6 shared destroyed, 8 and 1 shared probable, 8 damaged.

203 Keith William 'Bluey' Truscott was born in Prahan, Victoria, on 17 May 1916. After working as a clerk in South Yarra and playing Australian Rules football at senior level, he joined the RAAF in July 1940, undertaking most of his training in Canada. He reached the UK in March 1941, attending 57 OTU before being posted to 452 Squadron RAAF, as a Pilot Officer. During the cross-Channel sweeps of late summer and autumn 1941 he was credited with 11 destroyed and 3 probables. He was shot down into the Channel and rescued on 15 October. He was awarded a DFC. Meanwhile he had been promoted flight commander in October, whilst late in January 1942 he was given command of 452, receiving a Bar to his DFC. On 17 March 1942 he left for Australia where he converted to the Kittyhawk. On the night of 20/21 January 1943 he intercepted three bombers over Darwin and shot one down. On 28 March he took off to escort in a returning Catalina flying boat but flew into the sea and was killed instantly. His total score stood at 14 destroyed, 3 probables, 3 damaged.

204 Keith Brace Chisholm was born in Hobart, Sydney on 22 December 1918. A dental student at Petersham, NSW before the war, he joined the RAAF and sent to the UK and to 452 Squadron, the first RAAF unit in Europe. During late summer 1941 he made seven claims for aircraft shot down, receiving the first RAAF DFM in the UK. On 12 October he was shot down and bailed out into the sea and became a PoW in Stalag VIIIB in Czechoslovakia. In April 1942 he made several escape attempts, ultimately reaching Poland and remaining free in various parts of Occupied Europe until 1944. By then he had joined the French Forces of the Interior in Paris, where he was liberated in August 1944. He was awarded an MC and a Polish Gold Cross with Swords before returning to Australia. He was commissioned during his absence and was subsequently promoted to flight lieutenant. His score stood at 5 and 2 shared destroyed, 1 damaged.

205 Raymond Edward 'Throttle' Thorold-Smith was born in Manly, New South Wales on 30 June 1920, becoming a medical student prior to joining the RAAF. Posted to the UK on completion of his training, he joined the new 452 Squadron RAAF as a Pilot Officer in mid-1941. He was promoted flight commander late in October and in March 1942 became the CO, having received a DFC late the previous year. During the summer of 1942 he led the squadron home to Australia to form part of I Spitfire Wing at Darwin, but on the second occasion on which Japanese aircraft were intercepted, on 15 March 1943, he was lost in action. His score stood at 6 and I shared destroyed, 1 damaged.

206 Ratten, who was born in Sheffield, Tasmania on 13 November 1912, was working as a mining engineer before the w\ar. In January 1943 he attended the Fighter Leader's Course and at the end of May was promoted to lead the Hornchurch Wing, also receiving a DFC. His tour finished at the end of July. Later in 1943 he led the Peterhead Wing in north Scotland. He was reported to have died on active service on 27 February 1945. His score stood at 2 and 2 shared destroyed, 2 and 1 shared probable, 2 damaged. *Aces High* by Christopher Shores and Clive Williams (Grub Street, London 1994).

207 'Russ' Ewins was KIA on 15 August 1943.

208 464 Squadron RAAF CO Squadron Leader Gordon 'Peter' Panitz DFC of Queensland and Flying Officer Richard Williams of NSW were one of eighteen crews on 21, 464 and 487 Squadron RNZAF Squadrons who successfully attacked Bonneuil Matours, a collection of six buildings inside a rectangle just 170 x 100 feet, close to the village which had to be avoided, on 14 July, Bastille Day 1944.

209 Hampshire was a resident of Peppermint Grove, Western Australia. He was a regular officer in the RAAF prior to the outbreak of the war in the Far East, commanding 12 Squadron RAAF on Ansons and Wirraways when the Japanese attack commenced and at once he was given command of 6 Squadron RAAF on Hudsons, based at Port Moresby, New Guinea. During 1942 he was posted to 23 Squadron RAAF, also at Moresby, and also on Hudsons, but later in December when Boston light bombers became available, he was given command of 22 Squadron RAAF, the first Australian unit to be equipped with these aircraft, undertaking bombing and strafing sorties over New Guinea until July 1943, for which he was awarded a DSO during May. *Aces High* by Christopher Shores and Clive Williams (Grub Street, London 1994). He never married. On or about 17 November 1982 he died from injuries sustained when he fell from a beach cliff at Palos Verdes, California. The coroner recorded that his death was accidental.

210 Born in Encounter Bay, South Australia on 18 August 1915, Donald Hamilton 'Don' Smith worked as a farmer before joining the RAAF after the outbreak of war. On completion of training

he was posted to the UK. On 3 June 1942, now a Flying Officer, he flew a Spitfire off HMS Eagle as part of a force of 31 replacement aircraft for Malta. He was posted to 126 Squadron. During July he claimed three and one shared victories. On the 14th, after sending a Ju 88 into the sea, he was attacked by escorting Bf 109s and his aircraft was severely damaged, one bullet hitting his ankle and severing an artery. He managed to land without brakes or flaps and was rushed to hospital. On recovery he was evacuated to the UK, where in 1943, he served on 41 Squadron, becoming a flight commander. In April 1944 he took command of 453 Squadron RAAF, which he led during the Normandy Invasion. Awarded a DFC in September 1944, he left the squadron to return to Australia. His score stood at 5 and 1 shared destroyed, 2 probables, 2 damaged. *Aces High* by Christopher Shores and Clive Williams (Grub Street, London 1994).

211 Matoni was born on 27 June 1917 in Duisburg. Feldwebel Matoni was assigned to 9./JG27 in the summer of 1940 and his first claim, a Hawker Hurricane followed on 30 September. During mid 1941 Matoni operated over Russia and claimed three victories (Two DB-3s and an R-10). On 17 August 1941 Feldwebel Matoni was posted to 5./JG26 on the Channel front. He was soon transferred to 7./JG 2 in September. He was badly wounded in aerial combat resulting in a lengthy convalescence, following which he served as an instructor with Jagdgruppe West from October 1942 to February 1943, when Leutnant Matoni returned to II./JG 26. He shot down a Spitfire on 17 June as his fifth victory. On 31 August Oberleutnant Matoni's Focke Wulf 190A-5 was hit and he was wounded by return fire from B-17 bombers, force-landing at Montdidier. In December he claimed a Spitfire near Boulogne on 21 December as his 8th victory. In an action against USAAF B-26 twin-engine bombers on 14 January 1944 he shot down a Spitfire escorting the bombers, probably flown by Austrian-born Squadron Leader Franz Colloredo-Mansfeld DFC (3 destroyed) of 132 Squadron, who was killed. On 24 February Matoni shot down a USAAF B-24 bomber near Frankfurt for his 13th and JG26's 2,000th victory. Matoni was appointed Staffelkapitän 5./JG 26 in February 1944 and on 10 May was awarded the German Cross in Gold for 20 victories. On 15 August 1944, Hauptmann Matoni was appointed Gruppenkommandeur of I./JG11 before being appointed Gruppenkommandeur of I./JG 2 on 24 September. On 5 December Matoni was so seriously injured in a crash he was unfit to undertake any further combat flying. Despite this, he was appointed Gruppenkommandeur of II./JG2 in January 1945 until 28 February. Matoni was awarded the Knight's Cross of the Iron Cross on 2 January 1945.Walter Matoni was credited with 34 victories in over 400 missions. He recorded three victories over the Eastern Front, and of 31 victories claimed over the Western Front, 14 were '4-mots'. He ended the war at the Fighter Pilot's rest-home at Bad Wiessee. Matoni died on 26 June 1988 in Frankfurt.

212 Wing Commander Panitz and Flying Officer Williams were killed attacking railway communications near Dijon. Their Mosquito was flying extremely low when it struck the side of a hill. The aircraft was completely destroyed. Panitz and Williams were buried together in the Bona Communal Cemetery in Nièvre, France. Panitz was just 28 years old.

Chapter 19

The Battle Of Malta

'Laddie' Lucas

'There are twelve-plus 'big jobs' at angels twelve flying south from Sicily obviously heading for the ships. It looks as if the attack is timed to go in at last light. There are no little jobs about. I know it's late and will almost certainly mean night landings, but we'd like you to send out a section of four aircraft, with four experienced chaps, to see if the attack can be intercepted and broken up. The convoy has been taking a pounding all day and we'd like to try to give this support. The leader should start out on a heading of two-seven-zero degrees - due west - climbing fast to 14,000 feet. I'll contact him when he's airborne. He should be able to see the big jobs against the western sky.'

'OK, sir,' I said. 'I'll be going with my Tiger Red section. Jones, Linton and Watts will be with me. They're all clued up, sir and quite able to handle this sort of thing. We'll get off at once.'[213]

'Good show, Laddie,' said Woody,[214] *'I'll call you when you're airborne and give you other vectors.'*

Jones, my trusted No. 2 and Linton, at No. 3 were old hands by now. Les Watts was newer, flying at No. 4, but as sound a bit of brass as ever came out of Birmingham. He had come to us quite recently from the fire of 11 Group and the sweeps over northern France. I had been much impressed with his competence and dry and uncontrived humour. Wattie was a reliable trooper.[215]

It was one of Woody's virtuoso performances. Variations in vectors were given in that deep, measured and always confident voice. 'You should see them quite soon now against the western light. They're a little below you.'

Search as we might, we could not see them. If we were above them, I thought, we're trying to pick them out against the darkening sea down below. I dropped a couple of thousand feet which, anyway, gave us a bit of extra speed. Almost at once, I saw them, standing out plainly against the western sky.

'OK, fellers, I see them. Eighty-eights at two o'clock, flying south. Same level. About a dozen of them.'

The Ju 88s were flying straight and level in quite tight boxes of some four aircraft each. They hadn't seen us coming out of the darkening eastern sky. I gave the instructions. We would dive another 1,000 feet and, with all the speed we wanted, pull up from underneath and attack from the quarter into astern position. Lint and

Wattie would take the starboard box and Jonesie and I the one to port. Then both pairs would have a go at the centre formation if we could. This would give the best chance of breaking up the attack. After that, it would be each man for himself.

Our assault came off to a T. The rear gunners never saw us as we attacked upwards from underneath, against the dark waters below. It wasn't until we had closed to 150-200 yards' range and the flashes from the four cannons in our Spitfire VCs and the strikes from them began to drive home that the German crews realized what was happening. Then there was mayhem, with the 88s breaking all over the place, not knowing how many Spitfires were attacking them. There might have been a couple of squadrons of us for all they knew.

It was a splendid steal from which we extracted about as much as we could reasonably expect in the fading light.

It was difficult to see the results, but Wattie and I reckoned we had shared an 88 between us.[216] *Jonesie got another - a flamer - while Lint and I felt we had severely damaged an additional 88 apiece. But more important than the score was the fact that the attack had been thrown into disarray. The Luftwaffe really had little idea what had hit them.*

Woody came on the blower. 'Tiger aircraft, put your backs to the light and fly zero-nine-zero degrees for base.

Put the light behind you and steer due east for fifteen minutes. We'll see you home.'

'OK, Woody,' I said, 'message understood.'

***Malta; The Thorn In Rommel's Side - Six Months That Turned the War* by Laddie Lucas (Stanley Paul & Co, 1992) Percy Belgrave 'Laddie' Lucas was born in the old clubhouse at Prince's Sandwich Bay, Kent on 2 September 1915. His father Percy Montagu Lucas co-founder of Prince's Golf Club, Sandwich died when he was aged 11. Lucas was educated at Stowe School and Pembroke College, Cambridge where he read Economics. He also captained the University Golf Team. He was the top amateur golfer in the 1935 Open Championship and at 19 found himself hailed as 'the finest left-handed player in the world'. He was a member of the English International and Walker Cup Team in 1936. On graduation he joined Beaverbrook Newspapers to work on the *Sunday Express* in 1937, becoming involved in sports writing. In June 1940 he joined the RAF and was sent to Canada to train. On return to the UK he attended 52 OTU and then was posted to 66 Squadron in August 1941, being promoted flight commander after four months. In February 1942 he was posted out to Malta with a group of reinforcements, arriving in a Sunderland flying boat. Posted initially to 185 Squadron and then to 249 Squadron, he made a few flights in Hurricanes before the first Spitfires arrived in March. Twice during May he was flown to Gibraltar to lead flights of reinforcement Spitfires from the decks of aircraft carriers, once on 8 May and again ten days later. At the end of June he was promoted to command the squadron and shortly afterwards was awarded a DFC for three victories and seven damaged.**

The great battle for Malta, one of three decisive island battles of World War Two - the Battles of Britain and Midway being the other two - ran for two and a half years from 10 June 1940 until 31 December 1942. Yet few have recognised the strategic importance of Malta in the Allies' grand design for North Africa, the Mediterranean and southern Europe. It is difficult for anyone who was not there during those historic days to appreciate how a small piece of rock, 17 miles long by nine miles wide, isolated in the dead centre of the Mediterranean could mean so much to the Allied cause and to the Axis powers.

One person who recognised the importance of Malta was Churchill; he despatched two signals in quick succession to General Auchinleck, C-in-C land forces Middle East, on 8 and 10 May 1942. The signals left not the slightest doubt about Malta's significance. The opening sentences of the first message set the tone:

'The Chiefs of Staff, the Defence Committee and the War Cabinet have ... earnestly considered the whole war situation, having particular regard to Malta, the loss of which would be a disaster of the first magnitude to the British Empire and probably fatal in the long run to the defence of the Nile Valley. We are agreed that in spite of the risks you would be right to attack the enemy and fight a major battle (in its support).'

On 10 May Churchill referred to the same issue:

'The Chiefs of Staff, the Defence Committee and the War Cabinet have again considered the whole position. We are determined that Malta shall not be allowed to fall without a battle being fought by your whole army for its retention. The starving out of the fortress ... (and) its possession would give the enemy a ... sure bridge to Africa with all the consequences flowing from that. Its loss would sever the air link upon which you and India must depend ... It would compromise any offensive against Italy and (other) future plans. Compared with the certainty of these disasters ... the risks ... to the safety of Egypt are infinitely less and we accept them.'

Malta was vital on two counts; as a staging post for aircraft flying from Britain to the Middle and Far East and as a strike base from which the Island's submarines and offensive aircraft could hammer the Axis powers' seaborne convoys plying their way southwards across the Mediterranean to Libya.

The success of these attacks, signally aided by information provided by Ultra's unravelling of the enemy's coded cyphers, became a constant thorn in Rommel's side. With his lines stretched to the limit, Rommel and his Afrika Korps were fatally weakened as they faced Montgomery's Eighth Army on the Egyptian frontier.

I well remember, over dinner at the RAF Club, discussing the part which Malta had played in all these desert operations during the summer and autumn of 1942 with my good friend, Eduard Neumann, the popular and able commander of Jagdgeschwader 27, the Luftwaffe's group supporting Rommel's forces in the drive across Cyrenaica to Egypt. 'How much,' I asked, 'did Malta really matter to the Axis campaign in North Africa?'

'Malta,' Eduard said decisively, 'was the key.'

Against the advice of his High Command and that of Mussolini and the Italian General Staff, Hitler turned his back on Operation 'Hercules', the invasion of Malta, in the spring and early summer of 1942 when he might well have succeeded. Albert Kesselring, German C-in-C South and the Luftwaffe's commander in Sicily, made this quite clear after the war in his *'The War in the Mediterranean Part 1.'* 'To guarantee supplies (to the Afrika Korps in Libya) the capture of Malta was necessary. The abandonment of this plan was the first blow to the whole undertaking in North Africa. The one fatal blunder was the abandoning of this plan. When this happened the subsequent course of events was almost inevitable.'

The fact was, however, that to hold Malta we had first to win the battle for control of the air over the Island. Unless we won the fighter battle our strike and bombing aircraft could not be maintained safely at Luqa nor could we cover the convoys running the gauntlet from Gibraltar or Alexandria. The Island was close to starvation and critically short of essential stocks so the need for seaborne supplies was now imperative.

The future depended on the ability of the fighter defence, first to contain and then master the larger Luftwaffe force based in Sicily, especially the new Messerschmitt 109F and later the Me 109G. Our Hurricane IIs were now obsolete and all hope therefore rested upon the supply of Spitfire Vs.

With the enemy controlling much of the north and south coastlines, a passage by sea for these aircraft was out of the question; they would have to be flown in from aircraft carriers standing off some 650 to 700 miles to the west of Malta. These hazardous operations, which began hesitantly in March 1942 and gathered momentum through the following months, saved Malta. They represented a paragon of Royal Navy, US Navy and RAF cooperation in which the losses of Spitfires were less that 5%, a remarkable achievement in the face of the manifest risks that were there.

Early operations involved the Royal Navy's carrier *Eagle* which initially only allowed 16 or 17 Spitfires to be ferried at any one time - insufficient to influence materially the fighter battle against the numerically superior enemy. In a personal deal between Churchill and Roosevelt, the United States turned the tide by providing the large carrier, *Wasp,* which could carry 48 Spitfires in addition to her own aircraft.[217]

On 20 April 47 Spitfires of 601 (County of London) and 603 (City of Edinburgh) Squadrons, which had been loaded aboard *Wasp* at Greenock, were successfully delivered to Malta. Then disaster fell. With the Germans monitoring the reinforcements down the Mediterranean and with Luftwaffe bases only sixty miles away in Sicily, they struck as soon as the arrivals were on the ground and being refuelled. After a series of attacks over the following two days against the airfields of Takali and Luqa, only seven of the 47 aircraft were still serviceable. Undaunted *Wasp* tried again after a reorganisation of the Island's operational arrangements. Five Malta trained and experienced pilots were sent back to Gibraltar to lead in the next reinforcements with their 90-gallon drop tanks, across the intervening 650 miles of sea. None of us who had been entrusted with this task underestimated the responsibility.

This time, *Wasp,* after returning to Scotland to load up more Spitfires, sailed south to join forces in the Straits of Gibraltar with HMS *Eagle*. Together they sailed with a heavy escort to the familiar fly-off point, reached on 9 May. *Eagle* launched her aircraft and returned immediately to Gibraltar to take on another 16 Spitfires. By 17 May all was ready and after sailing eastwards through the night her precious cargo flew off to Malta the next morning to join the 64 aircraft which had made the journey nine days previously. Thus, in this brief spell the Island's fighter strength was increased by nearly eighty aircraft, an unprecedented uplift in Malta's defensive might. With these reinforcements being turned around on arrival, by Army, Navy and Air Force personnel working together, in less than 15 minutes and with each aircraft being taken over by an Old Malta hand, this new-found defence was ready and waiting for the Luftwaffe when its staffeln struck again with their usual speed and aggression across the Sicilian channel. Attack after attack was punched squarely on the nose as the defending squadrons tore into the invaders. Great air battles were fought out over the island to the cheers of the gallant inhabitants as they bore witness to the spectacular transformation which was unfolding before their eyes. For Kesselring and his spirited German and Italian cohorts, it was 'never glad confident morning again'.

The air battle had now been irrevocably turned. Long hot weeks of fighting, with increasing privations facing all on the Island, still lay ahead, but to the battle-hardened pilots in the squadrons, the island took on an utterly different feel. Gone was the evidence of the enemy's growing strength; gone too was the nightly threat of airborne invasion. In place was the knowledge that the balance of power had shifted in favour of the defence which was now on top of the job. Moreover, for the ground crews who, amid all the bombing, had kept the aircraft flying with a courage and purpose which set them apart, it seemed that a corner had been turned and the worst was now past. It was their total dedication in the arid temperatures of over 90 degrees Fahrenheit that had kept the aircraft flying, thus bringing glory to their trade. One question is often asked. How was it that in those darkest days, when the air defence was often outnumbered by 15 and 20 to 1 we were able to hold the line? The response must be all embracing.

The defending sections of aircraft, of which a pair flying fast in line abreast, 200 yards apart, was basic to everything, were brilliantly controlled by Group Captain Alfred Basil 'Woody' Woodhall whose genius marked him out as the Service's outstanding operations controller of the war. This, and a radar system incomparably superior to anything possessed by the enemy, gave us the edge and made it possible for a handful of Hurricanes and Spitfires to be pitted against raids of 50, 80 and 100 plus with a better than evens chance of survival if not of outright success.

Furthermore, command counted. In Air Vice Marshal Hugh Lloyd, AOC, Malta and Air Marshal Sir Arthur Tedder, C-in-C, Cairo, we had a pair of commanders who displayed a rugged 'John Bull' approach on one hand and an exceptional intellectual agility on the other. It was a combination which proved invincible. Later, Air Vice Marshal Keith Park arrived in mid July to make his immaculate and highly publicised contribution to success by changing, at a stroke, the ethos of the squadrons' work from defence to offence. True he now had an accumulated force of some 130 Spitfires but even so, it was no mean feat. However, Park did not win the Battle of Malta as some have claimed. In a command sense, the credit for that belonged to

Lloyd and Woodhall in Malta and Tedder in Cairo. The real victory had been won before Park arrived; but it was he who sealed the achievement. Many have their place in the Malta story; the indomitable ground crews working in all conditions; the army gunners who stood to their posts in the heaviest bombardments; the fighter pilots who slipped in to land under cover of the guns, refuelled, rearmed and took off again while under attack by the Me 109s; the strike and bomber crews and their brave Fleet Air Arm counterparts in their slow Swordfish and Albacore aircraft each of whose dangerous task was to stop the convoys getting through to Rommel; the important photo reconnaissance Spitfires flown by Harry Colbeck, Les Colquhoun and Jo Dalley; the exceptional officers and men of the Royal Navy's Fighting Tenth Submarine Flotilla; the crew of the mine-laying cruiser, Welshman, which disguised as a French destroyer, brought vital supplies by night from Gibraltar; and the Merchant Navy who, with their Naval escorts, braved the enemy's fury as they fought a passage through to Malta.

Finally, the near 300,000 strong Maltese population have to be singled out. They remained steadfast throughout the siege in the face of sustained attacks lasting two and a half years. Truly did they deserve King George VI's unique award of the George Cross and its embracing accolade: 'For Gallantry'. Malta GC survived Hitler's might with incredible fortitude. That we won battle was paramount, for the story of the North African campaign would have been quite different had we lost. There never was a combined operation like it in World War Two.[218]

In December 1941 the Luftwaffe made 169 air raids on Malta and in early 1942 Malta was blitzed daily by the Luftwaffe. In January 1942, the Luftwaffe made 263 raids on Malta and in February 1,000 tons of bombs were dropped. By April a peak of 283 bombing raids was reached and a total of 6,700 tons of bombs were dropped on the island. Many towns and cities were reduced to rubble. In April 1942 alone, more than 11,000 buildings were destroyed or damaged. Because of their proximity to the Naval Dockyards, the Three Cities were particularly badly hit. In Valletta too, many historic buildings were hit. The Royal Opera House, the Law Courts and some of the old Auberges were totally destroyed. On 15 April the morale of the Maltese people received a welcome boost. The following message arrived from King George VI: *'To honour her brave people I award the George Cross to the Island Fortress of Malta to bear witness to a heroism and devotion that will long be famous in history.'*

In June 1943 King George VI visited Malta and he received a tumultuous welcome. In September the Italian Fleet assembled in Maltese harbours and Marshall Badoglio signed Italy's final surrender document in Malta. In November Winston Churchill visited Malta and saw for himself the devastation inflicted by the enemy. Three weeks later, Franklin D. Roosevelt arrived. The second siege of Malta, like the first, four centuries earlier, won the admiration of the world. Out of both sieges, Malta emerged in a state of utter devastation but totally unscathed in spirit and honour. From the last siege, Malta also emerged with the firm resolve to become at last the mistress of her own destiny.

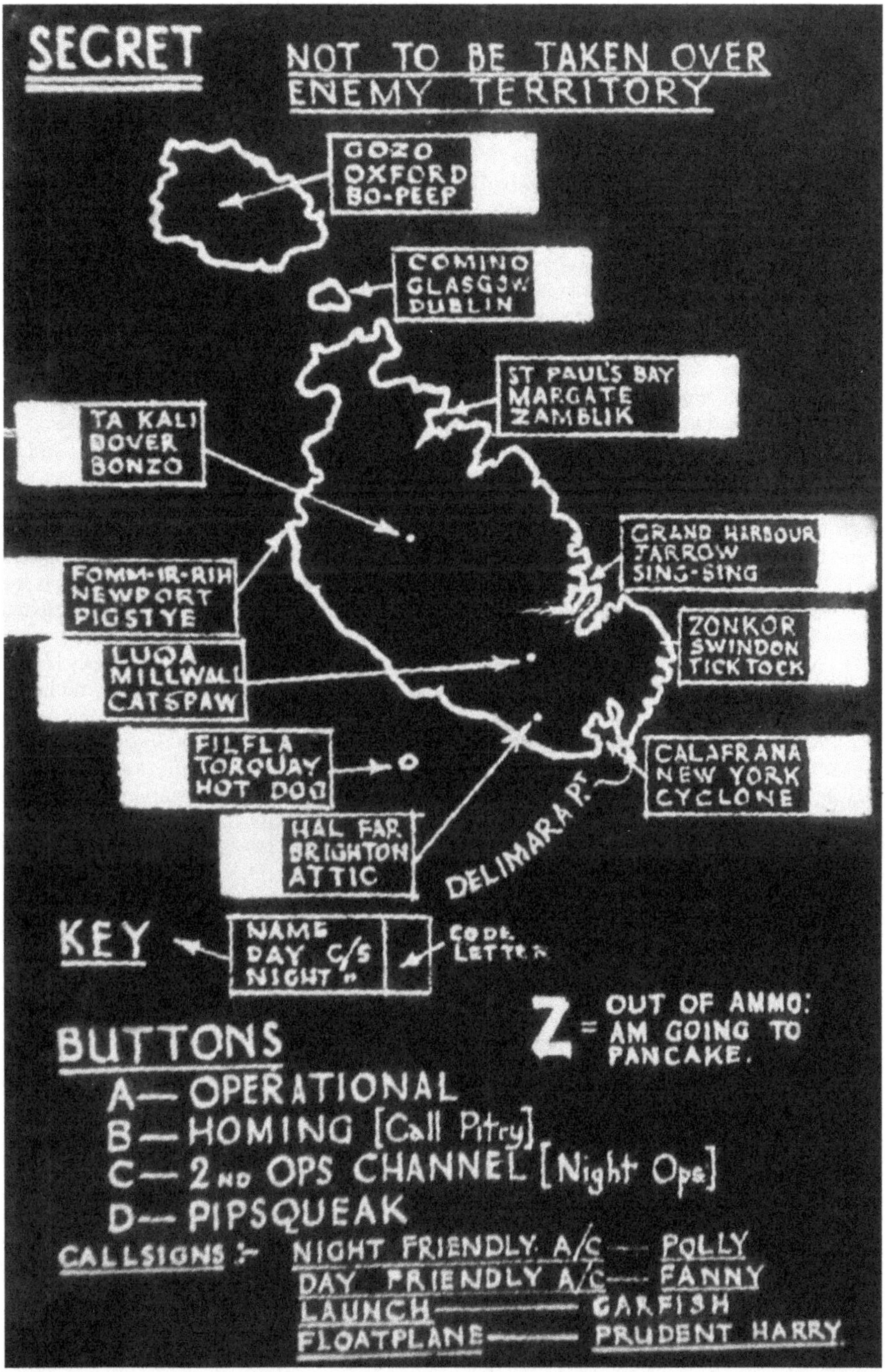
SECRET
NOT TO BE TAKEN OVER ENEMY TERRITORY
GOZO
OXFORD
BO-PEEP
COMINO
GLASGOW
DUBLIN
ST PAUL'S BAY
MARGATE
ZAMBLIK
TA KALI
DOVER
BONZO
GRAND HARBOUR
JARROW
SING-SING
FOMM-IR-RIH
NEWPORT
PIGSTYE
ZONKOR
SWINDON
TICK TOCK
LUQA
MILLWALL
CATSPAW
FILFLA
TORQUAY
HOT DOG
CALAFRANA
NEW YORK
CYCLONE
HAL FAR
BRIGHTON
ATTIC
DELIMARA PT.
KEY
NAME
DAY C/S
NIGHT "
CODE LETTER
Z = OUT OF AMMO: AM GOING TO PANCAKE.
BUTTONS
A— OPERATIONAL
B— HOMING [Call Pitry]
C— 2ND OPS CHANNEL [Night Ops]
D— PIPSQUEAK
CALLSIGNS :-
NIGHT FRIENDLY A/C — POLLY
DAY FRIENDLY A/C — FANNY
LAUNCH — GARFISH
FLOATPLANE — PRUDENT HARRY

Endnotes Chapter 19

213 'Big jobs' were bombers; 'little jobs, fighters. Angels 12 was 12,000 feet. The date of this encounter was 15 June 1942.

214 During the Battle of Britain and later in Malta the sector control rooms were presided over by experienced career officers like Wing Commander Alfred Basil Woodhall at Duxford. 'Woody' Woodhall was a South African who in 1914 had been a lance corporal in the Witwatersrand Rifles before joining the Royal Marines. During the early twenties he had flown biplane torpedo bombers before transferring to the RAF in 1929. When war came, Woodhall had a desk job at the Air Ministry and he was posted to Duxford on 12 March 1940 as senior controller. Ubiquitous WAAFs wearing headsets plotted the raids on table maps dutifully moving each one around the grids like in a board game with croupier rakes as the enemy raids developed. On the wall, a five minutes' coloured change clock ticked away and a 'tote' recorded all details of enemy raids and fighters sent to intercept. Sector station operations rooms were the nerve centre and crucial. After the Battle of Britain Woodhall went to Malta as senior controller on the island. He retired from the RAF on 14 July 1945.

215 Leslie 'Les' Watts served on 603 Squadron as a Pilot Officer early in 1942, accompanying the unit to Malta aboard USS Wasp, flying off to the island on 20 April. At the end of the month he was transferred to 249 Squadron, where in late July he was promoted flight commander.

216 Each was awarded a half share of a Ju 88. Les Watts' tour ended in mid-August and he returned to the UK. Early in June 1943 he joined 616 Squadron as a flight commander, but was then posted to 322 (Dutch) Squadron. The following month he was posted back to 616 Squadron as commanding officer, leading the unit for a year. He was also awarded a DFC at this time. In June 1944 66 became the first squadron to convert to Gloster Meteor I jets and Watts flew against V-1s that summer. On 29 April 1945 he collided with another Meteor in cloud, both pilots being killed. His score stood at 1 and 2 shared destroyed, 1 and 1 shared probable, 5 and 1 shared damaged.

217 On 7 March fifteen Spitfire Vbs were flown off the deck of the carrier Eagle and they landed at Ta'Qali. On 20 March 143 Ju 88s and Bf 109s made a massed attack on the islands and heavy raids continued for two more days before the Luftwaffe switched to bombing a convoy of merchant ships heading for Valletta. Airfields came under constant attack and soon the blockade of Malta began to have a telling effect on the Island's reserves of stores, munitions and fuel. Food was in very short supply and 'Victory Kitchens' were introduced to feed the starving population. Sugar was unobtainable and even soap and matches had to be rationed.

218 On 13 July 1942 Laddie Lucas' Spitfire was hit by four Bf 109s and it began to burn. He sought to bail out, but found the cockpit jammed, following which he was able to make a successful down-wind-landing. Five days later he left the unit and was flown home some days later. He became Squadron Leader Ops at HQ Fighter Command, until April 1943, when he was given command of 616 Squadron. In July he was to take over a Wing in North Africa, but this posting was cancelled as he prepared to leave and he went instead to lead the Coltishall Wing, where Wing Commander 'Sandy' Rabagliati had just been lost. At the end of the year Lucas returned to HQ Fighter Command, as Wing Commander Ops, being awarded a DSO in January 1944. He dropped rank to Squadron Leader to join 2 Group HQ in the prospect of an operational job after 'D-Day' and was soon promoted again, commencing a third tour in late 1944 as commanding officer of 613 Squadron, undertaking 'Night Intruder' sorties in Mosquito VIs. He led this unit until the end of the war, receiving a Bar to his DSO later in 1945. His total score was 1 and 2 shared destroyed, 1 probable, 8 and 1 shared damaged. Lucas was married in 1946 to Jill Addison, the sister of Thelma Bader, wife of his fellow flying ace Douglas Bader, of whom he wrote a best-selling biography. The couple had five grandchildren. Wing Commander 'Laddie' Lucas CBE DSO* DFC died on 20 March 1998.

Chapter 20

The Spits

Captain John R. 'Tex' McCrary

My boss on the Mirror *used to say I was a sucker for the British. I never really denied it. I always liked to tell on myself the story I invented and attributed to Freddie Lonsdale, about how he once said: 'The trouble with you, McCrary, is that you look down on the English with the profoundest envy.'*

***First of the Many* by Captain John R. 'Tex' McCrary (1943)**[219]

I don't deny that I'm a sucker for the British. Let me try to tell another story of a day spent with one of them not so long ago, one of the best of them. It begins with sound effects.

'What the bloody hell could be plainer than that, you bloody idiot! I said American Wing Headquarters. Wing!! Yes. Right. Put me through. Priority One. This is Wing Commander Johnson speaking.'

His hair was straight and strong and sweaty and flopping in his face, like that of a fighter whose seconds have just slopped a sponge of ice water across his head to cool him out after a tough round. He wore the rough wool battle jacket and faded blue breeches and quarter-length black boots of an RAF fighter pilot. On his jacket were the ribbons of the DSO and the DFC and Bar. His hands were thick, but nervous; his lips thin, but strong. His eyes did not look - they punched holes through what they saw. He sat on a map-littered desk in the canvassed caravan into which fed the control wires of a mobile RAF fighter station. The whole station was under canvas. This was dress rehearsal for the push across the Channel.

Johnny Johnson, twenty-seven, one-time civil engineer, veteran of the Battle of Britain, killer of 25 German planes - more over enemy territory than any other fighter pilot - was the boss of this Spitfire wing, a Canadian wing with a boss as British as a dropped-h.[220]

Savagely, he was hammering a scrambler phone, trying to penetrate the tangle of channels to get through and talk to the Commanding Officer of a Group of American Eighth Air Force Marauders, the medium bombers that Johnny's Spits had escorted on some thirty missions in the past six weeks. He wanted to get a couple of them down for the day for 'fun and games-practice attacks - get to know the plane - what she can do -'

Americans ought to get to know guys like Johnny Johnson, quite aside from the fact that they and their Spits nursed our Fortresses through their first shallow penetration missions and now are nursing the Marauders. In the period from April 15 to July 31 1943, RAF Spitfires flew 8,743 sorties escorting our Marauders, destroyed 123 enemy fighters and lost 61 Spits. We ought to get to know guys like Johnny, because they are England. The best of England.

'His boys think the sun rises and sets in his hip pocket and they're not so far wrong.'

Speaking was a gangling tall blond boy, about twenty-three - looked like Paul Hartman of the screwball dancing team of the Hartmans. He looked awkward - slightly sissy - but he wore the slant-striped ribbon of the DFC. You don't get that in the RAF for being awkward and sissy. Johnny called him 'The Nippler.' Treated him like a kid brother: 'Why dammit, I set up the Nippler the other day for a perfect shot at an Me 109 and the bloody idiot missed. Last night I set him up for a wizard shot at a bloody wonderful blonde and the bloody idiot missed again!'

The Nippler went into the Volunteer Reserves with Johnny back when the war broke out; they learned to fly together; were on the station with the American Eagles at one time. The Nippler was shot down once in the Battle of Britain, twice over Malta - got it in the hip out there, was grounded and now he's supposed to be on a ground job up in Scotland, but: 'I come down here with Johnny and he lets me sneak in a 'do' now and then.'[221]

Let's study the Nippler a little more. It gives you more respect for his opinion of Johnny. We were beating through some bushes out beyond the airfield, trying to scare out pigeons or grouse or rabbits, anything to shoot at. I flushed a grey squirrel out of the bush; the Nippler legged him as he raced toward a tall tree. He walked over to where the squirrel was kicking in the dust. He stopped to pick it up; his Adam's apple did nip-ups. He straightened, took careful aim and wasted a scarce shell to blow the squirrel's head off.

'I never could kill anything with my hands.'

We walked on and I tried to draw him further into talking; wasn't easy. He talked about the weary weeks he ferried combat planes across Africa after he got shot up over Malta and couldn't fight any more. He talked about the dim future of civil aviation for all the kids in the RAF - conceded the Air Age to America. What about a guy like Johnny? What will he do? Any airline in America would grab such a man.

'No, I don't think Johnny will ever leave the RAF. He's got a good career there. Everybody, all the big shots say that he's the best Wing Commander in the South and you can't top that, you know. Old Johnny has been on ops longer than anybody else, but if he doesn't watch, the big shots will ground him or the Jerries will, one or the other. He doesn't want either, but one or the other will get him...'

Johnny knew that 'the percentages' were after him, too. If he quit flying now and took over a station, like 'Sailor' Malan did down at Biggin Hill, nobody could say he had not done his share of fighting. Since he took over this Wing last April, he had lost fifteen planes and 'now we're on the last leg of a sweep for the 100th Jerry.' That's hot, brother. And all over enemy territory.

Johnny has a wife. Married last October. Picture of the wedding party is on his table in the old farm house by the field where he sleeps.

Johnny has had a tempting proposition dangled under his nose - 'Want me to go to Canada, maybe hop down to the States for a couple of days. I never did travel outside England before the war. I'd like to, that's why I was flat out for this idea.'

There was a 'but': he looked out across the field where the iron mats had mashed a runway out of the turf, where brown tents and camouflaged caravans and netted planes made this whole Spitfire field look exactly like dozens of them were to look when the Tactical Air Force pushed across the Channel, the way other airmen moved into Sicily. Johnny Johnson looked at all this and then came the 'but': 'Sure, I'd like to take a trip to Canada and the States, but I don't want to get too far away. I've flown over France so bloody much, when we hop the Ditch, I'd like to be around, flying over France - from France --'

First time I ever heard of Johnny was last winter. I wanted to cook up a newsreel that would show how the United Nations worked together in the air-Fortresses being escorted by Spitfire pilots from England and South Africa and Holland and France and Poland and Czechoslovakia and Australia and Canada and Norway. All these airmen who never saw each other, but only saw each other's planes - all these airmen who spoke in many languages and accents on the ground, but only one language in the air. I wanted to get pictures of Spitfires of the RAF flying with Forts of the US Eighth Air Force. The Canadians offered to co-operate and suggested that Wing Commander Johnson come up to a Fortress Station, talk to the CO, work out the deal.

Johnny came up; brought his flight and squadron leaders; they met the Fortress crews, ate and drank and talked and got to know each other. The Fortress CO said afterwards: 'Jesus, why can't there be more of this!'

Johnny had a wonderful time: 'Great chaps, your boys. Remember when they couldn't hit a thing with their guns or their bombs. Ought to see them now. We know - they clobber their targets proper.'

Johnny has 'clobbered' a dozen Jerries on the Fortress shows with the guns of his Spitfire.

'I copped a couple of your .50-calibre guns up there. Actually, they gave them to me. I wanted to try them out in my kite - wizard trajectory, your guns get - but the Stress & Strain boys said no go - said my kite couldn't hold the extra guns.'

Johnny's Spit guns have teamed up with the Fortress .50's on some thirty shows. Maybe more. His first was September 6 1942 to Amiens. Once, last spring, when Johnny's Spits were racing to cover a wounded Fort that was being hammered by a dozen Jerries out over the Channel, they got there a little too late - they did get two of the Jerries, but the Huns got the Fort, sent it spinning, blazing, down into the Channel. Johnny felt the loss of that Fort deeply; he gnawed his thin lower lip and cussed in crackling four-letter words. And when he got back to base, he bathed and shaved and drove through the night to find an American general and tell him how the Fortress had gone down in flames, with the top turret firing until the Channel waters closed over the guns.

That kind of fighting by Fortress crews makes Johnny Johnson want to 'know more about your guys.'

It was late afternoon before we got word through that the Marauders wouldn't be down for the 'fun and games''; they were going out on a mission; and Johnny's Spits of the Canadian Wing were 'laid on' to give top cover for their cousins. Instantly, there was tension. Men ducked in and out of tents. Johnny's lips became thinner, his hair straighter, his hands thicker; his eyes sharper - everything on the field that was strong became suddenly stronger. Where there had been hospitality, far more than any Englishmen ever got on a Fortress station, now there was preoccupation. Johnny stuck out his hand:

'Well, old boy, come down again, or we'll come up. Like to meet some of your popsies. Hear the Americans have all the best girls in hand. You know, I'd like to meet some of your chaps who have tangled with the Japs. Any of them over here? Like to talk to them. I'd like to have a crack at the Japs after the Jerries are done in. Bloody good sport that would be - bloody good.'

The day before, the King had announced the creation of a new British holiday -'Battle of Britain Day,' September 26, a day to remind the people of Britain of what Mr. Churchill once carved into granite, timeless words:

'Never in the field of human conflict has so much been owed by so many to so few.'

Our debt to the Spitfires is not quite so old as Britain's, but it's deep. Many a grey-faced, blue-fingered, frozen-eyed American boy has looked back over the tattered tail of a crippled Fort at the Focke-Wulfs queuing up for the kill and then seen the vultures scatter for home as the pilot's voice shouted into the intercom:

'The Spits! There they come! Hot damn, come-a-buzzin', cousin!'

Three weeks after I saw Johnny down at his station, I met him again in town. The Eighth Air Force was cooking up a decoration, a 'gong' for him. I asked him to come up to London and bring his log book with him so we could get the right figures for the citation. We went to Claridge's for lunch - a Canadian Squadron Leader, Buck [McNair] DFC and Bar, was with Johnny. Buck's face was burned dark, all the part not covered by oxygen mask and goggles. As we walked down Brook Street, his running commentary on the girls we passed made them blush and even Johnny squirmed. Inside Claridge's both looked around at the cold marble elegance of the place: 'What's this?' asked Johnny. Buck whistled.[222]

Johnny is the type of Englishman who has never been in Claridge's. We sat in a corner of the big room; he hauled out his log book; we went through a sparse record that concealed a dozen epics.

From August 1942 to September 1943, when they took him off ops and put him into a chairborne planning job, Johnny flew seventy-one escort jobs with the Forts and Marauders and four supporting sweeps.

On the slug-fests he shot down for certain thirteen enemy fighters; on the supporting umbrellas he got two. (Johnny Johnson had shot down 27 planes by May 1 1944. He had been put back on combat again, flying back over his favourite hunting grounds, the coast of France).

Doubt if that score will ever show up in the Lend-Lease accounts; it should, on the credit side for Britain.

Just the night before I had been down at a Marauder station; the CO gave me an interesting note on Anglo-American relations:

'When an RAF pilot drops in here and we take him up to the bar for a drink, we only pay for our own drinks for the RAF are on the house. Guess that's why all the Spitfires seem to give out of gas over our field, which is okay with us.'

At lunch, Johnny and Buck talked about Topics A and B - Girls and Flying.[223] It's hard to get these boys talking seriously; the first job is to make them talk at all - to a 'paddlefoot.' But you can always hook them, with this question: 'What happens to you after the war?' Buck's answer was quick and typical:

'The guy who pays me the most to do the least work gets me for keeps.'

But ten minutes later, he was solemn, his burned forehead was wrinkled in thought and he was talking like this: 'There's no capital in Canada, that's the trouble.'

Johnny confirmed what the Nippler had told me. He wanted to stay in the RAF. 'It's a good life, Tex. I've thought about going to your country. I want to go, when all you chaps get back and I know somebody there. But I don't think I could take it there. You live too fast in America.'

'Johnny, you're more like an American than anybody I ever knew who was born in America and I've never known any American with half your intensity.'

'Would you say that? Really? Hmmmm, you mean I'm high-strung? Would you say that, Buck, about me?'

Buck laughed at Johnny's puzzled face: 'Listen, Johnny, you're not high-strung. You're just punchy!'

And we let it go at that. Then we talked politics. Johnny ventured an idea that Arthur Brisbane once wrote a column about: 'You know what would be a wonderful idea - can't you find an American to marry Princess Elizabeth?'

He was serious, dead serious. We talked on about the Royal Family, about the House of Lords - and at that point, a girl sent over a note, a girl I knew, wife of an RAF pilot. The note read: 'You said you always wanted to see what a Duke looked like. Well, there is one sitting in that corner by the door.'

I showed the note to Johnny and Buck - they craned their necks as hard as I craned mine to look at a Duke. He was a boy, about twenty-eight, in an officer's uniform. Sandy-haired, pale. Said Buck: 'So that's a Duke.'

We talked about Douglas Bader, the great RAF pilot with the two aluminum legs. Johnny was his No. 2 man, was on his wing the day he was shot down over France. He must have been a great leader. The guys in his outfit must have worshipped him.

'It wasn't so much to fly with tin legs,' said Johnny. 'It wasn't that he flew with tin legs, anyway. It was just that he had so damn much guts. That was it.'

And we talked about 'Sailor' Malan, the man who shot down thirty-two planes, most of them over England in the Battle of Britain.

Listen, they gave Malan credit for thirty-two. I bet he shot down fifty. He was fighting in the days when he would come down, flop on his bunk for fifteen minutes' sleep while they checked his kite and got it ready and then go up again. All day, while there was light to see, he went up and fought. He never checked his kills. Some Intelligence bloke would ask him how many he had for the day and he would say, 'Make it a couple' and drop off to sleep as if he were slugged. But I bet he got fifty.'

After lunch we went by the PX and picked up my ration of cigarettes - which Johnny took and split with Buck. And then, so long:

'If you want to get hold of me before next Sunday, just ring through to Melton Mowbray 500 - that's the police station. We haven't a phone in our house. And ask for Mr. Johnson, the constable. He'll take a message. He's my father.'

A constable's son. Old Beaverbrook was so right when he said: 'Pilots - they are our new nobility. Not dukes or earls or lords, but pilots. Praise them and pray for their glorious survival.'

In March 1944 Johnny Johnson was posted as Wing Leader of a new RCAF Wing, 144, claiming a further ten victories with this unit by early July, having led the squadrons to Normandy when airfields became available after the invasion. A second Bar to his DSO was gazetted on 7 July. In August, however, the Wing was disbanded and he returned to 127 Wing with one of his squadrons, leading this formation until early 1945.

On 23 September 1944 an article entitled *Topscore Fighter Ace; An intimate story of Wing Commander J. E. Johnson DSO with two bars, DFC and bar and American DFC, as told by his wife to Illustrated reporter Elsie Marshall* appeared in *Illustrated magazine:*

'A man who is a hero in the headlines is sometimes not such a hero at home.

Wing Commander Johnny Johnson, triple DSO, double DFC and American DFC, destroyer of thirty-seven Nazi planes, mostly over France, is different. His people think he's fine, too. Listen to what his wife Pauline - Johnny calls her Paula - says about the evening just over two years ago when she met her husband:[224]

'I thought he was quite a hero. In fact I thought he was marvellous; and he only had one DFC then.'

Paula, a pretty girl with blond hair and big blue eyes, was eighteen when she met Johnny. It was at a party given by Lord Beaverbrook's son, Max Aitken, in Norwich, her home town, 'to celebrate something or other.' Max Aitken was wingco to Johnny in those days when the fighter ace was a squadron leader:

Three months later, on November 14 1942, Paula and Johnny were married.[225]

'We were never officially engaged,' she says, 'although Johnny's boys gave us an engagement party: I think they overheard him proposing. When I told mummy he wanted to marry me, she warned me not to believe everything these pilots told me. Johnny lived in awe of mummy in those days for she insisted that he should not keep me out later than ten o'clock; but he's such a lovable sort of boy that he soon wheedled his way round her, too.'

Johnny was then stationed not far from Paula's home[226] and after a brief honeymoon in London - Paula's first visit to the capital - at Blackpool and at Johnny's home in Melton Mowbray, where she met her in-laws for the first time, Paula came home again and Johnny went back to his station. Now, married for two years, they have spent only brief leaves together, for Johnny doesn't believe, in 'station wives.' He insists that his wife's nerves would go quicker than his. She agrees with him and says: 'Any time I've been at the station waiting for him to come back has been a nightmare.'

Of course Paula worries about her husband's safety; but superstitiously she says: 'He's got such a definite widower's peak that I feel he must outlive me!'

Johnny is not the reckless type. His wife finds him placid and decisive.

'If there's a fight going, he's sure to be in it,' she admits, but he always knows his method of attack beforehand. He's always been like that. His father has told me what a dreadful child he was, always in a scrap.'

Johnny's father is a War Reserve Police Inspector at Melton Mowbray. When Johnny was a kid, always in some scrape or other and someone used to threaten to 'tell a policeman,' he would grin disarmingly and say: 'That's all right, he's my dad' and get right on with the fight.

Now Mr. Johnson's chief worry is that his famous son will get into trouble driving his big open Lagonda car. But Johnny is a good driver.

'He's very careful;' recommends his wife. 'And he has a clean licence. I've never been nervous driving with him. But I wouldn't fly with him - I wouldn't fly at all - although when Johnny's flying I don't think he ever takes unnecessary risks, but if he sees a gap he'd try to get through it.'

Very reticent about his prowess in the air, Johnny never mentions flying to his wife. Recently, when he bailed out from the Spit he's had since the days of the Battle of Britain, she heard the news from his father.[227]

'When I ask him about flying, he just tells me that it's only part of his job; and when I ask him how he manages to shoot them down so well, he laughs and tells me that you can't miss when the things will get in front of you.'

Johnny Johnson has a lively sense of humour - it's obvious from his twinkly brown eyes and infectious grin. He dislikes the publicity that his fighting has brought him but all the same enjoys and laughs at some of the fan mail that pours in, mostly from teenage girls.

Autograph hunters haunt him, too and often when he's on leave at Paula's home, a queue will be sitting on the low brick wall of the garden, waiting with pencils and books at the ready.

Recently in France, where he is now stationed, a new type of pin-up girl was stuck on the wall of the mess. It was a naked baby lying on a sofa. A brassiere and panties had been pencilled in. It was a photograph of Wing Commander J. E. Johnson DSO DFC cut from a newspaper. Johnny took his teasing with good humour.

An enthusiastic horseman (Paula is keen on horses, too and for some time had a job exercising remounts for the Army), Johnny now has a horse of his own in France, captured from the Germans. He calls it Hans and whenever he has time he rides to the beach to bathe. Sally, his black Labrador, seen on this week's cover with her master; is also in France, flown there by a Canadian in Johnny's wing. Sally is intensely jealous of Hans and when Johnny is mounted the dog pretends to be asleep and will have nothing to do with him.

Johnny is a great sportsman. Rugger and soccer are his games, but nowadays squash and swimming are his main exercise.

A civil engineer before the war, Johnny hopes to stay in the RAF. His and Paula's post-war plans are to have a country cottage.

'Johnny loves the country and so do I,' she says. 'He spends most of his leaves rough shooting. He's even been shooting hares as well as Nazis in France. I don't shoot. I just stooge round with him and I like it. If he ever gets home for forty-eight hours' leave on the Twelfth I tease him that it's the grouse, not me, that's brought him back.'

When not in uniform, Johnny likes to wear country clothes. He's the pipe-smoking, out-of-door type. He wears tweed suits, shooting jackets, flannels and brogues.'

He likes his beer,' says his wife, 'but he doesn't drink spirits. He likes his food, too, little but good. Steak is his favourite dish and he likes fresh fruit instead of sweets.'

Soon there is to be an addition to the Johnson family. Both Johnny and Paula want it to be a girl, whom they will call Susan. If it's a boy, his name will be Richard - and he won't be allowed to fly; one flyer in the family is enough for Paula. Johnny hopes to get leave about the time of the birth and is already a' nervous father.' He swears that he'd rather fight fifty Huns than go up to that maternity home.'

But before then he has ample time to break his own record of thirty-seven Nazis. In France, his Canadian boys would, in their own words, 'follow him to hell and back,' He's waiting for a Hun rash enough to give him the chance.

Good luck to him![228]

Endnotes Chapter 20

219 Captain John R. 'Tex' McCrary was a war reporter (as well as a Photographic Officer) for 8th Air Force Public Relations. He had once worked on the *New York Mirror*, which always specialized in 'Rape, riot and ruin'. Born John Reagan McCrary in 1910 in Calvert, Texas, the son of a cotton farmer hurt by the Depression later attended Phillips Exeter Academy and Yale where he was a member of Skull and Bones. He started in journalism as a copy boy at the *New York World-Telegram*. He left to join the *Daily Mirror*, later becoming its chief editorial writer. After divorcing his first wife in 1939, McCrary began writing the column 'Only Human' and in 1941 met Jinx Falkenburg. When he interviewed her; she was starring in *Hold Onto Your Hats* on Broadway with Al Jolson. In 1945 he was one of the first Americans to visit Hiroshima after the atomic bomb was dropped. He advised journalists not to write about what they had seen because he did not think Americans could stand to know 'what we've done here.' After John Hersey published his account in the New Yorker, McCrary said, 'I covered it up and John Hersey uncovered it. That's the difference between a PR man and a reporter.' After the war McCrary edited the *American Mercury* magazine. He soon renewed his friendship with Jinx Falkenburg, who had become a star under contract at MGM and was one of the nation's highest-paid models. They were married in June 1945. Although they were separated years later, they never divorced. McCrary and his wife had two radio talk shows, *Hi Jinx* and *Meet Tex and Jinx* and a TV show, sometimes broadcasting from Gotham's Waldorf-Astoria Hotel where they could nab celebs, as they stopped to pick up their room keys. McCrary died aged 92 in New York.

220 'Johnnie' Johnson was born at Barrow upon Soar, near Melton Mowbray, Leicestershire, on 9 March 1915. He qualified as a civil engineer at Nottingham University in 1937, also attempting to join the Auxiliary Air Force, but being turned down. He was later called into the VR and commenced flying training. Late in August 1940 he joined 19 Squadron but on 5 September he moved to 616 Squadron. An old rugby injury now troubled him, a broken collarbone having been incorrectly set, trapping some nerves. He therefore entered hospital to have it reset, returning to 616 Squadron in December. During the summer cross-Channel sweeps of 1941 he made his first confirmed claims, frequently flying in the section led by Wing Commander Douglas Bader, the Tangmere Wing Leader. At the end of September he was awarded a DFC and promoted to command a flight. In June 1942 he received a Bar to his DFC and in July took command of 610 Squadron, leading this unit over Dieppe on 19 August. March 1943 brought further promotion to lead the Canadian Wing at Kenley on Spitfire IXs. In August this became 127 Wing in the new Tactical Air Force which was about to be formed. Whilst leading the Wing, he claimed 14 and five shared victories between April and September, receiving a DSO in June and a Bar to this in September. He was at last rested during September, spending six months with the Planning Staff at HQ, 11 Group. *Aces High* by Christopher Shores and Clive Williams (Grub Street, London 1994).

221 Philip Whaley Ellis 'Nip' Heppell, from Newcastle, joined the RAF after the outbreak of war and on completion of training was posted to 616 Squadron, seeing action during the summer of 1941. His father had been an RFC pilot in the First War, whilst his sister was to become a ferry pilot in the Second. Awarded a DFC later in the year after two victories, he was promoted flight commander in November. Early in 1942 he was assigned to fly one of the first Spitfires to Malta, taking off HMS *Eagle* on 9 March to the island, where he was posted to 249 Squadron. On 8 April, on his second sortie of the day, he was attacking a Ju 88 over Grand Harbour when his Spitfire was hit by an AA shell and he was thrown out of the aircraft, wounded in the head and legs, and badly bruised. He managed to get his parachute open and land at Floriana. After some weeks in hospital, he was evacuated to Egypt by air on 30 April. He returned to the island in April 1943 to command 229 Squadron, but during the following month was wounded. His score stood at 4 destroyed, 1 and 1 shared probable, 5 damaged. On recovery he flew briefly with 1435 Squadron but then returned to the UK. In January 1944 he became CO of 118 Squadron, subsequently converting the unit to Mustang IIIs and undertaking a number of escorts to Bomber Command heavy bombers over Germany by day. In March 1945 he received a Bar to his DFC after the conclusion of his tour. He died in 1987. *Aces High* by Christopher Shores and Clive Williams (Grub Street, London 1994)

222 Robert Wendell 'Buck' McNair was born in Springfield, Nova Scotia on 15 May 1919. In 1937 he joined Canadian Airways as a radio operator and handyman. He joined the RCAF in June 1940,

qualifying as a pilot in March 1941, when he was commissioned. Posted to the UK he attended 58 OTU and was then sent to 411 Squadron on 23 June 1941, remaining with the unit until February 1942. He was then posted to Malta, flying out in a Sunderland and arriving just before the first Spitfires reached the island. Posted to 249 Squadron, he became one of the unit's most notable pilots, being awarded a DFC in May for five destroyed and seven damaged. He left Malta in mid-June as a Flight Lieutenant, flying back to England where he immediately rejoined 411 Squadron, staying with this squadron until 21 September, when he was sent home on leave. After taking part in a war bonds publicity drive, he was posted to the Western Air Command to fly with 133 Squadron RCAF. He at once pressed for a return to operations, reaching the UK in April 1943, where he joined 403 Squadron. A month later he was given command of 416 Squadron, whose CO, Foss Boulton, had just been shot down. Within another month he took over 421 Squadron but on 20 July he was forced to turn back from a sortie to France due to his engine losing power. Over the Channel the engine burst into flames and he was obliged to bail out, his faced being burned. He was awarded a Bar to his DFC at the end of the month and a second Bar on 7 October. On 17 October he was promoted to lead 126 Wing RCAF. However the effects of the flames on his face had begun to affect his vision and on 12 April he relinquished his post, the award of a DSO being announced two days later. He returned to Canada on leave, but came back to take up a staff post at RCAF Overseas HQ, which he held until after the war had ended. His score stood at 16 destroyed, 5 probables, 14 damaged. He died on 15January 1971.

223 As a teenager Johnson became fascinated by speed and joined the Melton Car Club with two boyhood friends. Johnson enjoyed the lifestyle of cars and 'pacey' women.

224 Pauline Ingate worked in the Norwich operations room of the Auxiliary Fire Service.

225 On 14 November 1942 Johnson married Pauline Ingate in Norwich during home leave. Hugh 'Cocky' Dundas acted as best man and Lord Beaverbrook's son, Wing Commander Max Aitken also attended. Johnnie and Paula had two sons. (After the couple split up, Johnson lived with his partner Janet Partridge).

226 At RAF Coltishall, Norfolk.

227 Over Calais in August 1944 his Spitfire was hit by fire from a German fighter for the first and only time.

228 On 6 April 1945 Johnny Johnson was given command of 125 Wing as a Group Captain, his new command being equipped with the latest Griffon-engined Spitfire XIVs. At the end of the war, he was the RAF's officially-recognised top-scoring fighter pilot with 34 and 7 shared destroyed, 3 and 2 shared probables, 10 and 3 shared damaged, 1 shared destroyed on the ground in 515 sorties flown. Air Vice-Marshal Johnson CB CBE DSO** DFC* retired from the service in March 1966. He died on 30 January 2001 (aged 85) at Buxton, Derbyshire.

Chapter 21

Night Fighter Triumphs

David Masters

It was rumoured that his wife and children had been killed in one of the early bombing attacks on Manchester and this was the reason for his fanatical determination to hunt down the bombers. Stories told how he 'screamed like a man demented' whenever he went into the attack, after tracking the bombers by the AA bursts. It was reported that one bomber which blew up as a result of his attack, splattered the wings of his Hurricane with the blood and fragments of the crew, which he refused to allow the ground crew to wash off.

***Aces High* by Christopher Shores and Clive Williams (Grub Street, London 1994). Richard Playne Stevens was Born in Tonbridge, Kent, in 1909. In 1928 he was sent out to Australia as part of the 'Big Brother' movement, when an Australian family undertook to look after him and find him work, mainly as a grazier on a sheep ranch. In 1932 he left to enlist in the Palestine Police, where he served for four years. Finally returning to UK, he became a civil airline pilot, learning to fly at Shoreham in Sussex and then flying the early morning papers from Croydon to Paris each day. He was 32 when he joined the RAF, the maximum age for pilot training and clearly it was only his civil experience which allowed him to be accepted. Joining the RAF as a Sergeant, he was initially involved in army co-operation flying, but on 4 September 1940 he joined 151 Squadron in 12 Group, as this unit was about to become involved in night operations. Commissioned late in the year, he enjoyed some early success in January 1941 and was awarded a DFC at the start of February.**

His strong face and blue eyes were well-known on the air-route between Croydon and Paris before the war. Night flying was no new thing to him, for he had long experience as a pilot of commercial aircraft and often flew English newspapers over to the French capital in the dark hours, so his log indicated about 400 hours of night flying.

The night of 15/16 January 1941, when he achieved his first double success, was almost ideal for the purpose. There was bright moonlight and the earth was covered with a layer of snow against which an enemy bomber stood out to the night fighter pilot flying above it, while the snow reflected the moonlight to make the night even brighter. Listening posts all over the country were busy with their sound locators to catch the sound of the raiders so that the course and height could be plotted and warning could be given to the towns and cities which the raiders threatened to attack.

Pilot Officer Stevens and other night fighting pilots on his station awaited orders. They were ready to take off at any moment and their Hurricanes were serviced with ground crews standing by. Reports of enemy aircraft making for

London began to come in and just before 1 o'clock Stevens climbed into the cockpit, strapped himself in, had a look round to assure himself that everything was all right, closed the hood, signalled to the crew to pull the chocks from under the wheels and roared off into the moonlit sky. His clock on the instrument panel showed that it was 12.56.

Climbing steadily, he flew south, keeping in touch with his base by wireless. It was cold enough on the ground, but it was much worse in the air. The higher he climbed, the lower the temperature fell. It dropped to the zero mark and continued to drop as he rose.

Despite his warm clothing and the enclosed cockpit he began to feel a little cold. He kept a sharp look-out, weaving about at times to try to find the enemy, but he flew for half an hour without seeing anything at all. He was now over three miles high and feeling almost frozen. A minute or two later he saw the flashes of bombs exploding ahead of him. The magic voice whispered directions in his ears and he made a slight alteration of course. When he got near London the anti-aircraft shells bursting above him told him that the enemy was at a still higher altitude. Climbing another 500 feet, he began to weave up and down and sideways, as the magic voice told him that the enemy was somewhere near.

He looked around, but saw no signs, so he decided to follow the line taken by the bursting shells. It was then 1.30 am. A few seconds later he caught sight of the raider crossing his path. It was a Dornier 'flying pencil' [Do 17Z, of 4/KG3] turning and climbing very fast about 400 yards ahead.

At once the fighter pilot gave the Hurricane full boost to attain the highest possible speed in order to overtake the enemy, but after that momentary glimpse the Dornier vanished. Flying at top speed the fighter pilot sought his quarry. 'I picked him up again,' Pilot Officer Stevens remarked afterwards, 'climbing at 20,000 feet. He had dropped his bombs and was light. I climbed after him and chased him up to 30,000 feet. Throttling back to cruising speed as I closed, I swung out to make my attack between fifty and twenty-five yards. I saw my ammunition going home and striking him. Bits flew off and hit my aircraft. Oil came back on my windscreen and he just reared straight up. I thought I was going to crash into him, so I turned to one side to get away and only just managed to avoid him. As I did so he went straight down.

'Thinking he was trying to fox me, I went down after him flat out from 30,000 to 3,000 feet in a steep spiral. I've never travelled so fast before - you've no idea of speed when you are looking for a Jerry, you just notice when the ground is coming too close and then pull out. I saw him shooting away in a steep climbing turn, so I pulled everything back and did a gentle black-out. Owing to my excess speed I went well outside him and lost him again for a moment. Then I saw him still climbing and quickly closed on him. I gave him a burst from my eight guns and saw little blue flames dancing about his wings and fuselage. At the top of his climb, as he started to stall, I gave him another burst. Flames streamed from him as he went down and crashed [at Hart's Wood, Brentford] at 1.35 am among some trees which he set on fire. Circling round, I climbed to 15,000 feet and went home.'

The gentle black-out he referred to was caused by turning at such a high speed that centrifugal force drove the blood away from the blood vessels behind the eyes and caused him momentarily to go blind, although he remained fully conscious of what he was doing. This phenomenon was first suffered by Air Commodore A. H. Orlebar in training for the Schneider Trophy race[229] and he very courageously experimented and subjected himself to a complete black-out in order to see what happened. He found the senses were not otherwise affected, although he could see nothing at all. Medical researches proved the cause and found that the effects were in no way dangerous or permanent, so this was something else which the Schneider Trophy races taught the world.

So fast did Pilot Officer Stevens travel during his dive that the bottom of his aircraft cracked under the tremendous air pressure. Although the pilot did not know it at the time, he himself suffered in his zeal to overtake the enemy. At 30,000 the air pressure is only about 41 lbs per square inch, while at ground level it is 15lbs to the square inch. He dived so rapidly that the pressure inside his body could not adjust itself quickly enough to the increasing pressure outside his body, with the result that some fluid formed in one of his ear drums. Luckily it soon came right.

We can imagine how the news of further raiders broke up the discussion in the mess and sent Pilot Officer Stevens and the other night fighter pilots to fresh Hurricanes to take up the hunt once more. Pilot Officer Stevens, with his mind full of the unforgettable impression of the greatest city in the world dwarfed to microscopic proportions as he viewed it in the moonlight from a height of six miles and what appeared to be a torch, but was actually a fairly large fire, blazing amid the tiny buildings, sped away in the direction of the capital and climbed to about 17,000 feet. Alert ears listened at innumerable posts ·below to pass on information with which the voice on the radio-telephone helped him. For a time his search was fruitless. Suddenly he glanced round and saw a Heinkel 111 coming up on his tail. Opening his throttle wide, the night fighter made a steep turn to get round on the tail of the enemy and attack. As he approached to within a quarter of a mile, the enemy aircraft opened fire, but did not hit the night fighter.

Closing up, Pilot Officer Stevens squeezed the button on his control column to set his eight guns blazing away at the enemy. He saw his tracer going home, but this was a bigger, heavier aircraft that could take more punishment than the Dornier. Observing little result, he attacked again and saw the lines of tracer flying past him as the enemy fired back. Suddenly he noticed a parachute rip open almost on his wing. In a few seconds another parachute cracked open and floated away with the moon illuminating it and making it look quite beautiful.

Attacking again, Pilot Officer Stevens saw the Heinkel begin to lose height, but all the time a German gunner was firing back. Turning away, the night fighter closed and sent in another sharp burst as the Heinkel went down. Again the Hurricane turned away and coming in from another angle blazed away at the enemy. One engine of the Heinkel began to give out white smoke. Pilot Officer Stevens stuck grimly to his prey, following one attack by another from different angles as the Heinkel went smoking down.

'He continued to lose height, with both motors smoking,' the pilot said afterwards in describing the end. 'I ran out of ammunition and followed him down to 1,500 feet and then down to 1,000. A little later I lost him over a dark patch of water, so I did not actually see him land.'

But immediate confirmation was forthcoming that the Heinkel had crashed [He 111 of 2/KG53 crashed in sea off Holehaven, Essex] and Stevens joined that very select band of pilots who had shot down two enemy aircraft in a night and the even more select band who have been awarded an honour on the field in England, for it is said that within ten minutes of his victory, he was decorated with the Distinguished Flying Cross.

In the days of April 1941 when the full moon fell on Good Friday, conditions were extremely favourable for intercepting the German bombers. Then for a few nights the British night fighters struck heavily at the raiders and scored numerous successes, one pilot making history by being the first to shoot down three enemy aircraft in one night.

Pilot Officer R. P. Stevens DFC also made night-flying history. He was up hunting in the moonlit skies on the night of April 8th, when his keen blue eyes detected first one and then another German raider, each of which he shot down and destroyed.

Forty-eight hours later, on the night of 10 April, his lucky star was again in the ascendant as he climbed high to stalk the enemy by the light of the moon, for he was once more able to make contact with the foe and bring two of the raiders within reach of his avenging guns. Thus on three occasions he shot down two enemy raiders in a single night - a remarkable record which not only won for him the Bar to his DFC, but also a warm commendation for his great determination to attack the enemy and to fly in the most difficult weather conditions. 'His courage, determination, thoroughness and skill have set an excellent example to his unit,' ran the official citation - which Pilot Officer Stevens fully justified by excelling his own record and shooting down two more of the enemy on the night of 7 May 1941.

After he scored his first double success in January, he was rather peeved because the medical officer said he could not fly again until the fluid in his ear was absorbed, as it might disturb his sense of balance.

'I could fly on my side,' laughed the fair-haired pilot with the strong face.

That is the spirit of England.[230]

Endnotes Chapter 21

229 Air Vice Marshal Augustus Henry Orlebar CBE AFC* (born 17 February 1897) was a British Army and RAF officer who served in both world wars. After being wounded during the Gallipoli campaign he was seconded to the Royal Flying Corps and subsequently the RAF. He formally transferred to the RAF after the First World War and between the wars was involved in high speed flying, commanding the High Speed Flight RAF, competing in the Schneider Trophy seaplane races of 1927-1931. Britain, having won the 1927 race, became the subsequent host for the contests, which were based at RAF Calshot on the eastern entrance to Southampton Water. In 1929 Orlebar set an air speed record of 357.7 mph in Supermarine S.6 N247. By the outbreak of the Second World War he was in command of RAF Northolt. He briefly became Director of Flying Training in 1940 before going to HQ RAF Fighter Command. In July 1941 he became Air Officer Commanding, 10 (Fighter) Group and in March 1943 Deputy Chief of Combined Operations. He fell ill and died in hospital on 4 August 1943.

230 An ear infection then prevented him flying until April, but thereafter he was almost constantly in the air, hunting for German bombers in his Hurricane, without the aid of radar, but with the benefit of his years of civil night flying. By mid-May he had claimed eight more and two probables, receiving a Bar to his DFC at the start of the latter month. In November he was posted to 253 Squadron to begin undertaking 'Intruder' sorties over occupied Europe. On 12 December he was awarded a DSO. By July 1941 Stevens had become the RAF's top-scorer by night. No other pilot without the benefit of airborne radar was even to approach his extraordinary total. On the night of 15/16 December 1941, three days after his DSO was gazetted, he crashed near Gilze-Rijen airfield in Holland in his Hurricane and was killed. His score stood at 14 and 1 shared destroyed, 2 probables, 1 damaged. *Aces High* by Christopher Shores and Clive Williams (Grub Street, London 1994).

Chapter 22

A Magnificent Leader

David Masters

Much has been written about the air aces of the Second World War and there has been speculation about who was the so-called 'greatest'. How can such a judgement be made? Not by victories alone, of that I am certain. Sailor Malan had more than most, but it was his other attributes which scored so heavily in his favour... His leadership which manifested itself so early... His exceptional foresight in the development of fighter operations... These and other features, single him out, in my book, as the supreme among supremes.

Al Deere, Spitfire pilot on 54 Squadron.

Adolph Gysbert Malan was born at Wellington in South Africa on 3 October 1910. He showed definite leanings toward the sea, for after leaving Wellington Public School, in February 1924 he entered the South African training ship General Botha as a cadet and became an officer in the Royal Naval Reserve. Three years later he joined the Union Castle Steamship Line as a junior deck officer. From the sea, however, his attention turned to the air and late in 1935 he applied for a short service commission in the RAF, commencing his training in England at the start of 1936. Posted to 74 Squadron in December 1936, he was promoted Flight Lieutenant in March 1939. He was awarded a DFC on 11 June for five victories, two confirmed and three unconfirmed.

Official citations are factual, prone to understatement and very sparing in the use of adjectives, so if they go so far as to mention 'his magnificent leadership' and 'his brilliant leadership,' nothing can be more certain than the fact that the officer concerned is an outstanding leader; and if they disclose that he has shot down at least eighteen enemy aircraft, he is assuredly a pilot of exceptional skill and courage - which explains why Wing Commander A. G. Malan has won the DSO and Bar and the DFC and Bar. This fine South African fighter pilot, who trained for the South African navy and joined the Royal Air Force in 1936, was the first airman to shoot down two German bombers in one night over England.

He is a leader to whom the squadron comes before everything. It is the squadron which counts and the successes of the squadron that matter. The team spirit which he infused into the pilots whom he led in the days of May 1940 served in time to turn 74 Squadron into a band of cool and resourceful and fearless pilots whose toll of the German Luftwaffe by the end of 1940 raised them to eminence in the Royal Air Force. He knew how to handle young men with the temperament of fighter pilots, how to inspire them, how to lead them and draw the best out of them. He instilled into them something of the spirit of the Canadian North-West Mounted Police. When they followed him into battle, each went with the intention of getting his man. It was their duty to shoot down Germans without being shot down themselves and if the enemy escaped one day they could bide their time and knock him down the next.

Not until [21 May] did the South African see a German in the air. Having patrolled the French coast for some days without sighting the enemy, he was sent out from his base to intercept a formation of German bombers whose movements had been notified. The interception was controlled from the base by orders which reached him through the radio-telephone and he altered his course and height according to the information received. Visual evidence in the way of heavy anti-aircraft fire was of considerable help in enabling him to locate the raiders over the French coast. He was flying across the top of a great cloud hummock which heaped up in the sky like a snowy peak when he nearly flew into a Heinkel 111. The first German he had ever seen was no more than fifty yards away, while fifty yards further on was a Junkers 88. So fast was he moving that only by prompt handling of the stick could he swerve to avoid the Heinkel.

Terrified that the German might drop down into the cloud a hundred feet below and escape, the South African did a steep turn on to the tail of the enemy and actually started firing on his side with full bank on. His attack was shattering. 'As I straightened up I saw my bullets pouring in and large pieces flew off him. He belched heavy smoke, his undercart fell out and he fell down into the cloud,' he said afterwards.

Anxious to deal with the German bombers further ahead, he called his section together and then sank down into the clouds to stalk the enemy for fifteen miles on a compass course. Flying blindly under the surface of the cloud, just as a submarine moves under the surface of the sea, Wing Commander Malan concluded after a few minutes that it was time to bob up above the cloud surface to have a look round.

It gave him a second thrill within five minutes, for he came up slap underneath a Junkers 88. A quick glance revealed about ten German bombers ahead. Ordering the other two Spitfires to attack, he let loose on the Junkers 88, which he completely surprised. Opening fire from a distance of a hundred yards, he squeezed the button for six seconds and was amazed to see the Junkers literally blow up in the air. While he was firing, the camera which was synchronized with his guns took photographs of what was happening as his bullets went home and this film, now historic, was shown on all the news reels in cinemas all over Great Britain.[231] Needless to add, the other two pilots of his section seized their opportunity. One shot down a Junkers before the rest escaped in the clouds and it transpired that the other, Flight Lieutenant J. C. Freeborn, who now holds the DFC and Bar, managed to shoot down two of the Junkers [over the Dunkirk area on 21 May 1940]. Unfortunately he caught a bullet in the radiator which drove him down in France.[232]

The Germans were over-running the country all round him, but Freeborn was determined to elude them. The first thing he did was to push his Spitfire among the undergrowth where he landed and then he covered it up with branches so that it was completely concealed not only from the air, but from any passer-by on the ground. Having hidden his Spitfire from prying eyes, he set off to see whether he could secure some petrol to refill his tanks so that he could make the attempt to cross the Channel. For three exciting days he dodged the Germans and tried to obtain petrol from the friendly French. Not a drop of petrol could he obtain. Once he found a German supply tank full of petrol that was left unattended by the enemy. Boldly seizing the chance, he slipped into the seat and drove it off full speed towards the spot where he had hidden his Spitfire. He was just congratulating himself on his stratagem and concluding that at last he would be able to get away when he came face to face with a long German column. Promptly turning the petrol tanker into the ditch, he bolted for his life. His flying start enabled him to get away and later he was picked up at Calais by a Blenheim bomber which was sent out for him with an escort of Spitfires from his own squadron.

Another time the squadron came on fifteen Messerschmitt 109s flying in broken cloud at 8,000 feet. There was abundant cover for all and in the mix-up that followed Flight Lieutenant Freeborn shot down a Messerschmitt 109 and darted away into a cloud to climb quickly through it. Directly he poked his nose out of the top he saw three Messerschmitts diving on him.

He did not wait. Spinning round, he took a header into the cloud again and went down and down in a screeching dive, shaking off his pursuers in the cloud which blanketed him like a dense fog. As he dropped out of the bottom of the cloud the first thing he saw was a Messerschmitt 109 chasing a Spitfire and automatically he swept round on the Messerschmitt's tail and shot the enemy down before the German knew what was hitting him.[233]

As the German armoured divisions progressed along the coast, the fights of Wing Commander Malan and his Spitfire pilots grew more numerous. From Boulogne to Dunkirk they patrolled their beat up and down, while the guns below opened up on them at every opportunity. The pilots had no respite. The weather on the whole was good and on no day was it bad enough to give them a breathing spell. On 24 May, by which time Boulogne was in German hands, they came to grips in real earnest with the full weight of the Luftwaffe. The flight of Spitfires became split up into three sections, one of which was led by Wing Commander Malan who was under severe fire from the German anti-aircraft guns when he got a call over the radio-telephone from his base to say that the Germans were bombing Dunkirk. At once he screamed flat out along the coast, dropping down to water level so as to see the enemy against the sky. The sight which met his eyes at Dunkirk was amazing. Never before had he seen anything like it. Formations of twenty to thirty bombers flying at 20,000 feet were grouped together and seemed to stretch in an endless chain as they bombed Dunkirk docks. Above the bombers were countless fighters.

'All I saw was the sky black with bombers. I could not see the beginning or end of them,' he reported.

Climbing all out, he led the other three Spitfires up to the attack. The whole of the Luftwaffe seemed to be arrayed against them, but they did not falter. Straight into one large layer of bombers they sped with guns blazing, cutting deeper and deeper into the formation. The leader gave a Heinkel 111 a burst of five seconds and as he saw the enemy aircraft take fire he felt a hit by anti-aircraft fire on his starboard wing. At the same moment bullets took a bit out of his flying boot and cut all his electric leads. Turning steeply to starboard, he saw a Messerschmitt 109 firing at him. A glance in his mirror revealed a Messerschmitt 110 firing cannon shell at him from astern. His ring reflector sight with its magic circle of light was put out of action, so his guns were useless without it.

He was beset with enemies seeking to kill him, threatening to riddle him with their fire. Yet in that crisis he was so cool and calm that he remembered there was a spare ring and bead sight in his locker and he decided to fit it then and there in order to carry on his attack. Climbing steeply into the sun, he pulled the spare sight out of his locker and slipped it into place; but by the time he had accomplished this and turned to take up the attack, the battle had rolled on.

Looking down, he saw what he thought were three puffs from exploding anti-aircraft shells. A second look disclosed that they were three of the crew of the Heinkel he had destroyed bailing out. Those were the first parachutes he had ever seen open in the sky.[234]

It was such courage displayed by all the British fighter pilots, as well as the pilots and crews of the bombers, which sapped the morale of the German airmen and set the canker of doubt as to their invincibility gnawing in their brains. Wing Commander Malan and his fellow pilots gazed upon the fierce fires which showed how well the British naval units had destroyed Boulogne before giving it over to the enemy. Calais succumbed after the aircraft of the Royal Air Force had dropped water and food and ammunition into the beleaguered citadel from the air.

Then the whole might of the Luftwaffe was concentrated on Dunkirk. Every fifteen minutes large masses of German bombers flew over the port and dropped their loads of bombs. At first they kept formation. Then they began to break under the harrying of the Spitfires which seized on the stragglers and shot them down. Seeing their fellows go down in flames also helped to sap the German morale.

Nightly the Spitfires returned full of bullet holes. Those that could be patched by next day were patched; the others were discarded and 74 Squadron simply raked together all the aircraft it could and plunged at dawn into the struggle once more. They were getting too little sleep, they were working and fighting hard, but the passing of each May day brought with it the knowledge of their growing ascendency over the Germans. They saw the German aircraft begin to waver, then they saw them start to break formation and in their last days over Dunkirk, Wing Commander Malan and the other fighter pilots saw obvious signs of the loss of German morale, for the enemy bomber formations broke up directly they caught sight of the Spitfires and put their noses down and went screaming all out for their own lines and the protection of their anti-aircraft guns.

When the squadron of Spitfires was taken out of the line for a rest on 27 May, it had definitely destroyed over thirty German aircraft, besides a number that were undoubtedly destroyed, although they were not seen to crash because the pilots were compelled to evade the attacks of the enemy. The squadron's losses were three pilots, of whom one was killed and the other two were taken prisoner.

Among crowded days later on was one at Dover when Wing Commander Malan led his pilots on four sorties between dawn and 1 o'clock. During that morning they knocked down twenty-four German aircraft and damaged at least eighteen more. Their own losses were four aircraft and two pilots, while two of the pilots bailed out safely.

In June 1940 during a night attack by enemy aircraft, he shot down two Heinkel 111s. His magnificent leadership, skill and courage have been largely responsible for the many successes obtained by his squadrons,' was a part of the citation announcing the award of a Bar to the Distinguished Flying Cross of Flight Lieutenant Adolph Gysbert Malan, who has since attained the rank of Wing Commander and been awarded the DSO and Bar.

The war brought out his abilities and under his leadership 74 Fighter Squadron, which was the first squadron to knock down 600 enemy aircraft, has out-rivalled the deeds and reputation of the old 74 Squadron of the last war. One or two brilliant fighter pilots who fought under him have paid him spontaneous tributes - a fact which suggests that one of his qualities as a leader may be his ability to recognize the qualities of other pilots and give them full credit for their work. And his destruction of two enemy bombers within twenty minutes on the same night was a memorable feat.

It was on the night of 18 June 1940, a clear sparkling night with everything illuminated brightly by a moon almost at the full, when the enemy sent about thirty bombers at intervals up the Thames estuary. They began to drop their bombs and dozens of searchlights swept the skies and held them in their beams as the guns started to boom out.

At the time Mrs. [Lynda] Malan was in a nursing home and her husband must have been rather concerned about her, particularly as she was right in the area which was being attacked. The bombing continued and for some time the pilots on his station watched the searchlights picking up and holding the Germans. As they watched the enemy bombers coming over, they chafed to get into their Spitfires to attack, but the area was so heavily defended by guns that it was considered inadvisable for any pilots to fly there. Conditions were so ideal for attacking the raiders from the air; however, that permission was granted to send up one aircraft and Squadron Leader Malan was selected as the pilot.

According to an eyewitness, he called for his fitter and rigger, who happened to have turned in for the night. Without waiting to dress, they pushed their feet into gum boots, slung their rifles over their shoulders, put on their tin hats and reported for duty in their striped pyjamas. No one seemed to take much notice of their incongruous appearance. More vital things claimed their attention.

Along with the squadron leader, they were rushed out to the aircraft dispersal post.

While the rigger and fitter worked swiftly to start up the Spitfire, the pilot methodically buckled on the harness of the parachute. By the time he had got his gear on, the engine had started, so he climbed into the cockpit and strapped himself in, before opening up the throttle to warm the engine up a bit.

Meanwhile he looked up and tried to pick out a target ahead and saw a Heinkel 111 at 6,000 feet being held by the searchlights. It was making a straight run directly across him.

A second glance at the approaching bomber made him decide that discretion was the better part of valour and that the engine was quite capable of warming itself up. Leaping out of the cockpit with his parachute on, he made a dive for a little trench close at hand.

The last time he saw the trench it was only about eighteen inches deep. But unknown to him the men had continued to dig until it was about five feet deep. He dived in just as the bomber arrived slap overhead and landed on his face in the mud at the bottom.

When the Heinkel had passed over, he got in and cracked off and made straight for the same Heinkel, which was obviously blinded by the searchlights. Heading for the coast and climbing quickly, he intercepted it just as it was on a slow climb crossing the coast.

The beams of the searchlights made things very deceptive. The first thing he knew he was about fifty yards from it. One moment it looked like a moth in a candle flame, the next the wings suddenly took shape and he realized he was very close.

He gave signs to the guns to stop firing directly he was in a position to attack and they at once stopped firing - the whole thing worked like a charm - and in he went. He pressed the trigger, but after a three second burst he had to jam his stick forward to avoid colliding with the enemy. In this short time his screen was covered with oil from the bomber, which spiralled out of the searchlights and soon crashed on the beach, half in and half out of the water.

As the South African pilot returned to Hornchurch, he looked back and saw another Heinkel 111 held by the searchlights. Climbing in a spiral below the enemy he signalled the guns to hold off. Then he moved in to attack at 16,000 feet. This time he was a lot more cautious and determined not to overrun the enemy, so he opened fire at 200 yards and closed to 100 yards. As he passed, the Heinkel burst into flames and a parachute became entangled near the tail. Then the enemy aircraft went down in a steep spiral well on fire. The pilot of the Spitfire saw it crash in a vicar's garden near Chelmsford with a terrific sheet of flame that was seen all the way from Southend.[235]

So Squadron Leader Malan in twenty minutes brought down two of the enemy bombers out of the seven destroyed by British fighters that night. The following night three more of the enemy bombers were shot down by British fighters and directly the German bombers learned that the fighters were up they began to turn off to sea. The losses suffered by the Germans on these occasions curtailed their night attacks for some time.

By January 1941 74 Squadron under the leadership of Wing Commander Malan had destroyed 127 enemy aircraft, which were seen to crash, while its own losses totalled twelve pilots. The last thirty-three Germans were destroyed without a single loss to themselves.

That is why the official announcements relax their usual restraint and refer to his magnificent and brilliant leadership. Before the end of July 1941 his personal victories totalled at least thirty-five German aircraft which he had shot down and destroyed.

Lack of decision and incompetence are two of the human failings which the South African cannot tolerate, which probably explains why he has developed such a fine spirit in 74 Squadron. Fearlessly he led his winged crusaders against the German hordes in the Battle of Britain and every enemy they sent down in flames was another Torch of Freedom lit in the skies to dispel the darkness.

At the age of thirty, Wing Commander Adolph Gysbert Malan DSO* DFC* has already achieved high honour in the Royal Air Force and added another leaf to the laurels of South Africa.[236]

Endnotes Chapter 22

231 Malan's He 111, near Dunkirk, was unconfirmed. He was credited with a Ju 88 and a Ju 88 damaged.

232 From Middleton near Leeds, John Connell 'Johnny' Freeborn was born on 1 December 1919. He joined the RAF on a short service commission in January 1938 and at the end of October that year was posted to 74 Squadron at Hornchurch. On 6 September 1939 74 Squadron saw its first action only 15 hours after war was declared, sent to intercept a bomber raid that turned out to be returning RAF aircraft 'A' Flight was scrambled to intercept a suspected enemy radar track and ran into the Hurricanes of 56 Squadron. Believing 56 to be the enemy, 'Sailor' Malan ordered an attack. Paddy Byrne and John Freeborn shot down two RAF aircraft, killing one officer, Montague Hulton-Harrop, which became known as the 'Battle of Barking Creek'. At the subsequent courts-martial, Malan denied responsibility for the attack. He testified for the prosecution against his own pilots stating that Freeborn had been irresponsible, impetuous and had not taken proper heed of vital communications. This prompted Freeborn's counsel, Sir Patrick Hastings to call Malan a bare-faced liar. Hastings was assisted in defending the pilots by Roger Bushell who had become a barrister-at-Law of Lincolns Inn. The court ruled the entire incident was an unfortunate error and acquitted both pilots. Byrne would later be incarcerated with Bushell at Stalag Luft III.

Bushell was given command of 92 Squadron in October 1939 and his promotion to squadron leader was confirmed on 1 January 1940. During the squadron's first engagement with enemy aircraft on 23 May, whilst on a patrol near Calais, Bushell was credited with damaging two Bf 110s of ZG26 before being shot down himself (probably by future ace Oberleutnant Günther Specht). He crash-landed his Spitfire and was captured before he had a chance to hide. On arrival at Dulag Luft he was made part of the permanent British staff under the Senior British Officer Wing Commander Harry 'Wings' Day whose duty was to help newly captured Allied aircrew to adjust to life as a PoW. Escape, which was regarded as a duty of all PoWs of officer rank, was never far from his mind. Day placed Fleet Air Arm pilot Jimmy Buckley RN in charge of escape operations with Bushell as his deputy. Several escape tunnels, one of which was completed in May 1941, were started. On the day of the escape Bushell wanted an earlier get away so that he could catch a particular train, so he cut through the wire surrounding a small park in the camp grounds. He was recaptured on the Swiss border, only a few hundred yards from freedom by a German border guard. He was treated well and returned to Dulag Luft, before being transferred to Stalag Luft I with all the 17 others who had escaped in the tunnel (including Day and Buckley). After a short period he was transferred to Oflag XC at Lübeck where he participated in the construction of another tunnel. This was abandoned unfinished on 8 October 1941 when all British and Commonwealth Officer PoWs were removed from the camp and were entrained for transfer to Oflag VIB at Warburg. During the night of 8/9 October the train stopped briefly in Hannover where Bushell and a Czech officer Pilot Officer Jaroslav Zafouk jumped from the train and escaped unnoticed by the German guards. They made their way to Prague in occupied Czechoslovakia and made contact with the Czech underground movement, staying in 'safe houses' while arrangements for their onward journey was being made. However, following the assassination of Reinhard Heydrich in May 1942 the Germans launched a massive manhunt for the assassins; during the round-up Bushell and Zafouk were arrested. Both were interrogated by the Gestapo and were very roughly treated. Bushell was eventually sent to Stalag Luft III at Sagan, arriving there in October 1942. (Zafouk was sent to Oflag IVC at Colditz).

Bushell took over control of the escape organisation from Jimmy Buckley, who was being transferred to another camp, became known as 'Big X' of the camp escape committee and was the mastermind behind the mass escapes that occurred from the camp. He had developed an intense hatred for the Nazis and his plan was to strike back at them as best he could - by organising mass break-outs from the PoW camps he was in. In the spring of 1943 he masterminded a plot for a major escape from the North Compound from three tunnels 'Tom', 'Dick' and 'Harry' dug simultaneously. 'Tom' began in a darkened corner of a hall in one of the buildings. 'Dick's entrance was carefully hidden in a drain sump in one of the washrooms. The entrance to 'Harry' was hidden under a stove. More than 600 prisoners were involved in their construction. 'Tom' was discovered in August 1943 when nearing completion. Bushell also organised the 'Delousing' break out, which occurred on 12 June 1943 when 26 officers escaped by leaving the camp under escort with two PoWs disguised as guards supposedly to go the showers for delousing in the neighbouring compound. All but two were later recaptured and returned to the camp, with the remaining two officers being sent to Colditz for attempting to steal an aircraft.

After the discovery of 'Tom' construction on 'Harry' was halted. It resumed in January 1944 and on the evening of 24 March, 200 officers, all of whom wore civilian clothes and possessed a complete range of forged papers and escape equipment, prepared to escape but only 76 officers managed to get clear of the camp before the alarm was raised. Roger and his partner Bernard Scheidhauer were among the first few to leave the tunnel and successfully boarded a train at Sagan railway station. They were caught the next day at Saarbrücken railway station, waiting for a train to Alsace. Bushell and Scheidhauer were murdered three days later by members of the Gestapo. The perpetrators were later tried and executed by the Allies. Fifty of the 76 escapees were killed in the Stalag Luft III murders. Roger Bushell is buried at the Poznan Old Garrison Cemetery in Poznań, Poland. In 13 June 1946 he was posthumously Mentioned in Despatches for his services as a PoW.

233 This claim, on 24 May, was unconfirmed. 'Johnny' Freeborn was again shot down on 13 August 1940, but survived unhurt. He was awarded a DFC on that same date and was promoted to lead a flight on 28th. By the end of November he had been with his squadron longer than any other Battle of Britain pilot and had flown more operational hours. His continuous service would subsequently last from 29 October 1938 to 6 June 1941. He was awarded a Bar to his DFC on 25 February 1941. In June he was posted to 57 OTU as an instructor. He returned to operations as a flight commander with 602 Squadron in December 1942. Posted as CO of 18 Squadron in June 1943, he remained with this unit until June 1944, when he was appointed Wing Commander Flying of 286 Wing in Italy. His final score was 5 destroyed, 3 and 1 shared damaged. He left the RAF in 1946 as a Wing Commander. *Aces High* by Christopher Shores and Clive Williams (Grub Street, London 1994).

234 Malan was awarded a 1/6 share in a Do 17. His claim for a He 111 east of Dunkirk was confirmed.

235 Both claims were confirmed. The first Heinkel crashed at Foulness, the second, at Wickford-Chelmsford.

236 During the night of 19/20 June 1941 'Sailor' Malan was able to claim two German intruders shot down, for which a Bar to his DFC followed on 13 August. He was promoted to command the squadron on 8 August. The unit was then withdrawn to Kirton-in-Lindsey to rest and here he wrote his *10 Rules of Air Fighting* which was produced and distributed throughout Fighter Command. In October the squadron returned to the south and received some of the first Spitfire IIs. On Christmas Eve 1940 he received the award of a DSO, the citation crediting him with 18 confirmed and six possible victories. On 10 March 1941 he was appointed as one of the first Wing Leaders for the offensive operations planned for that year, leading the Biggin Hill Wing throughout the sweeps of May, June and July. A Bar to his DSO followed on 22 July, at that time recording his total as 28, plus 20 damaged or probables. In mid-August he was appointed CFI at 58 OTU, Grangemouth, by this time being listed as Fighter Command top scorer, with a total variously reported as 32 or 35 victories. In October he departed for the USA on a lecture tour, and to liaise with the USAAC, together with five other leading RAF fighter pilots. Returning to the UK in December, he became CO of the Central Gunnery School at Sutton Bridge, where he remained for a year, being promoted Group Captain in October 1942. On I January 1943 he returned to Biggin Hill as commanding officer, remaining until October, when he took command of 19 Fighter Wing in the new 2nd TAF. In March 1944, he moved to command 145 (Free French) Wing, which he remained with until after the Normandy invasion. He was then posted to command the Advanced Gunnery School at Catfoss in July. In 1945 he attended the RAF Staff College, but decided that the peacetime RAF was not for him and in 1946 he returned to South Africa with his family. His untimely death occurred on 17 September 1963.